Globalisation, Citizenship and the War on Terror

Globalisation, Citizenship and the War on Terror

Edited by

Maurice Mullard

Reader in Public and Social Policy, University of Hull, UK

Bankole A. Cole

Lecturer in Criminology and Deputy Director of the Centre for Criminology and Criminal Justice, University of Hull, UK

Edward Elgar
Cheltenham, UK • Northampton, MA, USA

Published by
Edward Elgar Publishing Limited
Glensanda House
Montpellier Parade
Cheltenham
Glos GL50 1UA
UK

Edward Elgar Publishing, Inc.
William Pratt House
9 Dewey Court
Northampton
Massachusetts 01060
USA

A catalogue record for this book
is available from the British Library

Library of Congress Cataloguing in Publication Data

Globalisation, citizenship and the war on terror / edited by Maurice Mullard, Bankole Cole.
    p. cm.
  Includes bibliographical references and index.
1. Globalization. 2. War on Terrorism, 2001–3. Citizenship. I. Mullard, Maurice, 1946– II. Cole, Bankole, 1954–
    JZ1318.G5785543 2007
    303.48′2—DC22

2007016158

ISBN 978 1 84542 740 5

Printed and bound in Great Britain by MPG Books Ltd, Bodmin, Cornwall

Contents

Figures and tables

FIGURES

TABLE

About the contributors

Terrence Casey is Associate Professor of Political Science at the Rose-Hulman Institute of Technology (USA) and the Executive Director of the British Politics Group of the American Political Science Association. His previous publications include *The Social Context of Economic Change in Britain* (Manchester University Press, 2002) and numerous articles on British politics and political economy in such journals as *Political Studies*, *Social Science Quarterly* and *Comparative European Studies*.

Bankole A. Cole is Lecturer in Criminology and Deputy Director of the Centre for Criminology and Criminal Justice (CCCJ) at the University of Hull. Prior to joining Hull in 2003, he was lecturer and senior lecturer in criminology at the University of Lincoln, UK, where he served for 13 years. His main publications are in the areas of comparative criminal justice, policing, race and crime and youth justice. His publications include 'Post-colonial systems' in R.I. Mawby (ed.), *Policing Across the World* (London: UCL Press, 1999); and 'Rough justice: criminal proceedings in Nigerian magistrates courts', *International Journal of the Sociology of Law*, **18** (3), 1990.

Michael S. Drake is Lecturer in Sociology at the University of Hull. He was formerly a lecturer in the School of Political, Social and International Studies at the University of East Anglia, Norwich. His areas of interest include the instrumentalisation of violence, historical sociology and the genealogy of military power.

Su-ming Khoo is a Lecturer in the Department of Political Science and Sociology at NUI Galway, Ireland. Her research interests are in globalisation, development theory and the political economy of development, with an emphasis on humanistic and ecological perspectives. She has a special interest in issues of environment, culture, decolonisation, democratisation and knowledge activism for development.

Simon Lee is Senior Lecturer in Politics at the Department of Politics and International Studies, Hull University. His teaching and research interests are principally in the field of political economy, with a particular emphasis upon the politics of globalisation and governance, and the political economy and national identity of contemporary England. His most recent research has been for *Politics of Prudence: The Paradox of Gordon Brown* (Oxford: OneWorld, 2007, forthcoming).

Michael McCahill is Lecturer in Criminology and Director of the MA Criminology course at the University of Hull. His main teaching interests are the 'sociology of deviance and social control' and his current research interests include the social impact of 'new surveillance technologies'. He has published widely on the topic of surveillance and social control including a book entitled *The Surveillance Web* (Cullompton: Willan, 2002) for which he received the British Society of Criminology book prize 2003. His most recent publications include C. Norris and M. McCahill (2006), 'CCTV: beyond penal modernism?', *British Journal of Criminology*, **46** (1), 97–118.

Maurice Mullard is Reader in Social and Public Policy at the University of Hull. He has published extensively in the academic areas of the politics of public expenditure, citizenship, globalisation, poverty and the war on terror. His publications include *New Labour New Thinking* (New York University Press, 2002); *Globalisation Citizenship and Democracy* (New York University Press, 2003); and *The Politics of Globalisation and Polarisation* (Cheltenham, UK and Northampton, MA, USA: Edward Elgar, 2004).

Andrew Robinson is Leverhulme Trust Early Career Fellow in the School of Politics, University of Nottingham. He has diverse research interests linked by concerns with oppression, resistance, everyday life and the discursive construction of exclusion. Previously published work includes papers on Gramsci and common sense, the construction of revolutionary subjectivities, militarist discourse after 9/11, horizontal and vertical tendencies in anti-capitalism, neo-liberalism in higher education, and critiques of the work of Ernesto Laclau and Slavoj Žižek. He recently completed his PhD on oppressive discourse in the work of John Rawls. He is currently working on the emergence of peripheral resistance in the world system. Andrew would like to acknowledge the Leverhulme Trust for enabling him to carry out the research for this book.

Stefan Skrimshire is Post-doctoral Teaching Fellow in Religion and Politics at The University of Manchester. His research and teaching focuses on contemporary responses to a 'politics of fear' by looking at the relationship between concepts of global crisis, apocalypse and utopian imagination. He has published in journals such as *Political Theology*, *Literature and Theology*, *Ephemera* and the *Red Pepper* magazine.

Colin Tyler is Senior Lecturer in Political Theory at the Department of Politics and International Studies, University of Hull. He has published on global governance and cultural diversity, and has a particular interest in Bentham and British idealism. He is, together with Simon Lee, Joint Director of the Centre for Democratic Governance. His most recent book is *Idealist Political Philosophy: Pluralism and Conflict in the Absolute Idealist Tradition* (London and New York: Continuum, 2006).

Tony Ward is Reader in Law at the University of Hull. He is co-author, with Penny Green, of *State Crime: Governments, Violence and Corruption* (London: Pluto, 2004) and has published extensively in the fields of criminology, criminal justice history and the law of evidence.

Peter Young is Professor of Criminology at the University of Hull. Previously he was Head of the School of Law and Director of the Centre for Law and Society at the University of Edinburgh and then Director of the Institute of Criminology, University College Dublin. His name is associated, internationally, with the emergence of the sociology of punishment and with the comparative study of crime and criminal justice. He has published essays on criminological and sociological theory, the analysis of punishment and penal sanctions and on comparative crime rates. His books include *The Power to Punish* (with D. Garland) (London: Heinemann, 1983), *Crime and Criminal Justice in Scotland* (The Stationery Office, 1997) and *Crime in Ireland* (with E. Clare and I. O'Donnell) (Dublin: National Crime Council, 2001).

Acknowledgements

Dr Andrew Robinson was in receipt of a Leverhulme Trust early career fellowship while writing the chapter for this book. He would like to thank the Trust for the opportunity. Dr Bankole Cole would like to thank Dr Kelvin Jones and the staff of the department of policy studies at the University of Lincoln for providing him with office facilities while editing the book. Dr Maurice Mullard would like to thank his wife, Eileen Mullard, for her continuing support.

1. Introduction

Maurice Mullard and Bankole A. Cole

BACKGROUND

This book seeks to explore the nature of globalisation and the 'war on terror' and how both processes are shaping and defining citizenship globally and within nation states. Citizenship does not obey a static definition. The concept is contestable and its meaning is located in changing economic, social and political contexts. Equally, civil, political and social rights are continually being politically defined. The war on terror has influenced issues of civil liberties and prioritised the need for 'security' over and above the protection of human rights. It has redefined the meaning of the rule of law. The nation state has become more and more coercive and the 'state of exception' is gradually becoming normalised (see Agamben, 2005). The wars in Iraq and Afghanistan are replays of colonial 'civilising missions' in Africa, clouded by deceit, corruption and corporate invasion of pacified homelands. Like the concessionaire and chartered companies in nineteenth-century Africa, the International Monetary Fund (IMF), the World Bank, the Development Fund for Iraq (DFI), and other international financial institutions (IFIs) are, as a consequence of the war on terror, actively involved in the corporate takeover and economic occupation of Iraq. Unlike in colonial times, in the war on terror the enemy is 'global' and the war is fought both abroad and at home. The enemy is within and without. The war is fought on all fronts. While the 'imperial' armies of the Allied forces are engaged in colonising missions abroad, significant changes are taking place with regard to the policing of communities at home. Colonial policing tactics, whereby the boundaries between civilian policing, military and security activities are blurred, are reborn and globalised, in the attempt to criminalise 'resistance' movements in pacified territories (Cole, 1999). Ethnic profiling replaces visual identification used in colonial times and has become a globalised method of policing (Editorial, 2006). Racist policing is normalised. One is a potential terrorist not simply because of one's colour but also because of one's religion and culture. Hallsworth (2006) argued that this is not simply about policing but is a reflection of the regimes of control that is characteristic of modes of governance integral to neo-liberal rule in late modernity. The impact goes beyond individual experiences (for example, of stop and search) to the marginalisation, regulation and control of 'suspect' communities.

The war on terror and globalisation both confirm the need to address the issue as to what constitutes appropriate political spaces between national boundaries and global concerns. Both point to the limits of the capacities of institutions located within the nation state and the recognition that politics in the context of the nation state still matters. The environment, climate change, migrations, world poverty and the wars in Afghanistan, Iraq and more recently Lebanon seem to require institutions that are global in nature. On the other hand, issues of income inequalities, provision of education and health services still require the capacities and the political will of the nation state.

THE ECONOMICS AND POLITICS OF GLOBALISATION

The classical debates between hyper-globalists and global sceptics have tended to put the focus on the issue of intensity and whether present globalisation is qualitatively different from other periods in history. Authors in the volume have argued on the need to separate global facts from global policy choices. While global facts point to inevitabilities, policy reflects choices. There are global facts that point to a world that is becoming more integrated, interdependent and increasingly aware of a common shared humanity. Through the media, the Internet and numerous forms of communication, there is now a continuing global sharing of images, stories and pictures, which also creates a context of increased expectations about economic prosperity, the potential of a shared global humanity and universal human rights. World poverty, the environment, migration, war and losses of human life become common shared experiences, which in turn make possible the idea of the global cosmopolitan citizen (Held and Archibugi, 1995; Kymlicka, 1995; Appiah, 2003; Beck, 2006). However, cosmopolitan citizenship is resisted since the idea of citizen is seen as belonging to the politics of the nation state.

These same processes also create the potentials for conflict, of seeing globalisation as a threat to national identity, culture and history; and of a globalisation that flattens out heterogeneity and enforces a new tyranny of sameness. Globalisation creates tensions around the distribution of resources, with those that have a vested interest in protecting the status quo resisting changes that are seen as undermining their privileges and ways of life. The arbitrariness of place of birth, parents, and social and financial inheritances shapes life chances so that some people are more citizens than others.

The discourse of globalisation is also a form of story telling. It is a story of 'sameness' in a world that is increasingly becoming unequal and polarised. As Cameron and Palan (2004, p. 154) put it: 'the narrative of globalisation as an homogenous, planetary force, provides ample plausibility for the political programme of "no alternative" constrictions of global inevitability'.

Globalisation is the exogenous variable to which the state has to respond; where there is no alternative but to create policy frameworks that correspond to the political and economic needs of globalisation. The basic argument is that globalisation is a process that threatens to overwhelm the nation state. Making the nation state increasingly irrelevant has resulted in further debate about citizenship and social exclusion and the shift towards the competitive state and the decline of the welfare state. In the context of the borderless economy, therefore, the nation state is often described as being hollowed out and losing relevance. Transnational corporations continue to shape global labour markets, demanding greater flexibility, long hours, low pay and the lowering of health and safety regulations. This model of economic globalisation has resulted in a situation whereby the income of the top 1 per cent of earners has increased 198 per cent over the past two decades, while for the other 99 per cent of income earners it has remained flat, stagnated or even declined.

THE NATURE OF THE WAR ON TERROR

Debates on the war on terror have centred on how to separate the real from the unreal and the facts from political manipulation. While on the real side are the victims of individual terrorist attacks in New York, Bali, Madrid, New Delhi and London, on the unreal side are the manipulative processes that seek to interpret facts in order to gain political advantage. The use of wars to gain political advantage is not new. Margaret Thatcher used the Falklands war to increase her political popularity in Britain in the 1980s. But the war on terror is a different kind of war. In the United States, the Republican Party strategist Karl Rove utilised the rainbow colours of the terror alert on the eve of the 2004 presidential election and the detentions of alleged terror suspects in the mid-term elections of November 2002 and 2006 to remind people that the USA was still at 'war', and that the nation was safer under Republican control since by implication the Democratic Party was soft on terror and not to be trusted with the nation's security. In all the three occasions in the USA, the Opposition (the Democrats) was defined as being soft and of coddling up to terror. Vietnam war heroes like presidential candidate John Kerry and Senator Jeff McClelland were put into photographs with Osama Bin Laden in the 2004 election while President George W. Bush reminded voters of how the democrats had voted against the Terror Bill in September 2006. The war on terror was also central to the Blair election campaign in 2005. It helped re-elect the Prime Minister of Australia for a fourth term and was central to the election campaign in Canada in 2005.

Of increased major concern must be how images and stories of the 'war' are constructed and communicated to the public. Since governments have the monopoly of such information, it is governments and their intelligence services that can give direction to stories. There are no independent checks and balances. In the war on terror, citizens have become the passive consumers of information. There is little room or space for independence of judgement. The questions usually come later. Democracy is replaced by the politics of trust, compliance and servitude. The question of the security of the state is beyond public scrutiny. In times of war the policy of government has to be taken on trust. The security of the state cannot yield to scepticism. Those who question state action are accused of treachery, madness or of literally supporting terrorism. According to Paul Krugman:

> The Bush administration and the movement it leads has been involved in an authoritarian project, an effort to remove all checks and balances . . . [An] almost equally important part of the project has been the attempt to create a political environment in which nobody dares to criticise the administration or reveal inconvenient facts about its actions. And that attempt has relied, from the beginning on ascribing treasonous motives to those who refuse to toe the line. (Krugman, *New York Times*, 7 July 2006, p. 12)

In effect, the extensive usage of the words 'the war on terror' initiated by President George W. Bush of the USA and echoed by ex-Prime Minister Tony Blair of the UK, has contributed to the polarisation of the world as belonging either within the camp of the good or with evil. The war on terror does not allow for complexity. The other is demonised. While Hamas and Hezbollah are defined by the USA and European countries as terrorist organisations in both Gaza and the Lebanon, these groups are perceived by their local communities as their resistance movements. In the war on terror the world is made simple. In the context of the war, resistance becomes a form of terrorism and furthermore all forms of terrorism are homogenised and defined as illegitimate whatever the cause.

More importantly, the war on terror has provided the context for a number of nation states to redefine the boundaries between security and civil liberties. The US Patriot Act passed in 2001 and revised in 2006 has provided a number of contexts that allows the President to confine detainees without trial, use surveillance orders, and wire taps on US citizens without seeking the consent of Congress. Major telephone companies have also had to surrender databases of telephone calls of US citizens. In the UK, the most recent anti-terrorism legislation (the Terrorism Act, 2006) has provided frameworks that allows the police to detain suspects for a period of 28 days without charge and also, despite opposition, introduced measures that deal with what has been legally defined as 'the encouragement of terrorism'. This includes acts which 'glorify' the commission or preparation of terrorism or acts from which members of the public could reasonably be expected to infer that terrorism is being glorified (section 1). This law went ahead in spite of the fact that a number of UK civil liberty groups and even Parliament have argued that this would seriously undermine freedom of speech and civil rights. The 'war' has provided an environment where the due process of law is perceived as more of a hindrance than a safeguard of civil liberties and human rights. Legal safeguards are defined differently for 'terrorist' suspects. For 'terrorists' it is often justice before trial. The case of the detainees at Guantánamo Bay clearly demonstrates this. On 17 October 2006, President Bush signed the Military Commissions Act into law. The law, which was passed specifically in relation to the war on terror, suspends habeas corpus for any alien (non-citizen of the USA) deemed to be an unlawful enemy combatant engaged in hostilities or having supported hostilities against the United States. Such detainees are considered an ongoing threat to the security of the United States. This law blocks the chances of these suspects ever being released, which means that they will remain in custody indefinitely without trial and their cases cannot be reviewed in US courts. The President already has the power, under the Presidential Military Order of 2001, to detain non-citizens suspected of connection to terrorists or terrorism as an enemy combatant, in which case, the person could be detained indefinitely, without charge, without a court hearing, and without entitlement to a consultation with a lawyer. In addition, contrary to the rules against torture under the Geneva Convention, evidence obtained though 'coercive interrogation' (torture and coercion) may be allowed in 'terrorist' cases.

Of even more significance are the 'moral' arguments that have been used to justify this war. Islamic fundamentalists are blamed for terrorist acts against predominantly Christian countries and President Bush (and his Christian Right followers), and ex-Prime Minister Blair, at various points in the debates on the war, have made reference to their own personal Christian convictions. The war is defined in terms of a struggle between 'good' and 'evil', in which God intervenes on the side of the 'good'. In various statements, Bush and Blair have maintained that the 'war' is a struggle of Western democracies against Islamic fascism and the threat of violence and ideological visions that seek to impose a specific form of intolerant Islam.

'Islamic' terrorism cannot be seen as individual criminal acts; it has to be located in the context of a global ideological struggle. Muslims all over the world are being lumped together as a homogeneous group. Homogeneity flattens differences and people as individuals become caricatures and stereotypes of images, which in turn undermines humanity and at the same time legitimises violence because the other becomes less human. Multiculturalism is under attack and anti-Muslim racism has increased at every level in most Western countries. But politicians have continued nevertheless to promote a politics of fear (see Sivanandan, 2006). In his speech on the HMS *Albion* in Plymouth, in January 2007, Tony Blair asserted that 'Put simply, September 11 2001 changed everything'. He described the war on terror as:

> [A r]adically different type of warfare requiring a radically different type of response. What we face is not a criminal conspiracy or even a fanatical but fringe terrorist organisation. We face something more akin to revolutionary Communism in its early and most militant phase. It adherents may be limited. Its sympathisers are not. It has states or at least parts of the governing apparatus of states that give it succour. Its belief system may be, indeed is, utterly reactionary. But its methods are terrifyingly modern. (Blair, 2007)

On terrorism, he said:

> Terrorism is an attack on our values. Its ideology is anti-democratic, anti-freedom, anti-everything that makes modern life so rich in possibility. When the Taleban murder a teacher in front of his class, as they did recently, for daring to teach girls; that is an act not just of cruelty but of ideology. Using force against them to prevent such an act is not 'defence' in the traditional territorial sense of that word, but 'security' in the broadest sense, an assertion of our values against theirs. (Ibid.)

As Sivanandan (2006) argued, this is new racism (anti-Muslim racism) thrown up by the processes of globalisation and modern empire. The war on terror is being sold to the world as a war against an emerging Islamic totalitarianism; a war of ideas between the science, rationality and reason to be associated with the Christian civilised West against the corrupt medieval world of Islam.

CONCEPTUALISING CITIZENSHIP

It is therefore important to ask what happens to ideas of democracy and citizenship in a world that is becoming increasingly significantly polarised and where dialogue is undermined. Ideas of citizenship are being continually constructed and deconstructed, influenced by deliberate policy choices but also by changes that reflect changing social, economic and political expectations. The narratives of globalisation and the war on terror have led to the construction of new landscapes that have given a different meaning to the concept of citizenship. The global context that, on the one hand, has created the awareness of human interconnectedness and of the potential of a 'cosmopolitan citizen' has, on the other hand, partially as a consequence of the war on terror, generated a meaning of citizenship that is defined by individualism, categorisation and the suspicion of the other. While Muslim communities and their representatives in Europe have come out to say that Muslims who commit acts of terrorism are in the minority, Muslim communities are being targeted as a whole. The war on terror is not about individual criminals but an attempt to defeat a 'movement', however ill defined. The war on terror has created racial tensions and has revived the colonial legacy of first- and second-class citizens. It is among the second-class citizens that one expects disloyalty. Muslim communities in the USA and Europe are retreating from public spaces and having to continually prove their innocence and loyalty. The war on terror has created a culture of fear, pessimism, passivity and silence. But the West presses on with legislation and surveillance technology that terrorises these citizens at airports and in their communities. The use of profiling in identifying potential terrorists at airports puts racism at the highest possible level in crime prevention. Now, connections are being made between terrorism and immigration; even asylum seekers who are Arab and Middle Eastern are themselves not immune from suspicion under anti-terrorism and immigration laws.

The war on terror is certainly influencing the meaning of citizenship. On the one hand, citizenship has become more than an ascription based, for example, on being born within a territorial space or on historic blood ties. It is consciously being racially defined. Immigrant citizens (especially Muslims), are increasingly being excluded from this definition and are having to define their citizenship outside the boundaries of their nation states, and in the context of their religion and culture. Citizenship has become a process and is taking the shape of resistance and struggles. On the other hand, the idea of the social citizen who is a member of a community with a sense of belonging is being replaced by that of the consumer citizen – where the government are trustees of the nation's interest and electors become consumers of policy. This neo-liberal thinking reduces citizenship for some, to almost 'bare life' (Agamben, 1998). The role of the state is redefined in terms of security and issues of human rights are reclassified. The symbolic politics of identity, cultural values and crime statistics fill the political agenda while policy aimed at the distribution of resources is downgraded.

THE BOOK

This volume is a collection of essays on the link between globalisation, citizenship and the war on terror written from various academic perspectives, incorporating ideas from sociology, criminology, political science and development studies. The book is divided into three interconnected parts.

In Chapter 4, Terrence Casey uses the Polanyian insight of market embeddedness to argue that how societies respond to globalisation, either through defensive resistance or proactive adaptation, depends on the extent to which societies (more or less) mimic underlying ideals of markets, creating a sense of citizenship within the economy as well as within the polity. Such market-responsive societies, he argues, are likely to exhibit superior economic performance and political stability as globalisation progresses. Simon Lee (in Chapter 8) provides an insight into how globalisation has been used as a weapon to justify and legitimise domestic and foreign policy choices which have had major implications for citizenship and communities internationally. He argues that the war on terror needs to be understood as the third of four distinctive phases in the politics of globalisation which have shaped international relations and domestic statecraft since the early 1970s. The common denominator of all four phases, he maintains, has been their domination by the neo-liberal perspective on globalisation.

Colin Tyler's and Lee's chapters (Chapters 3, 7, 8 and 9) provide a critical analysis of Bush's and Blair's positions on the war on terror and the impact these have had on the international community. In Chapter 3, Tyler considers the triumphant assertion of a senior adviser to George W. Bush that, during the 'war on terror', the US administration has acted as 'history's actors'. The chapter traces the origins of the Bush administration's post-9/11 policy towards Afghanistan and Iraq, to the concerns of neo-conservative lobby groups, especially the Project for the New American Century. After a critical analysis of Bush's policy on the war, Tyler argues that waging a war of righteousness, of the type the Bush administration has pursued post-9/11, has dangerous implications for the processes of international recognition and thereby international order. He concludes with the position that we should welcome the apparent decline of Bush's standing in the USA and the wider international stage, and have hope that the normal processes of international recognition will reassert themselves in the near future. This theme is pursued further by Lee in Chapter 9, where he explores the political economy of neo-conservatism. Lee shows how the

Bush administration's agenda for the World Bank and IMF has reflected an important economic dimension to the war on terror.

Tyler's second chapter (Chapter 7) examines Tony Blair's doctrine of international community, in both its political and economic facets. The former is shown to presuppose leadership of the international institutional architecture and the major developed states by a US administration that is on balance benevolent. The latter is shown to presuppose the extension globally of 'progressive' welfare capitalism. Tyler argues that Blair's excessive faith in the Bush administration and the collapse of the post-Doha talks has rendered Blair's doctrine of international community a very dangerous aspiration indeed. After examining Blair's anti-terrorist policies and their wider implications at the domestic level in the UK, Tyler concludes that Blair's doctrine has created highly significant problems, both internationally and at home. Further critique of Tony Blair's doctrine of 'international community' is provided by Lee in Chapter 8.

Contemporary understandings of the war on terror are underpinned by a series of powerful myths and narratives. These narratives, some argue, are orchestrated by the state and the aim is to delegitimise dissent (see for example, Jackson, 2005). In Chapter 2, Michael S. Drake assesses how the study of discourse can illuminate the dynamics of the war on terror. From the review of the work of Fairclough, the development of discourse analysis, and a critique of the writings of Jackson, Tilley, Baxi and Barkawi, Drake argues that the discourse of the war on terror appears to be driven either by the agency of external interest factors or by internal structural and ideational factors. The chapter concludes with a summary of the problems of discourse analysis as a means for assessing the effects of discourse in society and politics, and especially the dynamics of the war on terror, arguing that the problems reiterate some classical debates in social science over ideology and the function of ideas in history.

There are similar controversial debates on the definition of a terrorist or terrorism. Whatever definition is supported, the common denominator is the deliberate use of terror and violence or the threat of violence for a political goal. In Chapter 12, Tony Ward and Peter Young use the work of Norbert Elias as a framework for understanding the relationships between organised violence, legitimacy and terrorism, focusing on suicide bombers. They argue that Elias's work provides a useful device from which to construct a sociological perspective of this relationship. While not setting out to furnish a comprehensive account of the relationship between organised violence and terrorism, Ward and Young's position is that the use of Elias's work enables interesting questions to be asked. The chapter begins with a critical exposition of Elias's work that centres upon the role that the concept of pacified social spaces plays in his theory. Ward and Young then examine Elias's later work where he introduces the notion of decivilisation. It is in this context, they argue, that Elias provides an account of terrorism. The chapter then uses Elias's work to examine the relationship between decivilisation and terrorism and the relationship between terror, democracy and sensibilities. The analysis explores the relationship between the state's monopoly of violence, its own use of violence, conceptions of legitimacy and how terrorism and violence challenge these, often by mimicry and through symbolism. The chapter also examines the dynamics and complexities of the sensibilities of suicide bombers. The authors argue that contests over legitimacy clearly play a key role in understanding the sensibilities of terrorism and how and why terrorists use violence. Their analysis suggests that terrorism raises questions about how the state maintains control over its use of legitimate violence. The chapter concludes by looking at the relationship between state action and the construction of the terrorist as the 'other'.

It is generally accepted among commentators that the war on terror has been used to legitimate restrictive legislation and policing practices which encroach on civil liberties and citizenship rights, and which function as new conditions for power and resistance in the political sphere (see, for example, Lyon, 2003; Agamben, 2005; Beck, 2005). Mike McCahill (Chapter 11) explores the impact of the war on terror in terms of the global expansion of the use of surveillance technology before and after the September 11 attack in the USA. McCahill situates these developments within theoretical debates in the surveillance literature on 'panopticism' and 'post-panopticism' and argues that the rush to a 'technological fix' may not have the desired effects in terms of preventing 'global terrorism'. The chapter concludes by considering the likely 'social impact' of the 'globalisation' of surveillance, on issues of 'social sorting', 'discrimination' and 'community cohesion'.

Andrew Robinson (Chapter 13) continues with this line of argument by looking at the war on terror in the context of the spread of an increasingly pervasive form of state regulation of everyday life. This, he argues, exists in the demonisation of minor deviance and non-conformity and through the cultivation of fear of terrorism and a global state of war. Robinson shows how a new, especially insidious system of social control is being constructed in certain Western societies, instantiated by crackdowns on minor deviance and by the war on terror and its domestic correlates. This system, he maintains, is not simply a response to particular problems but rather, an attack on difference in general, and on the 'right to have rights'. More importantly, the system is constructed around a demonisation of others, mainly by means of Barthesian myth which, in turn, constructs social relations of voicelessness and domination. By constructing social problems in a way which precludes dialogue, this construction makes problems insoluble, and makes resistance both inevitable and necessary. Robinson concludes that this development should be viewed as an outgrowth of a state logic of control inherent to state power as such and inimical to horizontal association. In this context, everyday deviance can often be interpreted as *resistenz*, and an insurrection in everyday life is constructed as the only possible response to pervasive voicelessness.

In Chapter 14, Drake focuses specifically on resistance, looking at the issues from the angle of social movements. Specially, Drake looks at 'anti-globalisation' movements in the context of the war on terror. Through an analysis of the positions, tactics and responses adopted by actors in the events around the Gleneagles G8 Summit of 2005, the chapter investigates the contemporary relations between theories and practices of power and resistance. It shows how the new conditions of power and resistance have affected the 'anti-globalisation' movement and questions whether these new conditions are a consequence of the war on terror, or whether they represent deeper and longer-term developmental tendencies inherent in the condition of globalisation. A critical review of the sociology of power and of social movement theory in conjunction with analysis of the frames of interpretation of key actors in the events around G8 reveals how contemporary sociological analysis falls short of a capacity to engage with developments under the conditions of globalisation and the war on terror. Drake concludes that the war on terror illuminates a struggle over power itself, between constituted power in the globalised security state, and the constitutive power that networked global movement activism seeks to embody.

Stefan Skrimshire's chapter on citizenship (Chapter 6) describes how 'liberal democracies' have inherited the notion of a public sphere free for rational debate and political expression that has today all but disappeared, subsumed within a climate of acquiescence, consumption and fear. He discusses this with particular reference to the manner in which the 2003 US/UK invasion of Iraq was, and continues to be justified, but more generally to the institutional and discursive tactics of the war on terror as the ultimate paradigm of this de-politicised mode of citizenship. Skrimshire concludes with some suggestions of how this climate is producing alternative modes of political participation, including the reinvention of (political) public spaces through the emergence of global mobilisations of resistance and protest.

Further, on citizenship, Su-ming Khoo (Chapter 10) examines the impact of globalisation and the war on terror on the state of poverty and citizenship in 'developing' countries. She argues that the war on terror has led to structural tendencies towards maldevelopment, involving gross inequality, exceptionalism and subjection underpinned by injustice, violence and disproportionate militarism. She shows how globalisation and the rise of the 'competition' state are making it increasingly difficult for states in developing countries to deliver social citizenship. She concludes that a rights-based model of development is desirable and essential for the future development and realisation of social citizenship in developing countries.

Finally, Maurice Mullard (Chapters 5 and 15) provides a theoretical discussion of different models of citizenship. Mullard highlights the reasons why we should be concerned that in the context of globalisation and the politics of the war on terror, geographical spaces and boundaries of nation states no longer define what citizenship is.

REFERENCES

Agamben, G. (1998), Homo Sacer: *Sovereign Power and Bare Life*, Stanford, CA: Stanford University Press.
Agamben, G. (2005), *State of Exception*, translated by Kevin Attell, Chicago: University of Chicago Press.
Appiah, K. (2003), *Citizens of the World in Globalizing Rights*, Oxford: Amnesty International/Oxford University Press.
Beck, U. (2005), *Power in the Global Age*, Cambridge: Polity.
Beck, U. (2006), *The Cosmopolitan Vision*, Cambridge: Polity.
Blair, Tony (2007), 'Our nation's future: defence', Speech delivered on the HMS *Albion* in Plymouth, 12 January, London: 10 Downing Street.
Cameron, A. and R. Palan (2004), *The Imagined Economies of Globalisation*, London: Sage.
Cole, B. (1999), 'Postcolonial systems', in R.I. Mawby (ed.), *Policing Across the World*, London: UCL Press, pp. 88–108.
Editorial (2006), 'Ethnic profiling, criminal (in)justice and minority populations', *Critical Criminology*, **14** (3), 207–12.
Hallsworth, S. (2006), 'Racial targeting and social control: looking behind the police', *Critical Criminology*, **14** (3), 293–311.
Held, D. and D. Archibugi (eds) (1995), *Cosmopolitan Democracy: An Agenda for a New Global Order*, Cambridge: Polity.
Jackson, R. (2005), *Writing the War on Terrorism: Language, Politics and Counterterrorism*, Manchester: Manchester University Press.
Kymlicka, W. (1995), *Multicultural Citizenship: A Liberal Theory of Minority Rights*, Oxford: Clarendon.
Lyon, D. (2003), *Surveillance after September 11*, Cambridge: Polity.
Sivanandan, A. (2006), 'Race, terror and civil society', *Race and Class*, **47** (3), 1–8.

PART 1

Theoretical frameworks

2. Discourse analysis and the war on terror

Michael S. Drake

INTRODUCTION

This chapter assesses how the study of discourse can illuminate the dynamics of the war on terror. It commences with an overview of approaches to the study of discourse which identifies problems for discourse analysis that are then traced through a wider range of critical approaches to the discourse of the war on terror.

Since the concept of discourse itself remains contested or at least open (there is little even contentious dialogue between differing approaches), such an overview needs to begin with discussion of the 'discourse of discourse', or how approaches to the analysis of discourse construct their subject. Such attempts at overview conventionally begin by tracing the development of discourse studies to sources in structural linguistics and the work of Michel Foucault, but in so doing they partake of one of the principal shortcomings of discourse studies itself, which is to take a primarily textualist approach, despite theoretically extending the concept of discourse to social practice in some way or other.

APPROACHES TO THE ANALYSIS OF DISCOURSE AND SOCIETY

The analysis of discourse has proliferated over the past twenty years, penetrating into fields of social science that were previously dominated by empirical and even positivistic enquiry, and opening hitherto apparently peripheral phenomena as valid and significant data for analysis. It is of course contentious whether this is in fact 'new' at all, since most formulations of discourse analysis could include such classical work in social science as Karl Marx's critical analysis of classical political economy in conjunction with social practices in industrial finance and production, or Max Weber's Nietzschean analysis of Protestant doctrine and everyday social practice with particular focus on business. The difference is that the last two decades have seen the methodology of analysing texts in some relation to social practices elevated in status from general social scientific practice to specialist expertise.

However, this enormous extension of the scope and focus of the social sciences has not been accompanied by rigorous methodological development. Discourse itself remains an essentially contested concept and different approaches to discourse analysis have only recently begun to recognise one another, even critically, as engaged in comparable undertakings.

As Fairclough (1999) has noted, during that time we have also seen the emergence of a growing public awareness of the social effect of discourse. There is much greater awareness today than two decades ago of the effects of using particular terms of description of self and others, of the way that representations and structures of description can have wide-reaching social implications, such as the way the presentation of globalisation by its proponents as inevitable, or military reference to civilian casualties and destruction of civil infrastructure as 'collateral damage'.

The commonplace habit of 'bracketing off' words and phrases also indicates what Fairclough (ibid.) has called our contemporary 'critical language awareness', a societally shared understanding that the relationship between words and things is not immediate, but dependent on context and thus always potentially open to challenge, that is, political. Signs such as quotation marks around conventionally accepted terms have become commonplace in print to indicate that the usage of the term is up for question, contentious, and we have even developed hand signs as a supplement to indicate this in speech. Fairclough's concept of critical language awareness would suggest that complex strategies are increasingly open to agents within a discursively literate society. This raises a problem for analysis of the relation between discourse and society, that is, of how effective discourse can be in constructing social reality.

The concept of discourse is widely applied across all approaches in social science today, but what is considered as discourse can vary widely from one approach to another. However, we can draw out some key distinctions and some core assumptions which seem to be shared by most approaches. First, we can distinguish between usage which refers to 'discourse' as a process of ongoing communication, often involving exchange, and references to 'a discourse', indicating a particular system or framework of assumptions, conceptual associations and beliefs within which discourse in the first sense takes place. We could make this distinction terminological, differentiating between discourse as a practice and discourse as a field. Approaches deriving from linguistic techniques and those such as conversation analysis, for instance, may be reluctant to ascribe the fixity implied by the concept of 'a discourse', while some more macro-level approaches, such as Foucault's *Archaeology of Knowledge* (1972), do not consider interactions at all, but consider a discourse as the macro-level formation of specialist knowledge determining what can be said and thought around its discursively defined subject. Most approaches, however, use the term in both senses, interchangeably.

One further key distinction to be made is between approaches to discourse which understand it as representational (or expressive), and those which understand it as constitutive. Most current theories of discourse adopt the latter approach, a significant distinction from mainstream theories of ideology. The concept of ideology covers a range of usage in a similar way to discourse, but the extent of the concept is more constricted because ideology is considered as at most a distortion of underlying truths inherent in the world itself, so ideology is always a (mis)representation of reality which exists outside and independent of ideology and is therefore at least theoretically accessible to more 'scientific' forms of knowledge, while discourse theories can extend to more constructionist models of the social world, in which there is no intrinsic order independent of the structure given by discourse. However, the problematic of how discourse analysis can be critical without establishing grounds for its own 'truthfulness' continues to compromise much analysis of discourse in relation to wider social reality. Whenever discourse analysis seeks to move beyond description, to develop explanation or critique, it must make reference to an external grounding, whether normative or objective. This problematic is particularly acute in approaches to the discourse of the war on terror. Where discourse analysis collapses into analysis of ideological representations of a reality external to discourse, it becomes reduced to the older theoretical issue in the social sciences about the function of ideas in society and history.

The problematic of the relation between discourse and wider society is only tackled directly where some form of discourse analysis is explicit. For instance, Ernesto Laclau and Chantal Mouffe's discourse theory combines the concepts of discourse as field and as practice, so they see the meaning of discursive acts as dependent on discursive formations with structural forms that change over time in a process of the contestation of meaning within the margins of their parameters (Torfing, 1999, pp. 84–119; Nash, 2000, pp. 27–30).

For Laclau and Mouffe, politics is enabled by indeterminacy of meaning and consists of continuous attempts to 'fix' and to renegotiate meanings: 'indeterminacy of meaning is what makes politics possible' (cited in Nash, 2000, p. 29). While this shifts the focus of political studies away from strictly institutional processes and formally ideological pronouncements, it has the effect of restricting their analysis to discursive strategies and frequently to their textual formation, expression and contention.

In contrast, Norman Fairclough's development of critical discourse analysis (CDA), despite its textual engagement, consistently emphasises that: 'whereas all linguistic phenomena are social, not all social phenomena are linguistic . . . discourse refers to the whole process of social interaction of which a text is just a part' (Fairclough, 1989, p. 23). Fairclough is equally consistently critical of approaches to discourse which do not recognise the interpretative dimension of discourse, while acknowledging that interpretation is discursively framed, and is thus itself a discursive practice. Discourse is part of social practice in three ways: as part of the actual activity, in representations, and in the constitution of social identities, so that interpretation and re-representation feed back into discourse through reflexively informed social action (Fairclough, 2001, p. 4).

Thus, for Fairclough, discourse is at once both representational and constitutive, and the relationship between discourse and the non-discursive is thus, 'the dialectical relationship between discourse (including language but also other forms of semiosis, for example, body language or visual images) and other elements of social practices' (ibid., p. 1). However, Fairclough's applications of CDA lack the theoretical framework necessary to deal with the social side of the dialectic, and often consist of penetrating analysis of discourse which relates to wider society as ideology.

A strong case for the necessity of some form of discourse analysis as an adjunct to conventional methods in the social sciences can be drawn from Fairclough's observations that:

> As everyday lives become more pervasively textually mediated, people's lives are increasingly shaped by representations which are produced elsewhere, representations of the world they live in, the activities they are involved in, their relationships with each other, and even who they are and how they (should) see themselves. The politics of representation becomes increasingly important . . . (Fairclough, 1999, p. 75)

Fairclough's overall enterprise is concerned to show the role of discourse in large-scale social transformations (Fairclough, 1992), and he attempts to theorise some concept of agency in such processes, as well as discursive determination. His dialectical conception of the relationship between discourse and action enables him to see a potential for increased *critical* discourse awareness to enable transformation against the flow, because:

> People are not simply colonised by such discourses, they also appropriate them and work them in particular ways. Textually mediated social life cuts both ways – it opens up unprecedented resources for people to shape their lives in new ways

drawing upon knowledges, perspectives and discourses which are generated all over the world. (Fairclough, 1999, pp. 75–6)

Although Fairclough recognises that this opens up both life and representation to a two-way traffic of power in a 'colonisation–appropriation dialectic', there is always a tendency for the absence of social theory to turn the results of CDA in the direction of ideological determinism.

The next section of the chapter deals with a range of attempts to apply some forms of discourse analysis to the discourse of the war on terror. As all these approaches make clear, the war on terror depends heavily on particular discursive strategies since it effectively inaugurates new political relations, both domestically and internationally.

ANALYSING THE DISCOURSE OF THE WAR ON TERROR

Charles Tilly's (2004) short essay on the definitions of terms – 'Terror, terrorism, terrorists' – basically argues the objective normality of terror as a form of political action. The discourse of the war on terror posits a reified object – 'terror', effectively obscuring a complex reality of political processes with shifting positions and strategies, in which we need to accommodate ambivalence, rather than adopting the absolute value oppositions of US policy rhetoric. Using a wide range of examples, Tilly argues that, 'The strategy of terror appears across a wide variety of political circumstances, in the company of very different sorts of political struggle', p. 10, and is undertaken by a wide variety of kinds of political actors. Consistent with his broader theoretical conceptualisation of the state as in effect no more than a regularised form of extortion (Tilly, 1992, passim), Tilly argues that, rather than differentiating between the violence of state and non-state actors, we can more objectively differentiate between terror undertaken by specialists and that by non-specialists in coercion, since it is this distinction which will enable us to identify differential dynamics (Tilly, 2004, p. 9). The dynamics of terror tell us that we should be sceptical of the purported existence of 'a distinct coherent class of actors (terrorists) who specialize in a unitary form of political action (terror) and who thus establish a separate variety of politics (terrorism)', because specialisation in terror as a singular mode of action is typically transitory and 'accounts for a highly variable but usually very small share of all the terror that occurs in the contemporary world' (ibid., p. 5). We cannot demarcate terrorism as a unique field of political action because terror always relates to other strategies, claims and objectives; the 'terrorist' group or individual is not a coherent or durable identity, because terror is a strategy, undertaken by actors 'engaged in wider political struggles' and those specialising in wider practices of coercion (including both private and state-affiliated actors), with a relatively minor element conducted by groups, individuals and networks for which terror is a 'dominant rationale' (ibid., p. 5).

Although not addressing the discourse of the war on terror directly, Tilly's argument effectively consigns it to the status of a conceptual error which cannot be carried over into social science. He thus avoids direct confrontation with the political strategy of the discourse itself as an attempt to 'fix' identities and definitions, but thereby enables himself to defend the objectivity which for him grounds the claim to social scientific freedom of enquiry against the encroachments of ideological and political strategies. Tilly purposefully does not develop a critique of the discourse of the war on terror as a political strategy, but by demolishing its assumptions as a conceptual basis for social science, he re-establishes grounds from which such critique could be undertaken objectively. His essay corresponds to the undecidable debate in the social sciences over whether analysis can or should extend to the critique of politically normative descriptions of social reality, a debate classically articulated by the contrast between Weber's strict 'value-neutral' objectivity and Marx's confrontation of ideological representations with theoretical analysis. That debate is echoed in the contrast between Tilly's implicitly neo-Weberian casting of the role of public sociology in relation to the war on terror, and more normatively judgemental approaches, such as Noam Chomsky's didactic critiques (in the analytical tradition of 'vulgar' Marxism), or Ulrich Beck's projection (along the lines of Marx's historical materialism) of cosmopolitanism as grounds for response to 9/11.

There are three major problems with Tilly's analysis. First, his contradictory definition of terror as a means of political struggle extraordinary to the forms 'routinely operating within some current regime' (ibid., p. 5), which fails to encompass the origin he identifies for the term in the Jacobin policies of the French Revolution. Second, his argument that terror is a strategy, not an object, is undermined by his residual category of 'terrorists' as those for whom the undertaking of terror is a 'dominant rationale', since for them it has to be an end in itself, and is therefore both their strategy and their object. Third, Tilly's demolition of the discourse of the war on terror is only partial; he does not deal with its argument that networks of specialists in terror, even if relatively insignificant in numerical or quantitative terms, nevertheless exercise a qualitatively disproportionate capacity for destabilisation under conditions of globalisation. It is precisely this context that provides the grounds for Beck's analysis of the significance of 11 September 2001.

Beck (2003) points out how the difficulty of precise linguistic responses to September 11 indicates the condition of what he calls 'global risk society', in which, 'We live, think and act in concepts that are historically obsolete but continue to govern our thinking and acting' (Beck, 2003, p. 256). This discrepancy between language and reality is manifest in 'three dimensions of danger . . . each following a different kind of logic of conflict . . . first, ecological crises; second, global financial crises; and third – since 11 September 2001 – terrorist dangers caused by transnational terror networks' (ibid., p. 256). Beck's analysis is presented in terms of an idealist theoretical assertion of an existent 'global risk society', a context in which the terror attacks of September 11 reveal 'what globalization actually is: a worldwide community of destiny' (ibid., p. 257), an apparent occidentalism that is qualified by his recognition that the process involves different paths, and in itself historically transcends the 'European monopoly on modernity' (ibid., p. 258). In this context, Back prescribes the responses to September 11, 2001 that should be made by such a culturally diversified but historically universal, cosmopolitan 'global risk society', contrasting these to the impasse he diagnoses for neo-liberalism in the face of a situation requiring global regulation.

The idealism of Beck's response has become self-evident as neo-conservatism rather than cosmopolitanism has in reality become the ideology of response, with the effect of cementing cultural fundamentalisms rather than fostering universalism. However, Beck's idealism is underpinned by a critical analysis that we can extract from the evolutionary narrative in which it is presented, just as Marx's analyses can be extracted from the narrative framework of his historical materialism.

Beck argues that, 'The novelty of the global risk society lies in the fact that our civilizational decisions involve global consequences and dangers, and these radically contradict the institutionalized language of control – indeed the promise of control – that is radiated to the global public in the event of catastrophe' (ibid., p. 256). Such contact with reality, however, 'explodes' the very basis of authority of institutions that produce such legitimating rhetoric. The effect of September 11 is thus akin to Claus Offe's diagnosis of the 'legitimation crisis' of welfare capitalist industrial modernity (Offe, 1984). Beck clearly anticipates the demise of neo-liberalism in the same form of crisis that provided the conditions for its hegemony in the late twentieth century, but we can fruitfully disentangle the analysis from the normative framework of its presentation. We do not need to share his evaluation of the significance of September 11 as an indication of an immanent global risk society to follow his analysis of the effects of the meanings of the concepts of 'terror' and 'war' in the post-9/11 context.

The institution most severely exposed to delegitimation by September 11, 2001 is the territorial state, functionally reliant upon its claim to and exercise of the state monopoly of violence, since those attacks establish terror groups, 'as new global actors in competition with states, economies and civil societies . . . NGOs of violence' (Beck, 2003, p. 259) in which they function as agents of globalisation despite their apparent atavism (Beck, 2005, p. 89). In contrast to the old national liberation movements, these new deterritorialised, transnational terror networks, 'depreciate with a single blow the national grammar of the military and war' (Beck, 2003, p. 259). Rather than states, the new networks are conditional upon statelessness, or on the conditions of so-called 'failed states' such as Afghanistan, Somalia, Palestine and, most recently, Iraq since the overthrow of Saddam Hussein. When we look for states and figureheads of such networks we are engaging in the military thought that is part and parcel of the historically obsolete concepts whose continued existence indicates the immanence, the not-yet-quite existence of global risk society, in its contrast to the reality, that 'we are standing at the threshold of an *individualization of war*' (ibid., p. 259, original italics). Attempts to address this individualisation of war through the medium of the state inverts conventional relations and expectations: it becomes a condition of citizenship for an individual to prove that he/she is not dangerous, while governments unite together against citizens.

Beck thus shows how the discourse of war on terror is effective in producing the opposite of its purported aim. The death of democracy on a global scale is the eventual limit-result of the discourse of the war on terror in the condition of 'global risk society' understood as the obsolescence of the terms of that very discourse in the context of the very factors that the discourse aims to address: globalised terror networks. However, this incisive analysis is compromised by the idealism of the framework in which it is presented, an approach developed by Keith Spence's analysis of the discursive construction of the war on terror through 'outmoded vocabularies of national security and sovereignty' (Spence, 2005, p. 284). The effect of this process, Spence argues, marginalises the reasoned containment of risk in favour of a militaristic search for absolute security, displacing a model of negotiation with a model of war, and substituting the object of terror for the more diverse and relational concept of risk. The projection of global risk society thus provides us with a critical perspective, enabling analysis which 'challenges war against terror by addressing its underlying assumption and their consequences' (ibid., p. 285), showing that such responses in the context of a global risk society inevitably reveal the violence at the core of the modern state form (an argument that Spence attributes to Beck but which corresponds perhaps more strongly to Giorgio Agamben's philosophical critique of the political concept of sovereignty).

However, as with Beck's own analysis of the responses to September 11, 2001, it is questionable whether we need to accept the 'global risk society' framework, since Spence's analysis similarly uses the perspective offered by the projection to establish a normative point for evaluation, *beyond* critical analysis. In a more detailed engagement with the discourse, Spence points out how George W. Bush's description of the attacks of September 11, 2001 as 'more than acts of terror; they were acts of war' combined with his subsequent declaration of a war on terror worldwide to negate any absolute distinction between war and terror, since 'war', the act of a state, was now redefined and equated with the acts of individuals, while the recognition of territorial boundaries to legitimate sovereign state policy was swept aside in the declaration of a deterritorialised, worldwide theatre of operations, thus removing the vaunted status of war waged by sovereign states in its contrast to the terror waged by groups that refused to recognise state sovereignty (ibid., p. 288). The discourse of the war on terror thus from the outset undermined the very grounds of legitimating distinction to which it laid claim.

Further legitimating distinctions collapsed in the wake of this declaration; between civilian and combatant, collateral and non-collateral, innocents and implicated, attack and defence, emergency and normality, and between potential and actual threats and enemies. The blurring of the distinction between strategies and ends constitutes the war against terror as structurally unbounded, war without end, an infinite deferral of the model of absolute victory drawn from national military thought now redeployed in 'pre-emptive defence' on a global scale against potential threats. As well as this discursive, structural deferral constituting war without end, the means of national warfare employed globally also produce the same effect mechanically, collaterally producing new forces of revenge, resentment, solidarity and resistance which see the USA as their primary enemy.

Supposedly against critical perspectives on US imperialism, Spence argues that 'the response exemplifies the violence that inheres within the state as a political form' (ibid., p. 291), though this seems weak grounds to claim the insight for 'global risk society' and it is in any case doubtful that those accused would disagree with this proposition. The argument that terror has always been functionally necessary to the articulation of the modern nation state is not an insight of global risk society, but is commonplace among critical perspectives on the state, from Marx through Lenin, Weber, Walter Benjamin, Hannah Arendt and Norbert Elias, to Agamben today.

While his theoretical speculations thus outstrip the framework that Spence claims for them, his analysis generates original insights into the social effects of the discursive construction of the war on terror, in which, 'uncertainty is cultivated but remains unresolved as the act that completes the sequence – the event of terror – is defined in such a way that, although inevitable, its occurrence is always deferred into an unpredictable future rather than the foreseeable present' (ibid., p. 293). One of the great political utilities of the discourse of the war on terror is its capacity to invoke the ontological security of 'what if' – what if these restrictive policies were not in place, what if we refused this measure and so on, exemplified in the dichotomy, 'We can be afraid. Or we can be prepared' (Ridge, cited in ibid., p. 293), by which US Homeland Security operates as an endless self-replicating prophecy without requiring fulfilment. Again, this discursive structure is replicated mechanically in the rituals of security that pervade everyday life, just as the insecurity of the Cold War was fostered on a regular basis by the simulation of catastrophe.

Ultimately, however, Spence's analysis lapses into the instrumentalist model in which the discourse of the war on terror figures as an ideological 'means of shaping the beliefs and anxieties of malleable, self-regulating subjects who associate citizenship with conformity and patriotic duty' (ibid., p. 294). This instrumentalist reading produces the paradoxical argument that (following Beck) the terror of groups such as al-Qaeda advances globalisation, while the discourse of the global war on terror figures as an actually 'atavistic impulse' (ibid., p. 296). Beck himself, however, has developed this analysis beyond instrumentalism to argue that the task of deciding who is a transnational terrorist has today become constitutive of sovereignty (Beck, 2005, p. 295), transposing Carl Schmitt's formulation of the concept of sovereignty into the condition of the 'global risk society' in which he sees the construction of a transnational surveillance state as the precursor to 'a cosmopolitan despotism intent on dismantling the fundamental values of modernity in order to protect them' (ibid., p. 297; Weber, 2002, p. 452). In the difference between Beck's analysis of tendencies within the contemporary configuration and Spence's identification of an agent deliberately determining such an end lies the distinction between sociological analysis and conspiracy theory.

Beck's sociological analysis stands in stark contrast to other attempts to analyse the discourse of the war on terror. Where Tilly avoids direct confrontation with the political strategy of the discourse itself in favour of re-establishing the grounds for an 'objective' critique of that discourse and its practice, Beck's initial response idealistically projected a cosmopolitan global risk society as the grounds for a more normative critique. Subsequently, however, Beck has rejected the projection of a global risk society and its concomitant cosmopolitan idealism (and thus by implication rejects the instrumentalist critique of the war on terror discourse) by thinking through 'cosmopolitan realism' to arrive at a self-critical cosmopolitanism which is posited as both a normative and an objective perspective (Beck, 2005, pp. 110–11, 115–16, 306–7). The promise of Beck's approach to the discourse of the war on terror, to explain it sociologically by contextualising it in the context of a global risk society, thus collapses because he elevates his own analytical construct to a normative position from which to pronounce judgements and remedies. Nevertheless, underlying these claims, he develops a critique of the discourse of the war on terror and its social effects, through analysis of the processes of social change that are purportedly producing the global risk society and cosmopolitanism which he projects as grounds for normative evaluation.

These sociological analyses contrast with critical political science approaches to the war on terror which apply Norman Fairclough's CDA. Fairclough developed his method as an attempt to relate discourse – in his formulation restricted to hegemonic linguistic constructions – to wider social change (Fairclough, 1992). However, where the risk society perspective tends to obscure its own critical effectiveness by elevating its analysis of social change into speculative grounds for normative evaluation, CDA ultimately fails to connect linguistic constructions to wider social processes, so that it becomes little more than an 'exposé' of the instrumentalist deployment of discourse by those whose power is tautologically assumed as given in the hegemony of their discourse.

In both of the two essays considered here, Jackson begins his introduction to the discourse analysis method he applies to the discourse of war on terror by re-stating the premises of Fairclough's approach: 'Political discourses are not neutral reflections of social and political reality; rather, they are partly constitutive of that reality – they have a reality-making effect' (Jackson, 2005, p. 148). Despite apparently systematic research, Jackson illustrates clearly the methodological paucity of CDA where he sets out the twin objectives of his research, 'to uncover the primary discursive construction at the heart of the "war on terrorism" . . . and to assess the effects of discourse on democratic politics' (ibid., p. 148), since while CDA has recourse to linguistic analysis for the first objective, it does not provide a theoretical framework for analysing the effectiveness of discourse in relation to wider social reality, however narrowly that may be specified. In the latter part of the analysis, CDA thus falls back on a conception of ideology as an influential representation of reality that is in effect drawn from Marxism, but without adopting the Marxist theoretical framework, with its explanations of power, social contradiction and so on, CDA results in a tautological conclusion which sees ideological discourse as the source of the very power that is already assumed in the hegemonic status of that discourse. Nevertheless, just as Beck's approach produces insights into the relation between the discourse of the war on terror and wider social processes, so Jackson's analysis yields insights into the discursive construction of the war on terror.

Jackson's analysis identifies four main themes in the discourse of the war on terror: a fixing of meaning of '9–11' which constructed new identities as ontologically threatened by terrorism, thus legitimating 'good war' as the primary response, using a mixture of 'analogy, amplification, visual imagery, popular entertainment tropes, foundational meta-narratives and an overarching Manichaean frame' (ibid., p. 149). Jackson consistently refers to this discourse as a deliberately manipulative act, 'a powerful rhetorical strategy that can be reflexively and retroactively employed' (ibid., p. 163), thus producing conspiracy theory rather than explanation, while the account of the influence of the discourse is tautological. The discourse is thus not analysed as culturally and socially embedded, but as a conspiratorial and cynical use of culture and ideology to manipulate cultural dupes. The analysis thus results in the production of an account of a discursive exercise of power through a medium of culture and ideology where that power and those resources are already given and assumed as the precondition of the discourse. Jackson's analysis thus does not contribute towards understanding 'how discourses work to construct social processes and structures in ways that reproduce power relations' (Jackson, 2004, p. 4). Attempts to quantitatively assess the effect of the discourse of the war on terror on public opinion further undermine the central premiss of CDA that discourse is constitutive of political reality, not merely an influence upon it. The analysis lacks any sense of discourse being socially conditioned *or* socially constitutive because the notion of discourse employed is inherently asociological, with discourse entirely distinct from and operating upon a social reality external to it, emanating from an agent that is never explained but simply assumed, resulting in an instrumentalist account of the discourse of the war on terror verging on conspiracy theory and paranoia: 'Like the "red scares" of the past, the discourse of danger is deployed in this mode to enforce social discipline, mute dissent, and increase the powers of the national security state' (ibid., p. 11).

Jackson's analysis also produces contradictory conclusions. The 'shockwaves' produced by the photographs of abused Iraqi prisoners from Abu Ghraib gaol were 'the direct consequence of a discourse that constructs the other as inhuman and evil' (ibid., p. 14), yet his analysis of the discourse of the war on terror suggests that the abuse indicated by those photographs would have been perceived as acceptable and even righteous. Moreover, crucially, he wants to engage in normative critique by contrasting the discursive construction of the war on terror to its consequences in social reality, requiring him to introduce a distinction between discourse and social reality where CDA supposedly studies their interaction (this contradiction is built into

CDA, identifiable in the introduction to one of his analytical essays, which states: 'The "war on terrorism" is both a set of institutional practices . . . as well as an accompanying discursive project' (Jackson, 2005, p. 147). To establish grounds for normative critique contrary to this 'reality' of institutional practices, Jackson has to resort to the a priori position of 'a society supposedly built on the belief in human dignity, human rights and democratic participation . . . a universal and cosmopolitan vision of society' (Jackson, 2004, pp. 14–15). However, this seems to undermine his critical analysis of the effects of the discourse of the war on terror, which depends on the assumption that society and culture were permeated by the very different values and self-understandings that provided the rhetorical and ideological resources for successful discursive construction.

The faith of Jackson and even Beck in cosmopolitanism as a perspective which in itself enables effective normative critique is thrown into question by Anthony Burke's questioning of the very terms of moral discourse which such critique would utilise. In a critique of the 'just war' arguments in favour of strategic violence, as revived in the discourse of the war on terror, Burke enquires into the validity of the very tools of normative critique which Beck and Jackson deploy from their idealist positions. Burke asks, 'Are our moral discourses – whether they are couched in reality, "just war" or liberal/legal terms – adequate to the problem and phenomenon of war, and especially war against terror?' (Burke, 2004, p. 332), concluding that 'our frameworks for the moral justification (and limitation) of strategic violence have failed us' (ibid., p. 333).

Burke identifies in Bush's declaration of the war on terror the same Manichaean divide identified by Jackson, but rather than seeing this as a conspiratorial ruse on the part of the US presidential administration that enables it to claim the moral superiority and need of defence of the victim, as in Jackson's analysis, Burke points out how this language of morality constructs a subjective position for which force is an imperative response: 'Bush's address to Congress imagines a martial universe and a moral universe, and then unites them' (ibid., p. 334). This approach is clearly very different from Jackson's CDA, for which the effect of discourse is always external to the agent of discourse; in Burke's analysis, discourse constructs not only its objects, but also the subject.

Moreover, this approach provides a sense in which discourse constructs social reality, where as in Jackson's account discourse ultimately constructed ideology, a distortion of reality, enabling manipulation and producing public acquiescence, but always in contrast to the ideal of the 'real'. In Burke's account, the effects of moral discourse are powerful because they are also believed by those who utter them, enabling us to explain their discursive actions as part of social reality rather than as somehow distinct from it. For Burke, the disregard for international law in the discourse of the war on terror is not strategic, but a moral imperative for the discourse: 'built upon a particularly claustrophobic idea of moral community; a bifurcated moral universe which casts the US and its allies as virtuous and its enemies as ineradicably threatening and evil' (ibid., p. 336), producing the absolute struggle that Spence traced to the modern concept of military victory utilised in the discourse of the war on terror. Burke's analysis provides us with a deeper view that enables us to see how such a discursive configuration creates norms and makes war a norm in terms of international relations.

It is this function of the creation of norms that has exercised Upendra Baxi's essay, which provides also the most radical approach to the discourse of the war on terror that I shall consider here. Baxi's aim is to consider the war on terror in terms of its legal implications, but her approach thus also follows most closely Tilly's injunction that an objective approach to the discourse of the war on terror must eschew the temptation to claim idealist grounds for normative judgement.

Like Tilly, Baxi begins from the point that the very term 'war on terror' coins a discursive novelty, 'never before September 11 2001 ("9/11"), were acts of "terror" described in terms of a "war", nor were the practices of counter-"terror"' (Baxi, 2005, p. 8). The terms of Bush's declaration in fact defined two wars – a war of terror, indicated in the attacks of 9/11, and a war on terror, which he declared on September 12. In contrast to the approach of Jackson, which analyses the discursive statement only in terms of its enunciation and impact in the West, and even specifically in the USA, Baxi reminds us that this declaration did not take place in a context defined by Bush, or even by 'the West', but in a world divided into regimes corresponding to the implicit demands of the war on terror for legitimate control of violence within their borders, in which those 'failed states' or 'rogue states' became an implicit target of the US-led war on terror.

Baxi points out that much of the 'Third World' remains outside this construction of a world of states formed exclusively on the Euro-American model. Furthermore, the proponents of the 'war of terror' provide a counter-discourse, setting their actions in the context of long-term colonial oppression, another, prior 'war' in which terror in less spectacular forms has been frequently deployed against inhabitants of states that do not correspond to Euro-American norms. Since the US-led war on terror is experienced by inhabitants of excluded states as an extension of this war of terror, the counter-discourse therefore finds a receptive audience for their claim that theirs is a war on terror, using the only means available to them, while Bush's declaration simply tries to rebrand a prior war of terror that has a much longer history.

Tarak Barkawi's study (2006) similarly points out how the war on terror takes place within a broad discursive framework in which appeal to universal ideals such as 'humanity', 'civilisation', or 'justice' is a crucial strategy utilised by all participants, and so the struggle is not only over the deployment of violence, but also over its legitimation, over which organisation of violence can claim to be 'security forces', and which is deemed 'terror'.

CONCLUSION

The range of approaches examined above shows that discourse analysis in itself is inadequate because a social theory is required to understand how discourse relates to politics. Discourse theory is no more than a theory of discourse and leaves the non-discursive out of any analysis. CDA posits a dialectical relation between discourse and social reality, but its focus on discourse at the expense of social theory leaves it with a tendency to relate discourse to society as ideological determination, contradicting its theoretical claims. The concept of discourse is undefined, and the meaning of the term oscillates in most applications between discourse as formation and discourse as practice. Partly because of such fuzziness, the claims that are made for the relation between discourse and society do not even comprise stable positions, but may vary within any given analysis, so that the effectivity of discourse may be seen as ranged along a spectrum on which its relation to social phenomena can be constitutive (where there is 'nothing outside the discourse'), determinant (the subjects and objects of discourse are external to it, but are 'empty vessels'), manipulative (social reality is external to discourse but may be influenced by it), critically received, and even resisted by active agents of discourse.

However, the agent of discourse is rarely questioned in the analysis of the discourse of the war on terror; power is assumed to be there already, and discourse thus appears as the resource of power, rather than as a field of contention. Furthermore, the abandonment of the concept of ideology in its Marxist or Mannheimian sense, in which ideology is expressive of a socially structured perspective, leads away from questions about the external conditions of production of discourse, and towards conspiratorial, asociological conclusions that are particularly acute in application to the discourse of the war on terror, in which even critique tends to become participant in rather than resistant to the discursive construction of fear.

The problems raised by the examination of approaches to the discourse of the war on terror thus return us to more classical debates. One is the question of to what extent and in what sense specialist discourse – especially 'hegemonic discourse' – is distinct from ideology. Another is the extent to which debates over the relation between discourse and society simply reiterate the older issue in the social sciences over the function of ideas in history and society.

These issues produce the main question within the analysis of the discourse of the war on terror: whether its construction is an active, conspiratorial policy (the result of agency external to the process), or the inexorable expression of a structurally conditioned perverse moral imperative (and thus driven by internal dynamics). The two conclusions seem exclusive, but equally endless in their implications.

It is clear, however, that the war on/of terror is particularly dependent on fraught and imperilled discursive construction which produces its own conditions. The responses to the events of 9/11 no less than those events themselves seem to have flipped a domino effect, in which meaning has been disestablished. However, rather than empowering the contention of discursive constructions, this has produced conditions where actual violence, rather than its mediation, now becomes the primary mode of legitimation on a global scale.

REFERENCES

Barkawi, T. (2006), *Globalization and War*, Lanham, MD: Rowman & Littlefield.

Baxi, U. (2005), 'The "war on terror" and the "war *of* terror": nomadic multitudes, aggressive incumbents and the "new" international law', *Osgoode Hall Law Journal*, **43** (1&2): 7–43.

Beck, U. (2003), 'The silence of words: on terror and war', *Security Dialogue*, **34** (3): 255–67.

Beck, U. (2005), *Power in the Global Age: A New Global Political Economy*, Cambridge: Polity.

Burke, A. (2004), 'Just war or ethical peace? Moral discourses of strategic violence after 9/11', *International Affairs*, **80** (2): 329–53.

Fairclough, N. (1989), *Language and Power*, London: Longman.

Fairclough, N. (1992), *Discourse and Social Change*, Cambridge: Polity.

Fairclough, N. (1999), 'Global capitalism and critical awareness of language', *Language Awareness*, **8** (2): 71–83.

Fairclough, N. (2001), 'Dialectics of discourse', www.ling.lancs.ac.uk/staff/norman/2001a.doc, pp. 1–7, accessed 9 August 2006; also published in *Textus*, **14**: 231–42.

Jackson, R. (2004), 'Language power and politics: critical discourse analysis and the War on Terrorism', *49th Parallel*, **15**, www.49thparallel.bhma.ac.uk/back/issue15/jackson1.htm, accessed 28 December 2006.

Jackson, R. (2005), 'Security, democracy, and the rhetoric of counter-terrorism', *Democracy and Security*, **1**: 147–71.

Nash, K. (2000), *Contemporary Political Sociology: Globalization, Politics and Power*, Oxford: Blackwell.

Offe, C. (1984), *Contradictions of the Welfare State*, London: Hutchinson.

Spence, K. (2005), 'World risk society and war against terror', *Political Studies*, **53**: 284–302.

Tilly, C. (1992), *Coercion, Capital and European States, AD 990–1992*, Oxford: Blackwell.

Tilly, C. (2004), 'Terror, terrorism, terrorists', *Sociological Theory*, **22** (1): 5–13.

Torfing, J. (1999), *New Theories of Discourse: Laclau, Mouffe and Zizek*, Oxford: Blackwell.

Weber, S. (2002), 'War terrorism and spectacle: on towers and caves', *The South Atlantic Quarterly*, **101** (3): 449–58.

3. History's actors: insights into the 'war on terror' from international relations theory[1]

Colin Tyler

We're an empire now, and when we act, we create our own reality. And while you're studying that reality – judiciously, as you will – we'll act again, creating other realities, which you can study too, and that's how things will sort out. We're history's actors . . . and you, all of you, will be left just to study what we do. (A senior advisor to George W. Bush, 2004 quoted in Suskind, 2004; see also Ferguson, 2005, p. vii)

INTRODUCTION

The image of the Bush administration (at least prior to the 2006 congressional elections) as a self-interested elite leading a rogue nation – to some, even a right-wing terrorist force – is now popular among not merely the radical left, but even among moderate political commentators (Chomsky, 2003, 2006; Coleman, 2003; Prestowitz, 2003). Yet, such a polemical position obscures the crucial subtleties of the so-called 'war on terror'. This chapter argues that the aims of the Bush administration's 'war' are far from being restricted to the ruthless augmentation of US wealth and power in the world. The war also seeks to reassert the authority of the US state in the international system, to secure retribution, and to reassert the US body politic's own identity to itself domestically, as well as to pursue a neo-conservative moral mission. One thing that is notable about this list is that, in spite of the rhetoric, the different goals of US foreign policy serve the interests of different manifestations of 'the United States of America'. Sometimes it is US business interests, other times it is the current Bush administration, sometimes it is the US state understood as an entity that endures through changing administrations, and at yet other times it is the rather more amorphous notion of the US body politic.

This chapter assesses the likely impact on the international system and international society of each of these motivations for the 'war on terror'.

In part, it seeks to cast doubt on the chilling arrogance of the senior advisor to George W. Bush quoted at the start of this chapter. In part, it seeks to analyse the likely effects of the elite's attempt to manipulate international society. The next section highlights certain debts that Bush's war policy owes to neo-conservative think-tanks and lobby groups, especially the Project for the New American Century. The following section sketches a theory of state sovereignty which emphasises the dependence of sovereignty on official (particularly juridical) recognition by other state and non-state actors. It will be shown that this familiar model assumes an unrealistic theory of recognition. In fact, identity and sovereignty are derived from the inherently dynamic processes of intersubjective recognition. The section ends by noting that this revised theory is unlikely to produce significant order at the international level. The consequent need for institutional articulation and enforcement of the processes of dynamic recognition and their results is explored in the subsequent section. It is argued that institutionalisation must be led by powerful actors. The frequent absence of the great powers acting as 'great responsibles' and the clash of vitality and power together represent the tragic heart of international society (Bull, 1977, ch. 9; 1980). The penultimate section returns to the 'war on terror' with this wider perspective in mind. It argues that the theological presuppositions underpinning the present war policy will distort, not just the functioning of international society, but also the lives of the actors who together constitute that society. (I examine one instance of such distortion elsewhere in this volume.) The chapter concludes that any good that may come from any continuation of this 'war' in its current form will be more than offset by its long-run consequences. The chapter closes with the reflection that the policy already seems to be under pressure and so may pass away anyway with the conclusion of the Bush regime.

BUSH'S NEO-CONSERVATIVE WAR

The traditional criteria for waging a just war are familiar: a competent authority is justified in engaging in armed conflict with another state or non-state actor when that actor has deliberately, seriously and directly violated the authority's safety and integrity or that of its population; such conflict must be a last resort to secure peace, the response must be proportionate to the wrong, and the chosen strategy must have a good probability of success. When these conditions are met it is legitimate for the victim to respond against the perpetrator with organised and sustained violence.

The 'war on terror' meets few of these traditional criteria. The spectacular acts of aggression that, officially at least, sparked military actions by the 'coalition of the willing' against the Taliban in Afghanistan and the Ba'athist regime in Iraq were perpetrated by what is at most a loose terrorist network. The 'aggressor' is, in the words of the Bush administration, 'a far more complex and elusive set of targets' (White House, 2002, ch. 9) than is presupposed by traditional just war theory (Brzezinski, 2004, p. 215). In reality, al-Qaeda is probably more a symbol or rallying point for certain Islamic populations disaffected by the imposition of culturally arrogant and socially destructive Western capitalism, individualism and liberalism, than it is a military organisation with definite strategies and an effective command structure. There appears little possibility of the coalition winning a war against something as poorly defined, expansive and apparently endemic as 'terror' (ibid., pp. 215–16). Next, the former Iraqi state's alleged link to al-Qaeda is effectively non-existent (Ritter, 2002, pp. 45–6). The March 2003 Iraq invasion was not launched as an option of last resort, and indeed sanctions, diplomatic pressure and the weapons inspection regime were still supported by the United Nations (UN). Moreover, the coalition's 'shock and awe' policy entailed a rejection of any real sense of proportionality as well as of the sanctity of non-combatants. Furthermore, the US state did not have clear authority to commence military action in Iraq in the face of opposition by the UN (unlike the US-led action in Afghanistan which was UN backed).

The coalition of the willing side-stepped many of these worries by replacing the traditional just war doctrine with what has come to be called 'the Bush doctrine', according to which the US has the right unilaterally to conduct preventive action including preventive military action. Bush made this very clear in his now famous speech to the graduates of West Point military academy on 1 June 2002:

> The war on terror will not be won on the defensive. We must take the battle to the enemy, disrupt his plans, and confront the worst threats before they emerge. [Applause.] In the world we have entered, the only path to safety is the path of action. And this nation will act. [Applause.] . . . our security will require all Americans to be forward-looking and resolute, to be ready for preemptive action when necessary to defend our liberty and to defend our lives. [Applause.] (Bush, 2002a)[2]

In a final divergence from traditional just war theory, far from simply pursuing peace, it seems clear that several other goals also underlie current US foreign policy. These become more evident when one examines the origins of the Bush doctrine.

Despite the subsequent attempts of some neo-conservatives to distance themselves from the disastrous policy over Iraq (Burrough et al., 2004; Rose, 2007), the Bush administration's post-9/11 policy towards Afghanistan and

Iraq finds its roots in the concerns of certain US neo-conservative think-tanks such as the American Enterprise Institute and especially the Project for the New American Century (PNAC) (Bush, 2003). (I leave aside the question of the unity of neo-conservatism here, claiming merely that Bush adheres to a strand of the movement.) The PNAC's 1997 'Statement of Principles' boasts among its signatories Jeb Bush, Dick Cheney, Francis Fukuyama, Donald Kagan, Dan Quayle, Donald Rumsfeld and Paul Wolfowitz (PNAC, 1997). Since its inception, the PNAC's primary aim in lobbying the federal government has been to increase the US defence budget to a level that 'would maintain American security and advance American interests in the new century'. The 'Statement of Principles' continues,

> As the 20th century draws to a close, the United States stands as the world's preeminent power. Having led the West to victory in the Cold War, America faces an opportunity and a challenge: Does the United States have the vision to build upon the achievements of past decades? Does the United States have the resolve to shape a new century favorable to American principles and interests? (Ibid.)

Such solidly classical realist objectives are far from new in the international relations (IR) literature, of course. (The situation is rather different for structural realists.) Hans Morgenthau argued that every state has an innate tendency to be afraid of losing power relative to other states, through the latter's deliberate strategies, changed circumstances, or the state's own mistakes. For this reason, he argued, there is a perennial tendency for every state to try to increase its own standing and power relative to all other actors in the international system. Where a state achieves this goal, it will seek to strengthen its new position, possibly using diplomacy or war (Morgenthau, 1985, p. 228). The final section of the present chapter will show that neo-conservatives distance themselves from Morgenthau on other grounds (for example, Fukuyama, 1992, pp. 252–3). Yet, the PNAC has applied this reasoning vociferously to justify regime change in Afghanistan and Iraq. For example, in a letter to the *Weekly Standard* dated 28 September 1998, Robert Kagan (1998) urged the Clinton administration to use all necessary military force to support 'the Wolfowitz plan' (whereby the US would create and maintain a safe haven for indigenous anti-Ba'athist forces in southern Iraq) in order to counter the 'imminent and devastating threat to American interests' posed by Iraq's alleged possession of so-called 'weapons of mass destruction'. The PNAC kept up this type of pressure from its creation in 1997 until the invasion of Iraq in March 2003. In fact, its primary goal in the Middle East has always been to transform Iraq from a rogue state into a good neighbour in international affairs (Schmitt, 2005; see also Chomsky, 2006). This accords with a clear tradition in US foreign policy, the central claim of which found canonical expression in the Roosevelt Corollary of 1904, under the terms of which 'in the Western Hemisphere the adherence of the United States to the Monroe Doctrine [of 1823] may force the United States, however reluctantly, in flagrant cases of . . . wrong doing or impotence [by other states], to the exercise of an international police power' (Roosevelt, quoted in McCoubrey and Morris, 2000, pp. 102–3).

Since the Corollary was first stated, the great powers of the Old World have declined, the Soviet bloc has collapsed, technology has advanced, globalisation has intensified significantly and the US has rejected isolationism in favour of a new role as a global power. Together these factors have extended the US's backyard (a notion central to the Monroe Doctrine) to the whole globe. The US state's responsibilities and ambitions have expanded in line with its international pre-eminence. The PNAC has understood this for many years (PNAC, 1998).

America's post-9/11 war policy grows straight out of this line of thinking. Reflecting its endorsement of PNAC neo-conservatism, a key priority of the Bush administration's *National Security Strategy for the United States of America*, published in September 2002, is to repair failed states in order to protect US interests: 'As humanitarian relief requirements are better understood, we must also be able to help build police forces, court systems, and legal codes, local and provincial government institutions, and electoral systems' (White House, 2002, ch. 9). This document opens with the following statement of faith:

> [We in the United States] seek . . . to create a balance of power that favours human freedom: conditions in which all nations and all societies can choose for themselves the rewards and challenges of political and economic liberty . . . We will extend the peace by encouraging free and open societies on every continent. (Bush, 2002b)

The Bush administration will allow the Iraqi people to freely choose 'lasting institutions of freedom': in other words, liberal democratic free market capitalism (Bush, 2003; see also Chua, 2004; and Harvey, 2005, 'Afterword'). In this way, the Ba'athist state will be replaced by a neo-conservative ideal of the state and a civil society in which individuals enjoy, in the words quoted above, 'the rewards and challenges of political and economic liberty'. The international system will thereby be stabilised and US interests protected (Brzezinski, 2004, esp. part 2). (Some neo-liberals disaggregate free markets from the rule of law and democracy, looking to the former to bring international stability but not moral homogeneity; see Lal, 2004.)

Many neo-conservatives have acknowledged a classical realist basis for 'the war on terror'. Irving Kristol wrote in 2003, for example, that Thucydides'

History of the Peloponnesian War was 'the favorite neo-conservative text on foreign affairs' (Kristol, 2003, p. 35). Yet, the actual situation is not so straightforward (Kane, 2006). Famously and very influentially, Francis Fukuyama claimed Georg W.F. Hegel for the neo-conservative cause. In *The End of History and the Last Man*, Fukuyama argued that while all earlier political systems had contained 'grave defects and irrationalities', liberal democratic free market corporate capitalism had shown itself to be 'free from such fundamental internal contradictions' (Fukuyama, 1992, p. xi). In Bush's words, there is only one 'sustainable model for national success: freedom, democracy, and free enterprise' (Bush, 2002b). This model represents, in short, 'the end of History'. Fukuyama's work, and especially his 2004 book *State Building*, is pivotal here in that it foregrounds a core element of the neo-conservative mission beyond that of the pursuit of the interests of US businesses and the US state pure and simple: this is the inherently moral goal of developing currently non-capitalist (one is tempted to say 'barbarous') peoples (Fukuyama, 2004). Moreover, even though Fukuyama gives a poor interpretation of Hegel (see Tyler, 2006, introduction, and ch. 1), his work does allow one to recognise certain structural similarities between his justification of neo-conservative liberal democratic capitalism and the analytic frameworks employed by certain mainstream IR theorists, as will become clear shortly.

STATE SOVEREIGNTY AND THE CREATION OF INTERNATIONAL SOCIETY

Robert H. Jackson (1990) has done much to popularise the distinction between states in the full sense (what I shall also call, the state as such, or the ideal state) on the one hand and 'failed' or 'quasi-' states on the other (see Lawler, 2005). The former possess both negative and positive sovereignty in that, first, they enjoy predominant domestic authority and equality with other states ('juridical statehood'), and under normal conditions can enforce these claims (Jackson, 1990, p. 53). Second, they distribute the benefits attendant upon being governed by a state equitably to their members. Quasi-states, on the other hand, possess negative sovereignty alone: they enjoy the 'formal-legal condition' of being 'only deemed to be substantial and capable' in international law (ibid., pp. 27, 53). Their borders are respected in international law and they are accepted as members of the international system (are recognised in international negotiations, and so on). Quasi-states, however, lack positive sovereignty: they may not be endorsed by the domestic population and, by the standards of international law, they are institutionally immature. 'Their governments are often deficient in the political will, institutional authority, and organized power to protect human rights or provide socio-economic welfare' (ibid., p. 21). (Note that the Ba'athist regime may not have been a 'failed state' as it lacked only political will.)

The former conception of 'the state' underpins most contemporary analyses of the international system: at least as an ideal type or theoretical extreme in relation to which actual states are characterised, analysed and sometimes assessed (Bosanquet, 1923, pp. xv–lxii and ch. 11; Nicholson, 1976; *Review of International Studies*, 2004). In this chapter, the concept of the ideal state as a person is used in this way: that is, as a critical heuristic device. (While I think it unlikely to happen in practice, I do not deny the possibility that an actual state could live up to the ideal of the state as such, under certain circumstances.)

The ideal state has many facets. First, it exists as a unified rational actor (or 'person') in the sense that it possesses a clear and coherent internal structure for the making and implementation of political decisions. This structure is constituted by a systematic demarcation of departments and agencies, each with their own functions, relative autonomy and authority. Hence, although different aspects of one state engage in particular activities domestically and in foreign affairs, to the extent that they form part of an ideal state, they do so in conscious recognition of these systematic demarcations. The ideal state can have as many identities as it has facets, yet there must be effective conventions and procedures in place to determine the relative priority of each facet. Unresolved disjunctions and conflicts between the actions and dictates of the various facets of a particular state either domestically or internationally are signs of that state's failure to live up to its ideal. Ultimately, the state as such speaks and acts coherently. To the extent that a political unit fails to do so, it fails to be a state as such.

The state *qua* state possesses *de facto* domestic sovereignty over the inhabitants of its territory; that is, it exercises ultimate coercive power at home. Moreover, its will is complied with because it possesses this power, by a proportion of those inhabitants which is sufficient to secure a 'reasonable' level of social order (Ritchie, 1893). Furthermore, it is recognised by the appropriate international body or bodies as being able to promulgate and enforce its will over those inhabitants. Similarly, the state as such possesses *de facto* international sovereignty to the extent that it can exert its will in the international system. It possesses *de jure* sovereignty to the extent that it meets three further requirements. The first is that the domestic population recognises its rule over them as being legitimate. The second is that the domestic criminal justice system recognises the legislature and executive as being constitutionally entitled to issue authoritative commands which it (the criminal justice system) should enforce. The third is that the state is recognised by the appropriate international body or bodies as being entitled to represent its inhabitants and pursue its perception of their interests in the international system. Full sovereignty exists only to the extent that the same entity enjoys both *de facto* and *de jure* sovereignty. Thus conceived, statehood as a form of personhood is a matter of degree, not least because 'like all other human organizations states are conditional on leadership, cooperation, knowledge, resources, fortune, and much else. Absolute power is an impossibility' (Jackson, 1990, p. 53).

The internal structure of statehood has direct and dramatic consequences for the current international system. First, the centrality of recognition to both *de facto* and *de jure* sovereignty ensures that every encounter that a state has in the international system, no matter how routine, tends to either reaffirm or undermine its standing as a state. After the embarrassment of 9/11 (for it was that as well as much else), the Bush administration needed to reassert the authority of the US state in the international system and it chose to try to do this by prosecuting the 'war on terror' and particularly by high profile and vigorous military action in Afghanistan and the Middle East. Second, domestic political imperatives – especially the need for the administration to regain its standing with the US electorate – created a clear need for the administration to be seen to mete out retribution to some definite group that was perceived to bear significant responsibility for the 9/11 attacks, or at least could be made to do so.

This much is fairly obvious. Yet, a less apparent but significant problem confronts anyone who attempts to use a static, ahistorical conception of juridical and quasi-juridical recognition of the static sovereign state of the type outlined above, to understand the implications of 'the war on terror'. Writing in the context of Antonio Gramsci's theory of hegemony, the political economist Robert Cox has observed that '[a]ny fixed definition of the content of the concept "civil society" would just freeze a particular moment in history and privilege the relations of social forces then prevailing' (Cox, 1999, p. 98; see also Bieler and Morton, 2004). Cox's contention also obtains for 'the state'. Theories which effectively reduce international relations to the interaction of independent states are simpleminded in that they have 'too few thoughts and feelings to match the world as it really is' (adapting Williams, 1973, p. 149).

Given that 'the demands of political reality and the complexities of political thought are obstinately what they are' (ibid., p. 150), it is helpful to reconsider neo-conservatism in the wider interpretative context offered by theories of intersubjective recognition, employed by, for example, philosophical idealists, constructivists, English school theorists and critical theorists. From this more rounded and insightful cluster of perspectives, in addition to the undeniable considerations of enlightened self-interest, international society necessarily presupposes conventions, norms and laws that are for the most part routinely obeyed by states for irreducibly normative reasons. Such scholars reject the realist claim that the origins of a state's interests should be of little concern for international actors or to students of international affairs. On this view, there is no determinate identity which a state possesses prior to the ongoing processes of articulation and response entailed by its iterative interactions with other states and non-state actors.

An agent's identity and therefore its actions are intimately connected to the normative and ideational features of its existence, and not least the agent's sense of its own place and proper role within international society (Morris, 2005). In addition to holding true for bilateral relations, this applies at the global level (in relation, for example, to the UN), at the regional level (for example, the European Union: EU; and the African Union: AU), and the domestic level (for example, in relation to domestic non-governmental groups that monitor their government's foreign policies). This link between structure and identity extends even to the state's relations to terrorist organisations. Such considerations have momentous practical as well as theoretical implications. For example, Christian Reus-Smit (2005, p. 196) attributes to them the differences between the US's relations with Canada on one hand and Cuba on the other.

The dynamic between actor and system is not one-way, however. Structures do exert significant influences over the identities of actors, yet they cannot exist apart from the particular actions, interactions and intentions of particular actors. Moreover, this relational ontology helps to reinforce the authority of the particular elements, and changes in the agents' respective constituent meanings and values alter the nature of the system/society considered as a whole. Obviously there will be degrees of depth and specificity to these relations. Between an international society with thick and robust bonds and an international system based on the minimal structures required for communication and interaction, exists a hinterland in which, as Hedley Bull once put it,

> A sense of common interests is tentative and inchoate; where the common rules perceived are vague and ill-formed, and there is doubt as to whether they are worthy of the name of rules; or where common institutions – relating to diplomatic machinery or to limitations in war – are implicit or embryonic. (Bull, 1977, p. 15)

The expressive languages that help to determine such allegiances and animosities are found, for example, in the terms in which treaties are made and wars conducted (Hegel, 1821, secs 332 and 76A). The limits placed on the conduct of war, for example, by the Geneva Conventions presuppose certain things about those affected, whether they are individual combatants or civilians (namely, that they are to be treated with respect). Such languages help to constitute the concrete nature of a state's sovereignty, because they constitute the fields of meanings and values in which occur the multifaceted and inherently relational processes of judgement and international recognition which constitute the core identity of the state. These relations are based in praxis then: that is, in the communicative structure of one's particular deliberate actions. There is no realm of intentional practice which does not presuppose 'theoretical' claims and judgements to some degree, and the presuppositions of one's practices have significant consequences in intra- and inter-state relations.

Famously, Robert O. Keohane and Joseph S. Nye have stressed what they call the 'complex interdependence' of actors in the international system. They argue that contemporary IR is characterised by multifaceted reciprocal dependences between state and non-state actors (Keohane and Nye, 1977, p. 8; Ben-Porat, 2005). There are three key features of such a situation: first, actors interrelate through various routes ('interstate, transgovernmental, and transnational relations'); second, the relevant actors interact over 'multiple issues that are not arranged in a clear or consistent hierarchy'; and third, military force is used only against governments external to one's 'region' (Keohane and Nye, 1977, pp. 25–6). Complex interdependence links power to issue areas, such that an actor whose will tends to predominate in one area may be relatively weak in others. A large corporation may be very important in trade policy but have little influence over a state's decision to go to war. (Sometimes corporations play very significant roles in both areas, of course.)

At any one time, each participant acts in many spheres, and, even though Keohane and Nye neglect this fact, each therefore possesses a multifaceted and fluctuating self-identity. The State Department may understand 'the US' and its interests in one way, the Central Intelligence Agency understand them in another, the White House in a third and so on. Consequently, at any one time, these various facets of the actor's self-identity may be in tension if not outright conflict with each other. This means that the actor rarely lives up to the ideal of unity in final action which was noted earlier as the first essential characteristic of a sovereign identity (Mouffe, 2005, p. 20).

This is not to say that there are no centrifugal forces to the actors' identities. The most notable are found in being part of a common tradition, being within the same 'communities of fate', being subject to common international institutions, and being subject to the exercise of power (Falk, 1999). In regard to the first of these, only very rarely are states created *de novo*. Rarely does a new generation of citizens create its state anew and nor do administrations (Mao, Pol Pot and possibly Hitler are exceptions). They build on traditions that have been formed and gradually re-formed inter-subjectively over decades and often centuries. For example, 'new' states owe much to the preceding colonial traditions and any internal antagonisms between the groups brought under the new political system. Nigeria is a case in point here (Meredith, 2005, pp. 193–205, 574–87). Crucially, state identities are articulated and stabilised by the tendency of iterative interactions between actors to transform the international system of which they are parts into an international society. (For analyses of this process in the domestic context, see Rawls, 1993, lecture 4, esp. sec. 7 and lecture 6; d'Agostino, 1996.) Second, the development of issues and crises that do not respect current political boundaries has created what have been called international 'communities of fate' (Held et al., 1999, pp. 444–9). Most pressing here are drugs, AIDS, climate change and environmental degradation, none of which can be solved within traditional state-based structures (see Cammack, 2006). The subsequent efforts to address such issues require actors to redefine themselves – and especially their core powers, interests and values – more clearly.

Frequently, however, none of these is a strong source of unity when taken on its own. First, as Alasdair MacIntyre has argued (1985, p. 223), 'Traditions, when vital, embody continuities of conflict', and thereby have a tendency to disintegrate. Usually, there are also other significant countervailing pressures: most obviously, changing circumstances but also the multiplicity of spheres acted in by an actor's various facets. Second, communities of fate tend to have blurred and porous boundaries, making them fluid and subject to jockeying for advantage between groups. It is for this reason that states have looked to international institutions to provide stability. Yet, for much of the world international institutions are, in many senses, a 'precious bane' (Milton, 1667, bk 1, 1.690–9). They foster the semblance of peace and order that some countries have struggled for centuries to bring about domestically, and do so in a relatively short time. Yet, due to their reliance on asymmetries of power between the actors which make them up, of necessity they do so only imperfectly and with more than a tinge of injustice. The ambiguous character of international institutions is central to my analysis of the effects of the 'war on terror' on the future of international society, as will become clear now.

INSTITUTIONS AND POWER

Keohane and Nye see international organisations as playing a crucial role in the orderly functioning of the international system under conditions of complex interdependence. Keohane distinguishes three main institutional types, running from full articulacy and enforcement through international law, to customary manners of behaviour. He calls these 'Formal intergovernmental or cross-national non-governmental organizations' such as the UN, the EU or the AU, 'international regimes' such as the Bretton Woods regime, and 'conventions [which underlie] informal institutions, with rules and understandings that shape the expectations of actors' (Keohane, 1988, pp. 3–4). In the philosophical idealist Bernard Bosanquet's terms, every institution is an external manifestation ('fact') of sets of meanings and values ('ideas') which are arranged so as to facilitate the performance of a social function ('purpose') (Bosanquet, 1923, ch. 11; see also pp. xv–lxii). Reflecting this structure, for Keohane (1988, pp. 4–5), the strength of every institution is a function of three things. The first is 'commonality', or shared hermeneutic frameworks (ideas) within which actors develop critical expectations and interpret the actions of others. The second is 'specificity', the extent to which such expectations and modes of interpretation are formally articulated in norms, rules and laws (the extent to which they are facts and purposes). The third is 'autonomy', or the degree of control that an institution has over determination of the norms, rules and laws that frame its actions.

Keohane and Nye summarise the roles of international organisations in the following way: 'Organizations will set agendas, induce coalition-formation, and act as arenas for political action by weak states. Ability to choose the organizational forum for an issue and to mobilize votes will be an important political resource' (Keohane and Nye, 1977, p. 37). Keohane can be seen as developing further this aspect of complex interdependence, when he observed elsewhere that, 'the ability of states' – and here one might add all other actors in a scheme of complex interdependence – 'to communicate and cooperate depends on human-constructed institutions, which vary historically and across issues, in nature (with respect to the policies they incorporate) and in strength (in terms of the degree to which their rules are clearly specified and routinely obeyed)' (Keohane, 1988, p. 2).

Keohane and Nye wrongly regard concrete interests as prior to recognition (Wendt, 1992). When one remembers the previous discussion of identity formation, however, it can be seen that key international institutions are not merely superficial mechanisms through which states and non-state actors can pursue pre-existing interests. They help to structure the actors' multiple identities. More fundamentally, an actor's self-image, interests and therefore actions are partly determined by its sense of its actual place in the international society. Martha Finnemore and Stephen Toope (2001, p. 743; quoted in Reus-Smit, 2004, p. 3) have characterised international law, for example, as 'a broad social phenomenon deeply embedded in the practices, beliefs, and traditions of societies, and shaped by interaction among societies'. Starting from a similar point, other scholars have debated the 'Americanization' of international law (Keleman et al., 2004, 2005; Levi-Faur, 2005). Similarly, Edward Mansfield and Jon Pevehouse (2006) have highlighted the democratising pressures arising from joining international organisations, while Arturo Santa-Cruz (2005) has highlighted the effect of institutional election monitoring on notions of state sovereignty (see also Zün and Checkel, 2005). In these and other ways, when functioning at their best, organisations transform an international system based on enlightened self-interest and state power, into an international society based on shared norms of right and just behaviour.

Yet, most institutions are not 'natural' or automatically generated products of an organic international society. Instead, they are more or less consciously designed answers to such problems as the lack of trust or coordination between international actors. Moreover, it is very rare for the 'dialogue' that produces the commonality and specificity of international institutions to be a dialogue between equals. Often, they represent the articulation of arrangements and understandings already implicit within relations between actors, but even then the processes of articulating these norms are characterised by asymmetries of power (Hurrell, 2001; Foot et al., 2003; Morris, 2005; and Lee, this volume, chs 8 and 9). Many are created deliberately by the powerful, and usually to serve their own interests. Hence, international society contains hierarchies of authority arising from asymmetries of power. This has a number of consequences. First and most obviously, it blurs the distinction between *de facto* and *de jure* sovereignty, in that which body is to count as authoritative (the *de jure* concern) is in large part determined by the prior exercise of power (the *de facto* concern). The UN, the US and the People's Republic of China carry the day in the international non-recognition of the Taiwanese state in large part because they are more powerful, and not because they make a clearer or inherently more compelling normative case than those seeking recognition of Taiwan. Similarly, the former colonial states of the Middle East are recognised as discrete states by the UN, the US and in the system of international law which the UN and the US authorise. Yet, many individuals place far more significance on the notion of an Islamic/Arabic people in at least some of these states. Israel is recognised as an independent sovereign state (even if its precise borders are disputed) because the UN and importantly the US state and international law recognise it as such. Nevertheless, many actors do not recognise its legitimacy, and some including the Abu Nidal Organisation, Hizballah, Palestinian Islamic Jihad-Shaqaqi and of course al-Qaeda seek its overthrow (Home Office, 2006). This has substantive effects on the status of fighters from outside Iraq's borders, for example.

Are they interlopers or loyal participants in an Arabian military force? This question cannot be answered without presupposing certain normative judgements.

Ultimately, determining which bodies possess the moral authority to recognise an actor in the international system or society is an inherently normative matter rather than an empirical one (Goddard, 2006). Consequently, the mere fact of current institutional recognition does not and cannot by itself add moral weight to an agent's claims or even existence over that of any other, because one must first justify the authority of the recognising body (the UN, the US and so on) (see Edkins and Zehfuss, 2005). A Zionist's understanding of the state of Israel as the legitimate political manifestation of the Jewish homeland ordained by God has in itself no greater validity than a Palestinian's understanding of Israel as a legally sanctioned terroristic fiction, despite the fact of Israel's official recognition by the UN and most Western states. The idea that there is some neutral perspective or procedure that determines the 'objectively correct' (or 'scientific') position is a fiction which serves, sometimes consciously, to stifle fundamental debates about power and representation in IR.

A 'FAITH-BASED INITIATIVE': TALKING AMERICA'S LANGUAGE

Francis Fukuyama has claimed that 'Americans' believe that 'legitimacy at an international level' 'is rooted in the will of democratic majorities in constitutional nation-states and Europeans . . . [tend] to believe it is based on principles of justice higher than the laws of wills of particular nation states' (Fukuyama, 2004, p. 155). These assertions may fly in the face of recent evidence, yet, this contrast between praxis and moral universalism is an important one. It has been argued already that international institutions are required in order to stabilise and authorise the meanings and values underlying relations between actors in the international system. In this way, they help to build and sustain effective frameworks of communication and coordination between international actors.

Yet, these meanings and values tend either to become caricatures of their original selves, or to ossify into prejudices and dogma. (Witness the extension of the constitutional right of US citizens to bear arms from the nuanced need to provide a militia, to the current almost blanket permission to carry arms. Similarly, the Organization of African Unity was replaced by the AU when the former became a caricature of its founding principles.) Meanings and values avoid such fates only through the need to respond to new circumstances, the manipulation by large corporations and significant

international powers and their ilk, or as reactions to appalling and spectacular acts of violence by state or non-state actors. The clash between
the two tendencies inherent in institutions (vitality and articulation) is the
tragedy of international order. It is the clash of right against right, of the
need for the accommodation of the demands of praxis on the one hand and
the need for authoritative formulation on the other (Bradley, 1909).

Deepak Lal (2004, pp. 203–4; 2005) is scathing about the efficacy of
manipulating institutions to bring peace and about their tendency to
impose a single cultural model. Usually, he need not worry too greatly.
Rarely are individual actors sufficiently unified to achieve such coherent
and deliberate wholesale change of the significant parts of the ideational
structure of institutional institutions. Nevertheless, in exceptional circumstances and if it is sufficiently well-positioned and strong-willed, one
branch of a key actor can dominate the others internally. In such circumstances, deliberate manipulation of the structure of international society
becomes a realistic option. This has been the case in the US for several
years since September 11, 2001. The executive branch gained effective
control, and directed the reaction of every other significant arm of the US
state as well as the bulk of the voting population using the notion of a 'war
on terror'. (The US Supreme Court's recent rulings on the treatment of
prisoners at Guantánamo Bay offer hope that this control may be waning,
as do the 2006 congressional elections.) Indeed, it is unsurprising that this
idea has been particularly effective at galvanising popular support, given
that it combines security concerns, a moral vision, and the sense of superiority that will always tend to inspire the citizens of the superpower, especially where there is a widespread domestic belief in manifest destiny.
(President William Taft claimed once: 'The day is not far distant when
three Stars and Stripes at three equidistant points will mark our territory:
one at the North Pole, another at the Panama Canal, and the third at the
South Pole. The whole hemisphere will be ours in fact as, by virtue of our
superiority of race, it already is ours morally', (quoted in McCoubrey and
Morris, 2000, p. 102).

A number of factors worked in the US executive's favour in this regard.
First, in the aftermath of 9/11, the US people were suffering and continue
to suffer a collective existential crisis (Richardson, 2006, p. 175; Connelly,
2005). This manifests itself as a profound sense of the US's vulnerability to
people who previously the population had tended to regard as too poor,
disorganised and, for many, too uncivilised to inflict significant harm on
their hegemonic country. They came to realise that rather than improving
America's security, its hegemonic position made it the prime target for
disaffected groups. The shock was especially acute as the terrorists had used
asymmetric warfare so effectively to defile two of the most potent symbols

of US wealth and power, the Pentagon and the World Trade Center, and had done so with a significant loss of life. Moreover, the attacks shocked those who sincerely believed and still believe in America's world-historical importance (those who hold that, if spread, the 'American way' will bring freedom to all: 'These values of freedom are right and true for every person, in every society'; Bush, 2002b; see also Bush, 2002a). In this regard, what one leading scholar has called the 'Gothic' event of 9/11 (Devetak, 2005) has been answered by a myth of a war on 'terror' which serves to express and thereby to reaffirm the authority of basic American values to the American people themselves (an example of 'symbolic nonacquiescence' (Feinberg, 1994, pp. 78–9).

Given these existential dimensions to the attacks, obvious US oil interests in controlling Iraq (interests that are acknowledged by the Bush administration and the oil corporations themselves) and the ongoing Halliburton scandals should not blind us to the neo-conservative mission to 'liberate' Iraq and other 'underdeveloped' countries, a contemporary rather harsher Wilsonianism. I do not propose to analyse this morality in any depth, not least because of the publication of an excellent book on the subject by Peter Singer (2004; see also Mansfield, 2004; Pryce, 2006). What is important, however, is to trace out some of the wider implications of the way in which Bush believes that he comes to know the requirements of the coalition's moral mission.

We saw earlier that Bush was explicit in the 2002 *National Security Strategy* that, in practice, 'liberation' means fostering – using force if necessary – the only 'sustainable model for national success: freedom, democracy, and free enterprise' (Bush, 2002b; see further Lee, this volume, chs 8 and 9). In the West Point speech, Bush revelled in the crudity of his own moral universalism:

> Some worry that it is somehow undiplomatic or impolite to speak the language of right and wrong. I disagree. [Applause.] Different circumstances require different methods, but not different moralities. [Applause.] Moral truth is the same in every culture, in every time, and in every place. . . . There can be no neutrality between justice and cruelty, between the innocent and the guilty. We are in a conflict between good and evil, and America will call evil by its name. [Applause.] . . . America has a greater objective than controlling threats and containing resentment. We will work for a just and peaceful world beyond the war on terror. (Bush, 2002a; see also Bush, 2001)

This is God's plan for the world: 'Freedom is the Almighty's gift to every man and woman in this world . . . as the greatest power on earth we have an obligation to help the spread of freedom' (Bush, address to the nation 13 April 2004, quoted in Harvey, 2005, p. 214). This reflects the fact that

Bush operates in a divinely ordained, Christian, monistic universe of eternal and ultimate values, to which he has direct access through conscience. In this sense, it is correct to describe the war on terror as 'a faith-based initiative' (Suskind, 2004).

This theocratic, monistic and, importantly, univocal vision of diplomatic wisdom distorts the more careful and nuanced processes of recognition which, it was argued earlier, usually underlie international society. (While the latter processes are very far from perfect or just, at least they tend to be tempered by an acceptance of the need for some political and military humility.) First, it engenders a dangerously paternalistic attitude towards those without a direct line to God. Practically, for example, it supports the notion that, in Hegel's words (1821, sec. 351), 'The civilized nation is conscious that the rights of barbarians are unequal to its own and treats their autonomy as only a formality'.[3] Second, as Zbigniew Brzezinski has observed (2004, p. 215; see also pp. 215–16), it is likely to be self-defeating, with the US being seen as 'self-absorbed and . . . anti-American ideologies will gain international credence by labelling the United States as a self-appointed vigilante'.

The problem is not that Bush is motivated by simple self-interest, but that he is also guided by his particular form of moral universalism. It is significant, given what was noted in the second section, that even though many classical realists were committed Christians in their personal lives, they were very careful to warn against allowing faith to influence the foreign policies of states. The fifth of Hans Morgenthau's 'six principles of political realism' is emphatic on this point: 'There is a world of difference between the belief that all nations stand under the judgement of God, inscrutable to the human mind, and the blasphemous conviction that God is always on one's side and that what one wills oneself cannot fail to be willed by God also' (Morgenthau, 1985, p. 13). This message recurred throughout Morgenthau's writings, just as it did in the works of Reinhold Niebuhr and Herbert Butterfield. In fact, in 1954, Butterfield (1954, p. 96) attacked explicitly the notion of a 'war of righteousness' on the ground that one could never choose to end such a war, given that 'it soon becomes a sin to compromise' or even to disagree with judgements of the spiritual–military elite.

This thought takes on a special significance when one accepts the relational nature of identity set out above. From that perspective, even if one views the other participants in one's dialogue simply as enemies one must still at least see them as actors to be answered (Duff, 1986, p. 238). Necessarily implied in that perception of their agency is some recognition of their 'being a person like us': that is, some recognition of their status as a rational agent whom one can reform, or even with whom one can, at least in principle, compromise. If one demonises the enemy as has happened in the war on terror on the other hand, then there can be no recognition of status and legitimacy. It is for this reason that the war on terror is precluded from communicating US disapproval to the terror network. It cannot do this first, because that network is not part of America's discursive community (the Western-authorised international society). Second, communication is impossible because the network lacks unity and definition, and thereby lacks personality (it is an idea more than an organisation). Third, the indeterminacy of al-Qaeda's command 'structure' means that there is no head, not even Bin Laden himself, who is competent to negotiate a ceasefire and authorised to declare it. America cannot win the 'war on terror' within the latter's current terms. Moreover, it is not even acceptable to try merely to control those demonised groups and individuals as one would an aggressive dog,[4] because a demonised 'other' is necessarily seen as malevolent – it is simply the manifestation of evil. The only option is to seek to end their existence (Mouffe, 2005, pp. 5–6). Butterfield concludes, 'it is wiser not to be responsible for introducing a deep and permanent irreconcilability into the . . . [international] order'.[5] I trace out some of the far-reaching political effects of demonising one's enemy elsewhere in this volume.

CONCLUSION

This chapter has used strands of IR theory to show that international actors gain concrete identities from their interactions, many of which take place through institutionalised processes. Even though these interactions are framed by asymmetries of power, for the most part no one actor has the unity of purpose to shape identities deliberately. Yet, the current 'war on terror' allowed the Bush administration to gain the moral high-ground at home and so in the international community, at least temporarily. Hence, if a world-historical individual does exist at present, then it is George W. Bush, someone whose 'whole nature' is 'nought else but their master-passion' (Hegel, 1832, p. 31). Several commentators have argued that if the US continues to prosecute the 'war on terror', then the terroristic response of the US state will foster the collapse of the American 'empire' itself (Soros, 2004, ch. 2; Ferguson, 2005). If this is correct, then far from us reaching Fukuyama's 'end of History', we are approaching the fall of yet another world-historical nation.

Yet, ultimately one would do well to question the power of what Bush's senior advisor called at the start of this chapter, 'History's actors'. The insights gained from IR theory highlight the fact that recognition tends very strongly to be diffuse and multifaceted, and each of its processes has a discrete momentum. The Bush administration seems to be losing the upper hand as US courts decide against the treatment of fighters captured in Iraq, US deaths mount, and the war becomes more expensive in financial and diplomatic terms. It seems also that the November 2006 congressional elections have changed the domestic political balance against them very significantly. As neo-conservative forces also lose internal focus and impetus, it is likely that the traditions of recognition within international society will reassert something like their former predominance in key areas (for different opposing views, see Kennedy-Pipe and Renegger, 2006; Mead, 2006; Wheeler and Morris, 2006). The conclusion of Bush's second administration in 2008 should then mark merely the formal end of a policy that has already run out of steam. Nevertheless, the international society that remains will bear the scars as well as the inscriptions of the conflicts and policies that the Bush administration has pursued since 11 September 2001.

NOTES

1. I am grateful to Matt Beech, Tom Kane, Justin Morris, Noël O'Sullivan, Claire Thomas, Pip Tyler and Richard Woodward, for their comments on an earlier version of this chapter.
2. Bush's use of the term 'pre-emption' rather than 'prevention' is misleading as in international law the former requires the threat to be far more imminent and certain than he claims. Regarding the British case, see McLean and Patterson, 2006. The EU adopted the same position subsequently (European Commission, 2006).
3. For Hegel (1821, sec. 351) (and apparently Bush and Blair), nations are 'barbarous' to the extent that they 'lag behind [the more advanced nations] in institutions which are essential moments [sc. facets] of the state' (see Tyler, 2006, pp. 46–8).
4. 'A neutral sanction would treat offenders and potential offenders much as beasts in a circus, as creatures which must be conditioned, intimidated, or restrained' (von Hirsch, 1999, p. 69).
5. Butterfield (1954, p. 96). Butterfield referred to 'the European order'. He even argued: 'It is better to say that you are fighting for Persian oil than to talk of a "war of righteousness", when you merely mean that you believe you have a right to the oil; for you would be conducting an altogether unjust war if for a single moment you believed anything less than this' (p. 96).

REFERENCES

Ben-Porat, Guy (2005), 'Between power and hegemony: business communities in peace processes', *Review of International Studies*, **31**, 325–48.
Bieler, Andreas and Adam David Morton (2004), 'A critical theory route to hegemony, world order and historical change: neo-Gramscian perspectives in international relations', *Capital and Class*, **82** (Spring), 85–113.

Bosanquet, Bernard (1923), *The Philosophical Theory of the State*, 4th edn, London: Macmillan.

Bradley, Andrew C. (1909), 'Hegel's Theory of Tragedy', in his *Oxford Lectures on Poetry*, London: Macmillan, pp. 69–95.

Brzezinski, Zbigniew (2004), *The Choice: Global Domination or Global Leadership*, New York: Basic Books.

Bull, Hedley (1977), *The Anarchical Society: A Study of Order in World Politics*, London: Macmillan.

Bull, Hedley (1980), 'The great irresponsibles? The United States, the Soviet Union, and world order', *International Journal*, **35** (3) (Summer), 437–47.

Burrough, Bryan, Eugenia Peretz, David Rose and David Wise (2004), 'The path to war', *Vanity Fair* (May), 102–82.

Bush, George W. (2001), 'Address to a Joint Session of Congress and the American People', 20 September, www.whitehouse.gov/news/releases/2001/09/print/20010920-8.html, accessed 22 June 2006.

Bush, George W. (2002a), 'President Bush Delivers Graduation Speech at West Point', 1 June, www.whitehouse.gov/news/releases/2002/06/print/20020601-3.html, accessed 14 July 2002.

Bush, George W. (2002b) 'Introduction', in White House (2002), *National Security Strategy*, www.whitehouse.gov/nsc/nssintro.html, accessed 31 July 2006.

Bush, George W. (2003), 'President discusses the future of Iraq [with the American Enterprise Institute]', 26 February, www.whitehouse.gov/news/releases/2003/02/20030226-11.html, accessed 6 July 2006.

Butterfield, Herbert (1954), *Christianity, Diplomacy, and War*, New York: Abingdon-Cokesbury Press.

Cammack, Paul (2006), 'Global governance, state agency and competitiveness: the political economy of the Commission for Africa', *British Journal of Politics and International Relations*, **8** (3) (August), 331–50.

Chomsky, Noam (2003), *Hegemony or Survival: America's Quest for Global Dominance*, London: Penguin.

Chomsky, Noam (2006), *Failed States: The Abuse of Power and the Assault on Democracy*, London: Hamish Hamilton.

Chua, Amy (2004), *World on Fire: How Exporting Free Market Democracy Breeds Ethnic Hatred and Global Instability*, New York: Arrow.

Coleman, Vernon (2003), *Rogue Nation*, Barnstaple: Blue Books.

Connelly, William E. (2005), 'The evangelical–capitalist resonance machine', *Political Theory*, **33** (6) (December), 869–86.

Cox, Robert W. (1999), 'Civil society at the turn of the millennium: prospects for an alternative world order', in R. Cox with Michael G. Schechter, *The Political Economy of a Plural World: Critical Reflections on Power, Morals and Civilization*, London: Routledge, 2002, pp. 96–117.

D'Agostino, Fred (1996), *Free Public Reason*, Oxford and New York: Oxford University Press.

Devetak, Richard (2005), 'The Gothic scene of international relations: ghosts, monsters, terror and the sublime after September 11', *Review of International Studies*, **31**, 621–43.

Duff, R.A. (1986), *Trials and Punishments*, Cambridge: Cambridge University Press.

Edkins, Jenney and Maja Zehfuss (2005), 'Generalising the international', *Review of International Studies*, **31**, 451–72.

European Commission (2006), 'The EU fights against the scourge of terrorism', March ec.europa.eu/justice_home/fsj/terrorism/fsj_terrorism_intro_en.htm, accessed 31 July 2006.

Falk, Richard (1999), *Predatory Globalization: A Critique*, Cambridge: Polity.

Feinberg, Joel (1994), 'The expressive theory of punishment', in A. Duff and D. Garland (eds), *A Reader on Punishment*, Oxford: Oxford University Press, pp. 71–91.

Ferguson, Niall (2005), *Colossus: The Rise and Fall of the American Empire*, London: Penguin.

Finnemore Martha and Stephen J. Toope (2001), 'Alternatives to "legalization": richer views of law and politics', *International Organization*, **55** (3), 743–58.

Foot, Rosemary, S. Neil MacFarlane and Michael Mastanduno (eds) (2003), *US Hegemony and International Organizations*, Oxford: Oxford University Press.

Fukuyama, Francis (1992), *The End of History and the Last Man*, Harmondsworth: Penguin.

Fukuyama, Francis (2004), *State Building: Governance and World Order in the Twenty-first Century*, London: Profile.

Goddard, Stacie E. (2006), 'Uncommon ground: indivisible territory and the politics of legitimacy', *International Organization*, **60** (Winter), 35–68.

Harvey, David (2005), *The New Imperialism*, Oxford: Oxford University Press.

Hegel, Georg W.F. (1821), *Philosophy of Right* (1952), trans. T.M. Knox, London: Oxford University Press.

Hegel, Georg W.F. (1832), *Philosophy of History* (1956), trans. J. Sibree, New York: Dover.

Held, David, Anthony McGrew, David Goldblatt and Jonathan Perraton (1999), *Global Transformations: Politics, Economics and Culture*, Cambridge: Polity.

Home Office (2006), 'Proscribed terrorist groups', www.homeoffice.gov.uk/security/terrorism-and-the-law/terrorism-act/proscribed-groups, accessed 17 July 2006.

Hurrell, Andrew (2001), 'Hegemony, liberalism and global order: what space for would-be great power?', *International Affairs*, **82** (1), 1–19.

Jackson, Robert H. (1990), *Quasi-states: Sovereignty, International Relations and the Third World*, Cambridge: Cambridge University Press.

Kagan, Robert (1998), 'A way to oust Saddam', *Weekly Standard*, 28 September, www.newamericancentury.org/iraq-092898.htm, accessed 10 July 2006.

Kane, Thomas M. (2006), *Theoretical Roots of American Foreign Policy: Machiavelli and American Unilateralism*, Abingdon: Routledge.

Keleman, R. Daniel and Eric C. Sibbitt (2004), 'The globalization of American law', *International Organization*, **58** (Winter), 103–36.

Keleman, R. Daniel and Eric C. Sibbitt (2005), 'Lex Americana: a response to Levi-Faur', *International Organization*, **59** (Summer), 463–72.

Kennedy-Pipe, Caroline and Nicholas Renegger (2006), 'Apocalypse now? Continuities and disjunctions in world politics after 9/11', *International Affairs*, **82**, 539–52.

Keohane, Robert O. (1988), *International Institutions and State Power. Essays in International Relations Theory*, Boulder, CO: Westview.

Keohane, Robert O. and Joseph S. Nye (1977), *Power and Interdependence: World Politics in Transition*, Boston, MA and Toronto: Little & Brown.

Kristol, Irving (2003), 'The neoconservative persuasion: what it was, and what it is', *Weekly Standard*, 25 August; reprinted in Irwin Stelzer (ed.) (2004), *Neoconservatism*, London: Atlantic, pp. 31–7.

Lal, Deepak (2004), *In Praise of Empires: Globalization and Order*, Basingstoke: Palgrave Macmillan.

Lal, Deepak (2005), 'The threat to economic liberty from international institutions', *Cato Journal*, **25** (3) (Fall), 503–20.

Lawler, Peter (2005), 'The good state: in praise of "classical" internationalism', *Review of International Studies*, **31**, 427–49.

Levi-Faur, David (2005), 'The political economy of legal globalization: juridification, adversarial legalism, and responsive regulation: a comment', *International Organization*, **59** (Summer), 451–62.

MacIntyre, Alasdair (1985), *After Virtue: A Study in Moral Theory*, 2nd edn, London, Duckworth.

Mansfield, Edward D. and Jon C. Pevehouse (2006), 'Democratization and international organizations', *International Organization*, **60** (Winter), 137–67.

Mansfield, Stephen (2004), *The Faith of George Bush*, Lake Mary, FL: Charisma House.

McCoubrey, Hilare and Justin Craig Morris (2000), *Regional Peacekeeping in the Post-Cold War Era*, The Hague: Kluwer.

McLean, Craig and Alan Patterson (2006), 'A precautionary approach to foreign policy? A preliminary analysis of Tony Blair's speeches on Iraq', *British Journal of Politics and International Relations*, **8** (3) (August), 351–67.

Mead, Walter Russell (2006), 'God's country', *Foreign Affairs*, (September/October), 24–43.

Meredith, Martin (2005), *The State of Africa: A History of Fifty Years of Independence*, London: Free Press.

Milton, John (1667), *Paradise Lost, with variorum notes*, J. Prendeville (ed.) (1841), London: Samuel Holdsworth.

Morgenthau, Hans J. (1985), *Politics Among Nations: The Struggle for Peace and Power*, 6th edn, rev. K.W. Thompson, New York: McGraw-Hill.

Morris, Justin Craig (2005), 'Normative innovation and the great powers', in Alex Bellamy (ed.), *International Society and its Critics*, Oxford: Oxford University Press, pp. 265–81.

Mouffe, Chantal (2005), *The Return of the Political*, London: Verso.

Nicholson, Peter P. (1976), 'Philosophical idealism and international politics: a reply to Dr Savigear', *British Journal of International Studies*, **2**, 76–83.

PNAC (Project for the New American Century) (1997), 'Statement of Principles', 3 June, www.newamericancentury.org/statementofprinciples.htm, accessed 10 July 2006.

PNAC letter to Bill Clinton (1998), 26 January, www.newamericancentury.org/iraqclintonletter.htm, accessed 10 July 2006.

Prestowitz, Clyde (2003), *Rogue Nation: American Unilateralism and the Failure of Good Intentions*, New York: Perseus.

Pryce, Sue (2006), 'How many voices has America's god?', *British Journal of Politics and International Relations*, **8** (3) (August), 461–6.

Rawls, John (1993), *Political Liberalism*, New York: Columbia University Press.

Reus-Smit, Christian (2004), 'Introduction', in C. Reus-Smit (ed.), *The Politics of International Law*, Cambridge: Cambridge University Press, pp. 1–13.

Reus-Smit, Christian (2005), 'Constructivism', in Scott Burchill, Andrew Linklater, Richard Devetak, Jack Donnelly, Matthew Paterson, Christian Reus-Smit and Jacqui True, *Theories of International Relations*, 3rd edn, Basingstoke: Palgrave Macmillan, pp. 188–212.

Review of International Studies, **30** (2) (2004), special issue concerning Wendt's writings on the personality of the state.

Richardson, Louise (2006), *What Terrorists Want: Understanding the Terrorist Threat*, London: John Murray.

Ritchie, David G. (1893), 'On the conception of sovereignty', in his *Darwin and Hegel, with other philosophical studies*, London and New York: Swan Sonnenschein, pp. 227–64.

Ritter, Scott (2002), 'An interview with Scott Ritter', in S. Ritter and W. Rivers Pitt, *War on Iraq*, London: Profile, pp. 21–72.

Rose, David (2007), 'Neo Culpa', *Vanity Fair* (January), www.vanityfair.com/politics/features/2006/12/neocons 200612, accessed 12 December 2006.

Santa-Cruz, Arturo (2005), 'Constitutional structures, sovereignty, and the emergence of norms: the case of international election monitoring', *International Organization*, **59** (Summer), 663–93.

Schmitt, Gary (2005), 'Why Iraq's Sunnis won't deal', *Washington Post*, 13 September, www.newamericancentury.org/iraq-20050913.htm, accessed 10 July 2006.

Singer, Peter (2004), *The President of Good and Evil: Taking George W. Bush Seriously*, London: Granta.

Soros, George (2004), *The Bubble of American Supremacy: Correcting the Misuse of American Power*, London: Phoenix.

Suskind, Ron (2004), 'Faith, certainty and the presidency of George W. Bush', *New York Times Magazine*, 17 October, www.nytimes.com/2004/10/17/magazine/17BUSH.html?ex=1265346000&en=67e5e499d9ce0514&ei=5088, accessed 26 July 2006.

Tyler, Colin (2006), *Idealist Political Philosophy: Pluralism and Conflict in the Absolute Idealist Tradition*, London and New York: Continuum.

von Hirsch, Andrew (1999), 'Punishment, penance, and the state: a reply to Duff', in M. Matravers (ed.), *Punishment and Political Theory*, Oxford: Hart, pp. 69–82.

Wendt, Alexander (1992), 'Anarchy is what states make of it: the social construction of power politics', *International Organizations*, **46** (2) (Spring), 391–425.

Wheeler, Nicholas J. and Justin C. Morris (2006), 'Justifying the Iraq war as humanitarian intervention: the cure is worse than the disease', in R. Thakur and W.P.S. Sidhu (eds), *The Iraq Crisis and the World Order: Structural, Institutional and Normative Challenges*, Tokyo, New York, Paris: United Nations University Press, pp. 444–63.

White House (2002), *National Security Strategy of the United States of America*, www.whitehouse.gov/nsc/nss 9.html, accessed 23 July 2006.

Williams, Bernard (1973), 'A critique of Utilitarianism', in J.C.C. Smart and B. Williams, *Utilitarianism For and Against*, Cambridge: Cambridge University Press, pp. 75–150.

Zün, Michael and Jeffrey T. Checkel (2005), 'Getting socialized to build bridges: constructivism and rationalism, Europe and the Nation-state', *International Organization*, **59** (Fall), 1045–79.

4. The Polanyian image reversed: globalisation and economic citizenship in the New Great Transformation

Terrence Casey

Yes to the market economy; no to the market society
Former French Prime Minister Lionel Jospin

INTRODUCTION

Does globalisation herald a new dawn of growth and expanding prosperity across nations or increasing economic instability and political disorder? This chapter builds on the Polanyian insight of market embeddedness in order to establish a more useful theoretical framework for understanding the economic and political dynamics of responses to globalisation. The goal is to conceptualise how changes in the global system will be interpreted through the particular traits of diverse national systems. It is argued below that this is a function of whether the economic culture and economic institutions of these systems orientate individuals in either market-responsive (society-*cum*-market) or market-resistant (society-*contra*-market) directions. As such, how a society responds to the increased marketisation of social life – be it through defensive resistance or proactive adaptation – depends on the extent to which societies (more or less) mimic underlying ideals of markets, creating a sense of citizenship within the economy as well as within the polity. Economically this implies that market-responsive systems are likely to exhibit superior performance as globalisation progresses. Politically this implies that globalisation is not in itself a destabilising process, but rather cultural and institutional impediments at the national level serve to hinder adaptation and create conditions for political turmoil, alienation, a sense of disenfranchisement and, in its most extreme form, serving as a catalyst for terrorist movements.

COMPETING PERSPECTIVES OF GLOBALISATION

There is perhaps no better example of an 'essentially contested concept' than globalisation. Yet there has slowly emerged a relative consensus about the key aspects of this change in the international system. Far from being a specific change in the structure of the global economy, globalisation represents a series of interrelated processes. (The following discussion draws from Held et al., 1999; Berger, 2000; Mittelman, 2000; Scholte, 2000; and Held and McGrew, 2002.) It is the internationalisation of economic activity, represented by large and growing flows of trade and capital between countries, producing increasing economic interdependence. It is the process of global liberalisation, the removal of barriers to economic activity by governments within states and through international agreements. These are facilitated by technological changes. New technology, particularly computer processing and information technology (IT), as well as improvements in transportation (such as containerised shipping), allows corporations to maximise efficiency by adopting globalised production structures whereby elements of final products are made in the most economically beneficial locale and brought together in an integrated world production and marketing structure. Given the dominance of Western companies in international markets, particularly those for cultural products, it also represents the Westernisation or Americanisation of the world. These processes come together to create a situation whereby the barriers that physical distance presented to economic, political and social relations are reduced – what Jan Aart Scholte (2000) refers to as 'deterritorialization'. Across the breadth of the literature, including both the pro- and anti-globalisation perspectives, few authors would contest these factors as the basic elements that underlie the concept that we collectively label 'globalisation'. The disputes are interpretative, not definitional.

Contention turns on whether these processes create imperatives requiring significant alterations in the behaviour of private and public actors. There are two main axes of dispute: whether globalisation is an inevitable or contingent process, an empirical question, and whether the net results are likely to be positive or negative, a normative issue. Much of the reason why the analysis of globalisation is such a muddle is because of the difficulties in disentangling the empirical and normative questions. More often than not, empirical analysis is a function of normative interpretation.

At one extreme we have what may be called the 'hyperglobalists' (the descriptors used are from Held et al.), led initially by Kenichi Ohmae (1990, 1995), but since supplanted by Thomas Friedman (2000, 2005). From this perspective, globalisation changes everything. Friedman says this results from the 'triple convergence' (2005, ch. 3) of technological (that is, IT) and organisational (that is, outsourcing, offshoring) transformations that serve to 'flatten' the world; the reorganisation of business so as to fully reap the productive potential of these changes; and the true integration of vast swathes of the globe into the world capitalist economy, specifically China and India, rendering globalisation much more nearly 'global'. Whether one is talking about individuals, businesses or governments, this flattened world requires adaptation and adjustment or, as Friedman puts it, the 'golden straitjacket'[1] (or the 'convergence hypothesis'). State policy remains formally autonomous, but the potential costs of heterodox behaviour compared to the potential gains of being linked into the global market effectively forces liberalisation. A left-wing interpretation concurs with this view, but more to lament the social disruption and inequality created thereby.[2]

At the other end of the spectrum reside the 'sceptics', predominantly from the left, although Pat Buchanan in America and French Gaullists would comfortably fit into this camp. They refute the idea that globalisation dictates the dismantling of the core national values, namely the social welfare state (Hirst and Thompson, 1996; Callinicos, 2001). The idea of a fundamentally new economy is a myth. Levels of trade and capital flows prior to the First World War were similar to the present. Neo-liberalism, moreover, posits that open trade and capital mobility will punish those states that seek to excessively control their economies, leading to long-run convergence on economic policy, wages, and prices. Yet there is little evidence of this in practice. Foreign direct investment (FDI) is driven by productivity and infrastructure rather than by labour costs and, despite increased capital mobility, the vast majority of investment takes place within domestic economies. Social market economies that thrived in the past with higher wages and stronger social safety-nets can continue to do so into the future (Pontusson, 2005). Capitalism, therefore, is unlikely to converge on a single Anglo-American subspecies. Welfare states can be maintained if governments have the political will to do so (Hirst, 1999).

Both of these viewpoints start from the same initial question: has the international economy transformed in fundamental ways that require new behaviours on the part of key actors or has it not? The purpose of this chapter is not to attempt to come to a definitive conclusion as to what best represents the real material reality of globalisation. The working assumption is that globalisation encompasses a range of economic, social and cultural changes, all of which serve to alter the relationships of power and governance among national governments, major economic actors and international institutions, creating a more divided or shared political and economic sovereignty. Globalisation thus represents a genuine and momentous transformation of the international political economy, albeit not one that is complete or unique, having antecedents in the pre-First World War period. The present goes well beyond the past, however. The volume and velocity of capital movements dwarfs that in the early 1900s. The current phase of globalisation also has the economically and socially integrating aspects of advanced communication and information technology. We can retreat from technology, of course, but that leaves us to live like Ted Kaczynski (America's homicidal, techno-phobic 'Unabomber') or the Taliban, an option few would accept. The technological side of globalisation is for all intents and purposes irreversible. Conversely, sceptics rightly note that globalisation is driven by decisions made by the major players in the global economy (that is, policies of international and domestic liberalisation). What sovereign nation states can liberalise, they can also restrain – exactly as happened with the first era of globalisation. Such a reversal, while possible, is not probable. For a start, the strongest protests against globalisation often come from those least able to effect change. The most significant players in the international economy – the US, the EU, China, Japan, not to mention major multinational corporations – show no desire to halt the transformation of global markets. The last great reversal of globalisation, moreover, saw the Great Depression and the rise of fascism. Brink Lindsey (2002, p. 9) further makes the compelling point that the return to *laissez-faire* in the second half of the twentieth century resulted not from a sudden and widespread embrace of liberal ideals. Rather, it was a response to the repeated and sustained failures of collectivist solutions that led to the adoption of liberalism by default. It is the failure to construct an alternative that is not simply a rehash of failed policies of the past that hinders an anti-liberal counter-hegemony.[3] Taking all of these points together suggests that the globalisation is *largely* inevitable but *partially* contestable.

The core axes of dispute thus remain the range of strategies available to private and public actors given these changes, and the likely social, political and economic outcomes given differing responses of actors to globalisation. The problem with many analyses of globalisation is that they have difficulty weaving a logical connection between these points. Some works err in giving causal primacy to the international economic structure, and charting how these transformations drive actors to particular behaviours, a point most clearly seen among hyper-globalists, who largely welcome this change. Yet it is equally evident in many anti-globalisation views, which portray unconstrained globalisation as producing wrenching economic and social damage. Hence the calls for political struggle against globalisation in general and for reforms of the governance of the global economy (Mittelman, 2000, ch. 12; Scholte, 2000, ch. 12). In either view, the ultimate outcome for national political economies is a function of the imperatives created at the global level.

Others alternatively assume almost limitless agency for national actors. The purported convergence in capitalist regulation has failed to materialise (Berger and Dore, 1996). While recognising major shifts in the international economy, this perspective contends that the very institutional structures found in European corporatist welfare states (the main focus of interest among these authors) will serve to blunt the pressures of internationalisation (Swank, 2002). Some minor reconfigurations may be needed, but social democratic polities can survive globalisation relatively unchanged if they so desire (Krieger, 1999). In short, capitalism, even globalised capitalism, does not imply a single, optimal mode of regulation. Globalisation will not force Europe to become like America. States have choices as to how they structure their economies. One does not have to delve deeply, however, to recognise that not all choices produce equally favourable results (that is, North Korea, Cuba). That multiple capitalist paths remain is without question. The issue is whether they all still lead to the same promising end. The difficulty for the 'capitalist diversity' interpretation of globalisation is that in emphasising the elements of agency it disconnects choice from outcome.

What is needed is a conceptual framework that connects the dots for understanding the potential trajectories for national political–economic development in an era of globalisation; that is, one that logically links structure to agency to outcomes. The key question for globalisation is how the transformation of the global system is filtered through different national systems to produce either favourable or unfavourable economic and political outcomes. The next section begins to construct such a framework.

THE POLANYIAN VIEW OF GLOBALISATION

As the Second World War was drawing to its denouement, Karl Polanyi published one of the seminal texts in political economy, *The Great Transformation* (1944). In it he argued that the sources of the totalitarian horrors of the twentieth century were the free markets of the nineteenth century.[4] According to Polanyi, it was during this period that the dominant actors in the international system, specifically Great Britain, attempted to establish a self-regulating market system. Far from arising spontaneously as neoclassical economists imply, he argued that specific planning and legislation was needed to create free markets, particularly labour markets.[5] Self-regulating markets, moreover, reversed the traditional relation between economy and society. For most civilisations, economic relations were 'embedded' in a web of broader social values, including principles of reciprocity, redistribution, or 'householding', that is, production for family use (Carlson, 2006, p. 34). The capitalism of the late 1800s, however, attempted to 'disembed' economic relations from social relations by 'commodifying' all parts of the economy (that is, subjecting them to the price mechanism, including people via wage labour). To treat labour as a commodity regulated by price is dehumanising and unnatural; as such, it was a dangerously utopian exercise. Organic societies were rent asunder, destroyed by the atomistic and individualistic impulses of the market (Polanyi, 1944, p. 159). Faced with such an attack, society inevitably takes measures to protect itself from the market. This was Polanyi's 'double movement' – the expansion of self-regulating markets created a self-protecting backlash. Yet such protectionism only exacerbated the crisis of the market system, hastening its collapse (Lacher, 1999, p. 314). The fundamental message of Polanyi is that society cannot coexist with the free market; one or the other must break. And break European society did, as economic disruption led to the radicalisation of politics and society and the ascendance of reactionary forces.[6] The net result was Mussolini and Hitler.[7]

The world again finds itself in the midst of another great transformation and, for obvious reasons, Polanyi 'has emerged in recent years as a kind of patron saint of globalisation's critics' (Lindsey, 2002, p. 7). Neo-Polanyians like William Greider (1997), Dani Rodrik (1997) and George Soros (1998), among others, argue that a utopian faith in markets threatens a new cycle of international disasters. The most explicit application of this perspective is found in John Gray's *False Dawn* (1998). Today, *laissez-faire* utopianism is pushed by US economic hegemony and the 'Washington Consensus' of the International Monetary Fund and the World Bank. As always, uncontrolled markets threaten basic human needs of security and stability and Gray predicts a similarly pessimistic result. But Gray transforms the Polanyian argument into a more culturally specific form: 'The free market was – and remains – an Anglo-Saxon singularity' (p. 13). Free market capitalism is thus unique to a particular time and place. Trying to reproduce carbon copies of the American model in incompatible social environments is doomed to failure. It will instead produce new forms of social and political organisation as yet unknown. In a country like Germany, this might manifest as a relatively benign hybrid of the social market and neo-liberal models. In a place like Russia, the result will be an ever more virulent anarcho-capitalism. In the less-developed countries it may manifest as a fundamentalist backlash against modernity. Either way, the new version of global *laissez-faire* will undermine social and political structures wherever it takes hold, unleashing an era of deepening international conflict and anarchy. Only a new framework of global economic regulation can stave off such a catastrophe.

While there are empirical snags in this anti-liberal tapestry,[8] there are some useful conceptual insights that may be gleaned from the Polanyian perspective. The first is the idea of markets as social constructs.[9] In contrast to the neoclassical view of spontaneous market order, Polanyians maintain that markets require a supporting structure of institutions and laws in order to function.[10] Drawing these ideas into the global realm, this implies that, far from some unstoppable force, the actual trajectories of these processes of globalisation are contestable and malleable. Globalisation can thus become what we make of it (McNamara, 1998) – hence the appeal of this argument to sceptics. The second key insight is the normative connection between market structures and social structures. In the de-socialised neo-classical version of economics, markets are value neutral. In the Polanyian version, normative values are expressed in market relationships. In this sense Polanyi's argument is that pre-market, embedded economies are humane or moral economies (Booth, 1994, p. 653) while the disembedded, autonomous market economies are fundamentally destructive of the human spirit. Human beings were not, indeed could not be, treated as commodities. This violated basic human values. Globalisation thus represents a renewed attempt to disembed the economy from society, but one that promises a disastrous backlash akin to the 1930s (Birchfield, 1999, p. 38). To avoid this, political and economic struggle must aim at reigning in the market and re-embedding economic relations in societal relations: 'Such projects for reembedding the economy flow naturally from the picture of market society as ruled over by a disembedded, self-legislating economy coupled with a critical estimation of that society' (Booth, 1994, p. 658).

Both Marxists and Keynesians see crises of capitalism deriving from the inherent contradictions of the mode of capitalist production, be it overproduction or insufficient demand. From the Polanyian perspective, on the other hand, 'the core problematique is not a contradiction within the economy . . . but a social and cultural contradiction between a disembedded market and the conditions which make society, and social relations between human beings, possible' (Lacher, 1999, p. 315). Thus the Polanyian perspective on globalisation draws attention not so much to economic dynamics as to the intersection of economics with the particular institutions and values of different societies. The economy cannot be disconnected from society; economic interaction must be understood in the broader social and political framework in which it is embedded. The most useful means of elaborating this is through the 'varieties of capitalism' literature.

'VARIETIES OF CAPITALISM' AS COMPETING CONCEPTIONS OF THE MARKET

The varieties of capitalism (VoC) approach generally focuses on firms as the crucial actors in capitalist economies and examines how the particular institutional and regulatory structures in which those firms are embedded mould their strategies and interactions. (Representative texts include Berger and Dore, 1996; Crouch and Streeck, 1997; Hollingsworth and Boyer, 1997; Coates, 2001; Hall and Soskice, 2001; Pontusson, 2005.) Of course, all nations have some unique traits, implying myriad capitalist varieties. Yet Peter Hall and David Soskice (2001)[11] note that all firms must resolve some basic coordination problems in order to succeed – managing industrial relations, gaining access to corporate finance, securing a properly trained workforce, dealing with suppliers and clients and so on. The manner in which firms resolve these problems and the institutional structures that support that particular mode of coordination is what distinguishes different models of capitalism. Two broad categories predominate. In liberal market economies (LMEs), firms coordinate their activities through competitive market arrangements. In coordinated market economies (CMEs), firms rely on non-market relationships for coordination.

The United States is the prime example of an LME. Financing through the sale of equity shares requires managers to be attentive to current corporate earnings. Industrial relations are contractual and transient; managers can hire and fire at will. Conversely, management can autonomously craft corporate strategy in response to changing market conditions. Education and vocational training is decentralised and largely left to the worker to acquire, and is thus grounded more in general rather than in industry-specific skills. Close inter-firm networks, entailing not only cooperation, but insider knowledge, is discouraged by the regulatory structure (that is, antitrust). Technological innovations are thus treated as proprietary, allowing those developing new technologies to reap windfall profits from sales and licensing and putting a premium on innovation and being a 'first mover'.

Germany is the epitome of a CME. Firms in CMEs often have access to 'patient capital' through major banks or other corporations. Such investments are monitored less through profit reports and more through insider information. Banks often place representatives on the boards of directors of their customers and companies are linked through dense business networks coordinated by business associations. This allows companies not only to have knowledge of others' activities, but also to share technological and organisational know-how. In such an environment reputation is important, so openness and fair dealing with partners is a necessity. Additionally, corporate managers rarely have full freedom to shape corporate strategy. The structure of corporate governance and the dominant business ethos leads to consensus decision making, particularly including labour unions. Industrial relations are governed by industry-wide coordinated bargaining, which equalises wages across skill levels (generally at a high level), encouraging a committed and stable labour force. As a result, the training system focuses on developing industry or firm-specific skills without significant fear of employees being poached by other firms.

These traits tend to produce 'institutional complementarities', meaning that the development of particular forms of coordination in one sphere encourages similar practices in other aspects of the economy. Despite superficial differences, therefore, we see clear patterns of commonalities across clusters of states. The institutional structure in a given economy offers firms a particular set of opportunities and, since these are collective institutions, individual firms may be unable to alter this structure or create new coordinating structures. Companies are thus likely to gravitate towards strategies that conform to the dominant modes of coordination within an economy, be they market or non-market (Hall and Soskice, 2001, p. 15).

The main benefit of this approach is to illuminate how these differences alter comparative economic advantages. The most influential version of the theory of comparative advantage suggests that open capitalist economies will specialise in those products whose basic factors (land, labour or capital) they possess in relative abundance (Stolper and Samuelson, 1941). Developments in the global economy have not gone as this model would predict, however (that is, the expansion of intra-industry trade, the failure of capital mobility to equalise advantages and so on). A straightforward application of comparative advantage thus does not explain the geographic distribution of economic performance. The VoC approach suggests that the answer can be found in the idea of comparative institutional advantage:

> The basic idea is that the institutional structure of a particular political economy provides firms with advantages for engaging in specific types of activities there. Firms can perform some types of activity, which allow them to produce some kinds of goods, more efficiently than others because of the institutional support they receive for these activities in the political economy, and the institutions relevant to these activities are not distributed evenly across nations. (Hall and Soskice, 2001, p. 37)

The patterns of cross-national specialisation are less a question of factor endowments and more a function of political–economic institutions and how these influence corporate strategy.

Institutional variations thus translate into strengths and weaknesses in different types of economic activity. CMEs are strongest in terms of incremental innovations in existing product lines and production processes, markets in which quality is often more important than price (that is, capital goods, machine tools, consumer durables). Incremental innovations are easier to secure with a skilled and stable workforce and long-term relationships with other companies. LMEs have the converse strengths – radical innovations in fast-moving technology sectors that call for rapid product development. The flexibility of labour markets, the independence of managers, and the easy access to finance through equity markets allow for quick and flexible adaptation to new market opportunities. CMEs and LMEs are thus mirror images of each other. CMEs slowly and deliberately adapt to changing markets via incremental innovation, while LMEs flexibly and often disruptively focus on radical change. Hall and Soskice use patent data to show that this is not just theoretical speculation; indeed, the pattern of technological innovations for Germany and the US is that predicted by the CME/LME dichotomy (ibid., pp. 41–4).[12]

The emphasis on diversity within capitalism – and hence contingency in adjusting to the pressures of globalisation – as well as the focus on non-market forms of coordination as the key distinguishing trait among capitalist economies is the tissue that connects the varieties of capitalism argument with Polanyian perspectives. The idea of complementarities also suggests that these are not just 'grab-bag' collections of institutions, but interactive systems – true *models* of capitalism. Formal institutions are often not sufficient in themselves to produce a particular outcome; this is as much a function of a shared understanding of how those institutions are supposed to work.[13] In liberal systems, for example, management and labour are generally posed in conflictual terms; in coordinated systems they are portrayed as 'social partners'. Such differences are more than just semantics – they represent competing normative interpretations of economic interaction, or competing conceptions of the market. Thus the analysis is drawn back to Polanyi. It is not just the structure of markets that matter; it is how societies interpret the normative validity of markets that is key. The difference, of course, is that while Polanyi says that society cannot withstand the battering of the market, the VoC school suggests that the impact of free markets will be filtered through and mitigated by national institutional structures.

Further still, the idea of comparative institutional advantages suggests that different models of political economy have different strengths and weaknesses. In the near term, if we follow the Polanyian logic, it is those economies in which economic exchange remains embedded in the social fabric – that is, more coordinated economies – that are most likely to successfully weather the gales of globalisation. Further along, the logical supposition is that the way to avoid the disasters that followed the first era of globalisation is through the re-embedding of economies in society, usually expressed as some updated form of the post-Second World War social democratic 'embedded liberalism' (Ruggie, 1982).

The bigger issue is the relationship between these arguments and globalisation. The centripetal pull of institutional complementarities warrants against the necessity of radical change in the face of global pressures (see especially Rhodes, 2001 and Swank, 2002). Since globalisation is unlikely to revolutionise national institutional configurations, the comparative economic advantages derived thereby are unlikely to be transformed. This is fine as far as it goes, but the inference that follows is a continuation in trends in aggregate economic performance. Since different models of capitalism have prospered equally in the past, they can still do so despite globalisation. Or, to put the point more directly, coordinated economies will adjust and adapt to globalisation, but retain predominantly non-market forms of coordination without any skip in performance. However, to make such an argument is to raise the national institutional structure to causal prominence and to disconnect the linkages between structural changes in the global economy and national economic performance. It is to suggest that the institutional integrity at the national level is the fundamental determinant of not only the form of capitalist development, but also its relative functioning.[14] The broader environment of international markets and institutions, and how that system has changed over time, is far less relevant. The validity of this supposition is explored below.

ECONOMIC IMPLICATIONS

Before delving into the economic implications of this argument, it should first be noted that, for all the change that globalisation represents, the underlying logic of capitalist accumulation remains the same. National economic success is ultimately the result of the disconnected activity of firms buying and selling in order to maximise profits by establishing advantages in global competition (Porter, 1990). On the national level the ability to do this is primarily a function of the *productivity* of the economy, an 'old economy' rule that is alive and well.

What have been altered are the paths to productivity. The relatively stable technologies and Fordist mass-production methods of the post-war period heightened the benefits of incremental improvements in product and process technologies. Today's IT revolution has created whole new product lines (that is, personal computers, software), vastly expanded certain areas of activity (that is, consumer finance, communications, entertainment), altered the way that existing businesses operate (that is, computerised inventories facilitating just-in-time production), and created new market media (that is, e-commerce). Globalisation thus alters the scope and techniques of capitalist accumulation, as well as expanding the range of areas that can become commodified. The accelerated speed of product cycles places a premium on the accumulation of knowledge and the ability to transform this into competitive gains. Both at the company and the national levels, this demands an *innovative* environment with a steady supply of new ideas and the ability to redeploy resources to more productive areas of endeavour.

Yet deterritorialisation means that economic actors have a greater ability to exercise the exit option in seeking to upgrade performance and profits. If they do not like what they see at home – in terms of public policy, supplier performance, labour flexibility and so on – they can simply take their business elsewhere, either by moving operations or supply sources abroad. The ease of capital mobility, of course, is easily overstated,[15] but that does not mean that it does not have real impact. Even if capital chooses to stay put, it still must be able to effectively respond to changes in global markets. Companies or countries that are unable to *adapt* to changes in the global economy are likely to lose out as businesses either move to more productive locales or fall behind in international competition. Assuming that the trends in globalisation continue, national economic structures must be productive, innovative and adaptive.

One can, of course, accept that the trends of globalisation will continue, but as a prelude to its inevitable reversal – a new Polanyian double movement. The coming reaction will stem from the disruption caused by foolishly attempting – again – to establish unregulated markets in the global economy. Polanyi's call from the past, echoed in the present, is that such a system is inherently contradictory to basic human values. Thus the core problem with globalisation is not trade balances, or financial flows, or new technologies *per se*, it is the cluster of economic norms that it embodies. Specifically, it encompasses a set of ideas supportive of the economic utility and normative value of free markets – an ideology of 'globalism' (Steger, 2005).[16] Advocates of globalisation tend to err in portraying it in matter-of-fact, value-neutral terms, although some do offer a principled defence (Micklethwait and Woolridge, 2000; Lindsey, 2002). The portrayal of globalisation-as-norms is most easily seen in the writings of globalisation's critics: 'Market ideology is the necessary corollary of neoliberal economic globalisation', writes Vicki Birchfield (1999, p. 45), and 'a contestation of neoliberalism must begin by a dereification of the market which would demonstrate the fundamentally social and, therefore, public nature of economic relations'.

The key point of contention is the connection between the normative structure embodied in globalisation and its divergence from embedded social norms. Polanyi uncategorically argued that liberalism contradicts basic human values and is inappropriate for *any* society. Recent works tend to qualify their arguments to account for the vibrancy of the US economy. John Gray thus argues against extending American-style capitalism to other states because free market models will not work in more collectivist-orientated societies. One would think that reversing the equation would suggest that a free market works in the US because of America's individualistic and entrepreneurial culture. Yet the idea of 'successful free markets' repulses Gray. In his portrait America is a land where the middle class is being 're-proletarianized' and social stability is only maintained through mass incarceration (Gray, 1998, ch. 5).[17] American capitalism does not seem to work particularly well in America either. Similarly, despite a purported agnosticism regarding the optimal type of capitalism, most of the varieties of capitalism literature boils down to explanations of why coordinated economies manifest superior performance. What begins as a culturally specific critique of liberalism and plea for contingency in economic analysis morphs into a universal proposition: free market capitalism is inherently unstable because it undermines the social order.[18] There is a linkage between the norms of globalisation and the norms of society, and that linkage is destructive.

Yet what if these arguments are wrong? What if there are, in fact, multiple conceptions of the relationship between economies and societies? What if the normative values embodied in liberalism and globalisation are not at odds with the core values of a given society? If the dominant values of a given society accept the utility, efficacy and morality of (predominantly) market regulation of economic life, then would we still get a backlash, a new double movement? Polanyians, starting with Polanyi himself, do not explore this idea in a critical manner, but rather treat the opposition of society to unregulated markets as so self-evident as to not require elaboration. Yet if one treats this as a point that should be critically explored rather than asserting an inherent contradiction between society and the market, this opens up the hypothesis that the movement to less-regulated global markets has the potential to create a social and political backlash *unless* the values of the populace are accepting of market outcomes. That is, we need to look at the dominant *economic culture* within a given society – the empirical and normative values and preconceptions that individuals bring with them into economic interaction and how these might serve to alter behaviour in response to economic incentives. Such beliefs guide actors' behaviour and condition what they think are the feasible and acceptable outcomes. To put it in economic jargon, economic cultures alter individuals' utility functions, structuring how individuals respond to particular incentives. In Gramscian terms, it is a question of how much people have internalised the liberal hegemony. To put the matter in plain English, if people think that the outcomes produced by markets, including global markets, are acceptable, appropriate and just, then there will not necessarily be a backlash against increased marketisation of life. The point to be made here is that people in different contexts will react variably to similar external changes, such as globalisation, and the nature of their individual reactions helps to determine the collective performance of the national economy.

A *market-responsive* economic culture accepts market outcomes as just and appropriate, encourages entrepreneurialism and risk, and favours individual over collective interests. Such an ideological construction shifts the responsibility of economic adjustment from the social and political realm to the level of firms competing in product markets and individuals competing in labour markets. A *market-resistant* culture would, of course, do the opposite. Such an economic paradigm would question the efficacy and morality of unconstrained market outcomes, seek to socialise economic risk, and raise collective values above individual ones. A market-resistant context may specifically place values of social solidarity, equality and security above those of material gain. This may require greater regulation of economic life, more concentration of economic decision making, and a generally more rigid political–economic structure. The issue here is not the 'objective correctness' of these values, but rather how they change individuals' and policy makers' responses to economic conditions, specifically globalisation (Hay and Rosamond, 2002). The point is that the values embedded in a market-resistant economic culture discourage the very behaviours that are most likely to increase economic returns in a liberalised global economic environment.

Far more importantly, and relevant to the themes of this text, it is the underlying economic culture that serves to establish the sense of either economic citizenship or alienation. A market-responsive economic culture reinforces the idea that one is rightfully, justly an active part of – a citizen in – a market-orientated society. Feeling that one is an active participant in, rather than a passive victim of, a market system raises the potential for one to take actions appropriate to producing positive economic outcomes in a globalised economy. Conversely, a culture in which many feel that the advance of market imperatives is inherently corrosive to wider social values is likely to inculcate a sense of alienation from rather than citizenship in the economic system. Far from successfully adapting to globalisation, such collective sentiments may serve to discourage actions adaptive to market forces, further undermining economic performance and, in turn, embedding an even deeper sense of estrangement.

Take, for example, the response of an individual to say, the loss of employment. This may be significantly different in a social milieu where work is considered an individual responsibility as opposed to one where it is seen as a right of social provision. In short, if the social structure mimics the behavioural assumptions underlying liberalism, then that society is better suited to adjusting to a more liberalised international environment. A market-responsive context does just that by turning rationalistic material calculation into positive individual and collective values. How might behaviour vary in a cultural climate where the provision of employment is considered more of a social right than an individual responsibility? This is a crucial question for many European economies trying to deregulate their labour markets. If labour markets are deregulated and masses of workers are laid off, what are they likely to do? If they focus on seeking new employment, the results will be those intended by the government. If they live off the dole and focus on political activity to overturn such laws, there will be no net economic gain for these economies. Successful liberalisation is not just a question of policy, but also of people. It does little good to liberalise unless people change their behaviour accordingly. The economic culture that they hold determines how they will respond to liberalisation.

This is a crucial point in assessing the impact of globalisation, which entails a broad movement of liberalisation even if we can still distinguish meaningfully between liberal and coordinated economies. Both proponents and opponents of globalisation assume that individuals will respond in particular ways to the expansion of markets, either seeking protection (the double movement) or grasping the opportunities of the global marketplace. In reality, both behaviours are probable and the important question is the relative propensity of individuals in a given economy to respond one way or the other. Market-based adaptation, for example, is premised on the belief that individuals will take economic risks in pursuit of business opportunities and innovation; that is, they will become entrepreneurs. Is entrepreneurial propensity equivalent across capitalist economies? The Global Entrepreneurship Monitor (GEM), an international research programme directed by Babson College in the US and the London Business School, measures the level of 'Total Entrepreneurial Activity', the percentage of the adult population engaged in entrepreneurial activity (GEM, 2005). Among major developed economies, New Zealand and the United States stand out as having the most entrepreneurial populaces; Japan and Belgium as having the least. Nor is this simply a question of regulation; both the US and the UK are considered liberal economies, but rates of individual entrepreneurial activity are nearly double in America (Minniti et al., 2004, p. 17). Similar evidence was found in a Eurobarometer study of entrepreneurialism in the EU and competitor countries (Eurobarometer, 2004). Europeans were less likely to desire to be self-employed, or to see this as a viable possibility in the near future and tend to see more obstacles in the way of starting a new business, particularly in terms of administrative barriers. But they also weigh the psychological costs of failure much more heavily. American entrepreneurs are also more likely to have started a business in order to seize a business opportunity (71 per cent) compared to Europeans (55 per cent). Twice as many Europeans did so for reasons of necessity, that is, lack of other employment possibilities (Eurobarometer, 2004, p. 36). In sum, some social contexts are more likely to encourage the sort of productive, innovative and adaptive behaviour among firms, workers and entrepreneurs that is most likely to induce prosperity in an increasingly liberalised economy. In contrast, market-resistant societal contexts are attempting to swim against the tide. The economic behaviours encouraged within market-resistant contexts are not well suited to successful adaptation to globalisation.

It is not only a question of underlying economic cultures. The VoC approach highlights the determinative role of institutions, suggesting that complementarities have allowed coordinated systems to survive relatively unchanged despite globalisation. Unfortunately, this argument rests on a questionable assertion: not only will the institutional integrity of these models hold, but their comparative performance will be unchanged. The logical problem with this is that it disconnects economic outcomes from changes in international markets. The forms of capitalism may be diverse, but the prediction is for relative convergence in economic performance, globalisation or not. What is missing from existing accounts is a clear connection between models, globalisation and performance. What is missing is an understanding of the *global complementarity* of models of capitalism. The proper question to ask is whether changes in the structure of the global economy might alter the relative returns to be derived from different models of national political economy? This can be addressed by thinking not only in terms of comparative institutional advantages, but also how globalisation increases or decreases the relative costs and benefits of different institutional matrices. How does globalisation alter the opportunity cost of the alternative models of capitalism? The argument here is not that the competitive advantages of coordinated market economies will disappear; they will still likely have a strong position in incremental innovation in established technology. The point is more that increasing global competition and a greater emphasis on rapid innovation and technological change will serve to produce increasing institutional returns for liberal market economies. To state the point conversely, a globalising world economy imposes rising opportunity costs for continuing to pursue strategies of non-market coordination as opposed to market-orientated policies. Models that buck global trends pay a rising price for doing so, and this should be reflected in relatively poor performance.

How exactly do non-market forms of coordination increase costs? Globalisation, with its open and dynamic market, raises the salience of productivity, innovation and adaptability for national economic development.

The institutional advantages created in CMEs have reduced utility for effectively addressing these challenges. In terms of innovation, LMEs are noted for focusing on radical innovations while the strength of CMEs is on incremental innovation. Does incremental innovation have the same utility as in the past? One need only ponder the capabilities of their first computer compared to their current system to see how rapidly the core technologies of the present day are changing. Technological life cycles have been shortened to a few years or less. By the time such technologies become sufficiently stable for incremental innovation, the market has moved on to another good. Rapidly changing and fluctuating technological paradigms provide increased returns for radical innovation. Widespread adaptability is equally constrained by the emphasis on consensual decision making and cooperation among the social partners. Hence CMEs have developed relatively inefficient domestic and international service industries. Technology increases the range of services that can be exported, so falling behind in services means falling behind in a broad area of exportable products.

The economic implications are that countries with more 'embedded' (in Polanyian terms) economic cultures and that rely more heavily on non-market forms of economic coordination are going to face diminishing returns for maintaining such structures as globalisation continues apace, manifesting in declining relative economic performance. A fully fledged examination of this hypothesis is beyond the scope of this chapter (and is as much a question of future as of past performance), but evidence of recent economic performance supports this contention. While the distinction between coordinated market economies and liberal economies is not a perfect proxy for the market-responsive–market-resistant distinction described here,[19] Table 4.1 breaks down the economic performance of the major coordinated and liberal economies. The most obvious difference is in growth. From 1995 to 2005, LMEs grew on average nearly twice as fast (3.9 to 2.1 per cent) as CMEs. Even if one removes the high-flying Irish economy from the equation, LME growth was a full percentage point (3.2 per cent) higher. (Whether societies should favour economic growth over other metrics of performance, such as the social equity, is a separate question, although Benjamin M. Friedman (2005) has made a strong case that the fulfilment of solidaristic values is dependent upon continued growth.) This has translated into higher per capita GDP and higher overall levels of employment (note that there is much greater variation on this measure among the coordinated economies). The one bright spot for CMEs is on productivity, higher on average and with many individual countries even higher than the US. However, this requires some qualification. The high productivity of some countries, such as France, comes at the cost of employment; in essence, low-skilled workers are unable to find employment, which

Table 4.1   Comparative economic performance, 1995–2005

	GDP (growth %)[1]	GDP per capita[2]	Employment[3]	Productivity[4]
CMEs				
Austria	2.2	78.2	67.7	101.1
Belgium	2.1	75.1	58.6	103.1
Denmark	2.1	82.8	75.5	89.9
Finland	3.5	73.9	65.3	87.6
France	2.2	71.5	61.0	112.1
Germany	1.4	72.7	67.9	98.7
Italy	1.5	69.9	53.4	87.3
Japan	1.3	75.4	69.0	74.3
Netherlands	2.3	73.0	70.6	100.5
Norway	3.0	101.2	76.1	125.5
Sweden	2.8	71.3	73.1	89.3
Switzerland	1.3	77.3	77.7	85.7
CME average	2.1	76.9	68.0	96.3
LMEs				
Australia	3.7	76.3	68.2	79.1
Canada	3.3	81.9	70.0	78.3
Ireland	7.5	98.1	61.2	105.0
New Zealand	3.3	60.3	70.7	60.1
United Kingdom	2.8	72.5	71.6	88.9
United States	3.3	100.0	72.8	100.0
LME average	3.9	81.5	69.1	85.2

Notes:
1. Average percentage change in real GDP, 1995–05 (IMF).
2. Index of pc GDP at PPP, 2005 (CIA World Factbook, 2006).
3. Average employment/population ratio, 1995–2004 (OECD).
4. Index of real GDP per hour worked at PPP, 2004 (Groningen Growth and Development Centre, Total Economy Database).

boosts the productivity numbers. Even for those countries with both high productivity and high employment, such as the Netherlands, productivity performance has declined as of late. Dutch GDP per hour worked, about even with the US in 2005, was about 20 per cent *higher* in 1995.[20] The counterargument for proponents of CMEs is that the longer-term economic record is more favourable to coordinated economies. The problem is that the trends on a wide range of economic measures are moving in the wrong direction. Albeit hardly conclusive, the prima facie evidence suggests that liberal economies are indeed performing better as globalisation progresses.[21]

POLITICAL IMPLICATIONS

To end the discussion on economic questions would be incomplete since Polanyi's fundamental concern was not the economic failure of the Great Depression, but the political catastrophe of the rise of fascism and war. Analysts invoke Polanyi in the present because they foresee the same danger looming. The expansion of global markets will unleash social disruptions that might manifest in some new and horrific form of political reaction, unless, that is, steps are taken to limit markets and protect society. Those that do not heed the call to resist will be the ones to pay a terrible price; hence Polanyi as an anti-globalisation prophet.

The political implications of the Polanyian perspective, as the above analysis suggests, are not so straightforward. Indeed, the argument above implies an inversion of the Polanyian perspective. Despite claims to focus on how economic relations are embedded in particular cultures, neo-Polanyians ignore actual analysis of how different cultures might react to these trends. The characterisation of the reaction to globalisation is posed in universalistic terms – *all* societies *must* eventually protect themselves from the encroachment of markets on society. The argument here is genuinely contingent. Economic and political behaviour is embedded in particular social structures, and these will shape how people respond to globalisation. Some polities (those that are market resistant) are more threatened by the increased marketisation of social life, leading to social disruption and political discontent surrounding continued globalisation. But this will not be the reaction everywhere. The adjustment to globalisation in some countries (that is, those with market-responsive contexts) will be smoother because of a combination of positive economic performance and social structures producing behaviours that more directly mimic the imperatives of markets – generalised political acceptance of the benefits of liberalisation. For some places globalisation will be a 'false dawn', for others it will not.

Differentiating which countries will react in which ways is ultimately a rather large empirical question that is beyond the scope of this chapter. We are already seeing substantial variation, not only economically, but also politically, in response to globalisation across the globe.[22] Look, for example, within the developed world. Those countries that seem to be most accepting of and adaptable to globalisation (and equally seem to be thriving economically) would include the Anglo-Saxon liberal economies, but also the welfare states of Scandinavia. This is not to say that political discontent related to globalisation is lacking in these states; note complaints in the US, perhaps the epitome of a market-orientated society, regarding outsourcing and immigration. It is to suggest, however, that the 'default position' among policy makers and the general public alike is that global-isation is something to be accepted and managed, not resisted. (Discontent is also likely to be ameliorated by stronger economic performance in these states, *pace* the economic argument above.) For others, where institutional coordination and collectivist cultures are more entrenched – France, Germany, Italy and Japan – increasing globalisation has been matched with comparative economic stagnation and political alienation. While there has been some radicalisation of politics in these countries – the second-place finish of Jean-Marie Le Pen in the 2002 French presidential election being the most successful example – the historical legacies of fascism and communism on the continent would likely hinder a full turn to extremism. More probable would be political malaise and 'genteel stagnation' (Casey, 2006a).

In the developing world, emerging economies in China, India and Southeast Asia seem to be embracing the opportunities of globalisation – even in the wake of the 1997 East Asian financial crisis – and moving up the economic ladder. In sharp contrast, in the Middle East, globalisation has served to expose the underlying political and economic faultlines of a region lacking in both political democracy and widespread opportunity for economic advancement. It is no coincidence that Islamic extremism, terrorism and globalisation have all arisen concurrently.

Middle Eastern nations, for a wide array of reasons, have not been adept at acclimatising themselves to the transformation of modern world economic and social system. Latin America seems to represent something of a middling position, with (at least the leadership) of states such as Mexico, Brazil, Argentina and Chile implicitly inculcating the necessity of market adaptation. Others, mainly Venezuela and Bolivia, have moved in a more populist direction. Sub-Saharan Africa really is too weakly integrated into world markets to be meaningfully analysed in the terms of this discussion.

All of this also highlights the limitations of neo-Polanyian prescriptions. Polanyi is invoked to rationalise a return to the past, but the past envisaged is the social democratic settlement of the post-Second World War era. This actually is contrary to Polanyi's thinking. Remember that for Polanyi the extension of the market was the underlying cause of the cataclysm of the first half of the twentieth century. The proximate cause was the attempts at protection encompassed in the double movement which served to destabilise the market system. Re-establishing minimalist protections for society against the market is simply going to exacerbate the current crisis in this view. Hannes Lacher notes, moreover, that 're-embedding' means something much more than minimal state protections on an otherwise market-based economy. It means the complete de-commodification of land, labour and capital – an abandonment of the market system and a return to organic, subsistence-orientated, pre-market (and pre-modern) societies

(Lacher, 1999, p. 315). William James Booth (1994, p. 660) notes that those pre-modern societies for which Polanyi yearned maintained strong communities, but did so through rigid social structures and steep hierarchies, which would surely run counter to the democratic impulses of neo-Polanyians. More to the point, Polanyi shines a spotlight on the potential failings of the market system, but he offered no coherent alternative means through which scarce economic resources might be allocated. Any renewed call for 'embedded liberalism' needs to explain why this will not produce the same failing as in the 1970s. Lacher goes further to contend that globalisation requires a turn to democratic socialism (1999, p. 323), but the long-term record of 'real existing socialism' makes this suggestion much more hopeful than helpful. For all of the hand wringing over the failings of globalisation, one hears the distant echo of Margaret Thatcher – 'There is no alternative'.[23] Encouraging resistance to and protection from globalisation, far from protecting societies from globalisation's purportedly destabilising effects, will more likely serve to induce instability.

CONCLUSION

The idea of citizenship is usually posed in purely political terms. Using a Polanyian perspective emphasising the embeddedness of markets in social structures allows one to understand how the underlying values and institutions of a society influences individuals' connections to the economic structure, providing (or eroding) their sense of economic citizenship. The effects of globalisation are best understood within particular social contexts, but the Polanyian view is that free markets are implacably corrosive of the social fabric, everywhere and always. Economic exchange must, therefore, be 're-embedded' in the social structure (that is, de-commodified) in order to stave off imminent catastrophe. While accepting the idea of market embeddedness, a truly contingent approach to understanding the impact of globalisation is taken here. It is argued above that, to the extent that a society inculcates the values of the market – a more market-responsive social context – that society is more likely to thrive economically and maintain political stability as globalisation progresses. In contradiction to the traditional Polanyian view, those places where economic activity is most embedded in non-market institutions, those coordinated market economies in VoC terminology, are likely to have the most difficulty adapting, which will translate into sub-par economic performance, which in itself can breed further economic alienation and heighten political discontent. At the extreme, these dynamics may serve to breed support for or participation in terrorist movements. Only by understanding how both normative and institutional factors influence how societies adapt (or not) to changes in the international economy can we fully understand the dynamics of globalisation and the space for political action. The Lionel Jospin quote at the start of this chapter suggests that one can have a thriving market economy without concurrently 'marketising' society. It is a conception of a liberalised market coupled with a solidaristic view of society. The argument here is that society can collectively make that choice, but it is a choice that comes at an economic and political price. And that price is rising as a result of globalisation.

NOTES

1. Friedman (2000, ch. 6). This implies that states must reduce taxation and spending, deregulate the economy, establish price stability via relatively strict monetary policy, implement free trade and capital mobility, limit the number of state-run industries, cut back on industrial policy and so on. While this constrains the range of policy options, it opens up the potential for a steady flow of international investment and higher growth.
2. See the discussion of the Polanyian view of globalisation below for representative authors.
3. This is not to say that there is not resistance to the ideology of globalism. It is rather to say that that resistance is largely reactionary rather than counter-hegemonic.
4. In one of the great ironies of history, another Austrian exile, Friedrich Hayek, published *The Road to Serfdom* in the same year, drawing the diametrically opposite conclusion. 'Few are ready to recognize that the rise of fascism and naziism [sic] was not a reaction against socialist trends of the preceding period but a necessary outcome of those tendencies' (Hayek, 1944 [1994], p. 6).
5. He specifically examines the Poor Law reforms in Britain in the 1830s which sought to push people into the labour market by reducing the value of public relief.
6. Polanyi's entire argument is summarised early on in *The Great Transformation*: 'Our thesis is that the idea of a self-adjusting market implied a stark utopia. Such an institution could not exist for any length of time without annihilating the human and natural substance of society; it would have physically destroyed man and transformed his surroundings into a wilderness. Inevitably, society took measures to protect itself, but whatever measures it took impaired the self-regulation of the market, disorganized industrial life, and thus endangered society in yet another way. It was this dilemma which forced the development of the market system into a definite groove and finally disrupted the social organization based upon it' (pp. 1–2).
7. As a historical explanation of fascism and war, Polanyi's thesis is questionable. For a start, self-regulating markets as Polanyi described them never really existed. Europe, even England, was replete with protections and economic controls throughout this period (see Halperin, 2004, p. 271). If fascism resulted from the disruption of unregulated markets, furthermore, then one would assume that this would first arise in the most *laissez-faire* nations – Great Britain and the United States. Fascism arose instead in Italy and Germany, countries with mercantilist policies and weakly inculcated liberal values. Finally, he essentially discounts *the* intervening variable between nineteenth-century liberalism and twentieth-century fascism: the First World War. He falls back on a Leninesque economic interpretation – it was the failure of the international market economy that caused the war, not the rise of tight alliances, or aggressive German policies, or the instability in the Austro-Hungarian Empire and so on. With reasonable and proximate explanations readily at hand, Polanyi instead opts for tenuous and distant solutions.
8. The empirical problems with Polanyi are cited above. Current versions are no better. Gray offers little solid evidence to bolster claims about the declining standard of living

and social instability created by free markets. Nor does his suggestion of runaway markets hold: his own examples of *laissez-faire* economies (US, UK, New Zealand) still have public spending equivalent to at least one-third of GDP, and all have minimum wages (that is, price floors in labour markets). Among his liberal exemplars, government intervention in the economy and policies to counter the negative consequences of the market are quite prominent. Perhaps these are not to his satisfaction, but we are nowhere near the minimal government of the late nineteenth century.

9. For a more detailed elaboration of the intellectual development of this idea, see Swedberg (1994).

10. There is an inherent contradiction in Polanyian thinking: if free markets require an elaborate institutional edifice, then what is then meant by describing such a system as 'disembedded'? (see Booth, 1994, p. 661).

11. Hall and Soskice's typology is the most widely cited. While other authors use different categorisation schemes, the differences are organisational rather than substantive. As such, they are representative of the broader literature.

12. Using European Patent Office data for 1993–94, they showed that US companies had a higher percentage of patents in pharmaceuticals, telecommunications, semiconductors and so on. German patents were concentrated in machine tools, transport, engines and so on.

13. Hall and Soskice indeed argue for just such an emphasis on culture as the foundation of different systems (pp. 12–14), but then promptly drop it from further consideration. This is a surprising omission given the intellectual debt owed by this school to studies of corporatism in the 1970s and 1980s and especially Katzenstein's (1985) recognition that successful corporatism was dependent on the inculcation of an ideology of social partnership.

14. With his focus on the need to stabilise organic societies, Polanyi unashamedly does just that. Modern Polanyians, on the other hand, would be rather uncomfortable accepting what is in many respects a very conservative argument.

15. Multiple factors go into where to locate productive operations, labour costs often being one of the least significant. Hence the bulk of foreign direct investment remains within the 'triad' of North America, Europe and Japan.

16. Steger makes a sharp distinction between 'globalization – a set of real historical social processes of increasing interdependence . . . and globalism – a political ideology endowing globalization with market norms, values, and meanings' (p. 18).

17. The argument that the US only keeps unemployment low through incarceration is a farce. In 2003 the civilian workforce was 147 million with 8.7 million unemployed (5.9 per cent). If *all* of the approximately two million people in jail were released and *none* of them could find work, the unemployment rate would rise to 7.2 per cent, or 1.3 per cent increase. To suggest that social stability is hostage to a small jump in the unemployment rate is facetious!

18. Hall and Soskice try to maintain a veil of neutrality, but it is clear that they much prefer coordinated modes of regulation. Others are more direct in their critique of liberalism. David Coates for his part contends, 'it is not that particular models of capitalism fail to function in a satisfactory manner . . . It seems rather that capitalism itself, in whatever form, is capable of functioning with only sporadic effectiveness and always at considerable social cost' (2001, p. 234). Wolfgang Streeck, indeed, presents the bizarre formulation of 'the perverse outcome of the less well-performing Anglo-American model of capitalism outcompeting the better performing "Rhine model"' (Crouch and Streeck, 1997, p. 53), implying that CMEs should be held as 'superior' models while suffering from inferior performance!

19. Within both the CME and LME categories there is a good deal of variation in terms of economic culture. The US is more individualist than Great Britain, for example, while Scandinavian countries tend to be more entrepreneurial than continental CMEs. The same is true in terms of the extent to which market forces predominate in both product and labour markets (that is, the extent of employment protection legislation). Whether and at what level elements of non-market coordination between private actors (that is

centralised wage bargaining) occurs also exhibits extensive variation. Unfortunately, the approach adopted in most of the VoC literature is for thick description and analysis across (not within) typological categories rather than empirical assessments of similarities and differences within systems. (For an example of an empirical approach to categorising economies, see Casey, 2006b.)

20. Specifically, the index figure was 119.4. Data from the Groningen Growth and Development Center Total Economy Database.

21. It is fair to say that liberal economies have generally done well and many coordinated economies are in the doldrums, but there are also coordinated economies, especially in Scandinavia, that have been thriving. The empirical record does not neatly break down into a 'liberal/prosperous–coordinated/stagnant' dichotomy.

22. It should again be noted up front that the pattern that we see does not neatly fit the free market/liberal and embedded/coordinated dichotomy implied by both the globalisation and VoC literatures.

23. More accurately, there are alternatives, but none of them works terribly well!

REFERENCES

Berger, Suzanne (2000), 'Globalization and politics', *Annual Review of Political Science*, **3**, 43–62.

Berger, Suzanne and Ronald Dore (eds) (1996), *National Diversity and Global Capitalism*, Ithaca, NY: Cornell University Press.

Birchfield, Vicki (1999), 'Contesting the hegemony of market ideology: Gramsci's "good sense" and Polanyi's "double movement"', *Review of International Political Economy*, **6** (1), 27–54.

Booth, William James (1994), 'On the idea of the moral economy', *American Political Science Review*, **88** (3), 653–67.

Callinicos, Alex (2001), *Against the Third Way*, Cambridge, UK: Polity.

Carlson, Allan (2006), 'The problem of Karl Polanyi', *The Intercollegiate Review*, **41** (1), 32–9.

Casey, Terrence (2006a), 'Of power and plenty? Europe, soft power, and "genteel stagnation"', *Comparative European Politics*, **4** (4), 399–422.

Casey, Terrence (2006b), 'Mapping the "models of capitalism" among OECD countries', paper presented at the International Studies Association Conference, San Diego, CA, 22–25 March.

Coates, David (2001), *Models of Capitalism: Growth and Stagnation in the Modern Era*, Cambridge, UK: Polity.

Crouch, Colin and Wolfgang Streeck (eds) (1997), *The Political Economy of Modern Capitalism: Mapping Convergence and Diversity*, London: Sage.

Eurobarometer (2004), *Entrepreneurship*, Flash Eurobarometer 160.

Friedman, Benjamin M. (2005), *The Moral Consequences of Economic Growth*, New York: Knopf.

Friedman, Thomas (2000), *The Lexus and the Olive Tree: Understanding Globalization*, 2nd edn, New York: Anchor Books.

Friedman, Thomas (2005), *The World is Flat: A Brief History of the Twenty-First Century*, New York: Farrar, Strauss & Giroux.

GEM (2005), *Global Entrepreneurship Monitor: National and Regional Summaries*, Babson College, Wellesley, MA.

Gray, John (1998), *False Dawn: The Delusions of Global Capitalism*, New York: New Press.

Greider, William (1997), *One World, Ready or Not: The Manic Logic of Global Capitalism*, New York: Simon & Schuster.

Groningen Growth and Development Center Total Economy Database, University of Groningen, The Netherlands, www.ggdc.net/homeggdc.html, accessed 1 November 2006.

Hall, Peter A. and David Soskice (eds) (2001), *Varieties of Capitalism: The Institutional Foundations of Comparative Advantage*, Oxford and New York: Oxford University Press.

Halperin, Sandra (2004), 'Dynamics of conflict and system change: *The Great Transformation* revisited', *European Journal of International Relations*, **10** (2), 263–306.

Hay, Colin and Ben Rosamond (2002), 'Globalization, European integration and the discursive construction of economic imperatives', paper presented at the International Studies Association Conference, New Orleans, USA, 24–27 March.

Hayek, Friedrich von (1944 [1994]), *The Road to Serfdom*, Chicago: University of Chicago Press.

Held, David and Andrew McGrew (2002), *Globalization/Anti-Globalization*, Cambridge: Polity.

Held, David, Anthony G. McGrew, David Goldblatt and Jonathan Perraton (1999), *Global Transformations: Politics, Economics and Culture*, Stanford, CA: Stanford University Press.

Hirst, Paul and Graham Thompson (1996), *Globalization in Question: The International Economy and Possibilities for Governance*, Cambridge: Polity.

Hirst, Paul (1999), 'Has globalization killed social democracy?', *Political Quarterly*, **70** (Special Issue 1), 84–96.

Hollingsworth, J. Rogers and Robert Boyer (eds) (1997), *Contemporary Capitalism: The Embeddedness of Institutions*, Cambridge: Cambridge University Press.

Katzenstein, Peter (1985), *Small States in World Markets: Industrial Policy in Europe*, Ithaca, NY: Cornell University Press.

Krieger, Joel (1999), *British Politics in the Global Age: Can Social Democracy Survive?*, Oxford: Oxford University Press.

Lacher, Hannes (1999), 'The politics of the market: re-reading Karl Polanyi', *Global Society*, **13** (3), 313–26.

Lindsey, Brink (2002), *Against the Dead Hand*, New York: Wiley.

McNamara, Kathleen (1998), 'Globalization is what we make of it? The political construction of market imperatives', paper presented at the Eleventh International Conference of Europeanists, Baltimore, MD, 25 February–1 March.

Micklethwait, John and Adrian Woolridge (2000), *A Future Perfect: The Challenge and Hidden Promise of Globalization*, New York: Crown.

Minniti, Maria, William D. Bygrave, Andrew L. Zacharakis and Marcia Cole (2004), *National Entrepreneurship Assessment: United States of America*, Global Entrepreneurship Monitor, Babson College/Kaufman Foundation, Wellesley, MA.

Mittelman, James H. (2000), *The Globalization Syndrome: Transformation and Resistance*, Princeton, NJ: Princeton University Press.

Ohmae, Kenichi (1990), *The Borderless World*, London: Collins.

Ohmae, Kenichi (1995), *The End of the Nation State*, New York: Free Press.

Polanyi, Karl (1944), *The Great Transformation*, Boston, MA: Beacon Press.

Pontusson, Jonas (2005), *Inequality and Prosperity: Social Europe vs. Liberal America*, Ithaca, NY: Cornell University Press.

Porter, Michael (1990), *The Competitive Advantage of Nations*, New York: Free Press.

Rhodes, Martin (2001), 'Globalization, welfare states and employment: is there a European "third way"', in Nancy Bermeo (ed.), *Unemployment in the New Europe*, Cambridge and New York: Cambridge University Press, pp. 87–118.

Rodrik, Dani (1997), *Has Globalization Gone Too Far?*, Washington, DC: Institute for International Economics.

Ruggie, John Gerard (1982), 'International regimes, transactions, and change: embedded liberalism and postwar economic order', *International Organization*, **36** (2), 379–416.

Scholte, Jan Aart (2000), *Globalization: A Critical Introduction*, London: Routledge.

Soros, George (1998), *The Crisis of Global Capitalism: Open Society Endangered*, New York: Public Affairs.

Steger, Manfred (2005), *Globalism: Market Ideology Meets Terrorism*, 2nd edn, Lanham, MD: Rowman & Littlefield.

Stolper, Wolgang and Paul Samuelson (1941), 'Protection and real wages', *Review of Economic Studies*, **9**, 58–73.

Swank, Duane (2002), *Global Capital, Political Institutions, and Policy Change in Developed Welfare States*, Cambridge and New York: Cambridge University Press.

Swedberg, Richard (1994), 'Markets as social structures', in Neil J. Smelser and Richard Swedberg (eds), *The Handbook of Economic Sociology*, Princeton, NJ: Princeton University Press, pp. 255–82.

5. Citizenship, globalisation and the politics of the war on terror

Maurice Mullard

INTRODUCTION

Expectations of citizenship are at present being shaped and defined by the dual processes of globalisation and the war on terror. In the context of globalisation the nation state is perceived as passive, having to respond to offshore pressures and larger planetary forces which are beyond its control. Increases in income inequality reflect global markets. There is little that governments can do to reduce income inequalities since any attempts to improve wages might result in higher unemployment. The war on terror is equally explained as being a global war. The emphasis on fear, of the continued presence of an 'enemy within' of terrorists seeking weapons of mass destruction and chemical weapons provides the legitimacy for surveillance and policing which in turn leads to a chilling effect and quietism. This process narrows the spaces for dissent but also corrupts the democratic process as people stand in silence when the human rights of others are being violated in the name of security.

Citizenship is not a static concept that can be captured within a definition. Expectations and hopes of citizenship are located in social, political, economic and cultural contexts. Civil, political and social rights that shape and define citizenship are equally not static. The boundaries between the state and individual civil liberties are contestable. It is with increased frequency that governments have made the exceptional case to redefine privacy, freedom of speech and freedom of assembly. During the First World War, President Woodrow Wilson passed the Espionage and Seditions Acts of 1917 and 1918 to deal with those who were arguing against the war, which in turn resulted in the Palmer Raids against communists in 1921. Under the acts, Jacob Adams, a Russian émigré, Charles Schenk and Joseph Gilbert were all imprisoned for making protests against the war while Anita Whitney was convicted for joining the Communist Party in California and advocating the overthrow of the US government (Brinkley, 2003). In an important opinion judgment in the

Whitney v. California case in 1927, Justice Louis Brandeis gave the following opinion:

> Those who won our independence by revolution were not cowards. They did not fear political change. They did not exalt order at the cost of liberty. . . . The fact that speech is likely to result in some violence or destruction of property is not enough to justify its suppression. There must be the probability of serious damage to the State. Among free men, the deterrents ordinarily to be applied to prevent crime are education and punishment for violations of the law not the abridgement of the rights of free speech and assembly. (Brinkley, 2003, p. 38)

There are therefore historical precedents that confirm the tendency of the nation state to question and violate what seem to be taken for granted civil and political rights in the name of security. The opinion of Justice Brandeis in 1927 pointed out that free speech was an essential pillar of democracy even when it seemed to undermine the security of the nation state. The US Patriot Acts of 2001 and 2006 and the UK anti-terror legislation have in their own ways reshaped the relationships between the individual and the state.

The war on terror and globalisation are generating contexts and landscapes of thinking, public institutions and policy processes that seek to locate citizenship in terms of individualism, retreat from public spaces, increased fear of the other and safety. The war on terror is connected with the argument of good and evil that is increasingly demonising, isolating and marginalising Muslim communities in Europe and the USA.

In the following sections, it will be argued that the landscapes of the war on terror and globalisation are generating two possible models of citizenship. First, there is the model of the consumer/communitarian citizen where consumption confirms identity and membership of a community. In the context of the consumer society, consumer citizenship provides a sense of belonging in the sense that identity is defined by the possession of consumer goods. The war on terror seeks to trade off individual liberties for the safety and security of consumers. The emphasis on safety results in retreat and feelings of passivity. Arguments for community create the language of inclusion and exclusion. There is the underlying assumption that community actually exists. A number of UK politicians both Labour and Conservative continue to make statements on the failure of the Muslim community to integrate into British society, assuming first that there is a tangible and homogeneous British society and second that there is a homogeneous Muslim community and that there are identifiable Muslim leaders who can speak for that imagined community.

By contrast, the public citizen model seeks to reclaim the public spaces and to make present forms of globalisation accountable and transparent.

The argument for a global cosmopolitan citizen points to the increased human connectedness, the possibilities of a global morality, common humanity, universal human rights and cosmopolitan values. The public citizen model gives priority to participation and involvement in the democratic process. It points to the uniqueness of human life, and the importance of the democratic process.

DEFINING GLOBALISATION

Definitions of globalisation tend to conflate two separate themes. First, there is the process of 'globalisation' that can be connected to global forms of consumption, lifestyles, culture and identities. Within this context globalisation is defined in terms of the compressing and the stretching of geographical spaces, where technology, information exchanges, the knowledge economy and capital flows are defining the nature of the borderless economy (see Casey and Lee in this volume, for their review of the literature on globalisation). According to the hyper-globalists (Ohmae, 1995; Bhagwati, 2002), this form of globalisation is to be celebrated because it confirms the ascendancy of competitive markets, the expansion of free trade, and the break-up of monopolies and protectionist policies:

> The country to which they (the consumers) are all migrating . . . helped along the way by shared exposure to the English language to the internet, Fox TV, the BBC, CNN and MTV and by interactive tools . . . is the global economy of the borderless world. Using a telephone, fax machine or personal consumer linked to the internet, for example a Japanese consumer in Sapporo can place an order for clothing with Lands End in Wisconsin or LL Bean in Maine and have the merchandise delivered by UPS or Yamato and charge the purchase to American Express, Visa or MasterCard. (Ohmae, 1995, p. 39)

However, despite the many theories of globalisation, there is the argument that globalisation is a concept that still lacks a definition and that the continued search for global facts has generated a globalisation discourse that seeks to equate globalisation with geographic spaces that are occupied by the nation state. The concept of discourse in this chapter is used to denote the influence of language and narratives that seek to explain and interpret the world, and that within that discourse are implicitly woven ways of seeing but also policy options that correspond with the way the story is being told. The discourse of globalisation therefore seeks to provide a specific narrative on a series of processes, which are defined as being global. In arguing the case that globalisation exists as a concept, there is the implication that there is therefore a major flaw in equating globalisation as a concept with the nation state. While the latter represents a series of tangible institutions, globalisation is an abstraction that occupies a different epistemological space to that of the nation state:

> Strictly speaking, the relationship between globalisation and the state is one between a concrete institutional structure and a descriptive concept; that is to say, since they belong to separate epistemological orders, the extent to which they can interact is questionable. How could a mere concept change an institution as established and enduring, as real, as the nation-state. (Cameron and Palan, 2004, p. 55)

Within the context of this chapter, discussion of the concept of globalisation is treated as a narrative which seeks to frame the academic concept that still needs to be defined with real time and geographic spaces that are congruent with the nation state. Furthermore, the geographical spaces that make up globalisation are by definition described as being larger than the nation state, much larger even than the geographic spaces occupied by 25 countries in the European Union (EU) or the USA. This geographical essentialism reduces governments to that of passive observers, of being limited to construct policy frameworks that correspond with the perceived challenges of events that are beyond political control. Governments, within the narrative of globalisation, have no alternative but to construct policies that are compatible with the sentiments of financial markets where the magnitudes of daily flows are beyond the controls of the nation state, which means constructing macroeconomic policies that give priority to low inflation, low levels of government borrowing and low interest rates. The response to the challenges of global competitive labour markets is to ensure lower labour costs, which means reducing the costs of all forms of social provision since these are defined as increasing labour costs. The commitment to flexible employment and investment in human capital are also seen as essential in the reforms of labour markets.

However, rather than seeing the nation state as responding to an exogenous event called globalisation, globalisation represents a series of deliberate policy choices. It is governments and global institutions including the International Monetary Fund (IMF), the World Bank and the World Trade Organisation (WTO) that are defining and shaping the nature of globalisation. So, rather than globalisation being outside the control of governments it is made by governments. Market liberal policies, including the privatisation of gas, water or electricity, reducing social spending and competitive labour markets reforms, represent deliberate policy choices that are contributing to global and within-country income inequalities. The World Bank Report on South America and the Caribbean (World Bank, 2003) has pointed out that the region has the highest rate of inequality when compared with other industrialised economies. The Gini coefficient for 2001 in South America was 0.522 compared with the Organisation for Economic Cooperation and Development (OECD) average of 0.342. In South America the richest 10 per cent earn 48 per cent of the total income while the bottom 10 per cent earn 1.6 per cent, compared with the OECD average of 29 per cent for the top 10 per cent and 2.5 per cent for the bottom 2.5 per cent. Clientele politics continues to perpetuate the existing political elites. Politics in countries in Sub-Saharan Africa, Thailand, Bangladesh and Malaysia are dominated by political elites, serving the interest of strategic groups rather than the commitment to universal principles of rights and citizenship. Public spaces are corrupted. Positions in the public sector are rewarded as part of currying political favours. In these contexts the marginalised poor tend to retreat from the public space to the safety of families, tribes and communities:

> It is difficult to sustain a universalist account of human rights and citizenship, based in effect upon Western liberal philosophy, in societies where even the incorporationist version of civil society was underdeveloped through colonial behaviour, and nowhere more so than in Africa. Thus the idea of rights emanating from the legitimated state, serviced by intermediary organisations constituting civil society, is almost laughable as a responsible description of the evolution of political institutions of power and authority in sub-Saharan Africa. (Gough and Wood, 2004, p. 73)

In 1950, world exports totalled US$61 billion or 6 per cent of world GDP, which by 1970, had increased to US$317 billion or 12 per cent of world GDP to US$3770 billion in 2000, equivalent to 16 per cent of world GDP. While world exports as a total have expanded, the ratios for the less developed countries (LDCs) actually declined in 2000, to 0.3 per cent of world trade compared with 0.7 per cent in 1994. The same story can be told for most of the developing countries where the ratio of trade has fallen in 44 out of the last 48 years. Subsidies to agriculture that tend to benefit multinational corporations (MNCs) have resulted in the overproduction of food in the USA and the EU. The advanced economies now provide subsidies to agriculture that amount to approximately $360 billion per annum. Food production is now controlled by a very small number of US MNCs, including Cargill, ADM and Zen Noh, which between them control 75 per cent of the world cereal commodity market, while the top five US retailers control 42 per cent of all retail food:

> Wheat is selling for 40 per cent less than it costs to produce. For cotton the level of dumping for 2001 rose to a remarkable 57 per cent and for rice it has stabilised at 20 per cent. Developing countries need healthy agricultural sectors to eliminate poverty. Dumping is a gross distortion . . . it undermines the livelihoods of 70 per cent of the world's poorest people. (IATP, 2003, p. 3)

At present, the LDCs' social expenditure is around 2 per cent of GDP in contrast to 24 per cent of GDP in the OECD and 11 per cent in Latin America. Thirty-seven out of the 44 HIPC (High Indebted Poor Countries) countries are located in Sub-Saharan Africa. Total debt owned by these countries is around $230 billion which is the equivalent of $365 per capita while the per capita income for these countries is $305. While in the developed countries education spending per child is around $1980, in the LDCs it is $74. With regard to health, the average spending in Europe per person was $1675 and in Southeast Asia $196, compared with average spending for Africa of $52. In the LDCs, infant mortality rates are at present 157 deaths per 1000 compared with 37 in the OECD. Stiglitz (2002) has criticised the IMF and their standard Letters of Intent which seek to secure major reductions in social spending while not taking into consideration their social implications:

> The international financial institutions have pushed a particular ideology – market fundamentalism – that is both bad economics and bad politics. The IMF has these economic policies without a broader vision of society or role of economics in society . . . The IMF often speaks about the importance of the discipline provided by financial markets. In so doing, it exhibits a certain paternalism, a new form of the old colonial mentality. The arrogance is offensive but the objection is more than just to style. The position is highly undemocratic. (Ibid., p. 3)

In the UK, while income inequalities had tended to narrow between 1960 and 1974, the Gini coefficient has widened from 27 to 34 per cent since 1979, reflecting trends in earnings, policies on tax revenues and public expenditure (Glennerster, 2004). A recent survey of the earnings of the 100 highest-paid executives in the USA (*Washington Post*, 27 June 2005) found that executive pay and bonus payments in 2004 had reached $5.25 million, with top earners including Dale Wolf at Coventry Health Care receiving an income of £32.3 million. The national median earnings is $37 000. During the Bush presidency, 53 per cent of tax reductions have benefited the top 10 per cent of income earners and more than 15 per cent went to the top 0.1 per cent:

> Under the Bush tax cuts the 400 taxpayers with the highest incomes – a minimum of $87 million in 2000 – now pay income Medicare and Social Security taxes amounting to the same percentage of their incomes as people making $50,000 to $75,000. . . . From 1950 to 1970 for every additional dollar earned by the bottom 90 percent, those in the top 0.01 percent earned an additional $162. . . . From 1990 to 2002, for every dollar earned by the bottom 90 percent, each taxpayer at the top brought in an extra $18,000. (Paul Krugman, in *New York Times*, 5 June 2005, p. 12)

THE WAR ON TERROR

The language of the war on terror has generated symbolic generalisations about grievance and victimhood that both dehumanises and demonises the other (see Jackson, 2005). Islam has been described as a flawed religion that is connected to terror and violence:

> Religions bind people to one another and to God. They form a 'We' greater than the 'I'. They create, in other words, group identity. However the very process of creating an 'Us' involves creating a 'Them' – the people not like us, the other, the outsider, the infidel, the unredeemed . . . That is why, at the very time they are involved in creating community with borders, religions can create conflict across those borders. (Sachs, 2005, p. 114)

Implicit within the language is also the argument about the clash of civilisation between the West and Islam, between the progressive science and secularism of the West and the traditions and backwardness of Islam in the Middle East. However, a brief history of the West would show that it was Christians who were involved in the Holocaust, that Christians were slave owners who went to church on Sundays and received communion, that the Klu Klux Klan burned crosses after the lynching of blacks in the USA, that it was a Christian president who dropped bombs on Hiroshima and Nagasaki, that Christians were involved in the genocides of Rwanda and finally that Radovan Karadžić and Ratko Mladić who were involved in the slaughter of over 8000 Muslims were praised as heroes by the Serb Orthodox church.

Collective identities of Muslims and Islam implicitly legitimises violence against the other, since the other loses individualised identity and the claims of equality and humanity. The discourse of the war on terror points to an enemy within, thus narrowing the spaces for dissent and resistance:

> The discourse and practice of counter-terrorism inevitably leads to the delegitimation of dissent and the narrowing of the discursive space for political debate. In large part, this is because fighting the 'enemy within' requires strict discipline, patriotism, conformity, informers, loyalty pledges and the bifurcation of national life; it requires clear lines between good and evil, between self and the other, citizen and foreigner inside and outside – all of which is the antithesis of a healthy politics. (Jackson, 2005, p. 184)

The bombs and the loss of lives in New York, Bali, Madrid and London are connected with the language of the war on terror. The wars in Afghanistan and Iraq are also increasingly justified as being part of the war on terror. During the month of October 2006 it is estimated that around 3400 were killed in roadside bombings and in ongoing ethnic cleansings between Shia and Sunni communities in Baghdad. According to a *Lancet* estimate, some 650 000 Iraqi civilians have died since the end of hostilities.

The language of the war on terror has allowed the nation state to embark on counter-violence while the other has been defined in terms of collective identities of Muslim and Islam, which are continuously being utilised as the adjective to describe those who commit these outrages. The labels of Muslim and Islamic fundamentalists have become the collective identity of the other. The language of the war on terror requires the 'us' and 'them'. In the immediate three weeks following September 11, 2001 there were 700 reported hate crimes in the US against 'Muslims' (Maira, 2004). The British National Party (BNP) attracted between nine and 15 candidates in areas with Muslim communities during the 2005 election in the UK where issues of immigration and asylum became major issues in the election campaign. The war on terror is implicitly connected with ideas of community and homogeneity, patriotism, conformity, collective identities and shared histories while at the same time generating fear of strangers. Arguments for community create the language of inclusion and exclusion in terms of who is part of a community and implicitly who is not (see Robinson in this volume). It is also assumed that community actually exists. According to Human Rights Watch (2003), in the war on terror, human rights issues seem to have become less important in the name of security of citizens by national governments:

> In the context of anti-terrorism measures adopted after 11 September 2001, the legislation of some countries allows for long periods of detention of non-nationals, without basic guarantees, where the provisions of some new anti-terrorist legislation at the national level may not provide sufficient legal safeguards as recognized by international human rights law in order to prevent human rights violations, in particular those safeguards preventing and prohibiting torture and other forms of ill treatment. (Ibid., p. 7)

The prevailing discourse of the 'war on terror' provided the context for the US President to pass the Patriot Act of 2001 within five weeks of the attacks with little deliberation or dissent. Under the Patriot Act migrants from 25 countries mainly in the Middle East had to register with the immigration authorities even though they had resided legally in the US for a number of years. The legislation has provided the framework for increased surveillance and greater intelligence gathering. The President, through the National Security Agency (NSA), has embarked on wiretaps of US citizens without seeking judicial oversight. The Patriot Act has contributed to the making of a 'chilling effect':

I am now experiencing what American legal scholars call 'a chilling effect', and I was indeed aware of it as a sort of chill running up my spine a half second of anxiety . . . I feel that chill again when I realize that I now pause a moment before I write anything. I worried even when I wrote that last sentence, then I worried about my worry. (Hentoff, 2004, p. 135)

In seeking new anti-terror measures prior to the mid-term elections in November 2006, President Bush argued the case for increased presidential powers in dealing with issues of surveillance, defining non-combatants and the need to remove habeas corpus from detainees at Guantánamo Bay. Democrats who expressed reservations on granting unrestricted powers to the President were accused of coddling up to terrorism. Despite efforts to set limits and revise the Patriot Act of 2005, 16 out of the 18 clauses of the act have now been made permanent while the concerns with libraries and intelligence gathering will not be revised for another 10 years.

For some critics, the USA is increasingly seen as becoming lawless in ignoring or undermining international laws including the Geneva Convention and the International Convention on Torture. The abuse of detainees at Guantánamo Bay and Abu Ghraib were dismissed as the aberrant behaviour of a few soldiers who have been duly punished. However, there is increased evidence of the involvement of senior officers who imported tactics of stripping prisoners and threatening them with dogs from Guantánamo Bay to Iraq. During the court martial of a US soldier accused of the killing of two detainees at Bagram Control Point in Afghanistan, in his defence the soldier argued: 'I did what everybody else did . . . it was standard practice . . . that was how things were done' (*Los Angeles Times*, 23 March 2005, p. iv).

The European Parliament Temporary Committee on Illegal CIA [Central Intelligence Agency] Activity in Europe has pointed out that there has been a total of 1246 US flights from European airports carrying suspected terrorists 'kidnapped' by the US Intelligence Services. Known as 'extraordinary renditions', this allows for the transfer of terrorist suspects captured by the USA to be transported for questioning in Saudi Arabia, Egypt and Kuwait where the detainees are likely to be tortured. The report estimates that there were 176 such flights from the UK, mainly from Scottish airfields. The UK and Poland are cited in the report as being the most unhelpful in answering questions posed by the Committee. The report accuses European governments of acting in complicity with the Bush administration. The report shows how European governments acted as the willing facilitators of CIA abuses such as secret detentions and renditions to torture (Joanne Mariner, Director Human Rights Watch, 29 November 2006). The Italian courts have asked for the extradition of 13 CIA agents who, while on diplomat services in Italy, allegedly kidnapped the Cleric

Abu Omar outside a mosque in Milan and transported him to Egypt one month before the US-led invasion of Iraq in March 2003 (Human Rights Watch, 2006). According to Sands (2005, p. 230):

> Until the revelations at Abu Ghraib there was virtually no informed public dissent against the administration's (Bush Government) efforts to rewrite international law into irrelevance. In a climate in which the President could declare that those who were not with the US were against it, the proponents of the global rules were easily marginalised and mostly silenced. It took Abu Ghraib to end America's collective amnesia.

Under the British Anti-Terrorism, Crime and Security Act (2001), some 500 men have been detained of whom only two have to date been brought to trial. Under section 23 of the act, the UK government has sought to opt out of the European Convention of Human Rights. The House of Lords judgment in February 2003 found the detentions discriminatory against foreigners and migrants and in breach of habeas corpus. The UK government strategy since 2005 has been to disconnect and decontextualise suicide bombings from the wider contexts of the wars in Iraq, Afghanistan and the Palestinian–Israeli conflict. The government website points to a history of terrorism that pre-dates the Iraq war. The war on terror is shifting in focus towards a war on an Islamic ideology which implicitly means a war that goes beyond identifying the threats but includes a war of ideas and on winning hearts and minds. Ministers are now putting pressures on UK universities to provide intelligence on Muslim Student Union organisations. The worry for universities is that there could be a conflict between the encouragement of freedom of speech and discussion, which can be interpreted as justifying terrorism. In itself this approach creates a chilling effect since in future, academics will be very concerned about teaching topics on the war on terror. Writers seeking to connect terrorism with Iraq and Afghanistan could also fall within the categories of encouraging terrorism. Freedom of speech is undermined by the ambiguity of these measures. But it is that same ambiguity that contributes to uncertainty and silence.

THE CONSUMER–COMMUNITARIAN CITIZEN

The discourse of globalisation builds on the principles of market liberalism and is therefore inextricably linked with ideas of the rational individual, the priority of competitive markets and the need to put limits on the role of government. Implicit to the discourse of globalisation is consumer citizenship, which is defined and shaped in the marketplace where the rational individual makes continuous decisions about investment in education, health and prosperity. The primary role of government is therefore to make a commitment for individuals to keep more of their income and therefore to starve the beast of government of revenues and to enable greater individual choice. Governments are described as being corrupted as a result of using their arbitrary powers, and it is therefore safer for the individual to live with markets than with corrupted public spaces.

Globalisation and consumer citizenship inevitably involves issues of inclusion and exclusion. Inclusion in the consumer society means those who can participate in the shopping experience, and go to Starbucks and McDonalds. In the consumer citizen, identity is defined by consumption, where clothes, cars and furniture become part of one's identity and lifestyle. Leisure is defined by the theme of Disney parks. According to Bryman (2004, p. 172):

> Citizenship under Disneyization comes to be defined in terms of one's capacity to consume. Consequently, those without the capacity to consume or who are deemed to have limited capacity to do so, those who might hinder the consumption inclinations of consumers are often excluded or kept under the watchful gaze of security camera and guard.

Those excluded include poor families with a low income. They become the flawed consumers. Implicit in the language of exclusion is the idea of inclusion and how the excluded can become included in the consumer society. Social policies are targeted at social inclusion, which means identifying the excluded and setting up policies tailored to deal with exclusion. Within this language are therefore included single mothers and the vulnerability of children, the young and the long-term unemployed. Social policy is equated with human investment in terms of education and training as part of creating the knowledge economy. Policies are designed to enable single mothers to go to work and for provision of child care. The socially excluded are rational agents who have therefore implicitly made the wrong choices about investment in their human capital.

In contrast, the discourse on the war on terror seeks to build on the ethics of collective identity and community as defined by the nation state. The language of the war on terror identifies the collective identities of the imagined community in contrast to the identities of the other. The war on terror asks the individual to identify with responsibility, attachments, friendships and religion. Civil society is defined in terms of voluntary groups and charities. It is the attachment to collective memories and histories which gives the individual a sense of identity. President Bush seeks to associate American identity with commitments to liberty and freedom, to American generosity and Christian values. In the aftermath of 9/11, flags, anthems and other symbols become important in the war on terror. Patriotism, conformity, allegiance and loyalty become the normal expectations of the good citizen. Community is the anchor; it provides certainty, regularity and rhythm – within the community, people know their place and they know what is expected of them and equally what to expect of others. The community defines the individual. Life is stable and predictable and it is the stability, the durability and continuity of rhyme and rhythm that give people a sense of belonging, identity and citizenship.

In the war on terror communities with sizeable migrant populations are increasingly vulnerable to racial tensions, and conflicts between the commitment to the ideas of plurality and diversity and ideas of homogeneity, belonging and solidarity. Migration and race issues have resulted in the emergence of new nationalist movements and political parties in Europe. In the aftermath of the London bombings and the discovery that the perpetrators were British citizens, the language has become increasingly connected with issues of betrayal and loss of trust. In London and Scotland there have been a sharp increases in the abuse of people who look Muslim.

Thus, the discourses of globalisation and the war on terror seek to define citizenship both in terms of individualism and less government but also at the same time the acceptance of strong government, centralisation of intelligence, policing and surveillance. In this context, less government is associated with claims on governments in terms of social provision including health, education and social security. The ascendancy of the discourse of globalisation points to competition, reduced labour costs and flexibility. Embracing globalisation means lower expectations of governments but also that individuals should make more personal provision through insurance and savings. Public spending priorities shift from social provision to security against the perceived external threat.

The consumer–communitarian citizen discourse is also inherently contradictory. On the one hand, citizenship is contextualised in global labour markets, global competition, flexibility, the need for wage moderation and lower expectations of government. By contrast, the war on terror seeks to decontextualise the atrocities in New York, Bali, Madrid and London in denying possible connections and images that emerge in the wars in Afghanistan, Iraq and the abuses in Abu Ghraib and Guantánamo Bay. The war on terror seeks to create the other but at the same also delegitimises the existence of the other.

Consumer–communitarian citizens are expected to lead a normal daily life of work, travel and visiting shopping malls while at the same time being reminded that the war on terror is likely to become part of their daily life for many years to come. Politicians and law-enforcement agencies admit that they cannot provide safeguards and complete security in the war on terror.

The consumer citizen is also increasingly depoliticised. Political choices and ideology are being replaced by models of policy making that are perceived to be rational, based on evaluation and monitoring. There is little room for resistance movements since these are often described as irrational and not addressing issues of globalisation.

THE PUBLIC CITIZEN MODEL

In the context of the global economy the discourse of global citizenship has become associated with commitments to cosmopolitan ethics, universal human rights and greater transparency of environmental policies. Cosmopolitan democracy and cosmopolitan citizenship represent the alternative to the retreat from public space. The language of citizenship provides the potential universal language of resistance. Protests against water privatisation in Ghana, electricity privatisation in Mexico, anti-market liberal policies in India and Argentina and the unity of trade union action across borders in Mozambique and South Africa, reinforce the possibilities of linking industrial, environmental and human rights coalitions.

Rather than the retreat from public spaces to quiet privatised lives, globalisation and the war on terror provide the possible spaces for making claims for global citizenship and common humanity. The retreat from public spaces allows for political elites, financial and business interests, trade lobbyists, lawyers and experts to define the nature of globalisation. The alternative model of the public citizen is connected with the ideas of deliberative, thick democracy where the commitment to public space reflects the need to listen; to the 'other', to accept the presence of differences and therefore, to be involved in a dialogue of equals, compromise, honesty, sincerity and transparency. For Voet (1998, p. 137), participation is the cornerstone of citizenship:

> A full citizen in its most complete sense is someone who participates in legislation or decision-making in public affairs. It concerns participation through which one reflects upon the desirable new character of society and through which one rejuvenates society by cooperating with other people. It is participation whereby one discusses common affairs with others, reflects upon the common good, learns to bear responsibility to judge and to decide.

The public citizen model represents recognition and an urgency to democratise, to make accountable and transparent the international institutions that are at present defining and shaping the nature of globalisation including the IMF, the World Bank and the WTO. While the WTO makes claims for its democratic credentials in the sense that each member country has equal voting rights, the day-to-day bilateral and often complex trade negotiations in Geneva in reality means that poor countries do not have the resources and the capacities to ensure that their views are heard. It is estimated that there are on average over 50 meetings each week at the WTO. Influential lobby groups including the Transatlantic Business Dialogue (TABD) which is made up of CEOs in the EU and the United States have ready access and advise their respective trade ministers on day-to-day trade issues. Regulations on both TRIPS (Trade-Related Aspects of Intellectual Property Rights) and GATS (General Agreement on Trade in Services) reflected the priorities of financial agriculture and pharmaceutical interests in the US and Europe:

> Large private corporations purchase influence within all the so-called democratic societies. As all Geneva trade diplomats know, their influence over secretive international negotiations is also considerable, witness the role of the pharmaceuticals industry in intellectual property debates and the banking and financial sector. . . . The bulk of their activity is not transparent to the public . . . Their activities though usually formally legal, constitute a grave threat to the prospect of democratic and accountable global economic governance. (Helleiner, 2000, p. 12)

The criticism is that at present within the context of economic globalisation there is a global democratic deficit. In discussions about poverty and hunger in Africa there is a need to connect issues of aid with trade. Both the USA and Europe need to phase out their subsidies to agriculture. Protocols and agreements on universal human rights, universal labour standards, and greater accountability of multinationals are seen as important pillars to the making of the global citizen. As Held (1999, p. 106) puts it:

> In the context of contemporary forms of globalisation, for democratic law to be effective it must be internationalised. Thus, the implementation of what I call a cosmopolitan democratic law and the establishment of a community of all democratic communities – a cosmopolitan community – must become an obligation for democrats; an obligation to build a transnational, common structure of political action which alone, ultimately, can support the politics of self determination.

Globalisation creates the potential for greater human connectedness, of greater awareness and solidarity. Environmental degradation, abuses of human rights, child labour and sweatshops have generated new forms of protests and social movements that promote the possibility of citizenship as resistance. These social movements while still ephemeral seek to advertise the nature of political choices and the possibility for change.

The public citizen model points to the primacy of human life and the respect for human life where no one person or state has the right to make one person less human than another. The Iraqis losing their lives to suicide bombings are of equal value to those who lost their lives in New York or London.

The public citizen model seeks to create a possible dialogue among civilisations as opposed to creating the idea of the clash of civilisations. Dialogue requires listening and understanding while at the same time seeking to undermine absolutes and the enforcing of a truth on others:

> The aspects of cultures that have survived are those that have the capacity for exchange, and especially listening. Listening is a virtue to be acquired; its acquisition needs purposeful moral training, self-refining, and rational nurturing. Listening is not a passive act like silence it is, rather, an activity through which listeners expose themselves to the world of others, Without listening any dialogue is doomed to failure. (President Khatami, 2005, p. 74)

CONCLUSIONS

The discourses of the war on terror and the consumer citizen encourage a passive consumer citizen where citizenship is defined by consumption while at the same there is an attempt to create an anti-politics and a retreat from public spaces. At present, public spaces are corrupted. The silent takeover (Hertz, 2001) of public space by political and business elites leaves the majority as the quiet audience sitting passively in the darkness of the auditorium watching the political actors on the stage (Sennett, 1979). The audience of liberal democracy is encouraged to be passive.

Defining and shaping citizenship in the dual contexts of the politics of globalisation and the war on terror has to be located within people's specific lived experiences which in turn means the understanding of political struggles and compromises, of expectations, hopes and aspirations at a certain point in time. Marshall's (1950) attempt at a definition of citizenship represented a discourse which was emancipatory and had validity in the aftermath of the Second World War. The present-day challenge therefore is to construct a citizenship which is equally emancipatory in the context of surveillance, policing, loss of human rights, greater income inequalities and the emergence of new political and economic elites.

Human rights are assumed to be inalienable rights and are at the centre of the public citizen model. Terrorist bombs represent the most explicit denial of human rights. Citizenship has to confer a number of rights that are seen as universal and fundamental rights that cannot be negotiated away in the context of the war on terror. Those who kill and maim others are criminals and need to be defined as criminals within the due processes of law and justice which are central to the democratic process. The concept of citizenship is therefore undermined in the context of surveillance, which results in silence and retreat. However, universalism has to be combined with the right to be different. Within modern nation states there are now substantial minority ethnic groups, which derive their dignity from their communities. The right to worship and to be educated in separate Muslim, Jewish, Catholic or girls' schools confirm a new morality of pluralism, tolerance and freedom (Parekh, 1995). Pluralism in the context of a multicultural and multi-racial society means a diffusion of power, a break with the dominance of the 'in group' and a willingness to live with difference. The globalised economy requires a commitment to widening political accountability where people feel that they are part of the global community, involved in decisions which affect their lives, their environment and the world to be left to future generations.

Citizenship is about a sense of belonging and membership but it is also about differences and pluralities. Citizenship has to embrace the expectations of universal human rights but also the rights of differences. Citizenship is therefore more about dialogue, involvement and participation rather than a series of ascribed static rights. Citizenship has to include involvement in bringing about change – to shape change and alter priorities – rather than being just a passive consumer citizen.

REFERENCES

Ahmed, A. and B. Frost (ed.) (2005), *After Terror, Promoting Dialogues Among Civilisations*, Cambridge: Polity.

Bhagwati, J. (2002), 'Globalisation and appropriate governance', The 2000 WIDER annual lecture, Helsinki, 10 October, www.wider.unu.educ, accessed 14 January 2007.

Brinkley, A. (2003), 'A familiar story: lessons from past assaults on freedom', in Leone and Anrig (eds), pp. 23–46.

Bryman, A. (2004), *The Disneyization of Society*, London: Sage.

Cameron, A. and R. Palan (2004), *The Imagined Economies of Globalisation*, London: Sage.

Glennerster, H. (2004), 'Mrs Thatcher's legacy: getting it in perspective', *Social Policy Review*, No. 16, 231–50.

Gough, I. and G. Wood (ed.) (2004), *Insecurity and Welfare Regimes in Asia, Africa and Latin America: Social Policy in Development Contexts*, Cambridge: Cambridge University Press.

Held, D. (1999), 'The transformation of political community: rethinking democracy in the context of globalisation', in L. Shapiro and C. Haker-Cordon (eds), *Democracy's Edges*, Cambridge: Cambridge University Press, pp. 84–112.

Helleiner, G. (2000), 'Markets, politics and globalisation', 10th Paul Prebisch Memorial Lecture, UNCTAD, New York, 14 June.

Hentoff, N. (2004), *The War on the Bill of Rights and the Gathering Resistance*, New York: Seven Stories Press.

Hertz, N. (2001), *The Silent Takeover: Global Capitalism and the Death of Democracy*, London: Heinemann.

Human Rights Watch (2003), *In the Name of Counter Terrorism – Human Rights Abuses Worldwide*, New York: Human Rights Watch, www.hrw.org, accessed 14 January 2007.

Human Rights Watch (2006), Press Release on the European Parliament Report on Extraordinary Renditions, 29 November.

IATP (2003), 'US dumping on world agricultural markets: can trade rules help farmers?', Institute for Agriculture Trade Policy, Cancun Papers, South Minneapolis, MN.

Jackson, R. (2005), *Writing the War on Terror: Language Politics and Counter-Terrorism*, Manchester: Manchester University Press.

Leone, R. and G. Anrig (eds) (2003), *The War on Our Freedoms: Civil Liberties in an age of Terrorism*, New York: Public Affairs.

Maira, S. (2004), 'Imperial feelings, youth culture, citizenship and globalisation', in M. Suarez-Orozco (ed.), *Globalization, Culture and Education in the New Millennium*, Berkeley, CA and London: University of California Press, pp. 204–34.

Marshall, T. (1950), *Citizenship and Social Class*, Cambridge: Cambridge University Press.

Michie, J. (ed.) (2003), *The Handbook of Globalisation*, Cheltenham, UK and Northampton, MA, USA: Edward Elgar.

Ohmae, K. (1995), *The End of the Nation State: The Rise of Regional Economies*, London: Free Press.

Parekh, B. (1995), 'Ethnocentricity and the nationalist discourse', *Nations and Nationalism*, **1** (1), 25–52.

President Khatami Seyed Mohammed (2005), 'Dialogue among civilisations and cultures', in Ahmed and Frost (eds), pp. 72–8.

Sachs, J. (2005), 'Turning enemies into friends', in Ahmed and Frost (eds), pp. 112–18.

Sands, P. (2005), *Lawless World: America and the Making and Breaking of Global Rules*, London: Allen Lane.

Sennett, R. (1979), *The Fall of Public Man*, London: Faber & Faber.

Stiglitz, J. (2002), *Globalization and Its Discontents*, London: Allen Lane.

Voet, R. (1998), *Feminism and Citizenship*, London: Sage.

World Bank (2003), *Poverty in Developing Countries*, Washington, DC: World Bank.

PART 2

Issues

6. Citizenship after the death of the public sphere

Stefan Skrimshire

INTRODUCTION: THE GREAT PERSUADER AND THE VULGAR MASSES

> A Prince should take great care, therefore, that nothing issues from his mouth which is not imbued with the five aforementioned qualities. To see him and hear him, he should seem all-merciful, all-trustworthy, all-integrity, all-humanity, all-religion. Nothing is more important than to seem to have than this last quality. Generally speaking, men judge more by the eyes than by the hands, because everybody can see, but only a few can feel. Everyone sees what you seem, few feel what you are like . . . for the common people are always impressed by how things seem and by the way things turn out, and in the world there is nothing but common people. When the many are comfortably settled, the few will find no way in. (Machiavelli, 1995, p. 98 used by Edwards, 2003b)[1]

The day after Tony Blair delivered his impassioned speech to parliament calling for MPs to endorse an Anglo-American war on Iraq in March 2003, Britain's newspapers were unanimous in describing the speech as a defining moment in restoring the credibility and integrity of the prime minister and democracy. The *Daily Mirror*, for example, despite being in full swing of its anti-war 'phase', wrote:

> [W]e do not question [Blair's] belief in the rightness of what he is doing. It is one thing to have principles others disagree with, another altogether to have no principles . . . Mr Blair and Robin Cook have helped to restore the integrity of parliament at this crucial stage in the nation's history. Both have made compelling arguments on each side of this debate – and both have been listened to with respect. (Quoted by Edwards, 2003b)

The entire spectrum of mainstream media, irrespective of their views on the morality of the impending war, were so mesmerised by the rhetoric of one speech that they found its *effect*, that is, its ability to instil a confidence that 'he believes in what he is doing', to take precedence over what he actually said. Given that the main focus of the *Mirror*'s – along with most other anti-war commentators at the time – criticism of that integrity had been towards the lack of democracy in the government's stance on the war and the illegality of its independence from UN support, what could have changed in those respects from hearing two speeches? What kind of opinion of the role of parliament, traditionally the arena in which political experts are given the chance to test their ideas of governing against rational argument, is given credibility by a rhetoric that was never publicly challenged by experts on the issues pertinent to Iraq (such as UN inspections, the effects of sanctions, Middle-East politics and so on)?

Before that parliamentary speech, Blair appeared on BBC's *Newsnight* to various citizen groups in an attempt to 'engage with the public'. While what he said has been severely condemned by experts for its content,[2] what is remarkable is not the use of lies in generating public support but the fact that the structures of communication chosen to present these lies were taken to be a fulfilment of parliament's accountability and engagement of the public with the correct facts. The arena of discussion, therefore, was somehow able to present the decision to go to war as simultaneously outrageous and entirely ethical. If opinion polls are to be believed, and public opinion swung dramatically in favour of the war once it had started and was being 'won', it begs an enquiry into the assumptions behind this nebulous entity known as 'public opinion'. What processes, natural or manipulated, lay behind this movement? Was it really the impression that at the very least the decision makers had strength in their own convictions and had listened to the reasoning of the dissenters? And in the light of evidence that it was entirely *false* evidence that formed the basis for war, does anything fall from the perception of public confidence in a government's motivation? Does all become forgotten because the show was entertaining enough?

This chapter attempts to take seriously the question of *who* Blair thought he was fooling when he presented his 'compelling evidence' for the necessity of going to war, understanding the active popular resistance to the war on Iraq to be a significant shift in what people demand from the bearers of political truths. The tactics of New Labour spin doctors in fabricating the illusion of a consensual, engaged and democratic process in the run-up to what Edward Said has called 'the most unpopular [war] in modern history' (Said, 2003, p. 1) do not, perhaps, represent any radical change in the mode of electoral politics in a post-industrial age. But they do open up important questions about the recent transformations in modes of citizenship when juxtaposed with emerging alternatives to the popular conception of democratic participation in so-called liberal democracies.

Five months after Blair's 'sexed-up' dossier and one month before his commons speech, London saw arguably the biggest protest march of its history, alongside an estimated 30 million people worldwide, condemning war on Iraq.[3] When war began, continued marches, acts of civil disobedience, road blockades, strikes and occupations were organised around the country to attempt to disrupt 'business as usual' while the government waged war, but went largely unreported. The monumental efforts in 'public relations' from British and American governments after those protests showed the relationship between political information and public opinion entering a new phase. It could be said that, in comparison with wars in the past, the 2003 invasion significantly raised the stakes for the bearers of public truth: anti-war groups and individuals became experts in media lies and government propaganda, and the government went on an all-out offensive to produce (I do not use the term rhetorically) whatever 'hard evidence' its audience demanded. The war was opposed with arguments that not only preceded the invasion, but anticipated the use of propaganda before the government was able to execute it. Never before has the questioning of a politics of information and the manufacturing of consent[4] taken such a front seat in the discourse surrounding a war long before it had even started. It was also a kind of race to remain in step with a fast unravelling tragedy since September 11, 2001.[5] 'Typical' sites of critical debate and political information were read and seen alongside an explosion of multiple sources of information and the prominence of tactics in discrediting and satirising those of the mainstream sources of information such as government statements and the national media. What these outbursts of alternative information demonstrate is the desire to seek alternative sources and sites of 'opinion' to those that are assumed in social institutions. The traditional notion that 'the media' are a vehicle for public information and represent some semblance of public opinion therefore provokes a sense of identity crisis – what should we believe? What do we think? Who shall we allow to speak on our behalf? Does the 'mainstream' represent us any more? Tony Blair's desperate struggle since that challenge to maintain his reputation as the 'great persuader'[6] is testimony to this. But the development of his style of moral/political performances simply play an essential role in the wider transformations of political rhetoric since the birth of the 'war on terror'. It forges, that is, ever more reductionist assumptions about who the public are and what is expected of them. What it exposes, as I shall argue, is that citizen participation is today more analogous to the marketing of a product for popular consumption, than the practice of democratic, critical debate. The construction of public opinion involves important developments in the processes of production and consumption that occur beneath the surface level of who *speaks* and who *listens* in social life.

WHO ARE THE PUBLIC? WHERE DO THEY COME FROM?

> The things that are discussed [in government] are the things that [people] don't much care about, like questions of character or questions of reform, which they know aren't going to be implemented. So that's what's discussed, not what people care about. And that's pretty typical, and it makes sense on the assumption that the role of the public, as the ignorant and meddlesome outsiders, is just to be spectators. If the general public, as it often does, seeks to organize and enter the political arena, to participate, to press its own concerns, that's a problem. It's not democracy; it's what's called 'a crisis of democracy' that has to be overcome. (Chomsky, 2000, p. 3)

Hannah Arendt, in the context of discussing the infamous Pentagon Papers,[7] famously suggested that the only people at risk of 'complete manipulation' of information are presidents and prime ministers, since it is they who saturate their own political environment with advisors, spin-doctors and other interpreters of 'outside reality', leaving very little to see for themselves (Arendt, 1972, p. 8). If this is still, and perhaps much more so, the case, then where does that leave a believing public, and what remains for the engagement of the (post)modern citizen in political life? The Vietnam war triggered, in fact, the first major wake-up call to governments that waging unpopular wars meant, as Arendt observed, engaging with the concept of a public 'psychology' – predicting, in other words, with some precision, what it takes to achieve public acceptance. Over forty years on, this legacy takes on new dimensions within an international political environment many are rushing to categorise as 'post-democracy' (Crouch, 2004). The hallmarks of this categorisation are typically the gradual decline in traditional sites of citizen participation and the increasing association of the role of the 'autonomous' citizen as that of consumer, and whose influence on public policy is replaced by that of the financial markets. As Colin Crouch puts it, the 'commercialization of citizenship' simply fits into a perfectly logical progression of the specific model of *liberal* democracy whose first truly global marketing strategy came out of cold-war ideology. In the new post-democratic model of citizen participation:

> While elections certainly exist and can change governments, public electoral debate is a tightly controlled spectacle, managed by rival teams of professionals expert in the techniques of persuasion, and considering a small range of issues selected by those teams. The mass of citizens plays a passive, quiescent, even apathetic part, responding only to the signals given them. Behind this spectacle of the electoral game, politics is really shaped in private by the interaction between elected government and elites that overwhelmingly represent business interests. (Crouch, 2004, p. 4)

In what sense, then, is it still possible to speak of a 'public' attributable to opinions, consensus, participation or knowledge? Much social analysis implicitly assumes it to be a *tabula rasa*, a blank sheet upon which political truths become inscribed, and this is particularly problematic in the light of the concept of post-democratic citizenship. If participation is reduced to patterns of spectatorship and consumption, what hope is there that it might 'enter the political arena, to participate, to press its own concerns' (Chomsky, 2000, p. 3)? To consider the possibility that new modes of citizenship still reside in the problematic category of the public, we need a critique of those conditions, both institutional and discursive, that give rise to this apparently malleable and coercive subject. To reach below the surface level of the *effects* of public opinion involves asking not only what institutional means make possible the malleable world of 'a public', but the conceptual and discursive assumptions that make it possible for society's communicators to refer to an incontestable and homogeneous mass of moral and social viewpoints. How, for instance, in the context that I have chosen, was the UK's popular outrage at an illegal war transformed, as soon as the bombing began, so easily into an obligation towards patriotism – supporting 'our boys' and therefore no longer challenging the legitimacy of their actions – that dared not be challenged outside the most 'extremist' anti-war critiques? Are we talking about the same public in both instances?

Perhaps the first target of deconstruction should therefore be the principle vehicle of the communicators themselves, the 'mainstream media'. The notion of 'mainstream' is itself controversial in this respect, since its processes of excluding and including beliefs or information are perceived to be a principal element of the creation of an acceptable and identifiable 'public' and mode of 'publicness' (Pilger, 1998, p. 487). The concept of a mainstream has been closely identified with the collusion of power to form a homogeneous realm of the 'prevailing current of thought', linking the hidden agendas of news reporting with market interests and the politically established order (such as Rupert Murdoch's well-documented support for Tony Blair's election in 1997). John Pilger echoes a long legacy of journalistic experience when he claims that those who aspire to the freedom of the 'free press' 'risk becoming eased out of the "mainstream" . . . exiled to the margins' (ibid., p. 487). In the UK, examples abound in which the renowned 'liberal' press has attached itself to a prevailing ideology, by sanitising a fundamentally unjust world order and unjust acts in the vocabulary handed down to it. It is, however, predominantly in what the mainstream *fails* to say, rather than in what it says, that attracts the most criticism of its servility to power and the assumptions about the relationship of that power to a public.

Who decides what is newsworthy and what people want to hear or read? Why, for instance, is it the case that 'only 3 per cent of peak-time programmes feature *anything* about the majority of humanity' (ibid., p. 2, original italics) or that political analysis follows the demands, not of the 'big' issue's affecting people's lives but of marketable, sensational news? 'Democratic accountability and vision are replaced by a specious gloss, the work of fixers known as "spin-doctors", and assorted marketing and public relations experts and their fellow travellers, notably journalists. A false "consensus" is their invention' (ibid., p. 5). Televisation of the war on Iraq surprised no one in these respects, and, if anything, simply set new precedents for the war on terror as a whole, in the establishment of public relations as the simple fabrication of a palatable reality. More journalists than ever (around 7000 'in theatre') (see Fisk, 2003, p. 1) appeared, and yet were more censored by the military than ever. Large-scale dumbing-down of the gruesome reality of 'collateral damage' was replaced by sensationalist reporting of the 'siege of Baghdad', or the 'Battle for Babylon' by journalists, as Robert Fisk sees it, 'back to their old trick of playing toy soldiers, dressing themselves up in military costumes for their nightly theatrical performances on television. . . . The orchestration will be everything, the pictures often posed, the angles chosen by "minders" '.[8] After the statue-toppling sensation, opinion polls were said to have finally swung in Blair's favour in a 'patriotic surge' symbolising a 'sweet political moment for Blair' (London Reuters, 10 April 2003), and bitter anti-war feeling replaced by flowers on Blair's' doorstep. ICM polls showed that after the fall of Baghdad

> the proportion of those who disapprove of military action has dropped to an all-time low of only 23 percent – ess than half the level of eight weeks ago. In contrast, support for the war has risen from a low of 29% in mid-February to 63% . . . one of the most dramatic shifts in public opinion in recent British political history. (*The Guardian*, 15 April 2003)[9]

How should the 'spectacular' use of news reporting help us understand the new conditions of citizenship and the construction of a public consensus? Who is able to speak on its behalf? At the most basic level this can be explained in terms of *ownership* of the production of the truth of public opinion. As Pilger and others have argued, there is an instituted collusion of media with neo-liberal elites that own it, but also from the stealth by which the economic order that underpins them becomes part of a normal state of affairs to be conveyed through the appearance of 'news'. Normality can be produced by an omission of pertinent questions surrounding any issue, such as the massive inequalities of rich and poor that underpin the 'new world order' against the massive hikes in military spending of UK and US governments. It can also be produced by repeating the discourse of established authority, like the suggestive rhetoric of 'wars' on terrorism, on drugs, or on crime. There is still, therefore, a prevailing assumption in analyses of the 'production of news' and the 'editorial function' that inasmuch as it is able to affect public opinion, news follows a pattern of reproduction that favours 'the definitions of the powerful' (Hall et al., 1973, p. 351). These definitions fit more squarely with (for example) politicians or business elites simply because all news favours the structural and presentational convenience of having 'primary definers'. These are communicators well-versed and socially positioned to use the press as a vehicle for their discourse, who have already decided the terms of engagement, what issues are to be addressed and which omitted, to the effect that 'counter-definers' (such as protesters) are labelled as extremist and irrational because they fall foul of the 'closure of the topic around its initial definition' (ibid., p. 349). This suggests, moreover, that whatever the best intentions of journalists, the *process* of manufacturing news inescapably attempts to voice a 'common opinion' alongside that of a 'dominant ideology', a silent allegiance to power that greatly diminishes the critical intentions of a news-consuming public.

Even if we grant Pilger the right (which is far from obvious) to say that 'there is a critical intelligence and common sense in the way most people arrive at their values' (Pilger, 1998, p. 11), the production of a *public* value cannot be defined simply as the convergence of many individually reached conclusions, as if people were isolated from social life in order to reach their views. It can only be understood within the context of the contingent emergence of a public, constructed with specific tools and social sites given for that process. The historical roots of a concept of the 'public' are inseparable from a history of 'public information' and its collusion with a certain social and economic order. It did not arise outside of social privilege and domination. Thus, the word 'public', despite, etymologically at least, being generally descriptive of that which is open and accessible to all people in distinction to that which is 'private', is rarely intended to mean *generally* open.

As Habermas notes, the emergence of the concept within the organisation of the Greek *Polis* was bound to the distinction of 'citizens' (distinct from women and slaves, for instance) participating in the state and expressing 'freedom and permanence . . . an open field for honourable distinction' through the instituted public sphere (Habermas, 1989, p. 4). It seems that since those times the concept of 'public' has always had something to do with a hierarchical distinction: in the fifteenth century, European royals were the representative 'public body'. Again, in the bourgeois 'civil society' in the eighteenth century the public sphere was associated with the concept of a critically engaged public that could openly think for itself and was still defined by those that controlled the 'instituted' (and restricted to the reading classes) practices of publicity such as literary discussions, the publicising of letters, and secret societies and lodges (ibid., p. 35). This makes sense when it is considered that published 'news' reporting only emerged officially as an aid to the 'commercial traffic' of trade between regions (ibid., p. 16) and only became 'public' news when capitalist expansion took on a public dimension. But simply because the role of the press expanded to include a critical interest in political issues does not mean that it became independent of those originally economic concerns. The common interest of businesses and state authorities to be in control of what the press says can be traced, says Habermas, as far back as the seventeenth century where figures such as Cardinal Richelieu used the new 'Gazette' as an 'intelligence agency' in the service of court ordinances (ibid., p. 22). Despite the subsequent moves of press groups to be independent of state authorities, and the role that journals and pamphlets played in the Chartist and anti-absolutist movements, interpretations of a public voice have consistently been associated with property ownership. The rise of attempted democratic representations of the will of the 'people' since the French revolution held the contradiction of defining the public as the realm of universal rights alongside a bourgeois intellectual view that it was property-owning (male) individuals alone that had the right to direct that sphere. And so also have the institutions that turned private concerns into public ones (the rise of the welfare state) always been held in tension within the conditions of free market capitalism. The 'political' element of a critical public in a democracy depended on the freely competing reasoning of autonomous beings (in the Kantian understanding), but this notion was, in the nineteenth century, an autonomy that meant self-sufficiency, which in turn meant someone with property or land (ibid., p. 109).

Habermas describes the way in which an increasingly politically engaged public sphere, expressing the right to share in the 'universal' rational capacity of social contribution, and in places of early socialist experimentation defining public life as synonymous with political life (ibid., p. 129) was fatally undermined by the emergence of 'liberalism' as a dominant ideology. The *'laissez-faire'* ideology advocated by thinkers like J.S. Mill and Alex de Tocqueville and embraced by free market capitalism is essentially a rejection of the public sphere as a rationalised political domain. Political engagement, by contrast, was, according to liberalism, subsumed within a philosophy of history that presupposed a 'natural order' that the will of the people need not define other than to affirm the principle in general: 'there was to be a natural basis for the public sphere that would in principle guarantee an autonomous and basically harmonious course of social reproduction' (ibid., p. 130). It introduces the concept of hegemony, and importantly the hegemonic *process* by which a 'public' comes to endorse or *consent to*, the conditions of its own enslavement – that is, by a distinction between the public and private spheres dictated by authorities in whose interest it is to describe a particular political order as natural, normal and harmonious. The historical roots of a concept of the public are therefore instructive in so far as they show what limitations and 'hidden agendas' are contained in the institutions society has inherited as vehicles for a 'people's voice, or the access to political information. Habermas notes that the first publications of parliamentary debates have their origins in journalists being sneaked into parliamentary sessions and repeating whole transcripts from memory before their presence became legal. In the light of the amount of information that has brought Whitehall's weaknesses and scandals to light through leaked documents, little has changed in this respect. It is also clear that, despite the appearance of huge gains in a 'free' press in liberal democracies since the nineteenth century, the same obsession within state-craft of controlling, monitoring and using it to its own ends, and the same compulsions to restrict the social 'sites' of that critique, remain. Since their institutionalisation, places of political debate such as seventeenth-century coffee houses were eyed with fear by the authorities. In today's urban environment, public places for congregation, interaction and political expression that do not stand under the glare of state surveillance or private interests (the shopping mall replacing the public square) are becoming increasingly hard to find.

It is also important to see how the contemporary construction of a consenting public maintains itself through the illusion of defending popular democracy from the vagaries of individual or elite control. In the case of the nineteenth century, Habermas notes that liberals like Mill and Tocqueville feared the broadening public sphere because what had been, with the guarantee of the theories of thinkers like Jean Jacques Rousseau and Immanuel Kant, a social harmony based on the dissolution of conflict by the 'compulsion of reason', would turn into larger-scale social conflict powered by the coercion of mass opinion. The Danish philosopher Søren Kierkegaard was another bourgeois thinker horrified at the prospect of public opinion smothering the sovereignty of the individual. His life's work included a dedicated assault on the 'press' and the populist movements surrounding the nineteenth-century European revolutions. He laid the blame squarely on Europe's love affair with Hegelian philosophy, which, relativising the infinite value of the 'single individual' to the objective telos of the 'world-historical process', provoked a concept of citizenship obsessed with the 'ballot', a kind of deification of the majority (Kierkegaard, 1996, p. 305). But what makes Kierkegaard's anti-democratic[10] and often elitist stance instructive is his insistence that the 'established order' is only completely corruptive when it sanctions the absolute 'truth' of collective opinion, rather than any opinion in particular. The Public, then, simply doesn't *exist* as a bearer of truth, a domain reserved for the 'existential pathos' (Kierkegaard, 1992, p. 394) of the individual. The concept of a 'press' compounds this absurdity because it encourages everybody to be a nobody, to define truth by 'abstraction': 'even the most eminent individual is a trifle in the face of an abstraction, even if the latter notoriously arises through some individual's calling himself "the editorial staff"' (Kierkegaard, 1996, pp. 502–3). It was not the force of a majority, but the *illusion* of a majority that replaced the need for individuals to form a collective base for expressing their own opinions. And yet even if we take Kierkegaard's worries seriously, they only seem to pale in comparison with the consequences of what it means to 'be public' in today's post-democratic culture of mass media where almost everything seems to take on that role. It is clearly no longer a choice between a collective over individual form of citizenship but a collective against its own fabricated mirror image, misrepresented and misinformed through the vehicle of 'mass culture'.

The historical legacy of Europe's liberal agenda is the usurpation of the attempt of nineteenth-century reformers of the public sphere (through the labour unions, for instance) to extend its influence to the political realm, by defining the public sphere primarily as the free (even when regulated throughout the periods of 'interventionism' and 'protectionism') exchange of commodity with less interference from state authority. Habermas appears to be nostalgic for a time when the 'liberal' bourgeois public sphere expressed the freedom of private individuals to come together through certain sites of critical debate (the eighteenth-century 'world of letters' for instance), even when those sites privileged some over others (the reading classes). But this is because the demise of the 'public sphere' altogether through the sell-off of its political and 'regulating' responsibilities to the interests of capital, signalled the gradual privatisation, not only of the public sphere, but of life itself. The problem, in other words, with the identification of a public voice that is able to challenge or endorse the message of social power/the 'established order' goes far beyond Kierkegaard's worries because it has already been co-opted by the interest of an increasingly smaller circle of private interests. The single individual, through this ironic twist, is reinstated as sovereign, but that sovereignty is an illusion far removed from the freedom of an *existential pathos* – it is the illusion of a distinction between the world of private, family intimacy from the occupational 'world of work'. In a post-liberal or neo-liberal era, that amounts to the worst of both worlds: a private world which has withdrawn into itself and has no chance of becoming a critically engaged public sphere, and a private world of work, regulated not by the state but by the interests of a few individuals.

The absurdity of a vehicle of 'public opinion' therefore crystallises Blair's dilemma, alongside all the others trying to 'sell' the new political conditions of the war on terror to their own citizens: how to present a course of action that cannot (for security or diplomatic reasons, for instance) be challenged on the basis of rational, accountable debate with the appearance of exactly that – a rational, accountable debate. The first lesson to be learnt from Blair's success (putting aside how it may also have been the start of his downfall) is that the public whom Blair addressed were not poised on the edge of all the latest sources of information on world politics and therefore all the more critically aware for it.

There is still a common assumption that the explosion in mass media enterprise means a reduction in the hegemony of a few news sources. There is today a common perception that our 'network society' is characterised not by 'homogenised messages' but by the formation of multiple social identities that 'pick and choose' their sources of truth, but this impression is at best naive. Multiple sources of information, in the first instance, do not mean that a homogenised message is avoided, though it may force it to change shape to fit changing markets. Pilger, for instance, has long since argued that the veneer of 'neutrality' has been, in this country, the tactic by which left-of-centre news sources have prevented a huge number of the public from seeing exactly *what* is being legitimised, or 'allowed to be considered normal' by the media's 'not taking sides'. Many multiple news sources can do this in many different ways and still produce a message that is 'homogeneous' to the legitimation of one established order. Second, the public whom Blair had in mind to 'engage' with could rightly be said to be the public that has *ceased to exist*, if the original concern of defining public from private, that which is critically engaged in social life, is to be preserved. People's private lives do not contribute to the creation of a public domain because they are cut off from it, and the power of (particularly non-literary) mass media is making sure this rift widens: 'a pseudo-public sphere of a no longer literary public was patched together to create a sort of super-familial zone of familiarity' (Habermas, 1989, p. 162). In this sense the Iraq war could only become 'popular' through the everyday acceptance of a *non-debate* and the accompanying attempts, through staged discussions, expert panels, editorial letters and radio phone-ins, to assuage the anger of powerlessness that this might provoke. This is what makes Blair's last-ditch efforts to 'go live' on the BBC's *Newsnight* with his reasoned approach and moral integrity, so fascinating. Did anyone really believe that Blair saw the question and answer session as a two-way process, that he was hearing the concerns of his 'public' and was affected by them, or that he was willing to stake his reputation and career on the commons vote? Or are these the vehicles of a media-sensitive political spectacle, the distortion of an allegedly participative, 'rational' process into the more cynical notion: 'in a world of the de-politicised public, *what does this war have to do with you?*'.

CAPITALISING ON FEAR: A NEW MODEL OF CITIZENSHIP?

What makes people consent within this illusory public sphere? The popular assumption that people's political and moral judgements are simply at the mercy of a few powerful gatekeepers of information flows who control public belief like puppets is misleading. In an age where modes of communication are inseparable from structures of power, and those permeate not one-way flows of information but the infrastructure of culture itself, it is not enough simply to point to the modern-day vindication of Joseph Goebbels's insight that no matter how outrageous a statement is, if you state it loudly and often enough, it will become credible. Repetition, among other rhetorical tactics, is one aspect of influencing opinion, but presents only one side of the production–consumption relationship of consent. Also needed is an understanding of manipulation that draws more on Michel Foucault's concept of 'governmentality', that is, the proliferation of disciplining 'strategies' in which all are caught, including the way people govern themselves, or otherwise expect a certain level and mode of engagement with political life.

It is interesting to note, for instance, just how far the propaganda industry has come, by hearing Hannah Arendt suggest, in the context of the Vietnam war as 'PR campaign' that despite its aggressive form of psychological exploitation, still 'people . . . cannot be manipulated – though of course they can be forced by terror – to "buy" opinions and political views' (Arendt, 1972, p. 8). If the Iraq war demonstrated anything, it was that we now have both: the ability to instil the permanence of terror at the same time as a barely perceptible level of social normalisation. On the one hand, the way in which 9/11 has paved the way for a predictable ideology of 'national security' is nothing other than the logical application of the immanence of destruction, and fear of destruction, that is built into the very fabric of the imperial-style form of security that is Pax Americana. The new characteristic of our contemporary modes of governmentality, therefore, is the conscious manipulation of a 'politics of fear'. From the use of anti-terror legislation as a pretext for reducing civil liberties and demonising minorities, to the capitalisation of a climate of fear, such as the marketing of aggressive-looking SUVs (sport-utility vehicles) at the outset of war on Iraq,[11] the war on terror functions both as the new paradigm for social control, and as condition of political participation. It can be summarised as the controlled anticipation of terror, in all its manifestations as disaster, crisis, violence and apocalypse, as a precondition of social order. More fundamentally, the war on terror reveals precisely *what kind* of order it is conditioning. Here, the production of socially 'useful' fear marks a departure from the legacy of previous propaganda campaigns, such as the 'red scare' during the cold war or even the anti-German propaganda used to bring Americans into the Second World War.[12] To wage a war with no end, as even Dick Cheney has called the war on terrorism,[13] is to guarantee the legitimation of a state of permanent surveillance, control and social conditioning that was previously undreamed of, though its immanence to the political sphere of the 'new world order' has been obvious to many. As Gilles Deleuze and Félix Guattari wrote as far back as 1987:

> The war machine finds its new object in the absolute peace of terror or deterrence. It is terrifying not as a function of a possible war that it promises us, as by blackmail, but, on the contrary, as a function of the real, very special kind of peace it promotes and has already installed. It no longer needs a qualified enemy but, in conformity with the requirement of an axiomatic, operates against the 'unspecified enemy', domestic or foreign . . . There arises from this a new conception of security as materialized war, as organized insecurity or molecularized, distributed, programmed catastrophe. (Deleuze and Guattari, quoted in Massumi, 1993, p. 219)

On the other hand, the effects of a politics of fear in shaping the very norm of citizen participation necessary to maintain social order are achieved by the creation of a state of permanent emergency without the accompanying sense of hysteria that would threaten the social fabric upon which it is based. What distinguishes the paranoia of being watched from the paranoia of being permanently physically at risk, is that while the former tends to internalise the effect of fear, the latter effects a form of internalising *the fear itself*, in order to 'get on with life' in the face of constant risks. In the wake of the terrorist attacks on New York, President George W. Bush himself appeared in TV commercials, urging Americans to 'live their lives' by going ahead with plans for vacations and other consumer purchases: 'The president of the US is encouraging us to buy', wrote marketer Chuck Kelly in an editorial for the Minneapolis–St Paul *Star Tribune*, which argued that America was 'embarking on a journey of spiritual patriotism' that 'is about pride, loyalty, caring and believing' – and, of course, selling. 'As marketers, we have the responsibility to keep the economy rolling', wrote Kelly. 'Our job is to create customers during one of the more difficult times in our history' (*The Guardian*, July 2003).[14]

A politics of fear, in other words, is determining and not just deterring. The logic at work here is simply a continuation of the process of de-politicisation suggested throughout this analysis. The critical public is gradually transformed into a 'vulgar mass' of consumers, consumption being the definitive act of 'getting on with your life' in the face of disaster. Both the war on terror and the success of late capitalism represent the ability of people to internalise crisis and a kind of rationalised and even spiritualised violence through a redefinition of what 'public participation' means. Everyday life is *fearful* therefore in the sense that it embraces disorder and insecurity as the only option available to it. Habermas described it as a shift from a 'Culture-Debating to a Culture-Consuming Public' (Habermas, 1989, p. 159).

Brian Massumi's penetrating contemporary development of this critique in *The Politics of Everyday Fear* (1993) also suggests that what unites the character of the 'spectacle' in society with the identities cast by a culture of consumption is the ability to fight the inevitable passing of time, to guarantee, through one's acquisitions and purchases, the 'timeless' quality of buying the act that holds off the moment of accident, and 'insures against death'. (Massumi, 1992, p. 9). Does this mean that people desire 'things' as a means of putting off the fear of disappearing, of being nothing? A culture of acquisition and consumption – buying and having things – is therefore associated with the virtualisation of impending disaster. We fill in the present, becoming immortalised through commodities that we own and will go on having the right to own. How is fear used to pacify a sense of disorder and a loss of faith in the 'system'? An unstable capitalist world may make us keep falling, but by buying into the logic of consumption, we put off indefinitely the inevitable crash-landing. As Massumi says, 'When we buy, we are buying off fear and falling, filling the gap with presence-effects. When we consume, we are consuming our own possibility. In possessing, we are possessed, by marketable forces beyond our control. In complicity with capital, a body becomes its own worst enemy' (Massumi, 1993, p. 12). The selling of war, and especially the war on terror as a state of *permanent war* has therefore demonstrated very well how easy it is to buy opinions, and in doing so it has exposed the extent to which a logic of capitalist control in conditions of post-modernity – summed up by Hardt and Negri as 'every difference is an opportunity' (Hardt and Negri, 2000, p. 152) (for the market) – has permeated 'public life' to the extent that people are witnessing a selling off – or privatisation – of life itself. We might say that the function of social life has itself become incorporated, or co-opted, into the promotion of its own enslavement by that order, or the self-creation of a public that denies itself.

This is in part to vindicate Pilger's constant barrage of associations between the 'economic elite' and its 'media cohort', his way of defining the 'new world order'. But to another extent, Pilger only scratches the surface. For to understand why people consent is to ask not why people are only told certain things (the hegemony of a communications industry) but why they do *not* say things to the contrary (the disciplining of discourse). The mass protests against the war in March 2003, for instance, were a bandwagon that few newspapers wanted to miss, and they duly represented the 'public opinion' as anti-war and proactive. A few weeks later, when war had started, the continuation of protests, boycotts, strikes and road blockades opposing war fell off the media shelf of public observation. In the end, this tactic of turning a blind eye to dissidence and focusing on 'official' news once the war had become public property, worked. The momentum of the anti-war protests failed under the weight of disempowerment, but not simply because it had failed to stop a war. It failed to sustain a dissenting voice because it spoke it to an established order that does not allow those voices of dissent to function in the way that people conduct their lives, perceive themselves, or simply speak from day to day. This institutionalisation of passivity epitomises the 'publicity' of Blair before he declared war just as it does parliamentary politics itself. If it had anything at all to do with public debate then it was in the *discussion of the discussion*, the documentation of the parliamentary meeting, its myriad reporting, deconstruction of spin, analysis of who won and lost on points of rhetoric and opposition-bashing. The post-modern paradigm for Debord's original concept of the 'society of the spectacle' is indeed the masking of reality, the 'negation' of real life (Debord, 1992, p. 164). The real innovation, though, is not the reinvention of life as a cycle of productivity and consumption, but the affirmation of the reign of bio-power, the production of the illusion of choice and participation, manufactured by the appearance of diverse spectacles and the installation of 'trivial' oppositions, as much for sports entertainment as for elections (ibid., p. 40).

With the marriage of corporate control and the mass media, it is of little surprise that the subjects of 'public information' – people watching TV and listening to radio, day in and day out – cannot separate what they are told is 'information', and what is being sold to them, through advertising or sponsorship. Television, in particular, is, as Manuel Castells says, a 'leveller of content':

> The price to be paid for a message to be on television . . . is to accept being mixed in a multi-semantic text whose syntax is extremely lax. Thus, information and entertainment, education and propaganda, relaxation and hypnosis are all blurred into the language of television [the] normalization of messages, where atrocious images of real war can almost be absorbed as part of action movies. (Castells, 2000, p. 152)

Just as governments may sell off public services to private investment, means of communication follow suit, but in this case what is at stake is the very means of participation in the public realm and the possibility of criticising it. If the fabric of society is saturated by the logic of the markets and the imperative of consumption, the means of maintaining this 'order' are the concern of businesses no more than state authorities, because the interiorisation of private concerns and the creation of a 'pseudo-public' realm of critique has proven to be the most sustainable guarantee of a compliant, unquestioning 'public'. This, and not the use of 'terror' or the simplistic carrot and stick approach, is how to understand how a war could be sold to an anti-war 'public'. This is also why, for Hardt and Negri, 'communicative production and imperial legitimation march hand in hand and can no longer be separated. The machine is self-validating, autopoietic – that is, systemic' (2000, p. 34).

RECLAIMING THE PUBLIC: CITIZENSHIP AS PROTEST

So far, answering the question *why people consent* has led to an almost nihilistic exposition of public practice in post-democratic social life. The 'informational colonization of being' (Habermas, 2000, p. 34) that Habermas spoke about has triumphed, in this respect. The very language we use and concepts we employ get caught up in a legitimation of domination, from the use of concepts of 'normal' social behaviour and 'world order', to the concept of citizenship in terms of consumers, to the banalisation of violence through safe, acceptable 'just-war' language and the unavoidable hegemony of the reign of 'truth' in our speech. As Massumi says, 'democratic' society 'is not moral, just managerial. What it demands of its bodies is a practical acceptance of certain parameters of action, rather than a principled conformity to an absolute idea' (Massumi, 1992, p. 123). But this merely provokes the question of what happens when that containment is broken, when official news is disregarded or subverted, when public opinion fills streets and not radio phone-ins. In other words, when an alternative, engaged public attempts to reclaim its place. Today a truly fascinating opening of new social sites of critical debate is emerging through the Internet and other media, but is no less the target of police and intelligence agencies. The frequency by which police forces target communications offices of protest movements bears testimony to this, from the Indymedia offices that suffered violent police raids at the protest camps against G8 summits in Genoa and Evian,[15] to similar experiences at the offices of the International Solidarity Movement in occupied Palestine,[16] congregations sharing information that does not pass a censorship check is still one of the greatest threats to an authority's control of 'public' information. But despite the escalation of this form of repression, it at least demonstrates a latent desire on the part of citizens to re-invent modes of participation and 'being public'. Most large-scale demonstrations of the past few years have entertained a discourse that tries to redefine who the 'we' of the protests are, who the 'people' are, to the extent that a kind of reclaiming of the meaning of citizenship could be said to be at the heart of 'new social movements' in the twenty-first century. In a climate where more geo-political decisions are taken by fewer and fewer representatives than ever, it is appropriate that popular slogans have centred on this theme: 'we are the people'; 'this is what democracy looks like'; 'they are eight, we are millions'. Also representative of this desire for new public-ness is the emergence of 'World' and 'European' 'social forums', and a new wave of 'people's assemblies' that replace traditional sites of congregation and debate.

The emergence of these trends in protest movements also reflects a desire to challenge the continual erosion of public *spaces* as a sphere of contestation and debate. The process of depoliticisation that this chapter has outlined has an unavoidably spatial dimension, but is nowhere more evident than in the culture of obsessive security, the criminalisation of dissent and the creation of exclusion zones to deter the escalation of popular protest at symbolically critical sites such as the Houses of Parliament buildings or G8, WTO, IMF or World Bank summits, which as the summit in Gleneagles testified to, must rely on increasingly remote and impenetrable locations and the costly deployment of police and army resources from around the country. The palpable desperation of protest that wants to 'reclaim the streets' and 'reclaim the commons', is a significant reminder that even if global capitalist power has transcended geography, the popular consensus upon which it is founded still *lives* and works in those spaces. And what people are beginning to see in those spaces is an increasingly paranoid and violent erosion of the freedoms they were instituted to protect. Global protest movements are waking up to the disembodied reality of global politics, in response, through an exploration of mobility and fluidity of bodies. Not only the desire to be *seen* and *heard*, therefore, but the constant promise to be present and evade disappearance, to make known its political desires wherever power meets, is what constitutes the 'publicness' of public protest today. As Hardt and Negri put it, the 'multitude' is a source of constant antagonism to empire precisely because of its fluidity of movement across boundaries, *and* of ideas across social identities (Hardt and Negri, 2004, p. 44). Would Habermas want to say that the protesters of the past decade's global justice and anti-capitalist mobilisations are taking back something stolen from them in the nineteenth century? Just as in the nineteenth century European political issues were dominated by electoral reform, that is, the 'enlargement of the public' (Habermas, 1989, p. 133), and provoked a great mistrust by liberals of 'mass opinion', so the twenty-first century emphasis of anti-capitalist protests on reclaiming a (radical) political dimension to 'the public' is met with a suspicion that such an overspill of public resentment at the 'global order' should remain 'out of bounds' to the realm of public expression. It represents a 'crisis of democracy' to the established order.

If the 'success' of the new modes of citizenship enshrined in a depoliti-cising politics of fear is guaranteed by the apparent normality of that system and the lack of alternatives, then alternative modes of citizenship concerned to rediscover the space and discourse of public politics must reveal the absurdity and contingency of 'normal', acquiescent political life. Hardt and Negri's contention that the current world order engenders a manipulation of public consent through the 'local effectiveness of the regime' (Hardt and Negri, 2000, p. 343) sets out this task in terms that addresses my original problem, namely, how 'the most unpopular war in history' came to appear at times to tap into the semblance of 'public consensus'.

The appearance of an acquiescent, generally accepting public sphere to the most outrageous political decisions is possible because the barbarity of those decisions is hidden from the immediate, immanent grasp of the public sphere. There is an everyday appearance of order and naturalness of locally specific regimes – the functioning of a local economy, the institution of a police force 'doing their job', the integrity of 'our boys' obeying military commanders in a desert far away, and the disinterestedness of a journalist writing and taking photos about what they see in front of them. This fits entirely within the scheme of the bio-political production of information 'consumers' and 'spectators' in a society of control. The voice of dissent of two million citizens, as a response to Blair's reasons for waging war, however temporary and fragile, represented a breach in this internalised sense of 'order' in which consent is manufactured, and this is also why it did not last long. The daily consumption of mediatised atrocities has a powerful socialising effect, and the banalisation of the war once it had started, with the ever-shortening sound bites and homogeneously doctored 'safe' images reaching TV sets across the country, was no different from the process of normalising the morally outrageous that takes place on our screens and broadsheets everyday. What remained, however, and must be sustained in the momentum of the anti-war movement's broad-based popularity, was an awareness that the producers of public consent were visibly shocked by the demands of the public. This enlightenment, this surge in mistrust at the rationale of government policy, and proliferation of arguments, enquiries and analyses of the *structures* by which public consent has been manipulated, is nothing so revolutionary or utopian as a mass awakening, a breaking of chains or stepping outside the 'matrix' of bio-power propaganda. Nevertheless, it can be said that it accompanies a gradual decline in perceptions of democracy that is emerging in response to the manipulative style of publicity politics or the practices of post-democracy. We might also ask whether recent electoral signals of opposition to the war on terror also represent a consensus of dissent. In the case of the US, overwhelming opposition to the Republican Party in the 2006 mid-term elections might well represent a surprise vote of no confidence in Bush's foreign policy and the visions of the 'Project for a New American Century' (of which Donald Rumsfeld was a prominent advocate) in general. And while critics of both parties point to the political compromises made by the Democrats in order to achieve this, citing their commitment to 'bipartisanship' above all and cooperation in common 'security' goals, the reclaiming of the Senate and the House of Representatives undoubtedly represents some popularised desire to move the debate over Iraq and the war on terror beyond the Republican rhetoric of 'prevailing' in a 'war with no end'. Does Blair's sharp downturn in popularity and credibility, with his party also losing control over 300 local councils in 2006, represent a similar trend? If this chapter has revealed anything it is that the relationship between a dissenting population and the notion of 'active' voter participation is in a steady state of crisis, attested to by decreasing voter turnouts in almost all 'liberal democracies'. Recent protest votes may nevertheless indicate a parallel observation that the 'mythical' realm of a dissenting, rational public sphere continues to be a *contested* one, an idea that will not go away entirely, though it finds itself increasingly in need of changing shape. Alternative mobilisations of 'public opinion', of which global protest is only one experiment, attest, if nothing else, to a common realisation that electoral victories can only be the beginning of a much larger task to recapture the popular imagination of a freely speaking, acting and dissenting, public.

CONCLUSION

I have shown that the concept of a public sphere free to critically debate and articulate social and political concerns autonomously of the state, has been surreptitiously removed, while maintaining its illusion within the construction of a consuming and spectating public sphere. The conditions of these 'normal' modes of citizenship are therefore the legitimation and repetition of a highly controlled and selective means of communication as well as the physical production of social spaces. Periodic breaches of a lack of confidence in these locally 'successful' regimes, however, such as mass demonstrations, strikes and riots, are always important evidence that this grip of normalisation is not absolute: after friction, cracks appear, people refuse the self-perpetuating cycle and challenge the legitimacy of a certain social logic. If communication, as Hardt and Negri suggest, subsumes structures of education, culture and public information into the 'continuous and complete circulation of signs' (Hardt and Negri, 2000, p. 347) that effectively disables the motivation to *change* anything, then the possibility for a critical public consensus, or at the very least its disentanglement from a passive, unreflective one, is only possible where these breaches of participation in ordinary, ordered and 'safe' channels of communication occur. A mistrust of the mainstream media and the established order that it fails to question or undermine is only one small aspect of this, but it is a beginning. A whole grid of symbolic tactics of pacifying and marketising the public sphere is in place and only really becomes apparent when individuals attempt to break its symbolic normality, whether that means the anti-capitalist satirical 'subvertising' of advertisement space, or mobilising millions of people to articulate opposition and make accountable government decisions, or the campaign to 'reclaim the media' in the work of Indymedia and other information sources. Those breaches, which are occurring all the time, are not grand awakenings from a matrix of domination, but they do represent the creation of places of exchange and expression in which a public sphere is finally able to see its own antagonistic place in social life and therefore have some control over its future.

Pilger's hope is being partly vindicated by these processes. Given the chance, people do not believe only what they are told. 'Giving the chance' is the challenge this study has thrown up, however, because it is founded on a critique of social communication that inscribes self-enslavement, through a spectacular logic of acquirement and consumption, into the very discourse from which opinions and beliefs can be formed. In this sense Arendt was wrong to say that opinions cannot be sold; they were sold on a massive scale to Blair's favourite audience – those who found invading Iraq to be morally outrageous, and yet somehow normalised into a scheme of world order that praised Blair for his moral courage and upheld their faith in the integrity of parliament. But she was right in saying that, at least for Vietnam, the grounds upon which people will consent against their own judgement are continually open to miscalculation. Support for the 2003 invasion of Iraq was also miscalculated, as the upsurge of protests and sustained criticism testified to. And if miscalculations of the strong are always an assurance that the weak continue to raise the stakes and 'learn their game', the next gamble of consent-producing communicators will be this: will the demands for truth and an increasing semblance of public accountability have risen, will the rush to the streets (as one of the only spaces of critical publicity left, perhaps?) anticipate the next war even quicker and hit the country even harder? Or will the imperial logic have been to let people rage for a while and then, after the dust has settled, frustrated and dejected at the impotence of their banners and speeches, become acclimatised to perpetual war, and the passive consumption of the morally outrageous?

NOTES

1. I owe much of the media analysis of this section, including critiques of Jeremy Paxman's *Newsnight* and *The Daily Mirror*, to David Edwards (2003a).
2. Blair was consistent in contradicting, publicly, the statements of former UN weapons inspector Scott Ritter that Iraq was 'fundamentally disarmed' by December 1998, that his team was not forced out but withdrawn amid admissions of CIA infiltration and spying (intelligence that was used to bomb Iraq in Operation *Desert Fox* in December 1998) and that before he was asked to leave Hans Blix had reported that more time was needed and that Iraq was being more cooperative with them than they ever had been (see Edwards, 2003a).
3. 'Millions worldwide rally for peace', *The Guardian*, 17 February 2003, www.guardian. co.uk/antiwar/story/0,12809,897098,00.html, accessed 23 April 2007.
4. The phrase is taken from Noam Chomsky and Edward Herman, *Manufacturing Consent: The Political Economy of the Mass Media* (1988), New York: Pantheon Books.
5. The Stop The War Coalition was formed only ten days after the twin towers were attacked, when 2000 people met in London in response to a newspaper advertisement, anticipating the US programme of retaliation and seeing the urgency of mobilising resistance before the public became brainwashed into accepting wars as the only solutions to hand. Subsequent demonstrations against the bombing of Afghanistan did not take long to read between the lines of UK/US diplomacy and oppose a planned invasion of Iraq, at least a year before it actually occurred. Actions of resistance to the war were planned, mobilised and reported by independent media sites such as Indymedia, Active Resistance to the Roots of War (ARROW), Stop the War Coalition, CND, AntiWar.com, Act Now Stop War End Racism (ANSWER), Media Workers Against War, Iraq Body Count, and many others, including local groups and religious organisations.
6. See Polly Toynbee, 'Did Blair lie to us?' *The Guardian*, 30 March 2003, www.guardian. co.uk/Iraq/Story/0,966735,00.html, accessed 23 April 2007.
7. The Pentagon Papers were leaked US government documents detailing the US involvement in the Vietnam war, in particular the admission that the US had no plan to end the war. It had a huge influence on the deterioration of public confidence in the US government.
8. Nothing characterised this orchestration better than the farcical toppling of Saddam's statue in the 'fall of Baghdad' that baited the whole spectrum of waiting media. The *Mirror*, once again showing a preference for jingoistic sensationalism over a consistency of its views, showed a close-up of the American soldier draping the Stars and Stripes (taken from the Pentagon after the September 11 attack) over Saddam's figure with the words 'STATUE OF LIBERTY' (*Daily Mirror*, 10 April 2003) and, like most other papers, proceeded to discuss how the 'Pax Americana' would unfold, as if the prize scoop signalled an end to the conflict, at least in terms of 'big news'. It was referred to as 'their Berlin wall moment' and compared to the toppling of statues that marked the mass uprisings in Hungary in 1956 (despite the fact that the people of Iraq did not do this – an invading force did). The *Daily Telegraph* printed that 'The tyrannical rule of Saddam

Hussein was brought to an end by the American-led coalition yesterday amid wild scenes of jubilation in Baghdad from many of his own people . . . Thousands of ecstatic Iraqis gave US forces a tumultuous welcome in the capital before turning on the symbols of the regime that had lasted for 24 years, tearing down statues and pictures of the old dictator, pelting them with rocks and smashing them to pieces' (*Daily Telegraph*, 10 April 2003, www.telegraph.co.uk/news/main.jhtml?xml=/news/2003/04/10/war10.xml, accessed 23 April 2007). In fact, aerial photos show that there were approximately 150 people in the plaza, which was sealed off by Marines who are suspected to have 'chosen' the pro-American Iraqis who celebrated, incidentally, right next to the Palestine Hotel where the international media were based ('The Photographs tell the Story', www.informationclearinghouse.info/article2842.htm, accessed 20 October 2006). Days later, against the wishes of US forces, the Kurds in Kirkuk toppled another statue of Saddam themselves (NBC11, 10 April 2003), but this was not 'our' news and was therefore ignored by mainstream media.

9.   www.guardian.co.uk/antiwar/story/0,12809,937040,00.html, accessed 23 April 2007.
10.   According to Kierkegaard, the idea of 'people's government' is the 'true picture of hell' (Kierkegaard, 1996, p. 302), worse even than dictatorship, since a tyrant can be toppled or opposed in the silence of one's heart. In a democracy, the tyrant *is* the masses and drowns out that silence with the 'untruth' of 'ten thousand roaring people' (ibid., p. 292). Another, more helpful insight is the parallels he draws with herd mentality and the press. Kierkegaard vilified the press as much as he did – and for the same reasons – the established 'clergy', for its claim to represent public opinion and thereby express opinions that 'belong to none and yet to all' (ibid., p. 335).
11.   'Psychiatrist Clotaire Rapaille, a consultant to the automobile industry, conducted studies of post-war consumer psyches for Chrysler and reported that Americans wanted "aggressive" cars. In interviews with Keith Bradsher, the former Detroit bureau chief for the New York Times, Rapaille discussed the results of his research. SUVs, he said, were "weapons" – "armoured cars for the battlefield" – that appealed to Americans' deepest fears of violence and crime', Sheldon Rampton and John Stauber, 'Trading on Fear' in *The Guardian*, 12 July 2003, www.commondreams.org/views03/0712-01.htm, accessed 23 April 2007.
12.   Chomsky points out that the first 'coordinated propaganda ministry' was set up by the British government during the First World War to try to convince American intellectuals of the 'nobility of the British war' and draw the nation into it. The Wilson government's contribution was to follow suit, setting up its own propaganda agency (the Committee on Public Information) which succeeded in 'turning a relatively pacifist population into raving anti-German fanatics who wanted to destroy everything German. It reached the point where the Boston Symphony Orchestra couldn't play Bach. The country was driven into hysteria' (Chomsky, 2003, p. 3).
13.   As Richard Cheney puts it: 'It is different than the Gulf War was, in the sense that it may never end. At least, not in our lifetime' (Cheney, quoted by Bob Woodward, *Washington Post*, 21 October 2001, www.washingtonpost.com/ac2/wp-dyn?pagename=article&node=&contentId=A27452-2001oct20, accessed 23 April 2007).
14.   www.commondreams.org/views03/0712-01.htm, accessed 23 April 2007.
15.   See 'Indymedia Offices Raided Across Italy', *StateWatch*, February 2002, www.statewatch.org/news/2002/feb/15italy.htm, accessed October 2006.
16.   See 'ISM Offices Raided', *Peace News*, 10 May 2003, www.peacenews.info/news/article/154?PHPSESSID=7a7147a4d8e02c4fcd22ab722698f5ed, accessed 20 October 2006.

REFERENCES

Arendt, H. (1972), *Crises of the Republic*, New York: Harcourt Brace Jovanovich.
Castells, M. (2000), *The Rise of the Network Society*, 2nd edn, London: Blackwell.

Chomsky, N. (2000), 'Control of our lives', Lecture in Kiva Auditorium, Albuquerque, New Mexico, 26 February, www.zmag.org/chomskyalbaq.htm, accessed 20 October 2006.

Chomsky, N. (2003), 'Collateral damage', interview by David Barsamian, *Arts and Opinion*, **2** (4), www.artsandopinion.com/2003_v2_n4/chomsky-2.htm, accessed 13 March 2006.

Crouch, C. (2004), *Post-Democracy*, Cambridge: Polity.

Debord, G. (1992), *La Société du spectacle*, Paris: Gallimard.

Edwards, D. (2003a), 'Blair's betrayal, part 1', *Media Lens*, 10 February, www.zmag.org/content/AntiWar/edwards_blairpt1.cfm, accessed 20 October 2006.

Edwards, D. (2003b), 'Falling at the feet of power: Blair's sincerity and the media', *Media Lens*, 21 March 2003, www.zmag.org/content/showarticle. cfm?ItemID= 3301, accessed 20 October 2006.

Fisk, R. (2003), 'The war of misinformation has begun', *Zmag*, March, www.zmag.org/content/showarticle.cfm?ItemID=3241, accessed 20 October 2006.

Habermas, J. (1989), *The Structural Transformation of the Public Sphere*, trans. Thomas Burger, London: Polity.

Habermas, J. (2000), *Theory of Communicative Action*, quoted in Hardt and Negri, pp. 33–4.

Hall, S., S. Cohen and J. Young (1973), 'The social production of news: mugging in the media', in S. Cohen and J. Young (eds), *The Manufacture of News: Deviance, Social Problems and the Mass Media*, London: Constable, pp. 335–67.

Hardt, M. and A. Negri (2000), *Empire*, Cambridge, MA and London: Harvard University Press.

Hardt, M. and A. Negri (2004), *Multitude*, New York: Penguin.

Kierkegaard, S. (1992), *Concluding Unscientific Postscript*, ed. and trans. Howard V. Hong and Edna V. Hong, Princeton, NJ: Princeton University Press.

Kierkegaard, S. (1996), *Papers and Journals: A Selection*, trans. Alastair Hannay, Harmondsworth, Middx: Penguin.

London Reuters (2003), 10 April, http://uk.news.yahoo.com/030410/80/dxgz4. html, accessed 1 March 2006.

Machiavelli, N. (1995), *The Prince and Other Political Writings*, trans. and ed. Stephen J. Miller, London: Everyman.

Massumi, B. (1992), *A User's Guide to Capitalism and Schizophrenia*, Cambridge, MA and London: MIT Press.

Massumi, B. (1993), 'Everywhere you want to be', in Brian Massumi (ed.), *The Politics of Everyday Fear*, Minneapolis, MN: University of Minnesota Press, pp. 3–37.

Pilger, J. (1998), *Hidden Agendas*, London: Vintage.

Said, E. (2003), 'Who is in charge?', *El Ahram*, 6 March, http://www.weekly.ahram. org.eg.2003/628/op 2.htm, accessed 1 March 2006.

7. Citizenship, rights and Tony Blair's doctrine of international community[1]

Colin Tyler

INTRODUCTION

G.W.F. Hegel observed in 1821 that, 'the declining nation . . . loses its autonomy, or it may still exist, or drag out its existence, as a particular state or a group of states and involve itself without rhyme or reason in manifold enterprises at home and battles abroad' (Hegel, 1821, sec. 347R). Alex Callinicos (2001, p. 96, also chs 3 and 4) has made much the same point in a contemporary context: 'Britain has waged a series of colonial wars since 1945. Carrying these on in the name of human rights may help give its rulers a sense that they continue to bestride the globe. Continuing also to act as Washington's closest and most obedient ally . . . may strengthen this illusion. But an illusion it remains'. In May 2003, Tony Blair was even awarded a Congressional Gold Medal in recognition of the UK's support of US-led action in Afghanistan and Iraq. Even though the bill's sponsor claimed that 'Tony Blair is a hero', the Prime Minister did not collect the award, possibly out of fear of the potential domestic political damage doing so might cause (Hollingshead, 2006).

With these thoughts in mind, this chapter analyses Tony Blair's doctrine of the international community, which, for many years, has been the ideology officially underpinning much of New Labour's foreign policy. In this way, it assesses the Blair government's self-image as a civilising power in the world. The next section argues that the political dimensions of this ideal of international relations are surprisingly coherent even if, in the abstract at least, they are not particularly sophisticated and even if they rest on certain highly controversial presuppositions. The following section raises very serious concerns about the economic dimensions of the model and highlights a fundamental incoherence in the doctrine as a whole. The penultimate section traces some implications of the restrictions on civil liberties imposed domestically by the UK government, and which are justified by reference to Blair's model. The final section concludes.

BLAIR'S DOCTRINE OF INTERNATIONAL COMMUNITY

Tony Blair set out the political aspects of his 'doctrine of the international community' in five speeches that he has given since becoming UK Prime Minister in May 1997. The first was given to the Economic Club in Chicago on 24 April 1999, against the background of (North Atlantic Treaty Organisation (NATO) action in Kosovo (Blair, 1999). The second was a speech to the US Congress on 18 July 2003, in the context of the invasion of Iraq by the 'coalition of the willing' in March of that year (Blair, 2003). The next three were planned and delivered as a set in 2006, with the first being given on 21 March at Reuters in London under the auspices of the progressive think-tank, the Foreign Policy Centre (FPC) (Blair, 2006b). The second was given on 27 March to the Australian parliament in Canberra (Blair, 2006c), and the final speech was given at Georgetown University, Washington, DC, USA on 26 May (Blair, 2006d).

Blair recognises that international community is more an ideal than a reality at present, although elements are evident in the current international society even if only in a nascent form. He began his FPC speech by noting:

> The basic thesis [of these five speeches] is that the defining characteristic of today's world is its interdependence; that whereas the economics of globalisation are well matured, the politics of globalisation are not; and that unless we articulate a common global policy based on common values, we risk chaos threatening our stability, economic and political, through letting extremism, conflict or injustice go unchecked. The consequence of this thesis is a policy of engagement not isolation; and one that is active not reactive. (Blair, 2006b)

It is useful to begin this critical assessment of the political dimensions of Blair's doctrine by distinguishing its ontological dimensions from its normative ones. Blair ended his 1999 Chicago speech by stressing the historic need for the US and Europe to 'fashion . . . the design of a future built on peace and prosperity for all, which is the only dream that makes humanity worth preserving' (Blair, 1999). This was in line with the claim later made by George W. Bush in his 2002 West Point speech that, 'The 20th century ended with a single surviving model of human progress, based on non-negotiable demands of human dignity, the rule of law, limits on the power of the state, respect for women and private property and free speech and equal justice and religious tolerance' (Bush, 2002).

The normative dimensions of Blair's doctrine of international community are slightly more nuanced than these simplistic statements imply. (The same cannot be said for Bush's position; see Tyler, ch. 3 in this volume.) Blair holds that the interests and values of states are derived from the fundamental interests and values of its citizens. At the most fundamental level, these interests and values are held by all progressive individuals and groups, irrespective of their wider cultural, economic or political upbringing or their age, gender or genetic inheritance. The most important of these 'common values' are respect for claims of justice, personal dignity, individual freedom and social order.

These values justify a form of domestic society that is rights based and non-discriminatory, governed by a political structure founded on elected representative democracy, the rule of law, civil liberties, liberal economic freedoms tempered by welfare concerns, and freedom from fear. (Crucially as we shall see, in the post-9/11 world, Blair accords freedom from fear lexical or absolute priority over civil liberties.) These common values justify 'moderation' and tolerance both within the culturally diverse peoples that characterise a peaceful yet interdependent world, and between the member states of the international community (both must accommodate numerous religious faiths, for example, in a non-sectarian manner). The main problem, as Blair sees it, is to foster these values in the face of sustained opposition from terrorists as well as those in all countries who sympathise with terrorists' grievances if not with their methods.

One should not underestimate the ambition of Blair's agenda, nor indeed its arrogance (Will, 2004, p. 137). In his FPC speech, he claimed:

> Ours are not Western values. They are the universal values of the human spirit and anywhere, any time, ordinary people are given the chance to choose, the choice is the same. Freedom not tyranny. Democracy not dictatorship. The rule of law not the rule of the secret police. . . . Just as the terrorist seeks to divide humanity in hate, so we have to unify it around an idea and that idea is liberty. We must find the strength to fight for this idea; and the compassion to make it universal. (Blair, 2003)

These values inform the ideal ontology of Blair's international community. Specifically, the doctrine holds that, when realised, the international community is constituted by relations between peoples expressing themselves politically through states. There are several points to notice. First, Blair distinguishes between 'states' and 'regimes', with the former being relatively legitimate political manifestations of the peoples they govern, founded on the rule of law and individualistic economic freedoms. States are also relatively benign even if ultimately they remain self-interested international actors. 'Regimes' on the other hand are illegitimate tyrannies, characterised by arbitrary government and sustained by oppression. Where they have the power, they tend to be rogue actors in the international system. For Blair, 'states' are civilised, democratic and peaceful, whereas 'regimes' are barbaric, tyrannous and bellicose. Even though the positing of this dichotomy is partly a rhetorical device, it is also indicative of his underlying, polarising tendency.

Blair draws a relatively sharp and related distinction between peoples and states. Routinely, he justifies international intervention on the grounds that the target regimes do not pursue the interests of the people they govern. That was one of his main concerns in relation to both Kosovo and Iraq. The following remarks concerning Afghanistan, which he made on 25 September 2001, are also typical in this regard:

> [O]ur fight is with that regime [that is, the Taliban], not with the people of Afghanistan. These people have also suffered for years: their rights abused, women's rights non-existent, poverty and illness ignored, a regime without respect or justice for its own people. A regime founded on fear, and funded largely by drugs and crime. (Blair, 2001b)

The next ontological feature of Blair's doctrine of international community is the unavoidability of interdependence between countries' economies, societies and environments. Such globalisation brings with it many benefits and is inexorable in these three areas. This process has created and continues to create political interdependence, by establishing and strengthening the bonds of the nascent international community between states. Three dimensions can be identified here. The first is positive, arising from the opportunities for states and their peoples to pursue their interests and further their values more effectively through interaction than they could do in isolation. Primarily, Blair characterises these opportunities in economic terms. The second dimension is negative, arising from shared actual dilemmas and potential risks. Increasingly, states are becoming members of interlocking communities of fate, especially in relation to issues of health, the environment and of course security. The third type of bond between states in the international community is ideational, being founded on 'common values'.

In spite of this inescapable interdependence, Blair holds that a state's fundamental interests and values exist independently of the state's membership of the international community (see Tyler this volume, ch. 3). Counterfactually, interactions between states do not change those states' most fundamental self-conceptions and goals. Essentially contingent patterns of international interaction will have profound implications for the means by which a state's interests and values are best furthered at any particular time, but, on this view, fundamentally the basic goals are not shaped by them.

These bonds gain stability through the coincidence of the 'universal values of the human spirit' (Blair, 2003), not merely within and between peoples but at all levels of the international community. They also serve to underpin other lower-order values: 'Globalisation begets interdependence. Interdependence begets the necessity of a common value system to make it work. In other words, idealism becomes real politik' (Blair, 2006d). (Even in his first Commons statement following the 9/11 attacks, Blair mixed moral principle with economic self-interest: 'We will act . . . for the protection of our people and our way of life, including confidence in our economy . . . We act for justice', Blair, 2001c). In practical terms, this means that the leaders of the nascent international community must address issues of injustice, tyranny, poverty and environmental damage at the same time as they liberalise international trade. Only by so doing can global economic growth be sustained and security be enhanced.

Even though the international community is constituted by the interactions of individual states, it still requires shared authoritative points of orientation and leadership. Hence, Blair stresses the vital importance of international institutions, primarily the United Nations (UN), the World Trade Organisation (WTO), the International Monetary Fund (IMF), the European Union (EU), and particularly in relation to the Balkan conflicts of the 1990s, NATO. He outlined his preferred sets of reforms to these organisations in his Georgetown speech (Blair, 2006d). The first set relates to the UN. The permanent membership of the Security Council should be enlarged to include Germany, Japan and India, with 'proper representation' being given to Latin America and Africa; the Secretary-General should be given greater powers 'over the appointments to the Secretariat', over UN expenditures and to suggest solutions to resolve enduring disagreements (which particular powers are not made clear); the UN 'should streamline radically' its 'humanitarian and development operations' so that it can pursue coherent policies on the ground ('single UN offices, with one leader, one country plan and one budget'); and an agency should be created within the UN to predict and plan responses to future humanitarian disasters.

Next, Blair holds that a politically independent IMF should concentrate 'on surveillance, both of individual countries and the wider system', and should also include 'emerging economic powers and give greater voice to developing countries' (see Lee, this volume, chs 8 and 9). The Executive Board of the World Health Organisation should be strengthened. Blair called also for the International Atomic Energy Authority to supervise 'a multilateral system for "safe enrichment" for [sic] nuclear energy'. Next, the G8 should become officially the 'G8+5' (Brazil, China, India, Mexico and South Africa should be made permanent members). Lastly, Blair called for the creation of 'a UN Environment Organisation'. (Hence, the 'G8+5

Climate Change Dialogue' was established on 24 February 2006, under the auspices of the Global Legislators Organisation for a Balanced Environment; GLOBE, 2006.)

For Blair, each of these organisations exists (or would exist) and is (or would be) legitimised by treaties freely entered into by individual member states. States (namely, legitimate representatives of their people, as opposed to regimes such as the Taliban and the Ba'ath party) bestow authority on international organisations, *not* vice versa. Nevertheless, echoing Callinicos's point, Blair is emphatic that, as currently the only superpower, the United States of America has a duty to exercise – in alliance with a reformed and strengthened EU and other leading nations such as Australia – leadership in the international community. Blair has repeated this point forcefully many times. For example, it recurred throughout his Chicago speech to the Economic Club in April 1999: 'America's allies are always both relieved and gratified by its continuing readiness to shoulder burdens and responsibilities that come with its sole superpower status'. He developed the point in the conclusion of the speech:

> You are the most powerful country in the world, and the richest. You are a great nation. You have so much to give and to teach the world; and I know you would say, in all modesty, a little to learn from it too. . . . [T]hose nations which have the power, have the responsibility. We need you engaged. We need the dialogue with you. Europe over time will become stronger and stronger; but its time is some way off.

> I say to you: never fall again for the doctrine of isolationism. The world cannot afford it. (Blair, 1999)

Such laudatory remarks are more than their context might suggest: namely, more than simply a pragmatic attempt in one speech to shore up middle America's support for the then-ongoing intervention in Kosovo. In fact, it accords perfectly with the observation that Blair made halfway through his 2006 FPC speech that the upshot of increased global interdependence 'is a policy of engagement not isolation; and one that is active not reactive' (Blair, 2006b). He reiterated the point in Canberra: 'I do not always agree with the US. Sometimes they can be difficult friends to have . . . [Yet] the reality is that none of the problems that press in on us, can be resolved or even contemplated without them' (Blair, 2006c). Blair accepts then that the UK is, in Callinicos's words quoted above, 'Washington's closest and most obedient ally'.

Thus the drive to develop a true international community originates in our very humanity. Referring to the notion of 'progressive pre-emption' at the end of his Georgetown speech, Blair argued that 'the best of the human spirit, that which, throughout the ages, has pushed the progress of humanity along, is also the best hope for the world's future. Our values are our guide' (Blair, 2006d). The conflict between progressive and non-progressive forces takes on a profound significance in this way. Blair characterises the battle as at best a struggle between recognition of the moral and prudential need to develop on one hand and naive non-recognition or error regarding this need on the other. In more pointed cases, the battle is between freedom and vested interests, and, as with Bush, in its most acute form it is the demonising battle between good and evil. Yet, this does not mean that Blair has a unique affinity with the Bush administration, as will become clear in the next section.

PROBLEMS WITH THE ECONOMIC ASPECTS OF BLAIR'S DOCTRINE

Blair frames his doctrine of international community within the context of what he calls his 'progressivism', the ideology with which famously New Labour replaced its 'old' socialism and of which the Third Way is one manifestation. Relatedly, in December 2000, together with the then-President Bill Clinton and various other world leaders, Blair helped to launch the Policy Network, which aims to bring together centre-left politicians and the wider policy community from Europe and North America. In his contribution to a 2006 special issue of the network's journal *Progressive Politics*, Blair stated,

> We believe in solidarity, in social justice, in opportunity for all, in tolerance and respect, in strong communities and standing up for the weak, the sick and the helpless. What has, however, changed is the policy agenda needed to deliver a fairer society that is rooted in these values. (Policy Network, 2003)

At the conceptual level, two key elements of progressivism are, first, a set of guiding ideals by which all economic, cultural, social and political changes should be measured, and, second, the belief that an elite with a clear vision can generate systemic pressure that can push societies to manifest that ideal more perfectly. Blair characterises the first of these elements as a movement towards modernity, and contrasts it with the failure to adapt to globalisation. As one might expect, this 'struggle about values and about modernity' seeks to promote internationally an ideal of liberal democratic welfare capitalism. Blair's progressivism is shown also in the stress he places on the need for a welfarist twist on what could otherwise easily be a neo-conservative ideal. Unlike most previous socialist models, Blair's mechanism of welfare reform is based on the notion of public–private partnerships, and the distinction implied therein between planning and purchasing by the state, and then delivery by the private sector (Blair, 2006c; Marquand, 2004, pp. 22–5). Blair's ideal, then, is not inherently neo-conservative in the manner that some have suggested it is (Stelzer, 2004, pp. 4, 9–16, passim, 23–4). (Yet, I shall argue below that it has collapsed or will collapse into neo-conservatism in practice.)

Blair extends this domestic agenda on social justice into the economic dimensions of his doctrine of international community. In the very first of his five international community speeches, he claimed: 'We need to begin work now on what comes after our success in Kosovo. We will need a new Marshall plan for Kosovo, Montenegro, Macedonia, Albania and Serbia too if it turns to democracy' (Blair, 1999). Even in 1999 this idea was not a new one for Blair. Speaking on 29 May 1997 during an official visit to the meet the new UK Prime Minister, Bill Clinton called for such a scheme to form a cornerstone in the fight against terrorism (Blair and Clinton, 1997). After coming to office, Blair and his spokespeople highlighted the plan's centrality to the problems of EU accession countries (Blair, 2000; PMOS, 2005) and African economic development, through the Commission for Africa (Blair and Zenawi, 2005). In December 2001, Gordon Brown, then the UK Chancellor, made clear to the Press Club in Washington that: 'America's post-Second World War achievement in what we now call the Marshall Plan should be our inspiration in this post-cold war world – not just for the reconstruction of Afghanistan but for the entire developing world' (Brown, 2001).

In February 2002, Brown published a pamphlet in which he set out the details of this 'new Marshall Plan'. (For helpful background and analysis, see Payne, 2005, especially ch. 6.) The first of the 'four building blocks of this global new deal' are 'new rules of the game in codes and standards' for the international economy (HM Treasury, 2002, pp. 7, 10–7; also, for example, Brown, 2005a). These aim to increase transparency in developing governments' economic circumstances and to speed up the international flow of capital (primarily by fostering economic integration and fighting political corruption in the developing world). Moreover, Brown argues that there need to be better mechanisms with which to monitor member economies in order to anticipate problems and tackle crises, as well as there being reform of the international institutional architecture, and greater public investment in the development of foreign economies. A central role is played here by international institutions such as the IMF and the World Bank. The second 'building block' is the implementation of good governance measures in developing countries and education programmes to develop human capital (HM Treasury, 2002, pp. 7, 18–22). Dissemination of best practice will be encouraged via the creation of 'investment forums between public and private sectors' in developing countries. The aim is to make developing countries more attractive to private foreign direct investment. Businesses will also operate within a more demanding code of corporate ethics. The third 'building block' is the development of 'an improved trade regime', a process that began at the WTO's Fourth Ministerial Conference held at Doha in 2001 (ibid., pp. 7, 23–6). This process of trade liberalisation should be managed so as to help developing countries to participate more equally in the world economy. The fourth 'building block' of Brown's global New Deal is 'a substantial transfer of additional resources from the richest to the poorest countries in the form of investment [in new productive capacity] for development' (ibid., pp. 7, 23–6). The key elements here are debt relief, meeting the Millennium Development Goals, effectively targeted aid from developed countries, and more effective use of aid, so as to make developing countries more attractive investment opportunities for multinational corporations, once again.

Different elements of the new Marshall Plan have met with different levels of success since Brown's pamphlet appeared in 2002. The UK government pushed the scheme at the G8 Summit held in Gleneagles in July 2005 (Brown, 2005b). Unfortunately, the negotiations for a fairer trade regime finally collapsed towards the end of July 2006, leaving the plan as a neo-conservative scheme rather than a social democratic, structuralist one. Even if the negotiations had succeeded however, trade liberalisation, rather than either significant improvements in trading regimes, localism or sustained and substantial public investment by developing countries, would have remained at the heart of the new Marshall Plan, and therefore of Blair's doctrine of international community.

Indeed, many of the plan's structuralist presuppositions are highly controversial (see Harrison, 2005, passim; Slaughter, 2005, especially chs 1 to 3). First, even managed liberalisation presupposes that almost all countries have economically valuable resources and the technical and human capacities to make effective use of them. Yet, the capitalist neglect of significantly less productive countries condemns to continuing poverty almost everyone who is unfortunate enough to be born, for example, in Sub-Saharan Africa. Second, even when multinationals do invest abroad this can lead to serious distortions in the country's development, by tying up resources that otherwise could have been used to develop a diverse, integrated and robust national economy. Only with a solid domestic base can a country go on to weather the storms of global economic life. Premature liberalisation and openness to foreign competition make it far harder for indigenous secondary and tertiary sector activities to replace the frequently volatile and vulnerable primary activities that previously generated the country's wealth.

Moreover, where there is significant foreign direct investment, many corporations work very hard indeed to prevent the transfer of technical resources and knowledge to the essentially indigenous sector, not least through the use of copyright laws and intellectual property rights (for example, seed patenting and the denial of the permission for others to produce generic anti-HIV/AIDS medicines), and, on the business's withdrawal from the country, through the transfer abroad of their most skilled indigenous employees. Even while the corporation remains in the country, however, governments know of its power to move away and, in the absence of alternative foreign investment, grant these businesses special treatment and rights. Frequently, even those economically vulnerable governments that are not positively corrupt take on a client relationship to the corporation. In especially extreme cases, however, such as the Nigerian state's suppression of the Ogoni for Shell plc, they act as little more than the multinational's military wing (Obi, 2000, pp. 280–94).

In spite of their best intentions then, the failure of the post-Doha trade regime negotiations and the scheme's structural imperatives mean that the new Marshall Plan is likely to accelerate significantly the exploitation of the economically poorer countries. The absence of an effective monitoring and enforcement mechanism to moderate the behaviour of profit-driven multinationals (the absence of an international welfarist Leviathan) means that the liberalising dimensions of Blair's doctrine of international community are very likely to condemn less developed and vulnerable countries to the worst ravages of global corporate capitalism (Stiglitz, 2002).

There is another fundamental problem here, though. Certainly, the new Marshall Plan is to be commended for acknowledging that sustainable social development (the creation of robust and integrated civic and economic structures) needs to be kick started through targeted public expenditure on infrastructure such as roads and programmes to secure an adequate supply of basic utilities such as water and electricity, as well as the education of the indigenous population. Yet, the implementing institutions such as the WTO, the IMF and the World Bank, have shown remarkable enthusiasm for dogmatic, 'top-down' manipulation, most famously by attaching market liberalisation conditions to development loans. The underlying ideological faith in corporate capitalism has done much to stifle the efforts of local communities and has crushed many alternative approaches to economic development. It flies in the face of the great successes of local projects throughout the world, without the intervention of multinational corporations. Even the New Labour leadership has acknowledged such successes on many occasions (Feffer, 2002a; Brown, 2004; Kelly, 2006). John Feffer has noted: 'Sustainable economic development takes place in specific cultures and [where successful] has therefore been *culturally appropriate*. What works in one country or region may not work in another' (Feffer, 2002b, p. 18, original italics).

The structures that foster this type of nuanced support will have to be similarly nuanced, as I have argued elsewhere (Tyler, forthcoming). Local solutions tend to work best when they are planned and executed by engaged local communities themselves. Yet, the sort of liberalisation conditions that have been attached to previous loans from the various Bretton Woods institutions would have to be severely curtailed for many decades if agrarian economies were to be allowed to develop into robust industrialised ones. Where such large-scale development is required, regional planning and implementation is also needed, led by those whose circumstances are to be developed. George C. Marshall (1947) saw this far more clearly when he set out the original Marshall Plan in 1947 than either Brown or Blair do today.

There is yet another equally important problem, though. The new Marshall Plan presupposes the existence of certain civil conditions that in reality are not present in underdeveloped countries, or it assumes that it will foster them in the medium term. It assumes stable pre-industrial social structures, founded upon widespread allegiance to common norms of right conduct and structures of authority. Relative to the capitalist profit motive, such pre-existing and independently authoritative structures would act as countervailing social forces, thereby moderating and managing the development of new economic structures. While, as Amy Chua (2003) has shown, they can contribute to very significant problems, they can also help to lay the foundations for more formalised institutional structures by which a state could coordinate and regulate production and exchange both within its own territory and as a national economy within the wider, international economic systems (Hollingsworth and Boyer, 1997; Tyler, forthcoming).

Yet, indigenous civil associations, focused around and in part sustained by non-capitalist norms[2] of right conduct and responsibility, are frequently absent from contemporary underdeveloped countries. In part, this absence of independent authority structures is an inheritance of the decolonisation process, in the course of which often traditional cultural structures were destroyed and previously antagonistic indigenous groups were forced to attempt to achieve collective goals within shared political and 'national' structures. The result was frequently at best a fragmentary body politic (more an adminstrative category than a vibrant self-conscious people). Given the various effects that multinational corporations have on such economies (sketched above), it seems very unlikely that the liberalising facet of the plan will allow these civil conditions to develop in the future. In fact, the deliberate 'divide and rule' policies of the decolonisation period are now sustained (often ruthlessly) by the spread of multinational corporations, and a terrible state of affairs ensues for the local population (witness the recent history of many of the central and southern African states and not least the Democratic Republic of Congo; Hochschild, 2006).

These pressures expose a fundamental contradiction within Blair's doctrine of international community, between the values of liberty, democracy and security on the one hand, and the realities of global capitalism on the other. In the context of armed exchanges between Israel and Hezbollah in August 2006, Blair argued that there was an 'arc of extremism now stretching across the Middle East and touching, with increasing definition, countries far outside that region' (Blair, 2006f). He went on,

> To defeat it will need an alliance of moderation, that paints a different future in which Muslim, Jew and Christian; Arab and Western; wealthy and developing nations can make progress in peace and harmony with each other. My argument to you today is this: we will not win the battle against this global extremism unless we win it at the level of values as much as force, unless we show we are even-handed, fair and just in our application of those values to the world. The point is this. This is war, but of a completely unconventional kind. . . . [U]nless we revitalise the broader global agenda on poverty, climate change, trade, and in respect of the Middle East, bend every sinew of our will to making peace between Israel and Palestine, we will not win. And this is a battle we must win.[3]

Blair is probably correct when he argues that, from his point of view, this is the most significant conflict in relation to fostering his international community. The problem is that corporate interests are almost certain to frustrate the realisation of his 'broader global agenda'.

DISTORTING CITIZENSHIP: UK PUBLIC CULTURE POST-9/11

Less-developed countries are not the only ones that have been affected by the 'war on terror' and its various spin-offs, of course. Following 9/11, Blair's government passed many laws restricting civil freedoms in the UK. Three days after the attacks, Blair made it very clear in a statement to the House of Commons that he was willing to sacrifice civil liberties in the name of more effective counter-terrorism measures: 'Civil liberties are a vital part of our country, and of our world. But the most basic liberty of all is the right of the ordinary citizen to go about their business free from fear or terror' (Blair, 2001a). Eleven days after that, he made another statement, this time outside Number 10 Downing Street, in which he presaged these reforms:

> [A]s all countries look to their own domestic laws, we have been looking very carefully at issues such as the financing of terrorism, extradition laws, asylum

and immigration, as well as our own specific anti-terror laws. I am in no doubt of the need to strengthen our laws in the fight against terrorism. (Blair, 2001b)

Since that time, the UK government has pushed laws through parliament that restrict trial by jury, allow suspects to be held without charge for up to 28 days (and the government is still seeking an extension of up to 90 days), allow it to deport asylum seekers on the grounds of being suspected terrorists, and, until recently, they have restricted the right of citizens to protest within half a mile of the Houses of Parliament. Police have been given far greater powers to collect fingerprints and DNA from suspects as well as ordinary citizens and travellers, to engage in telephone tapping and to secretly inspect the financial records of individuals and groups, as well as to store and use the resulting data in future investigations and to share it with other EU states. Very famously, the Prevention of Terrorism Act 2005 replaced the state's detention powers with control orders (Carlile, 2006 summarises these powers). Before the Court of Appeal judged (on 1 August 2006) that the key provisions of control orders violated suspects' human rights, the act allowed police to restrict the freedom of association, movement and expression of any individual suspected of committing terrorist acts, or of aiding or abetting those who were suspected of doing so. Crucially for the Court of Appeal, these measures included the imposition of a curfew (making control orders a form of house arrest without the need for conviction) (Liberty, 2006). Section 1(9) of the act even allowed control orders to be applied to those who, among other things, are suspected of 'conduct which gives encouragement to the commission, preparation or instigation of such acts, or which is intended to do so'.

Many other measures have followed. Reinforcing the 2005 Act, in the Home Office's words, the Terrorism Act 2006 'makes it a criminal offence to directly or indirectly incite or encourage others to commit acts of terrorism. This will include the glorification of terrorism, where this may be understood as encouraging the emulation of terrorism' (Home Office, 2006). The 2006 Act also greatly extends police powers to search and detain those suspected of committing or encouraging terrorism, including those who distribute literature which 'encourages terrorism, or provides assistance to terrorists', and makes it a criminal offence to plan 'serious acts of terrorism' (apparently, no matter how ill-thought-out or spurious such 'plans' actually are). There are crucial and dangerous ambiguities throughout much of this legislation. For example, in both the 2005 and 2006 Acts, it is very unclear what constitutes 'encouragement', or what literature is proscribed by the 2006 Act. Crucially, many of these powers are granted even where the individual concerned has not been convicted by a court of committing any illegal act.

Blair and many of his ministers went on the offensive to defend such measures. On 22 June 2006, Blair gave the first of a series of speeches entitled 'Our Nation's Future', designed to complement his speeches on international community. He argued that the transformation of crime in an era of globalisation and global terrorism 'raises . . . profoundly disturbing questions about liberty in the modern world' (Blair, 2006e). A little later, he argued that 'it is time to rebalance the decision ['about which human rights prevail'] in favour of the decent, law-abiding majority who play by the rules and think others should too'. He called for four main changes in thinking about crime and justice: new laws are needed; the whole system must be 'clear' and 'tough' on criminals; the offenders' reasons for offending must be targeted, especially in relation to drug addiction; and the criminal justice system must be made to honour its primary role – namely, 'to protect the public by dispensing justice'. Blair was clear about the implications. For example, in relation to anti-social behaviour he argued in one chilling passage:

> We need far earlier intervention with some of these ['hard to reach'] families, who are often socially excluded and socially dysfunctional. That may mean before they offend; and certainly before they want such intervention. But in truth, we can identify such families virtually as their children are born.

We, the state, will use various measures to control you because we know you – who have always acted well in past – will offend in the future. 'Pre-crime' comes to the UK (Dick, 1956).

Reacting to media debate, Blair was emphatic that the most important problems with the criminal justice system come from neither the Human Rights Act nor sentencing policy:

> I am afraid the issue is far more profound: it is the culture of political and legal decision-making that has to change, to take account of the way the world has changed. It is not this or that judicial decision; this or that law. It is a complete change of mindset, an avowed, articulated determination to make protection of the law-abiding public the priority and to measure that not by the theory of the textbook but by the reality of the street and community in which real people live real lives. (Blair, 2006e)

In reality, Blair is asking not merely for a reappraisal of the terms in which the relationship between security and civil liberties are conceived in the UK. He is arguing for them to be reconceived along the definite lines that he himself endorses. There are many arenas in which he seeks this reappraisal, ranging from the hermeneutic context in which legislative proposals are framed and defended in parliament and the ways in which the general public think about crime and security generally, as well as the terms in which political and especially judicial decisions are made. In Rawlsian terms, Blair was attempting to manipulate and homogenise the public political culture, public reason, and the background culture of the civil society (namely, the internally complex citizen body) (Rawls, 1999, pp. 132–8, 152–6).[4] As such, Blair's was a Gramscian hegemonic project, although, remembering his belief in the coincidence of economic interests and moral realities that was highlighted earlier, moral factors play a more integrated role than one would normally expect in such a project (Bieler and Morton, 2004).

Robert Goodin has pointed out that such strategies are often adopted in response to terrorist attacks (Goodin, 2006, ch. 7; the whole book can be read with great profit). The 'war on terror' has been used as a device by which the executives in both the UK and the USA bolster their authority for extraordinary unilateral action at home, under conditions akin to a state of emergency (ibid., pp. 26–9). If justified, this tactic would place significant restraints on the moral legitimacy of civil criticism and active dissent, even by loyal citizens. The quasi-state of emergency is, in this sense, a fiction to which the executive appeals when attempting to manipulate the legislature and the wider public (witness the response of John Reid, the UK's then Home Secretary to attempts to hijack British airliners bound for America in August 2006, Reid, 2006). Yet, such a tactic makes it very difficult indeed to return to normality, not least because the characteristic lack of stable authority and command structures within terrorist organisations such as al-Qaeda means that there is no one with whom to negotiate a ceasefire or surrender: 'the sun will never set on terrorism and the fear it provokes' (Goodin, 2006, p. 28).

In reality, however, Blair's approach was not simply a response to terrorism. His political methods in this regard after 2001 accorded perfectly with the manner in which he transformed the Labour Party into 'New Labour' between 1994 and 1997, and, once elected prime minister in 1997, the manner in which he centralised control of all major political organs in his own hands and those of the Treasury. It is another example of what David Marquand has called 'the decline of the public' (Marquand, 2004). It shows a deep distrust of civil society and of more formalised public structures such as political parties and parliament. It is a profoundly apolitical approach to governmental decision making.

It is this which worried many of us so greatly (Chakrabarti, 2006). In each arena, Blair failed to respect the principle of reciprocity which is central to constitutional democratic government. The latter requires that the reasons appealed to when justifying political and legislative decisions are given weight only to the extent that one's fellow citizens could reasonably accept them as binding imperatives, given their deeper moral and epistemic commitments (see Tyler, 2006). This does not mean that we all have to share the same deeper commitments, because politically and as citizens we concern ourselves only with our shared public principles. These shared public principles are those that shape our collective life as citizens, even though our private, religious or wider moral commitments differ markedly. As obtaining between free and equal persons, our shared public principles possess authority only to the extent that they can be freely endorsed by such persons on the basis of their deeper commitments.

Blair's messianic self-confidence neglects the fact that, as Robert Cox has observed (1999, p. 102), a healthy civil society 'is not just an assemblage of actors, i.e. autonomous social groups. It is also the realm of contesting ideas in which the inter-subjective meanings upon which people's sense of "reality" are based can become transformed and new concepts of the natural order of society can emerge'. As I have argued elsewhere in this volume, it is in the affirmations and struggles with our significant others over our various identities that each of us conceives and revises those identities. As Mouffe observes (2005, p. 20), we are 'always multiple and contradictory subjects, inhabitants of a diversity of communities . . . constructed by a variety of discourses, and precariously and temporarily sutured at the intersection of those subject positions'. Blair's homogenising faith in his morality and the market denies this. It denies also the fact that political decisions are better made when they arise out of a multitude of ongoing debates and the exercise of critical judgement. The latter requires in turn both in the domestic and international arenas 'a full awareness of our own limits, our contradictions, our unevenness, our "mere humanity" – by which, of course, I mean our sense of ourselves on the borderline of difference and change' (Bhabha, 2003, p. 178).

As with Bush's efforts to transform the norms of international society into a neo-conservative paradise, the success of Blair's related 'progressive' project is far from assured. The custodians of the UK's constitutional freedoms have won significant victories, not least the Court of Appeal's ruling that control orders are illegal as they violate the 1998 Human Rights Act. Other countervailing pressures exist, including the UK's membership of the EU and the fact that it has been a signatory of the European Convention on Human Rights (ECHR) for many years. Politically, it would be very difficult to withdraw from these agreements, even in part, especially given initially Blair's and now Brown's desire to be seen as the leader of a civilised nation. (Indeed, both Blair and the then Home Secretary John Reid were careful not to blame the Human Rights Act which incorporates the ECHR into UK law, citing what they claimed to have been poor judicial applications of the act instead.) Moreover, there are significant protests by groups such as Liberty, and other marches and protests against specific measures around the UK as well as in the press and television media. Obviously, it still remains to be seen whether or not the normal modes of politics will be successful in reasserting themselves against the new Brown government and its descendants.

CONCLUSION

There is a further disturbing undertone to Blair's doctrine of international community and all that follows from it. Even though he believes that 'democratic values . . . do not belong to any race, religion or nation, but are universal', he seems to have his own clear understanding of the justification for using force to spread them (Blair, 2006b). Referring during a television interview to his decision to send troops to Iraq in support of the 'war on terror', Blair said (2006a), 'if you have faith about these things then you realise that judgement is made by other people'. Asked by the host to clarify this claim, he continued, 'I mean by other people, by, if you believe in God it's meant by God as well'. Indeed, there are clear similarities between Blair's doctrine of international community and Catholic teachings on international relations (see Pope John XXIII, 1963, parts 2 to 4; also Dearey, 2003, esp. pp. 26–7). (Blair's conversion to Roman Catholicism has been widely anticipated in recent times.) Given his particular justification for the creation of his ideal of international community, however, it seems that even though Blair's God may not be as vengeful as Bush's, He (God) does remain a rather muscular and aggressive deity. Yet, as the collapse of the post-Doha negotiations indicates in the economic realm at least, it is likely that Blair's God will be pushed aside by the holders of economic power. The effects will extend beyond even the consolidation of corporate political power. As Joel Bakan has observed (2005, p. 138),

> Increasingly, we are told, commercial potential is the measure of all value, corporations should be free to exploit anything and anyone for profit, and human beings are creatures of pure self-interest and materialistic desire . . . [I]n a world where anything or anyone can be owned, manipulated, and exploited for profit, everything and everyone will eventually be.

This applies to both international politics and the UK's constitutional culture. Hopefully, those who implement Blair's doctrine, whether under the auspices of the UK government or of the Quartet, will come to recognise their partial but still significant responsibility for the immense miseries that the system causes to the most vulnerable people of the planet and to the UK's political culture. Perhaps it is too much to hope that they will ever really feel guilty about the effects of their policies, even after the inevitable future atrocities.

NOTES

1. I would like to thank Matt Beech, Robert E. Goodin, Justin Morris, Pip Tyler and Richard Woodward for their help in relation to this chapter. None of them bears any responsibility for the use made of this help or for the opinions expressed herein.
2. 'Non-capitalist norms' does not necessarily mean 'anti-capitalist norms', of course. It is simply that they prioritise goals other than profit maximisation.
3. Goodin (2005) provides a useful framework in which to think about such statements.
4. There is insufficient space to contrast Rawls's position with Blair here, although much is brought to light about the latter's deficiencies through such a comparison.

REFERENCES

Bakan, Joel (2005), *The Corporation: The Pathological Pursuit of Profit and Power*, rev. edn, London: Constable.

Bhabha, Homi K. (2003), 'On writing rights', in M.J. Gibney (ed.), *Globalizing Rights: The Oxford Amnesty Lectures 1999*, Oxford: Oxford University Press, pp. 162–83.

Bieler, Andreas and Adam David Morton (2004), 'A critical theory route to hegemony, world order and historical change: neo-Gramscian perspectives in international relations', *Capital and Class*, **82**, 85–113.

Blair, Tony (1999), 'Prime Minister's speech: Doctrine of International Community at the Economic Club, Chicago', 24 April, www.number10.gov.uk/output/Page1297.asp, accessed 17 August 2006.

Blair, Tony (2000), 'Speech by the Prime Minister: Committed to Europe, Reforming Europe – Ghent City Hall, Belgium', 23 February, www.pm.gov.uk/output/Page1510.asp, accessed 17 August 2006.

Blair, Tony (2001a), 'Prime Minister's statement to the House of Commons following the September 11 attacks', 14 September, www.number10.gov.uk/output/Page1598.asp, accessed 1 August 2006.

Blair, Tony (2001b), 'Prime Minister's statement at 10 Downing Street', 25 September, www.number10.gov.uk/output/Page1604.asp, accessed 1 August 2006.

Blair, Tony (2001c), 'Prime Minister's statement to Parliament on the September 11 attacks', 4 October, www.number10.gov.uk/output/Page1606.asp, accessed 1 August 2006.

Blair, Tony (2003), 'Prime Minister's speech to the US Congress', 18 July, www.number10.gov.uk/output/Page4220.asp, accessed 2 August 2006. Subsequently removed from the Number 10 website, but still available as Tony Blair, 'Address to Congress Accepting Congressional Gold Medal' [the title is misleading], 18 July 2003, www.americanrhetoric.com/speeches/tblaircongressionalgoldmedal.htm, accessed 12 December 2006.

Blair, Tony (2006a), Interview on *Parkinson* chat show, recorded 2 March; broadcast 4 March 2006, http://parkinson.tangozebra.com/transcript.phtml?show_id=43, accessed 22 June 2006.

Blair, Tony (2006b), 'Clash about civilisations', 21 March, www.pm.gov.uk/output/Page9224.asp, accessed 2 August 2006.

Blair, Tony (2006c), 'Global alliance for global values', 27 March, www.pm.gov.uk/output/Page9245.asp, accessed 2 August 2006.

Blair, Tony (2006d), 'PM's foreign policy speech – third in a series of three', 26 May, www.pm.gov.uk/output/Page9549.asp, accessed 2 August 2006.

Blair, Tony (2006e), 'Our Nation's Future – Criminal Justice System', 23 June, www.pm.gov.uk/output/Page9737.asp, accessed 4 August 2006.

Blair, Tony (2006f), 'Speech to the Los Angeles World Affairs Council', 1 August, http://pm.gov.uk/output/Page9948.asp, accessed 23 August 2006.

Blair, Tony and Bill Clinton (1997), 'Speech by the Prime Minister and President Clinton', 29 May, www.pm.gov.uk/output/Page1025.asp, accessed 17 August 2006.

Blair, Tony and Meles Zenawi (2005), 'PM's Africa Commission Press Conference', 24 February, www.pm.gov.uk/output/Page7220.asp, accessed 17 August 2006.

Brown, Gordon (2001), 'Globalisation: speech given by the Chancellor, Gordon Brown, at the Press Club Washington', 17 December, www.hm-treasury.gov.uk./newsroom_and_speeches/press/2001/press_146_01.cfm, accessed 17 August 2006.

Brown, Gordon (2004), 'Our Children Are Our Future – Joseph Rowntree Lecture', 8 July, www.hm-treasury.gov.uk./newsroom_and_speeches/press/2004/press_65_04.cfm, accessed 21 August 2006.

Brown, Gordon (2005a), 'International Development in 2005: the challenge and the opportunity', 6 January, www.hm-treasury.gov.uk./newsroom_and_speeches/press/2005/press_03_05.cfm, accessed 17 August 2006.

Brown, Gordon (2005b), 'Speech by the Rt Hon Gordon Brown MP, Chancellor of the Exchequer at a DfID/UNDP seminar – "Words into Action in 2005" Lancaster House, London', 26 January, www.hm-treasury.gov.uk./newsroom_and_speeches/press/2005/press_09_05.cfm, accessed 17 August 2006.

Bush, George W. (2002), 'President Bush Delivers Graduation Speech at West Point', 1 June, www.whitehouse.gov/news/releases/2002/06/print/20020601-3.html, accessed 14 July 2002.

Callinicos, Alex (2001), *Against the Third Way*, Cambridge: Polity.

Carlile of Berriew, Lord (2006), *First Report of the Independent Reviewer Pursuant to Section 14(3) of the Prevention of Terrorism Act 2005)*, 2 February, www. homeoffice.gov.uk/security/terrorism-and-the-law/prevention-of-terrorism/?version=1, accessed 23 August 2006.

Chakrabarti, Shami (2006), 'Liberty calls for sensitivity over censorship', 10 February [Liberty press release], www.liberty-human-rights.org.uk/resources/articles/freedom-of-expression-feb-06.PDF, accessed 23 August 2006.

Chua, Amy (2003), *World on Fire: How Exporting Free-market Democracy Breeds Ethnic Hatred and Global Instability*, London: William Heinemann.

Cox, Robert W. (1999), 'Civil society at the turn of the millennium: prospects for an alternative world order', reprinted in R. Cox with Michael G. Schechter, *The Political Economy of a Plural World: Critical Reflections on Power, Morals and Civilization*, London: Routledge, 2002, pp. 96–117.

Dearey, Paul (2003), 'Catholicism and the Just War tradition: the experience of moral value in warfare', in Paul Robinson (ed.), *Just War in Comparative Perspective*, Aldershot: Ashgate, pp. 24–39.

Dick, Philip K. (1956), 'The Minority Report', reprinted in his *The Minority Report: Volume Four of the Collected Short Stories* (2000), London: Gollancz.

Feffer, John (ed.) (2002a), *Living in Hope: People Challenging Globalization*, London and New York: Zed Books.

Feffer, John (2002b), 'Challenging globalization: an introduction', in Feffer (ed.), pp. 1–21.

GLOBE (Global Legislators Organisation for a Balanced Environment) (2006), 'G8+5 Climate Change Dialogue', 24 February, www.globeinternational.org/home-page.html, accessed 4 August 2006.

Goodin, Robert E. (2005), 'Toward an international rule of law: distinguishing international law-breakers from would-be law-makers', *Journal of Ethics*, **9**, 225–46.

Goodin, Robert E. (2006), *What's Wrong with Terrorism?*, Cambridge: Polity.

Harrison, Graham (ed.) (2005), *Global Encounters: International Political Economy, Development and Globalization*, Basingstoke: Palgrave.

Hegel, Georg W.F. (1821), *Philosophy of Right* (1952), trans. T.M. Knox, London: Oxford University Press.

HM Treasury (2002), *Tackling Poverty: A Global New Deal. A Modern Marshal Plan for the Developing World*, HM Treasury, www.hm-treasury.gov.uk/mediastore/otherfiles/globalnewdeal.PDF, accessed 17 August 2006.

Hochschild, Adam (2006), *King Leopold's Ghost: A Story of Greed, Terror and Heroism*, London: Pan.

Hollingshead, Ian (2006), 'Whatever happened to Blair's Congressional Medal?', *The Guardian*, 20 May, www.guardian.co.uk/comment/story/0,,1779306,00.html, accessed 12 December 2006.

Hollingsworth, J. Rogers and Robert Boyer (1997), 'Coordination of economic actors and social systems of production', in Hollingsworth and Boyer (eds), *Contemporary Capitalism: The Embeddedness of Institutions*, Cambridge: Cambridge University Press, pp. 1–47.

Home Office (2006), 'Terrorism Act 2006', www.homeoffice.gov.uk/security/terrorism-and-the-law/terrorism-act-2006/?view=Standard, accessed 23 August 2006.

Kelly, Ruth (2006), 'Local government and democracy', Secretary of State for Communities and Local Government, at the Local Government Association Conference, 5 July, www.labour.org.uk/index.php?id=news2005&ux_news[id]=rklga&cHash=17536f1a0d, accessed 21 August 2006.

Liberty (2006), 'Press Release: Government told to lift "house arrest" restrictions on control orders', 1 August, www.liberty-human-rights.org.uk/press/2006/government-told-to-stop-house-arrest.shtml, accessed 23 August 2006.

Marquand, David (2004), *Decline of the Public: The Hollowing-out of Citizenship*, Cambridge: Polity.

Marshall, George C. (1947), 'Marshall's Harvard Speech', reprinted in Scott Sullivan (nd), *From War to Wealth: Fifty Years of Innovation*, Paris: Organisation for Economic Cooperation and Development, pp. 14–15.

Mouffe, Chantal (2005), *The Return of the Political*, London: Verso.

Obi, Cyril I. (2000), 'Globalization and local resistance: the case of Shell versus the Ogoni', in Barry K. Gills (ed.), *Globalization and the Politics of Resistance*, Basingstoke: Macmillan, pp. 280–94.

Payne, Anthony (2005), *The Global Politics of Unequal Development*, Basingstoke: Palgrave Macmillan.

Policy Network (2003), 'About Us', www.policy-network.net/php/section.php?sid=1, accessed 8 August 2006.

Pope John XXIII (1963), *Pacem In Terris. Encyclical of Pope John XXIII on Establishing Universal Peace in Truth, Justice, Charity and Liberty April 11, 1963*, especially Part III 'Relations Between States', www.vatican.va/holy_father/john_xxiii/encyclicals/documents/hf_j-xxiii_enc_11041963_pacem_en.html, accessed 24 August 2006.

PMOS (Prime Minister's Official Spokesman) (2005), 'Afternoon press briefing from 8 December 2005: EU Budget', www.pm.gov.uk/output/Page8740.asp, accessed 17 August 2006.

Rawls, John (1999), 'The idea of public reason revisited', in his *The Law of Peoples, and 'The Idea of Public Reason Revisited'*, Cambridge, MA and London: Harvard University Press, pp. 129–80.

Reid, John (2006), 'Security, freedom and the protection of our values', 9 August, www.labour.org.uk/index.php?id=news 2005&ux_news%5Bid%5D= freedomandvalues&cHash=9dba458100, accessed 23 August 2006.

Slaughter, Steven (2005), *Liberty Beyond Neo-Liberalism: A Republican Critique of Liberal Governance in a Globalising Age*, Basingstoke: Palgrave Macmillan.

Stelzer, Irwin (ed.) (2004), *Neo-Conservatism*, London: Atlantic.

Stiglitz, Joseph (2002), *Globalization and Its Discontents*, London: Penguin.

Tyler, Colin (2006), 'Contesting the common good: T.H. Green and contemporary republicanism', in M. Dimova-Cookson and W.J. Mander (eds), *T.H. Green: Ethics, Metaphysics, and Political Philosophy*, Oxford: Clarendon, pp. 262–91.

Tyler, Colin (forthcoming), 'Human welfare and the future of the WTO', in Simon D. Lee and Stephen McBride (eds), *Neo-liberalism, State Power and Global Governance*, New York: Springer Kluwer.

Will, George F. (2004), 'The slow undoing: the assault on, and underestimation of nationality', in Irwin Stelzer (ed.), *Neo-Conservatism*, London: Atlantic, 2004, pp. 127–39.

8. The politics of globalisation and the war on terror

Simon Lee

INTRODUCTION

The politics of globalisation constitutes an ideological battleground. To understand the contemporary war on terror, and the debates that continue to wage about its legitimacy and efficacy, it needs to be placed in context. Building upon Colin Tyler's analysis of citizenship and rights in the previous chapter (Chapter 7), this chapter shows how globalisation has been used as a weapon to justify and legitimise domestic and foreign policy choices which have had major implications for citizenship and communities, both at home and internationally. For example, John Reid, the former Home Secretary in the Blair government, claimed that the terrorist threat posed by the new breed of 'unconstrained' and 'fascist individuals' meant that 'We are probably in the most sustained period of severe threat since the end of World War Two' (Reid, 2006). Reid's thesis was that the international problems now confronting the United Kingdom, not least porous borders, failed states, civil wars and ethnic tensions were part of a chain reaction set off by the end of the Cold War that had made the world a very dangerous place. Against this context, the chapter will illustrate how a moral crusade both to establish liberal democracy as a universal blueprint for governance and individual freedom, and to build political institutions appropriate for an Anglo-American model of global capitalism, has permeated the politics of globalisation since its genesis in the demise of the post-1945 Bretton Woods system of fixed exchange rates and capital controls.

The chapter explores different ideological perspectives on the politics of globalisation to show how the war on terror needs to be understood as the third of four distinctive phases in the politics of globalisation which have shaped international relations and domestic statecraft since the early 1970s. In each of the four phases, the chapter draws upon the politics of Francis Fukuyama to illustrate the dynamic nature of the debate about globalisation, and how the thinking of even the most influential commentators has manifested major and rapid changes, as events have unfolded before them. The common denominator of all four phases has been their domination by the neo-liberal perspective on globalisation. This is not surprising since the neo-liberal orthodoxy emanated from the New Right's reaction to the perceived failure of economic and social policies at home, the threat posed by the 'evil empire' of communism abroad, and the profitable opportunities for entrepreneurship arising from rapid innovations in information and communications technology. Consequently, it is argued that the first phase of globalisation witnessed a rolling forward of the frontiers of global markets on a tide of liberalisation, deregulation and privatisation, that succeeded in bringing about the collapse of communism.

While the collapse of communism was held triumphantly to mark the 'end of history' and the universal triumph of liberal democracy and capitalism, the chapter then demonstrates how, during the 1990s, a second phase emerged in the politics of globalisation that was preoccupied with identifying the appropriate political and market institutions to sustain prosperity and development in the face of increasing global competition. The chapter then argues that the election in November 2000 of President George W. Bush and the 9/11 terrorist attacks on the World Trade Center and the Pentagon ushered in a third phase of the politics of globalisation. Whereas earlier phases had been preoccupied with the globalisation of the movement of capital, goods and services, and their consequences for the role of the state, international competitiveness and living standards, the most salient feature of the third phase of the politics of globalisation has been the war on terror.

This phase has also been marked by a reaffirmation of the sense of moral purpose that had inspired the New Right during the first phase of the politics of globalisation. The chapter identifies the growing debate both within and without the 'coalition of the willing' about the legitimacy and effectiveness of the war on terror, before concluding that the politics of globalisation are now entering a fourth phase. This phase is witnessing an intense battle of ideas between, on the one hand, those who still believe that the war on terror should be fought and can be won by a coalition of states, that on occasions must act unilaterally or bilaterally, and with only limited recourse to the United Nations. Confronting this perspective, on the other hand, are those who point to the mounting evidence that the war on terror is doomed to failure, and who therefore seek greater multilateral cooperation and a restoration of the public domain as a bulwark for citizenship, both at home and abroad.

THE PROJECT FOR THE OLD AMERICAN CENTURY

The war on terror reflects a battle of ideas about how the world should be governed and by whom in the twenty-first century. The dominant liberal perspective on globalisation has envisaged that, with the demise of communism and the increasing isolation of 'rogue' states and regimes, there will be a progressive convergence towards the institutions, norms and values of liberal democracy and open market capitalism as the basis of human civilisation. The origins of this project may be traced to the first phase of the politics of globalisation that began with the eclipse of the Bretton Woods international order during the late 1960s and early 1970s. The existing system of fixed exchange rates and controls on the movement of capital across national borders had been steadily undermined by market innovations, notably the eurocurrency markets. At the same time, US administrations during the 1960s pursued a policy of benign neglect, in relation to maintaining the stability of the dollar in its role as the international reserve currency. The preoccupation of financing urban regeneration at home and the Vietnam war abroad, but without recourse to major tax increases, served only to accentuate the flow of dollars overseas. With the eventual suspension of the convertibility of the dollar in 1971, followed by the drift to floating exchange rates and, most importantly, the decision of the United States to remove controls on the movement of capital, a new global political economy became possible, and with it the possibility of a redefinition of long-held assumptions about the respective roles of the state, market and citizen.

This transition was in turn facilitated by innovations in computer technology, and the recycling of Arabian oil revenues to developing economies through the international banking system. However, the key to the onset of a new politics of globalisation was ideological. Based upon the ideas of Friedrich Hayek and Milton Friedman, and driven politically by Margaret Thatcher in the United Kingdom and Ronald Reagan in the United States, during the late 1970s an ideological assault was launched upon social democratic conceptions of citizenship, and the role of the state and citizen that followed on from such assumptions (King, 1987). According to this agenda, 'In this present crisis, government is not the solution to our problem; government is the problem' (Reagan, 1981). Domestically, the New Right sought to roll back the frontiers of the social democratic Keynesian welfare state, and thereby to reduce the political and moral dependency culture that it held to have been fostered by the extension of state-funded social welfare and citizenship rights. By rolling forward the frontiers of the market as a discovery process for entrepreneurship, innovation, competition and profit, through policies of privatisation, liberalisation and deregulation, citizenship would be reduced to narrower political and civil rights.

The New Right's domestic agenda was encapsulated in the speeches of Margaret Thatcher during the late 1970s. To reverse 'the trend to the Left', and the politics of socialism and collectivism, Thatcher engaged in 'a battle of ideas' to launch 'a new renaissance' of free enterprise and entrepreneurship. She claimed: 'The reaction against Socialism is based on moral considerations as well as economic ones'. A free economy was necessary to restore individual freedom and human dignity, to foster 'a moral society' of freedom of choice, generosity and compassion, and 'not a society where the State is responsible for everything, and no one is responsible for the State'. For Thatcher, Victorian Britain, which had been 'the heyday of free enterprise', had also been 'the era of the rise of selflessness and benefaction'. Through a restoration of self-reliance, free association and responsible citizenship, the free capitalist societies of the Western world would triumph over the collectivist socialist–statist philosophy, in the battle of ideas, because of the ultimate superiority of their economics and moral philosophy (Thatcher, 1977).

The New Right's global ambition was nothing less than the defeat of the one alternative project to global capitalism, namely Soviet communism. This agenda was encapsulated in President Ronald Reagan's 1983 speech before the National Association of Evangelicals. Reagan portrayed global politics in terms of a political and moral struggle between, on the one hand, the God-fearing and freedom-loving democratic forces of the Judeo-Christian tradition, and, on the other hand, the totalitarian and class-war-driven Soviet Union. Reagan cautioned against ignoring 'the facts of history and the aggressive impulses of an evil empire'. The politics of globalisation had engendered a crisis, manifested in military confrontation, but where the real crisis was 'a spiritual one; at root, it is a test of moral will and faith' (Reagan, 1983).

When the Reaganite arms race had helped to economically bankrupt the Soviet Union, and Mikhail Gorbachev's policies of perestroika and glasnost exposed the political and moral bankruptcy of the communist project, the fall of the Berlin Wall was marked by triumphalism, unprecedented since Daniel Bell had forecast the 'End of Ideology' (Bell, 1962). This triumphalism was encapsulated by Francis Fukuyama's thesis of 'The End of History', where he claimed:

> What we may be witnessing is not just the end of the Cold War, or the passing of a particular period of post-war history, but the end of history as such: that is, the end point of ideological evolution and the universalisation of Western liberal democracy as the final form of human government. (Fukuyama, 1989, p. 3)

Despite Fukuyama's triumphalism, it soon became apparent that the collapse of communism had not brought about the end of ideology, and a universal adherence to a common model of liberal democracy and market capitalism would not characterise a new phase of the politics of globalisation.

BUILDING INSTITUTIONS FOR THE MARKET

During the 1990s the politics of globalisation entered a second phase that was shaped by a vigorous ideological battle over two aspects of globalisation. First, there was an intense debate over the nature of the challenge posed to both national prosperity in the industrialised world and to development in the industrialising world by a world characterised by increasingly liberalised and deregulated markets. In the industrialised world, a new wave of literature emerged that sought to define a political economy of globalisation that would sustain international competitiveness (for example, Porter, 1990; Reich, 1991; Tyson, 1992). For his part, Fukuyama abandoned his previous triumphalist perspective, contending instead that future competitiveness would be founded upon the presence or absence of societal trust. This was because wealth-creation was a social process that depended upon cooperation rather than the isolated pursuit of individual self-interest (Fukuyama, 1995).

In the industrialising world, a new neo-liberal political economy of development emerged, based upon privatisation, liberalisation and deregulation, and neatly summarised by John Williamson's thesis of the 'Washington Consensus' (Williamson, 1993). This became the official orthodoxy in the policies advocated by the international financial institutions, as illustrated by the World Bank's 1997 World Development Report, *The State in a Changing World*. Here, the World Bank endorsed the neo-liberal conception of the role of the state which confined politics to the task of building institutions for the market and entrepreneurs (World Bank, 1997). At the same time, a second and parallel debate developed in the politics of globalisation about the nature and implications of globalisation for the role of the state, international institutions, and citizenship at all levels from the local to the global. Three principal perspectives were identified (Held et al., 1999). First, the 'hyperglobalisers', for whom globalisation had rendered national politics largely redundant (Ohmae, 1995). Second, the 'sceptics', for whom the notion of the powerless state had been exaggerated to the point of mythology (Weiss, 1998). Third, the 'transformationalists', for whom globalisation had unleashed an unprecedented period of social change upon states and societies (Giddens, 1998). These three perspectives

were accompanied by a further parallel discourse about the possible transition from government to governance in policy making, at all levels from
the local to the global (Pierre, 2000).

Among the 'transformationalists', this period was also marked by a concerted attempt to reconcile progressive politics with the neo-liberal legacy
of the New Right. A Third Way was fashioned in the United States by the
New Democrats, led by Bill Clinton, and in the UK by New Labour, led by
Tony Blair. It was Clinton who asserted, in his 1998 State of the Union
address:

> We have moved past the sterile debate between those who say government is the
> problem and those who say government is the answer. My fellow Americans, we
> have found a third way. We have the smallest government in 35 years, but a more
> progressive one. We have a smaller government, but a stronger nation. (Clinton,
> 1998)

The fact that Clinton did not publicly embrace the notion of the Third Way
until midway through his second administration is indicative of how mar-
ginal it was to his overall political project. Indeed, in 957 pages of Clinton's
political memoirs, the Third Way received only the most cursory of men-
tions (Clinton, 2004, pp. 381–2, 878–9). By contrast, for Tony Blair the
Third Way was central to a new politics of globalisation that promised
nothing less than the renewal of social democracy itself (Blair, 1998).

The conceit of Third Way thinkers such as Blair and Anthony Giddens
was that they had identified a project of social democratic renewal that
would facilitate national modernisation, but simultaneously reconcile that
political project with the constraints of globalisation. Giddens asserted
that globalisation was 'not only, or even primarily, about economic interdependence, but about the transformation of time and space in our lives'
(Giddens, 1998, p. 30). Blair argued that, in the face of global markets,
global culture, and an unprecedented rate of technological advance, the key
challenge for progressive politics would be to use the state as an enabling
force to create a dynamic knowledge-based economy; a strong civil society
enshrining rights and responsibility; a modern government based on partnership and decentralisation; and 'a foreign policy based on international
co-operation' (Blair, 1998, p. 7).

However, as critics have noted, in Blair's Third Way politics, both 'globalisation' and 'the new global economy' are represented as accomplished
facts rather than partial or uneven tendencies, and 'change' is represented
as the inevitable movement in the direction of globalisation' (Fairclough,
2000, p. viii). Rather than presenting globalisation as a contestable political choice, the Third Way assumed that globalisation was a process that
was 'given and achieved', from which no country, including Britain, would

be immune, and that the neo-liberal model of globalisation was somehow inevitable and irreversible (ibid., pp. 27–8). Despite the onset of major financial crises in Korea, Thailand and Russia, the Third Way failed to question the benefits of globalisation, principally because it had 'no analysis, still less critique, of the modern capitalist system' (ibid., 2000, p. 29).

THE PROJECT FOR THE NEW AMERICAN CENTURY

As part of the foreign policy component of the Third Way, Tony Blair outlined his own new 'doctrine of the international community'. This asserted that, because of the growing interdependence brought about by globalisation, there was now a need for 'new rules of international co-operation and new ways of organising our international institutions'. Blair argued that states should not intervene in the affairs of undemocratic regimes or those 'engaged in barbarous acts' unless they were sure of their case; had exhausted all diplomatic options; could 'sensibly and prudently' undertake military operations; be prepared for a long-term commitment; and could identify the involvement of national interests (Blair, 1999a). Blair's analysis appeared to have been vindicated by the relationship between US foreign policy and the international community during the 1990s. A strategy of cooperation had been manifested in the Oslo Peace Accord between Israel and the Palestinian Liberation Organisation; the NATO intervention in Kosovo; Bill Clinton's high-profile role in the negotiation of the Downing Street Declaration of Principles on the future of Northern Ireland; and the policy of containment of Saddam Hussein, through the US–UK enforcement of a no-fly zone in Iraq, and pre-emptive strikes against Iraq's biological and chemical weapons stocks.

Cooperation among the international community could not guarantee homeland security. In February 1993, a bomb had exploded at the World Trade Center killing six people and wounding many hundreds more. Six of the Middle East terrorists responsible for this act were duly captured and imprisoned. Such acts persuaded certain influential conservative and Republican strategists that domestic security would not be possible for the United States, in the face of a global terrorist threat, unless the Clinton administration abandoned its strategy of threat containment through international cooperation. What was needed instead was a more proactive foreign policy that exploited the United States' huge military advantage as the world's sole remaining superpower to engineer regime change in those states deemed to be sponsoring terrorist networks. During Clinton's second term, the clearest and most unequivocal statement of the need for

American global leadership emanated on the 3 June 1997 from a newly established neo-conservative think-tank, the Project for the New American Century (PFNAC, 1997).

The project sought a restoration of the three principles of the Reagan administration's approach to global strategy, namely 'a military that is strong and ready to meet both present and future challenges; a foreign policy that boldly and purposefully promotes American principles abroad; and national leadership that accepts the United States' global responsibilities' (ibid.). This agenda was based upon the conviction that the history of the twentieth century had demonstrated that American foreign policy should embrace proactive, global leadership in order to deliver peace and security in Europe, Asia and the Middle East, and to avoid the crises that have arisen whenever Washington had failed to exercise its global responsibilities. Most significantly, on 26 January 1998, the PFNAC had written to Bill Clinton arguing that a strategy based upon 'the steadfastness of our coalition partners and upon the co-operation of Saddam Hussein is dangerously inadequate'. As a consequence, this meant that 'the aim of American foreign policy' should become the elimination of 'the possibility that Iraq will be able to use or threaten to use weapons of mass destruction'. This in turn meant regime change for Iraq through the removal of Saddam Hussein (PFNAC, 1998).

With the election of George W. Bush in November 2000, and the terrorist attacks on the World Trade Center and the Pentagon on 11 September 2001, a third phase in the politics of globalisation became possible, in which the objectives of the project became more visible. In September 2002, *The National Security Strategy of the United States of America* confirmed that the Bush administration's vision for the world would be based upon a 'single sustainable model for national success: freedom, democracy, and free enterprise' (USGOV, 2002, p. iii). However, this agenda would not be entrusted to multilateral institutions, but would instead be augmented by 'Coalitions of the willing' (ibid., p. v). Within six months, this doctrine was put into practice on 20 March 2003 with the launch of 'Operation *Iraqi Freedom*', the invasion of Iraq by a 'coalition of the willing' led by US and British armed forces.

However, from the very outset, there was a huge public unease and vehement protest in the UK about the war on terror and the British role in it. The justification given to the British people for the war given by Tony Blair to Westminster on the 18 March 2003 was that:

> The United Kingdom must uphold the authority of the United Nations as set out in Resolution 1441 and many Resolutions preceding it, and therefore supports the decision of Her Majesty's Government that the United Kingdom

should use all means necessary to ensure the disarmament of Iraq's weapons of mass destruction. (Blair, 2003, p. 760)

There were no weapons of mass destruction (WMD). Public anger increased when it was revealed that the assertion made in the Blair government's September 2002 'dossier' on Iraqi WMD, about the ability of the Iraqi military to deploy chemical and biological weapons within 45 minutes, had actually been referring to battlefield chemical weapons, rather than long-range missiles (Sands, 2005, p. 186). Much of the intelligence upon which the dossier was based, and which Blair himself described as 'extensive, detailed, and authoritative' (BBC, 2005, p. 8), was so discredited that it was later withdrawn.

Subsequently, a leaked 10 Downing Street memorandum from Matthew Rycroft, an aide to David Manning, the Prime Minister's foreign policy adviser, revealed that as early as 23 July 2002, the Bush administration had decided to launch an invasion of Iraq. UN Resolution 1441 had not been unanimously backed by the UN Security Council until 8 November 2002. In effect, the Bush administration had decided unilaterally to launch a preemptive strike against Saddam Hussein, and Tony Blair had unilaterally told Bush 'I'm with you' (Woodward, 2004, p. 178), committing both his government and armed forces to war months in advance of any Cabinet decision or parliamentary vote. Moreover, the widely held belief that the war on terror was being conducted upon the flimsiest of legal bases was confirmed when it emerged that Lord Goldsmith, the Attorney General and the British government's highest-ranking legal adviser, had seemingly changed his mind at the last minute about the legality of attacking Iraq without a second UN resolution. On 7 March 2003, Goldsmith had warned Blair that only a 'reasonable case' could be advanced for attacking Iraq on the basis of Resolution 1441. However, on the 17 March, Goldsmith then adamantly told both the Cabinet and Parliament that a material breach of UN Resolution 687 would revive the authority to use force against Iraq under Resolution 678 (Sands, 2005, p. 265).

ONWARD CHRISTIAN SOLDIERS

Disregarding its dubious legality in international law, Bush and Blair have shared a common belief that the war on terror is about the global exercise of moral purpose. Theirs is 'both a battle of arms and a battle of ideas' (USGOV, 2006, p. 9). This project is not just about the universalisation of the Anglo-American concept of liberal democracy. It is also founded upon a common Christian conviction. The moral underpinning and the role played by Christian values in Bush's agenda was long ago confirmed in his July 1999 'Duty of Hope' speech, when he argued that prosperity must have a purpose, namely to include everyone in a different form of affluence, that is, the wealth of 'justice and compassion and family love and moral courage' (Bush, 1999). However, the role of Christianity in Blair's decision to support the war on terror was not definitively confirmed until 4 March 2006. During a television interview, Blair confessed that his decision to go to war in Iraq would be judged, not only by other people and history, but also by God (BBC, 2006a). That sense of moral purpose was vitally expressed in a key qualification to Blair's 'doctrine of international community', when he had stated, 'The international community has a responsibility to act . . . but when the international community agrees certain objectives and then fails to implement them, those who can act, must' (Blair, 1999b).

The moral certainty that has arisen from these convictions has enabled Blair and Bush to advance onwards as Christian soldiers on the basis of a world whose politics may be divided between good and evil. For Bush, this moral crusade is a war that must be fought 'on a global scale' and in which 'there is no middle ground'. On one side stand the democratic free nations that offer 'the hope of freedom' to failed states such as those of Iraq and Afghanistan. Opposing those free nations are the terrorists who have 'nothing positive to offer' other than barbarity and brutality. For Bush, the war on terror constitutes the third ideological war between freedom and evil. The first war had been fought between free nations and 'the ideology of fascism' during the Second World War. The second ideological or Cold War had seen freedom defeat the ideology of communism.

The war on terror is simply the third ideological war, where freedom is confronting 'the followers of a murderous ideology, and like the hate-filled ideologies that came before it, the darkness of terror will be defeated', according to Bush's prediction (Bush, 2005). Therefore, 'victory in Iraq is a vital US interest' because 'The war on terrorism is the defining challenge of our generation'. Iraq must be acknowledged as 'the central front in our war on terror'. The United States and its Iraqi partners cannot afford to cede ground to terrorists or their 'perverse ideology' because to do so would be to 'threaten the world's economy and America's security, growth, and prosperity, for decades to come'. Indeed, failure in Iraq would mean not only a vindication of 'their tactics of beheadings, suicide bombings, and ruthless intimidation of civilians', but also the destabilisation of the Middle East, and a clearing of the way for further terrorist attacks at home (NSC, 2005, p. 4).

For his part, Blair's thesis on the politics of globalisation and the war on terror continues to be based upon three key tenets. First, the definitive characteristic of the contemporary world is its interdependence. Second, 'whereas the economics of globalisation are well matured, the politics of globalisation are not', and therefore urgent action is necessary. Third, unless 'a common global policy based on common values' is articulated, there is a risk of chaos 'threatening our stability, economic and political, through letting extremism, conflict or injustice go unchecked'. Consequently, this scenario demands 'a policy of engagement not isolation; and one that is active not reactive'. Global terrorism can be defeated through 'a broad global alliance to achieve our common goals', but that this in turn requires 'radical reform' of international institutions to render them 'capable of implementing such an agenda, in a strong and effective multilateral way' (Blair, 2006a).

The enemy is the 'revolting terrorist barbarity' of 'radical Islam', be it practised in Iraq, Afghanistan, Chechnya, Kashmir, 'or half a dozen other troublespots', including Algeria. The world is now divided between, on the one hand, 'an arc of extremism', that now stretches across the Middle East to touch 'with increasing definition, countries far outside that region' that must be met, on the other hand, with 'an alliance of moderation' (Blair, 2006b). For Blair, Islamic extremism is 'a posture of weakness, defeatism and most of all, deeply insulting to every Muslim who believes in freedom, i.e. the majority'. It is a global ideology whose 'attitude to America is absurd'; whose concept of governance is 'pre-feudal'; whose position of women and other faiths is 'reactionary and regressive'; and whose 'extremist view of Islam is not just theologically backward but completely contrary to the spirit and teaching of the Koran' (Blair, 2006a). Iraq and Afghanistan constitute 'existential battles for Reactionary Islam' where the objective is not just regime change but 'values change'. The battle must be won to give 'Moderate Mainstream Islam' the chance to modernise Muslim countries rather than retreat into 'a semi-feudal religious oligarchy' (Blair, 2006b). This politics of globalisation 'is not a clash between civilisations. It is a clash about civilisations. It is the age-old battle between progress and reaction'. Indeed, 'This is, ultimately, a battle about modernity' (Blair, 2006a).

Blair has argued that global citizenship will only be possible through the construction of 'a global alliance for these global values' (Blair, 2006c), and action in turn through that alliance to pursue those global values of 'liberty, democracy, tolerance, justice' (Blair, 2006d). But the time to have assembled that alliance was in the immediate aftermath of 9/11, when world opinion was so united in its condemnation of the terrorist attacks on the World Trade Center and the Pentagon. If Blair had wanted 'an active foreign policy of engagement not isolation' (Blair, 2006c), it should have been constructed through multilateral cooperation at the United Nations, in parallel with concerted action through the WTO, the IMF and the World Bank. Blair has forgotten the lesson of his own strategy in Northern Ireland. Preventive detention and aggressive military action had served as the best spur to recruitment for the paramilitaries. The rapid cessation of hostilities, decommissioning of paramilitary weapons, and the de-militarisation of Ulster by the British Army would not have been possible had the British government decided to pursue its own unilateral strategy, or acted only in bilateral concert with the Irish government. Peace and stability has been possible because a much broader strategy has been implemented, encompassing all constitutional political parties, paramilitary organisations and external parties, notably a high-profile role for the Clinton administration, led by the former President himself. Instead of standing shoulder to shoulder with a neo-conservative Bush administration, Blair could have chosen to advocate a consistently multilateral approach to global governance, and set his face firmly against pre-emption and aggressive unilateralism. Regrettably, he chose a different politics of globalisation that is based upon the neo-conservative 'war on terror'.

A RENAISSANCE OF MULTILATERALISM?

The admission by Blair that there must be a commitment to 'a complete renaissance of our strategy' (Blair, 2006b) amounts to a not so tacit admission that the previous strategy for winning the war on terrorism has failed. Uncertainty about the legitimacy and effectiveness of the war on terror has been reflected in a vigorous debate among prominent conservative strategists. It is especially notable that one of the PFANAC's early supporters, Francis Fukuyama, has disengaged from the neo-conservative project. He has, however, subsequently become embroiled in a bitter ideological debate with Charles Krauthammer over the war in Iraq and the prospects for successful nation-building. Fukuyama's scepticism has been matched only by Krauthammer's neo-conservative certainty that the invasion was both necessary and legitimate.

Krauthammer has argued that the Bush/Blair strategy of what he has termed 'democratic globalism' has been 'too ambitious and too idealistic'. The universalism of its 'world-wide crusade would overstretch our resources, exhaust our morale and distract us from our central challenge', which for Krauthammer is the Arab/Islamic radicalism stretching from North Africa to Afghanistan. His alternative of 'democratic realism' proposes a return to Cold War strategy, in that it 'is "targeted, focused and limited"', and 'intervenes not everywhere that freedom is threatened but only where it counts' (Krauthammer, 2004, pp. 16–17). Krauthammer believes that the war in Iraq 'was and is' central to the war against radical Islam (ibid., p. 22). Before 9/11, the United States could afford to wait passively for the Arabs to achieve the 'democratization, modernization and pacification' that had previously been achieved in Europe, East Asia and the Americas, with the assistance of American (often military) intervention. His thesis now is that 'After 9/11 we no longer have the luxury of time' (ibid., p. 24).

Fukuyama has contested Krauthammer's 'democratic realism', as the appropriate ideological basis for American foreign policy and a new politics of globalisation, by suggesting that it is 'disconnected from reality' (Fukuyama, 2004, p. 58). Fukuyama has pointed to seven reasons why 'the Iraq War – the archetypal application of American unipolarity' has failed. First, the failure to discover weapons of mass destruction in Iraq. Second, 'the virulent and steadily mounting anti-Americanism throughout the Middle East'. Third, the growing insurgency in Iraq. Fourth, the failure of a strong democratic leadership to emerge in Iraq. Fifth, the huge financial and growing human cost of the Iraq war. Sixth, the failure to use the war to facilitate progress on the Israeli–Palestinian front. Finally, the general failure of the United States' fellow democratic allies 'to fall in line and legitimate American actions *ex post*' (ibid., p. 58). Fukuyama's thesis is that the war on terror is 'a classic counter-insurgency war, except that it is one being played out on a global scale'. This war necessitates 'a tricky mixture of precisely targeted force, political judgement and extremely good intelligence: a combination of carrots and sticks'. Unfortunately, before launching the war in Iraq, the United States failed to undertake the necessary diplomacy and coalition-building, and was unrealistic about its capacity to undertake nation-building and social engineering 'in parts of the world it does not understand very well' (ibid., pp. 66–7).

Krauthammer has responded by reaffirming that, 'My approach to Islamism is identical to the muscular approach I consistently advocated against our previous global challenge, Soviet communism' (Krauthammer, 2005a, p. 9). Furthermore, Krauthammer has contended that there has been a 'neo-conservative convergence' in American foreign policy which has seen neo-conservatism move from its former status as 'a position of dissidence, which it occupied during the first Bush administration and the Clinton years, to governance'. The ultimate proof of its maturity, and that 'it is no longer tethered to its own ideological history and paternity', is that the current practitioners of democratic realism are Bush himself, Dick Cheney, Condoleeza Rice and Donald Rumsfeld, who 'have no history in the movement, and before 9/11 had little affinity to or affiliation with it' (Krauthammer, 2005b, pp. 22, 26). Thus, one possible course for the fourth phase of the politics of globalisation is to strengthen and deepen the ideology of neo-conservatism, and to reaffirm the war on terror in accordance with the March 2006 National Security Strategy (USGOV, 2006).

There is an urgent need for an alternative. There is overwhelming evidence that the war on terror is failing. In a leaked memo, the outgoing British ambassador to Iraq, William Patey, has warned that 'The prospect of a low intensity civil war and a de facto division of Iraq is probably more likely at this stage than a successful and substantial transition to a stable democracy' (BBC, 2006b). This analysis has been affirmed in evidence to the US Senate given by General John Abizaid, the head of US Central Command in Iraq. When asked to comment on Patey's memo, Abizaid stated, 'I believe that the sectarian violence is probably as bad as I've seen it in Baghdad in particular, and that if not stopped, it is possible that Iraq could move toward civil war'. This analysis in turn was supported by General Peter Pace, the chairman of the US Joint Chiefs of Staff, who concurred that 'we do have the possibility of that devolving into civil war' (Borger et al., 2006).

Fukuyama has now concluded that 'neo-conservatism, as both a political symbol and a body of thought, has evolved into something that I can no longer support' (Fukuyama, 2006, p. ix). He has noted how the Bush administration created the Department of Homeland Security, passed the Patriot Act, invaded Afghanistan, proclaimed 'a new strategic doctrine of pre-emptive action – actually, a doctrine of preventive war – that would take the fight to the enemy', and then invaded Iraq to depose Saddam Hussein (ibid., pp. 1–2). However, the failures of the approach which he initially supported are now manifest, for in anticipating 'a quick and relatively painless transition to a post-Saddam Iraq', Fukuyama asserts that the Bush administration 'gave little thought to the requirements for post-conflict reconstruction and was surprised to find the United States fighting a prolonged insurgency' (ibid., p. 3).

Fukuyama claims that the three major errors of the Bush Doctrine have been 'errors of prudential judgement or policy implementation, rather than reflections of underlying principles'. First, there was an error in threat assessment. After September 11, the Bush administration justified its strategy of 'preventive war' in terms of a mischaracterisation of the threat posed by WMD and radical Islam. Second, there was a failure by the administration to anticipate 'the virulently negative global reaction to its exercise of "benevolent hegemony"' and the wider 'strong undertow of anti-Americanism' that was enflamed by the 'seemingly contemptuous brush-off of most forms of international co-operation'. Third, there was a further failure 'to anticipate the requirements for pacifying and reconstructing Iraq', compounded by the administration's 'wildly over-optimistic' assessment of 'the ease with which large-scale social engineering could be accomplished not just in Iraq but in the Middle East as a whole' (ibid., pp. 5–7).

To redefine American foreign policy, and to move beyond the Bush administration's legacy, Fukuyama has advocated what he has termed 'realistic Wilsonianism'. This departs from classical realism, but does not amount to a complete abandonment of neo-conservativism, because Fukuyama's latest position is premised upon twin neo-conservative tenets. First, realistic Wilsonianism seeks to concern both American foreign policy and the international community 'with what goes on *inside* other countries, not just their external behaviour' (original emphasis). Second, it assumes that the exercise of 'power – specifically American power – is often necessary to bring about moral purposes'. Fukuyama's contention is that, before the invasion of Iraq and the project to affect regime change, neo-conservatives forgot that 'ambitious social engineering is very difficult and ought always to be approached with care and humility'. Fukuyama's new doctrine is therefore denoted as 'realistic Wilsonianism', because it seeks to restore to American foreign policy that necessary care and humility, and to better match 'means to ends in dealing with other societies' (ibid., p. x).

However, it should not be thought that Fukuyama's 'realistic Wilsonianism' amounts to an advocacy of global governance in general, or a greater role for the United Nations in particular. On the contrary, while he claims his approach differs from both neo-conservatism and Jacksonian nationalism, because 'it takes international institutions seriously', Fukuyama is adamant both that national sovereignty should not be replaced with 'unaccountable international organizations', and that 'the United Nations is not now nor will it ever become an effective, legitimate seat of global governance'. What Fukuyama now advocates is 'an agenda of multiple multilateralisms appropriate to the real, existing world of globalization' (ibid., pp. 10–11).

This will require nothing less than 'a new team and new policies' (ibid., p. 183). The United States must now promote 'both political and economic development, and it should care about what happens inside states around the world'. This in turn can only be accomplished 'by focusing primarily on good governance, political accountability, democracy, and strong institutions' (ibid., p. 185). At the same time, just as unchecked power can be corrupting domestically, there must equally be checks and balances on the exercise of power on the international stage. This is because 'The hegemon has to be not just well-intentioned but also prudent and smart in its exercise of power' (ibid., p. 193).

Given its previous evolution, it is to be hoped that Fukuyama's thought will evolve through one further phase. If there is to be any prospect that lasting homeland security will be sustained not only for the United States but also for Israel, Iraq and Afghanistan, then there must be not just a refinement, but an actual abandonment of neo-conservatism. There is an urgent need for a renewal of the public realm of international cooperation through multilateral institutions in order to secure global public goods, and a rejection of a worldview in which the only superpower has an effective veto over how the world is ordered. As Will Hutton has contended, globalisation and global governance should no longer be based upon the principle that 'the international order should privilege American autonomy of action and its capacity to act unilaterally, both as a matter of self-interest and as a matter of conservative ideology'. This is because 'The lesson of the last decade, a warning for the twenty-first century' is that 'Security, prosperity and justice are global public goods'. These goods 'cannot and should not be provided as any one country dictates, or as a by-product of what it considers its interests' (Hutton, 2002, p. 9).

HOMELAND INSECURITY AND THE WAR ON TERROR

The consequences for the United Kingdom's citizens of the Blair government's 'shoulder-to-shoulder' support for the Bush administration and its war on terror have been very damaging on a number of fronts. Rather than enhancing homeland security, the war on terror has materially contributed to homeland insecurity in the United Kingdom. This was especially so on 7 July 2005 when 52 people were killed in the terrorist bombings on London's transport system, and on 10 August 2006, when 24 people were arrested in England on suspicion of plotting to blow up passenger aircraft departing UK airports for destinations in the United States. It is extremely difficult to guarantee homeland security to a population of 60 million people, when there are 30.8 million visits to the UK annually by overseas residents (ONS, 2006), and when terrorist bombers are themselves likely to be UK citizens. In those circumstances, winning the hearts and minds of potential terrorist recruits at home and abroad has assumed a particular significance. There is increasing evidence that the war on terror has been losing those hearts and minds.

Parliamentary select committee scrutiny has identified major flaws in the Blair government's role in the war on terror. For example, the House of Commons Foreign Affairs Committee has concluded that 'despite a number of successes targeting the leadership and infrastructure of al Qaeda, the danger of international terrorism, whether from al Qaeda or other related groups, has not diminished and may well have increased'. Despite Blair's repeated denials of a link between British foreign policy and the London bombings, the Committee has found that 'the situation in Iraq has provided both a powerful source of propaganda for Islamic extremists and also a crucial training ground for international terrorists'. At the same time, the continuing existence of Guantánamo Bay and 'detentions without either national or international authority work against British as well as US interests and hinder the effective pursuit of the "was against terrorism"'. Indeed, the moral authority of the US and the UK has been further undermined by the 'possible complicity' of the British government in the 'possible use of rendition to countries where torture can take place' (HCFAC, 2006, p. 3).

Parliamentary scrutiny has concluded that 'there has been a worrying deterioration in the security situation in Afghanistan, and that there are signs that the tactics that have brought such devastation to Iraq are being replicated in Afghanistan' (ibid., p. 10). The commitment of significant numbers of troops in the southern provinces of both Iraq and Afghanistan has left the UK's armed forces dangerously overstretched. The House of Commons Defence Committee has expressed its concerns about the deterioration of the security situation in southeastern Iraq and its implications for UK forces. British troops are vulnerable because of the lack of armour on their Snatch Land Rover patrol vehicles, the shortage of helicopters, and the extreme temperatures and long hours to which they have been exposed (HCDC, 2006, p. 3).

The consequences for civil liberties and human rights in the UK have been equally damaging. Both the Bush administration and the Blair government appear to have forgotten that theirs is not only a war *against* terror but also a war *for* liberal democracy, citizenship and human rights. In relation to detention powers, the House of Commons Home Affairs Committee has failed to identify any evidence to suggest that the maximum of 90 days pre-charge detention sought by the Blair government is 'essential, rather than useful' (HCHAC, 2006, p. 4). Moreover, the government had experienced difficulty in securing the passage of its Terrorism Bill largely because of the speed with which the legislation was presented to Parliament, and the failure of the Home Office to examine the police arguments for extended detention (ibid., p. 47). Rather than enhancing homeland security, the passage of the legislation had been 'divisive and did not increase public trust in the police or the Government' (ibid., p. 53). The then Home Secretary, Charles Clarke, had stated that he found the case advanced by the police for greater preventive detention 'compelling', but the Committee criticised Clarke's 'instinctive judgement'. Such a major issue, with 'significant human rights implications', should have been based upon evidence-based analysis (ibid., p. 13).

On 22 July 2005, an innocent Brazilian, Jean Charles de Menezes, was shot dead by anti-terrorism officers from the Metropolitan Police's CO19 specialist firearms team on the London Underground, because he was mistakenly thought to be a suicide bomber who would blow up the train he had boarded. However, one year after de Menezes's death, the Crown Prosecution Service announced that, while the police had made errors, none of the officers concerned would be prosecuted. In a similar vein, on 2 June 2006, a force of 250 police officers had mounted a counter-terrorist operation against two houses in Forest Gate, East London, during which a man, against whom no terrorist charges were to be brought, was shot with a police firearm.

The Independent Police Complaints Commission concluded in its investigation of the shooting of Muhammad Abdulkahar that the officer who had fired the shot 'had committed no criminal or disciplinary offence', and there was 'no evidence of intent or recklessness'. Consequently, a public prosecution would not be brought against the officer (IPCC, 2006, pp. 5–6). The failure to mount public prosecutions following the shooting of two men innocent of being terrorists has weakened public faith in the police, and been detrimental to community relations, at a time when the police and security services have actively sought the assistance of multicultural communities in the fight against terrorism. The British state cannot expect its citizens to believe in the rule of law, both at home and internationally, if those charged with its implementation are seen to be beyond its sanctions.

The war on terror has been fought upon the basis of the occupation of the moral high ground by the Bush administration and the Blair government, but there is clear evidence that hearts and minds are being lost in increasing numbers. When George W. Bush first took office, he enjoyed a net approval rating of more than 20 per cent, with his personal approval rating never falling below 50 per cent. In the immediate aftermath of 9/11, that net approval rating soared to 84 per cent, as Bush's personal approval rating rose to 90 per cent (with only 6 per cent disapproving). In March 2003, following the invasion of Iraq, Bush saw his net approval rating rising again to 45–46 per cent (71 per cent approving and only 25–26 per cent disapproving) (CNN, 2006, p. 2).

With mounting American casualties in the face of the insurgency in Iraq, Bush's net approval rating has evaporated. Indeed, since the fourth anniversary of the terrorist attacks on the World Trade Center and the Pentagon, Bush has experienced a consistently high level of public disapproval in opinion polls that have assessed the President's overall job rating. With the exception of one single rogue poll in December 2005, which gave Bush a net 3 per cent approval rating, every opinion poll has registered public disapproval. A Gallup poll for USA Today, undertaken between 5 and 7 July 2006, recorded a net 34 per cent disapproval rating (with 31 per cent approving and 65 per cent disapproving). Indeed, throughout 2006 the

President's best performance has been a net disapproval rating of 9 per cent (Polling Report.com, 2006). Public scepticism about the efficacy of the war on terror has been further reflected in a CBS/New York Times poll, where 60 per cent of respondents indicated that they did not think Bush was respected by world leaders. Only 27 per cent thought that the United States was winning the war in Iraq, with no fewer than 58 per cent regarding the situation as a stalemate. Most intriguingly, 58 per cent thought that solving conflicts between Israel and other Middle East nations was not America's responsibility, with 59 per cent thinking that such crises should be solved by the United Nations or other countries (CBS, 2006).

Public opinion has been equally unfavourable for Tony Blair. In June 2006, the Labour Party's opinion poll rating recorded its worst performance since June 1987. Labour's support had fallen to only 32 per cent, compared to the Conservative Party's 37 per cent (Wintour, 2006). This followed the June 2005 General Election which saw the Blair government returned to office for an unprecedented third time, but with only 35.2 per cent of the votes cast and the support of only 22 per cent of the electorate. For the United Kingdom, the war on terror has become a test of the viability of its progress towards the creation of a harmonious multicultural society. The Blair government continued to propose further domestic terrorist legislation to redefine the relationship between the citizen and the state. However, as a string of all-party select committee reports had demonstrated, and as Blair's own Muslim MPs had urged (BBC, 2006c), what was needed instead is a wholesale review of the Blair government's foreign policy goals, and in particular its slavish support for the war on terror. There are other alternatives when engaging with the politics of globalisation, notably the principles of Blair's original April 1999 'doctrine of international community'. These should be urgently revisited.

CONCLUSION

The war on terror is being lost. Iraq has become 'a self-fulfilling prophecy' and a replacement for Afghanistan as 'a magnet, training ground, and operational base for jihadist terrorists, with plenty of American targets to shoot at' (Fukuyama, 2006, p. 181). Despite its unrivalled resources of hard power, America's armed forces are once again bogged down and overstretched in 'a long-term guerilla war' (ibid., pp. 181–2). Hearts and minds among Islamic nations and communities have been turned against the project of universal human rights and political freedoms, based upon a particular Anglo-American conception of liberal democracy and market capitalism.

This has occurred not least because Tony Blair did not follow the five major considerations of his own 'doctrine of the international community' before supporting the invasion of Iraq. On the available evidence at the time, he could not be sure of the existence of WMD. Not all diplomatic options, notably the return of UN inspectors to Iraq, had been exhausted. There were no military operations that could be sensibly and prudently undertaken, because they were bound to elicit a terrorist backlash. The 'coalition of the willing' had not prepared for the long term. There was no British national interest involved. By supporting the war on terror, Blair made London and England a target for terrorist reprisals. Moreover, Blair's own reward for his loyalty to the Bush administration's moral crusade has been personal and political humiliation.

As an overheard conversation between Bush and Blair at the July 2006 G8 Summit in St Peterburg revealed, Blair now occupied a subservient role in the conduct of the politics of globalisation. After greeting him with the derisory 'Yo, Blair', Bush dismissed Blair's offer to act as an intermediary in the Middle East, entrusting the role to his Secretary of State, Condoleeza Rice (McSmith and Castle, 2006). The myth of the 'special relationship' had been most cruelly exposed.

Ironically, Blair's own analysis of globalisation remains a very persuasive one. The thesis that 'Globalisation begets interdependence. Interdependence begets the necessity of a common value system to make it work' (Blair, 2006d) is one with which many concur. Equally, his insistence that 'it's the system itself that is at fault . . . the structures of 1946 trying to meet the challenges of 2006' (ibid.) is a widely held critique of the institutions and processes of global governance. It is, however, an agenda that has been advanced almost five years too late to be credible. Between 9/11 and its fifth anniversary, the politics of globalisation have been irrevocably affected by the Bush administration-led war on terror, with its underpinning principles of pre-emption and aggressive unilateralism. Whether the politics of globalisation can now enter a new fourth phase, defined by a renaissance in global citizenship, remains highly improbable because of the events that have shaped the moral crusade that is the war on terror.

REFERENCES

BBC (2005), 'Iraq, Tony and the Truth', *Panorama Transcript Text*, London: British Broadcasting Corporation, 20 March.
BBC (2006a), 'In full: PM on Iraq war judgement', *BBC News*, 4 March.
BBC (2006b), 'Civil war warning for Blair', *BBC News*, 3 August.
BBC (2006c), 'Full Text: Muslims' Groups' Letter', *BBC News*, 12 August.

Bell, D. (1962), *The End of Ideology: On the Exhaustion of Political Ideas in the Fifties*, New York: Free Press.

Blair, T. (1998), *The Third Way: New Politics for the New Century*, London: Fabian Society.

Blair, T. (1999a), 'The Doctrine of International Community', Speech to the Chicago Economic Club, 22 April.

Blair, T. (1999b), 'Facing the Modern Challenge: The Third Way in Britain and South Africa', Speech, Cape Town, 8 January.

Blair, T. (2003), 'Iraq', *Hansard* (Official Record of the British Parliament), London, 18 March, cc.760–64.

Blair, T. (2006a), 'Clash about Civilisations', Speech, London, 21 March.

Blair, T. (2006b), Speech to the Los Angeles World Affairs Council, 1 August.

Blair, T. (2006c), 'Global Alliance for Global Values', Speech to the Parliament of Australia, Canberra, 27 March.

Blair, T. (2006d), 'We must modernise institutions to meet challenges', Speech at Georgetown University, Washington, DC, 26 May.

Borger, J., A. MacAskill and R. Norton-Taylor (2006), 'Top US generals and British diplomat warn Iraq could slide into civil war', *The Guardian*, 4 August, www.guardian.co.uk/Iraq/Storyio,,1837088,00.html,

Bush, G.W. (1999), 'Duty of hope', Speech, Indianapolis, IN, 22 July.

Bush, G.W. (2005), 'President Addresses Military Families, Discusses War on Terror', Idaho Centre, Nampa, ID Washington, DC: Office of the Press Secretary, 24 August, www.whitehouse.gov/news/releases/2005/08/print/20050824.html, accessed 7 August 2006.

CBS (2006), 'Poll: World Doesn't Respect Bush', *CBS News Polls*, 10 August, www.cbsnews.com/stories/2006/07/26/opinion/polls/main183662.shtml, accessed 10 August 2006.

Clinton, W. (1998), 'The State of the Union', Washington, DC, 27 January, www.clinton4.nara.gov/textonly/WH/SoTu98/address.html,

Clinton, W. (2004), *My Life*, London: Hutchinson.

CNN (2006), *CNN/USA Today/Gallup Trends*, Washington, DC: CNN, 21–23 April.

Fairclough, N. (2000), *New Labour, New Language?*, London: Routledge.

Fukuyama, F. (1989), 'The end of history', *The National Interest*, Summer, 3–18.

Fukuyama, F. (1995), *Tryst: The Social Virtues and the Creation of Prosperity*, London: Hamish Hamilton.

Fukuyama, F. (2004), 'The neoconservative moment', *The National Interest*, Summer, 57–68.

Fukuyama, F. (2006), *After the Neocons: America at the Crossroads*, London: Profile Books.

Giddens, A. (1998), *The Third Way: The Renewal of Social Democracy*, Cambridge: Polity.

HCDC (2006), *UK Operations in Iraq*, Thirteenth Report of the House of Commons Defence Committee, Session 2005–06, HC.1241, London: The Stationery Office.

HCFAC (2006), *Foreign Policy Aspects of the War Against Terrorism*, Fourth Report of the House of Commons Foreign Affairs Committee, Session 2005–06, HC.573, London: The Stationery Office.

HCHAC (2006), *Terrorism Detention Powers*, Fourth Report of the House of Commons Home Affairs Committee, Session 2005–06, Vol. 1, HC.910-I, London: The Stationery Office.

Held, D., A. McGrew, D. Goldblatt and J. Perraton (eds) (1999), *Global Transformation: Politics, Economics and Culture*, Cambridge: Polity.

Hutton, W. (2002), *The World We're In*, London: Little Brown.

IPCC (2006), *IPCC Independent Investigation into the Shooting of Muhammad Abdulkahar in 46 Lansdown Road, Forest Gate on Friday 2 June 2006*, London: Independent Police Complaints Commission.

King, D. (1987), *The New Right: Politics, Market and Citizenship*, London: Macmillan Education.

Krauthammer, C. (2004), 'In defense of democratic realism', *The National Interest*, Fall, 15–25.

Krauthammer, C. (2005a), 'Letters: Krauthammer responds', *The National Interest*, Spring, 9–11.

Krauthammer, C. (2005b), 'The neoconservative convergence', *The National Interest*, Summer, 21–6.

McSmith, A. and S. Castle (2006), ' "Private" chat heard by the world ends a disastrous summit for Blair', *The Independent*, 18 July, www.independent.co.uk/world/politics/article1183389.cce, accessed 17 April 2007.

National Security Council (NSC) (2005), *National Strategy for Victory in Iraq*, Washington, DC: National Security Council.

Ohmae, K. (1995), *The End of the Nation State: The Rise of Regional Economies*, London: Harper Collins.

ONS (2006), 'Travel and Tourism: Visits to the UK from overseas up 5%', *News Release*, 9 August, www.statistics.gov.uk/cci/nugget.asp?id=352, accessed 11 August 2006.

PFANAC (1997), *Statement of Principles*, Washington, DC: Project for the New American Century, 3 June.

PFANAC (1998), 'Letter to the President, 26 January', Washington, DC: Project for the New American Century.

Pierre, J. (ed.) (2000), *Debating Governance: Authority, Steering and Democracy*, Oxford: Oxford University Press.

Polling Report.com (2006), 'President Bush-Overall Job Rating', www.pollingreport.com/BushJob.htm, accessed 10 August 2006.

Porter, M. (1990), *The Competitive Advantage of Nations*, London: Macmillan.

Reagan, R. (1981), Inaugural Address, West Front of the US Capitol, Washington, DC, 20 January.

Reagan, R. (1983), Remarks at the Annual Convention of the National Association of Evangelicals, Orlando, FL, 8 March.

Reich, R. (1991), *The Work of Nations: Preparing Ourselves for 21st-Century Capitalism*, New York and London: Simon & Schuster.

Reid, J. (2006), Speech delivered to the think-tank, Demos, London, 9 August.

Sands, P. (2005), *Lawless World Making and Breaking Global Rules*, London: Penguin.

Thatcher, M. (1977), 'The New Renaissance', Speech to Zurich Economic Society, University of Zurich, Switzerland, 14 March.

Tyson, L. (1992), *Who's Bashing Whom? Trade Conflicts in High-Technology Industries*, Washington, DC: Institute for International Economics.

USGOV (2002), *The National Security Strategy of the United States of America*, Washington, DC: United States Government.

USGOV (2006), *The National Security Strategy of the United States of America*, Washington, DC: United States Government.

Weiss, L. (1998), *The Myth of the Powerless State: Governing the Economy in a Global Era*, Cambridge: Polity.

Williamson, J. (1993), 'Democracy and the "Washington Consensus"', *World Development*, **21** (8),1329–36.

Wintour, P. (2006), 'Labour slides to 20-year poll low', *The Guardian*, 20 June, www.politics.guardian.co.uk/polls/story/O,,18019,00.html, accessed 17 April 2007.

Woodward, B. (2004), *Plan of Attack*, New York: Simon & Schuster.

World Bank (1997), *The State in a Changing World: World Development Report 1997*, Oxford: Oxford University Press.

9. Building institutions for freedom: the economic dimension of the 'war on terror'

Simon Lee

INTRODUCTION

Since September 11, 2001, the study of global governance has tended to focus understandably on the political and military consequences of the Bush administration's aggressively unilateralist approach to fighting the 'war on terror'. The desire to reintroduce Reaganite moral leadership to the process of global governance and the assembly of a 'coalition of the willing' has been associated with the influence upon American foreign policy of neo-conservatism (PFANAC, 1997, 1998, 2000). Comparatively little attention has been paid to the extent to which neo-conservatism has influenced the Bush administration's agenda for world economic development and the international institutions that seek to govern that process. Paradoxically, the Bush administration has defined the war on terror as 'both a battle of arms and a battle of ideas' (USGOV, 2006, p. 9). That battle of ideas has included a distinctive neo-conservative political economy, in relation to the role played by the World Bank and the International Monetary Fund (IMF) in the process of global economic development and governance. However, until the nomination of Paul Wolfowitz to become President of the World Bank in March 2005, the relationship between neo-conservatism and the foreign economic policy of the Bush administration, both in terms of personnel and ideology, had been much less transparent than that between neo-conservatism and national security policy (which Colin Tyler has addressed in Chapter 3).

This chapter explores the political economy of neo-conservatism and seeks to identify how the Bush administration's agenda for the World Bank and the IMF has reflected an important economic dimension to the war on terror. The chapter asserts that, from the very outset, the Bush administration has possessed a distinctive agenda for the international financial institutions (IFIs). Based upon its general belief in the moral superiority of capitalism, and its particular faith in economic growth as a source of personal and moral growth for the individual, the administration has sought a number of discrete policy objectives. First, it has sought to redefine the role of both the World Bank and the IMF to a limited number of core objectives. Second, it has sought to focus the IFIs' policies upon a results-orientated framework that better accords with the administration's notions of effective democracy and economic freedom. Third, it has sought to limit large-scale funding to the IFIs, and thereby prevent the risk of policy failure and moral hazard. All of these objectives have served the Bush administration's wider aims of achieving a repatriation of policy from the IFIs to national policy and a greater role for the market. This has been symbolised by the creation of the Millennium Challenge Account (MCA), and the promotion of personal self-reliance and independence, at both home and abroad, through a reduction in welfare dependency upon publicly funded programmes, in favour of those sourced from corporations and private charitable donations.

Following this introduction, the chapter is divided into six sections. First, the chapter explores the foundations of the economic dimension of the war on terror. Second, it focuses upon the administration's particular agenda for the multilateral development banks (MDBs). Third, it analyses the administration's policies towards the World Bank. Fourth, it then addresses the administration's attempts to redefine the role of the IMF. Fifth, it analyses the repatriation of development policy through the creation of the MCA. Sixth, it concludes by asserting that the administration's agenda has been fundamentally flawed. By abandoning multilateral cooperation in favour of a multinational 'coalition of the willing' that limits cooperative action to 'other main centers of global power' (USGOV, 2006, p. 1), including the world's major financial markets and transnational corporations, the Bush administration has undermined its attempts to secure both homeland and international security.

ECONOMICS AS A MORAL IMPERATIVE

Since 1945, American capitalism has been shaped by at least four political settlements. The first settlement was that of the 'Washington Consensus Mark I', in which an Atlanticist doctrine of domestic and international cooperation for reconstruction was enshrined in the Bretton Woods institutions and the Marshall Aid Plan. The second, and counter-revolutionary settlement was that of Reaganomics (and its Anglo-Saxon counterpart, Thatcherism), founded upon the simplistic conviction that the political and economic crisis of the 1970s had demonstrated that 'government is not the solution to our problem; government is the problem' (Reagan, 1981, p. 61). This gave rise to the 'Washington Consensus Mark II' in global governance, with its emphasis upon privatisation, deregulation and liberalisation. The third phase was that of Clintonomics and the Third Way political settlement of the New Democrats (duly followed by Tony Blair and New Labour in the United Kingdom), in which the heirs of an earlier social democratic settlement chose to further dismantle their inheritance in order to win the swing votes of an affluent middle class. During the presidency of George W. Bush, American capitalism has entered a fourth post-1945 phase of 'compassionate conservatism'.

A constant underpinning throughout these four political settlements has been a transatlantic adherence to the doctrine of liberal militarism, that is, a grand strategy based upon a defence of open markets through the use of superior military technology – whose earlier naval-, air-force- and nuclear-based technologies have been supplanted since the first Gulf war by the cruise missile-led smart weaponry of a post-Cold-War 'Pax Technologica' (Edgerton, 1991). Since 1945, the British and American warfare states have been as 'developmental' as their East Asian and continental European competitors. On the one hand, their technocratic industrial policies have promoted military technologies rather than the productive powers of the civilian manufacturing industries preferred by their competitors (Edgerton, 2005). On the other hand, their increasing homage to the market as a discovery process for entrepreneurial innovation, economic growth and development has seen their macroeconomic policies shaped by the commercial interests of Wall Street and the City of London, and their economies driven by increasing consumer borrowing- and debt-fuelled demand.

To fashion an agenda consistent with the tenets of liberal militarism, Bush has claimed that 'Often the truest kind of compassion is to help citizens build lives of their own. I call my philosophy and approach "compassionate conservatism"' (Bush, 2002a, p. 3). Domestically, this has meant reducing state welfare dependency but 'The same principles of compassion and responsibility apply when America offers assistance to other nations'. Indeed, Bush has claimed that 'the old ways of pouring vast amounts of money into development aid without any concern for results have failed, often leaving behind misery and poverty and corruption' (Bush, 2002b, p. 4). However, little or no evidence has been offered to sustain this particular analysis. The fact that a 50 per cent or $5 billion proposed increase in core development assistance over three years could be hailed by Bush as a record amount of spending, is indicative of the extremely low base from which it was increasing. At the March 2002 Monterrey Financing for Development Conference, Bush repeated his mantra that past aid programmes had been mistakenly measured in terms of 'resources spent, not the results achieved'. The duty of developed nations was now 'not only to share our wealth, but also to encourage sources that produce wealth: economic freedom, political liberty, the rule of law and human rights'. Greater aid would now be tied to political and legal reform, because 'by insisting on reform, we do the work of compassion'. Development aid must be used to unleash the universal spirit of enterprise, 'to build the institutions of freedom, not subsidize the failures of the past' (ibid., pp. 1–2).

The Bush administration's international economic agenda from the start therefore has been guided by the twin principles of increasing economic growth, as measured by improvements in productivity and higher income per capita, and improving economic stability, as measured by 'a reduction in the severity, length, and frequency of economic downturns and crises'. The philosophy has been that 'each country, by following basic policy principles and considering its own circumstances, should be encouraged to contribute in its own way to economic growth and stability'. This model should be applied to economic policy reform whether in Japan, Russia or the United States (Taylor, 2001, p. 1). Global growth should be driven by the engine of free trade. Indeed, the US Treasury claimed that a one-third cut in the barriers to trade in goods and services would boost the US economy by $177 billion per year, equivalent to a tax cut of $2500 per year for the typical American family. The Free Trade of the Americas (FTAA) alone could provide an additional benefit of $53 billion or about $800 per year per family (ibid., p. 6).

Great claims were made for the Bush administration's foreign economic policy in the wake of the events of September 11. Indeed, of the three 'essential and interlocking blocks' of the Bush administration's foreign policy, that is, the military, the political and the economic, the last was held to be 'by no means in third place', as evinced by the nomination, in the President's first National Security Presidential Directive (NSPD-1) of the Secretary of the Treasury as a formal member of the National Security Council Principals Committee, together with the Secretaries of Defense and State. It was claimed that this formal inclusion of economics in foreign policy had resulted not only in the elevation of economic issues but also 'a government inter-agency mechanism – from principals, to deputies, to technical staff – that allows for novel synergies between economic issues and military/political issues' (ibid., p. 2).

The relationship between the broader 'war on terror' and the political economy of the Bush administration was then confirmed in the September 2002 document, *The National Security Strategy of the United States of America*, where the relationship between markets and liberty was a central theme. In his preface, Bush identified 'a single sustainable model for national success: freedom, democracy, and free enterprise', and further asserted that 'In the twenty-first century, only nations that share a commitment to protecting basic human rights and guaranteeing political and economic freedom will be able to unleash the potential of their people and assure their future prosperity' (USGOV, 2002, p. iii). Bush specifically suggested that September 11 had demonstrated that 'weak states, like Afghanistan, can pose as great a danger to our national interests as strong states', for although 'Poverty does not make poor people into terrorists and murderers', nevertheless 'poverty, weak institutions, and corruption can make weak states vulnerable to terrorist networks and drug cartels within their borders' (ibid., p. iv). Bush then qualified a statement that 'multilateral institutions can multiply the strength of freedom-loving nations', by suggesting that 'Coalitions of the willing can augment these permanent institutions' (ibid., p. v). The strategy committed the United States 'to ignite a new era of global economic growth through free markets and free trade' and 'to expand the circle of development by opening societies and building the infrastructure of democracy' (ibid., pp. 1–2).

The strategy was unequivocal that 'The lessons of history are clear: market economies, not command-and-control economies with the heavy hand of government, are the best way to promote prosperity and reduce poverty' (ibid., p. 17). Indeed, a universal, one-size-fits-all approach would be appropriate because 'Policies that further strengthen market incentives and market institutions are relevant for all economies – industrialized countries, emerging markets, and the developing world' (ibid., p. 17). A repeated theme of the strategy was the moral dimension of this political economy. Thus, the strategy noted that 'The concept of "free trade" arose as a moral principle even before it became a pillar of economics'; that 'an expanding circle of development – and opportunity – is a moral imperative'; and that there was 'a moral obligation to measure the success of our development assistance by whether it is delivering results' (ibid., pp. 17, 18, 22).

This agenda has been reaffirmed in the March 2006 statement of *The National Security Strategy of the United States of America*. In his introduction, Bush has claimed that, as part of 'a wartime national security strategy', the US has 'dramatically expanded our efforts to encourage economic development and the hope it brings – and focused these efforts on the promotion of reform and the achievement of results' (USGOV, 2006, p. i). However, in stating that 'Effective multinational efforts are essential to solve these problems' (ibid., p. ii), Bush has signalled his administration's preference for multinational 'coalitions of the willing' that act in strict accordance with the central tenets of US foreign policy but not necessarily in accord with the institutions of global governance, like the United Nations, where the capacity to dictate the international agenda according to US interests continues to be hampered by the constraints of multilateral cooperation.

Rather than seeking a more inclusive process of global governance, the Bush administration has preferred to limit its ambition to the development of 'agendas for cooperative action with other main centres of global power' (ibid., p. 1). According to this vision, the world has now been divided into two. On the one hand, there are the free nations whose effective democracies and indivisible freedom honour and uphold basic human rights; are accountable to their citizens; exercise sovereignty and maintain internal order; and limit the reach of government by protecting 'the institutions of civil society', including a market economy. On the other, there are pariah states, namely 'the Democratic People's Republic of Korea (DPKK), Iran, Syria, Cuba, Belarus, Burma, and Zimbabwe' whose tyrannical governments persecute their own populations at home, while threatening freedom's expansion overseas and 'our immediate security interests', through their 'pursuit of WMD [weapons of mass destruction] or sponsorship of terrorism' (ibid., pp. 3–4).

According to this worldview, 'Economic freedom is a moral imperative', where 'America's national interests and moral virtues drive us in the same direction: to assist the world's poor citizens and least developed nations and help integrate them into the global economy' (ibid., pp. 27, 32). To this end, the Bush administration has pledged itself to 'harness the tools of economic assistance, development aid, trade, and good governance to help ensure that new democracies are not burdened with economic stagnation or endemic corruption' (ibid., p. 4). While its attempts to complete the domestic dismantling of the New Deal welfare state settlement, which was initiated by Reaganomics and continued by the Third Way of Clinton's New Democrats, have largely faltered, overseas the Bush administration has discovered that the salience of national security and foreign policy has given greater opportunity for compassionate conservatism's principles to be practised on a broader, global canvas.

THE BUSH ADMINISTRATION AND THE MULTILATERAL DEVELOPMENT BANKS

Despite the moral certainty expressed in the National Security strategy, at this juncture, it should be noted that the President does not operate autonomously in foreign economic policy, especially with regard to the role of the MDBs. With the guidance and consent of the Senate, the President nominates individuals to represent the United States on the executive boards of the five MDBs of which the US is a member. In theory, there they then serve fixed terms for between three to five years, depending upon each MDB's Articles of Agreement, but their tenure depends upon presidential pleasure. Under US law, it is the President who has the ultimate authority to direct US policy and to instruct US representatives at the MDBs. However, this authority is delegated to the Secretary of the Treasury, where the Assistant Secretary of the Treasury for International Affairs manages US participation in the MDBs. It is the US Treasury Secretary who serves as US Governor (or member of the governing board) at each MDB (Sanford, 2001).

In terms of congressional authorisation and scrutiny, the Senate Foreign Relations Committee and the House Committee on Financial Services have jurisdiction over MDB authorisation legislation, while the House and Senate Foreign Operations Appropriations Subcommittees handle MDB appropriations. Under the Bretton Woods Agreement Act (1945), each administration is supposed to submit an annual report on the operations and policies of the MDBs via an interagency body called the National Advisory Council (NAC) on International Monetary and Financial Policies. However, because Congress greatly expanded the number of issues to be included in the report, successive administrations have had difficulty in submitting NAC reports. For example, the Clinton administration submitted its report for FY1992 in 1996, and then failed to file a single report thereafter (Sanford, 2001).

Nothwithstanding these constitutional constraints, from the very outset reform of the MDBs was identified as 'a key priority' for the Bush administration (O'Neill, 2001a, p. 3). In accordance with its key assumption that 'To reduce poverty, there is no alternative to increasing productivity' (US Treasury, 2001, p. 5), the Treasury Department identified three priorities for the IFIs. These were, first, to 'concentrate on countries that demonstrate their commitment to sound policies that encourage productivity'. Second, to 'focus on activities that improve the productivity of the economy and/or remove economic constraints that hamper such productivity'. Third, to 'enhance the capacity of individuals (e.g. by better education and health services) to contribute to countries' economic activities' (ibid., p. 6). The focus in the Bush administration's first term would be to improve the performance of the IFIs by focusing their objectives and enhancing their effectiveness (O'Neill, 2002a, p. 1). Secretary to the Treasury Paul O'Neill had previously argued that 'the less the IFIs are associated with fire-fighting and crisis, the more support they will have both internationally and here in the United States' (O'Neill, 2001b, p. 1).

During the early months of the first Bush administration, O'Neill made the administration's critique of the MDBs abundantly clear. He identified how the World Bank had expended $470 billion during its history, and $225 billion in the past decade, but there was 'too little to show for it', and consequently it was time for 'a new approach to poverty'. This approach would be built upon the insight that almost all the differences between the $90 a day income of Americans and the 1.2 billion people living on less than one dollar a day could be attributed to differences in productivity. The challenge was therefore to raise productivity by spreading the principles that had made Americans prosperous around the world (O'Neill, 2001c, p. 1). The immediate problem with this argument was that it neglected how physical and human infrastructure had been built up over the decades by more developed economies, often behind protectionist trade barriers, and with the comparative advantage of massive natural resources and abundant and cheap migrant labour.

O'Neill also noted the association of the IFIs with crisis conditions or failure and the calls of unidentified 'respected elder statesmen and scholars' for the IMF to be closed down. The major 'repair and restoration' job would be based upon improved standards of living in the developing world based on productivity growth; the IMF providing careful monitoring and prompt decision before financial crisis conditions could destabilise the world economy. The Millennium Development Goals (MDGs), while 'a very useful set of objectives' had omitted the goal of higher productivity growth (Taylor, 2002a, p. 2). Taylor advocated quantitative targets for the productivity growth of poorer economies, for example, a country with productivity of only 1 per cent of that of the United States, might be set an objective of productivity growth 9 per cent greater than that for the US (ibid., p. 2). The impediments to productivity growth, and thus the escape from poverty, were 'capital per worker and the level of technology'. The key to 'catch-up' was to remove 'impediments to the use and accumulation of capital (including human capital) and technology'. After all, poor states in the late nineteenth century like Texas and Florida had grown more rapidly in the twentieth century than more affluent states such as New York and California (ibid., p. 2). However, this pattern had not been repeated elsewhere in the world. At one stroke, this was to overlook and discount the unique circumstances of the United States, the impact of two world wars, and the massive state investments in Texas and Florida by the Department of Defense and the North American Space Administration.

REFORMING THE WORLD BANK

In July 2001 President Bush told the World Bank that 'Debt relief is really a short term fix' and proposed that 50 per cent of the IFIs' funds should be devoted to grants for education, health, nutrition, water supply, sanitation and other human needs (Bush, 2001, p. 2). In a similar vein, in congressional testimony, when specifying the Bush administration's wider IFI reform agenda, US Treasury Secretary Paul O'Neill indicated that he believed the scope of the World Bank's activities to be 'too diffuse', and that its focus should be reduced to the core objective of raising income per capita (O'Neill, 2001a, p. 2). The US would provide guidance in the areas that could be 'scaled back' because O'Neill was not of the view that 'each MDB must be a full-service "supermarket" for the developing world' (ibid., p. 3). From now on, every project, programme, loan and grant should be judged by how much it increased productivity. This was because research and experience had taught the Bush administration that 'improved education and health, competitive and open markets, and the rule of law are central to boosting productivity' (Taylor, 2001, p. 4).

In its subsequent statements on global poverty and development, the Bush administration has sought to redefine the role and policy objectives of the World Bank such that they more fully accord with the administration's own sense of economic freedom as a moral imperative, and the specific benchmarks of good governance and economic performance that arise from that particular sense of moral purpose. First, the proximate cause of poverty has been identified as low productivity (Taylor, 2002a, p. 1). This has been linked by the administration to the 1959 Eisenhower proposal for the International Development Association (IDA), whose key goal was higher productivity, 'to promote economic development, increase productivity and thus raise standards of living' (ibid., p. 2). However, in emphasising productivity, the administration has deliberately overlooked more salient causes of poverty, notably unemployment, illiteracy, inequalities in the distribution of income and wealth, and the inability to sell farm produce and textiles on world markets because of trade barriers and agricultural subsidies.

The second theme of the Bush administration's approach to the World Bank has been an emphasis upon outputs rather than inputs and 'other flawed measures of compassion', a focus upon policy results rather than resources, and the alleviation of poverty through 'partnership, not paternalism' (Bush, 2005, pp. 2, 4). In this regard, the administration has championed a new measurable results system at the Bank, incorporating timely and high-quality diagnostic analyses. These have included public expenditure reviews; financial accountability assessments and investment climate assessments; and measurements of education (aggregate primary school completion rates), health (increase in measles immunisation coverage across IDA countries, and the increase in those countries with 80 per cent coverage) and private sector development (reduction in the number of days and costs required to start businesses). To these ends, the administration initially committed itself to providing an additional $100 million to supplement its three-year, $2.5 billion contribution to the IDA (Dam, 2002,

p. 4). Subsequently, there was a further pledge totalling $2.85 billion to the IDA-14 over three years, which represented a $100 million annual increase over the IDA-13 base level, but a reduction from 20 to 13 per cent in the US share of IDA funding, although the US remained the largest cumulative donor at 22 per cent of total contributions (Adams, 2005a, p. 3).

The third theme of the Bush administration's approach to the World Bank has been its promotion of the principle of 'the primacy of a country's own policies in determining its economic destiny' and a repatriation of responsibility for development from the multilateral agencies to national governments. This is because 'we can foster growth and development only by supporting and encouraging sovereign governments that rule justly, invest in their people and expand economic freedom', for 'we simply cannot bring about success from the outside' (O'Neill, 2002a, p. 1). In this way, by using a language of autonomy and responsibility, the administration was in effect detaching itself from and abandoning its moral responsibilities to help fund the development of poorer countries.

To help cut expenditure by the World Bank, and to increase the efficiency of that expenditure, the Bush administration has advocated a great reliance upon grants instead of loans 'to break the cycle whereby the poorest countries pile on more and more debt' (Taylor, 2001, p. 4). The US duly concluded replenishment negotiations for the Bank's IDA, the African Development Fund (ADF), and the Asian Development Fund, which saw these institutions increase their share of funding allocated to grants rather than loans, to about 45 per cent for the IDA and ADF, and 21 per cent for the Asian Development Fund (Executive Office, 2005, p. 225). At the same time, and to cut the misallocation of resources through corruption at the Bank, there would be greater disclosure of Bank Board minutes, and a focus upon internal control procedures, disclosure and accountability. At the project level, the bank would focus upon designs that reduced the opportunity for corruption. At the country level, it would focus upon enhanced transparency and accountability for recipient countries' governance systems (Adams, 2005a, p. 4).

A final theme of the Bush administration's policy on the World Bank, and the one most closely aligned to the tenets of compassionate conservatism, has been its emphasis upon a much greater role for the market and the funding of private compassionate donations by individuals and corporations. This was justified on the grounds that 'Economic development will falter and fail without a strong private sector' (Taylor, 2002b, p. 2). Trade and investment, rather than aid should become the engines of development through liberalised markets. There should be convergence towards the universality of freedom as liberal democracy. A more compassionate society, both at home and abroad, would be supported by the President's

Emergency Plan for AIDS Relief, outlined in his 2003 State of the Union Address, which promised a five-year, $15 billion commitment, including $2.4 billion in 2004, $2.8 billion in 2005 and $3.2 billion requested for 2006 (Executive Office, 2005, p. 227). Poverty would now be alleviated by private 'armies of compassion' staffed by non-governmental organisations (NGOs) and other voluntary associations, rather than by the World Bank and other IFIs. The task of the IFIs would now be to use their resources to write off existing debt and not to provide loans that will allow additional debt to accumulate in the future.

During its second term of office, the Bush administration has pursued its agenda for reform of the World Bank in a more open and aggressive manner. For example, in November 2005 the administration signed a law which withheld 20 per cent of its annual funding for the World Bank Group. The funding was withheld for only the second time by Congress because of the Bank's failure to comply with anti-corruption measures. Indeed, in congressional testimony, it was claimed that approximately $100 billion of the $525 billion Bank funding had been lost to corruption since 1946. This action followed critical reports from the US Treasury and the Government Accountability Office which had identified the Bank's failure to comply with modern standards of transparency and accountability in its auditing, internal control, whistle-blower protection and accountability (Center for Economic Justice, 2005).

Of even greater symbolic and substantive importance for the Bush administration's determination to reform the World Bank was its nomination of former Secretary of Defense Paul Wolfowitz to become the tenth World Bank President. This was unanimously confirmed by the Bank's Board of Executive Directors on 31 March 2005. Following this confirmation, Wolfowitz claimed that his new colleagues had recommended that 'I review the right balance between loans and grants; the Bank's role as lender versus technical advisor; lending to middle income countries versus support for the poorest nations; and timely, high quality delivery of financial support versus the need for conditions, accountability and safeguards' (World Bank, 2005a). This appeared to be little more than a rationale for an action plan justifying Wolfowitz's nomination by the Bush administration.

Wolfowitz's appointment inevitably proved controversial. The Group of Eleven (G11) countries, while welcoming the chance to meet Wolfowitz in advance of his appointment, nevertheless emphasised the need for 'a more global and transparent nomination process' and reiterated concerns about the need for their due representation in the World Bank's senior management appointments, on the principle of merit-based national diversity (World Bank, 2005b). However, when set against the Bush administration's wider grand strategy, the quest for a more democratic, transparent and inclusive process of good governance has not even registered on the radar screen.

PUTTING AN END TO 'MISSION CREEP' AT THE IMF

The Bush administration has played an even higher profile in relation to the redefinition of the role of the IMF. Here, it has sought to return the IMF to its core mission; a reduction in the IMF's funding; a repatriation of responsibility for policy making to national economies; a narrowing of the IMF's terms of conditionality to better align them with the US Treasury's conception of good governance; and an expansion in the role of the private sector in the governance of markets in general, and the resolution of financial crises in particular. The most interesting aspect of this approach to the IMF is the degree to which it has attributed the causes of recent financial crises to a failure of multilateral surveillance and moral hazard caused by the 'mission creep' of the IMF, rather than the reckless behaviour of private market actors. As a consequence, the administration's whole agenda for the IMF has rested on the twin assumptions that market actors will behave in a rational manner, when given the appropriate technical information, and will accept the responsibility for solving financial crises through collective action, rather than waiting for public authorities to bail them out. Recent financial crises in Mexico, Korea, Thailand, Russia, Turkey and Argentina have tended to point to the very opposite conclusion, namely that market actors tend towards irrational herding, contagion and panic in crises situations, and have a proclivity for collective inaction in the face of crises due to the constraints of market competition and their possible own fraud or bankruptcy.

The Bush administration's approach to the IMF has been much more in accordance than the Clinton administration with the recommendations of the report of the International Financial Institutions Advisory Commission, chaired by Professor Allan Meltzer (IFIAC, 2000). Most notably, the US Treasury has endorsed the Meltzer Commission's recommendation to sharpen the focus of the IMF, limiting its role to the core objectives of promoting sound monetary, fiscal, exchange rate and financial sector policies; surveillance, by carefully monitoring economic conditions; and dealing with critical problems in the international financial system as soon as they are detected. The Treasury noted how, because of 'mission creep', the IMF had intruded into areas such as privatisation, public sector management and social safety-nets which overlapped with the mandates of other IFIs (US Treasury, 2001, p. 2). Attending his first spring meeting of the IMF and the World Bank, US Treasury Secretary Paul O'Neill told the International Monetary and Financial Committee (IMFC) that there was the need 'to create an institution that is ever more focused, effective and accountable'. The IMF needed to sharpen its capacity 'to respond to financial disruptions swiftly and appropriately, and do so less frequently because it has succeeded in preventing crises from developing in the first place' (O'Neill, 2001d, p. 1).

From the outset, the Bush administration was confident that 'The big money IMF packages and high-profile, formal bureaucratic commissions are a thing of the past' (Taylor, 2001, p. 7). The objective of the Treasury was 'to continue to reduce reliance on official sector resources over time' (Dam, 2002, p. 3). To this end, in March 2003, the IMF Board agreed on four specific criteria that had to be met before large-scale funding beyond certain limits could occur. These were, first, the presence of balance of payments pressures on the capital account; second, a high probability of debt sustainability; third, good prospects of regaining access to private markets, so that the IMF financing would only be providing 'a bridge'; and fourth, the implementation of 'good economic policies'. Moreover, where exceptional access to funds was to occur, the IMF Board would have to prepare and publish a report to provide some degree of accountability for its actions (Taylor, 2004, p. 4).

At the same time, the Bush administration sought to reduce the risk of moral hazard, whereby the prospect of an IMF rescue package to bail out investors might provoke irresponsible market behaviour, by proposing the development of an international insolvency mechanism. This would ensure that, in the face of a financial crisis and the prospect of widespread bankruptcy, financial restructuring would be orderly, treat creditors fairly, and reduce 'the scope for arbitrary, unpredictable official action' with policies owned by the countries themselves and 'not the US, not the G7, not the IMF' (Taylor, 2001, p. 5). In April 2002, O'Neill's initial approach was a twin-track strategy. First, the Treasury's preference was for a decentralised, market-orientated approach to restructuring. Second, the Treasury also supported approaches to sovereign debt restructuring which might require legislation, but they would take time. To avoid debtors defaulting, the key was held to be greater clarity, order and predictability in dealing with debt servicing, through cooperation between the official and private sectors via 'a market-oriented contractual approach to the sovereign debt restructuring process' (O'Neill, 2002b, p. 2).

This would provide an alternative to the large IMF official packages of the late 1990s, because there had been little motivation for policy makers to make 'the tough choices that are necessary to maintain stability and achieve sustained growth'. However, O'Neill at this juncture did not rule out such packages altogether, stating that 'exceptional' levels of IMF financing would require strong justification (ibid., p. 2). Later, he stated that 'official resources are limited and that multiple, large-scale official financing packages will not be feasible or desirable in the future' (O'Neill, 2002a, p. 3). The ultimate objective would be 'investment grade sovereign debt' through a contractual, 'decentralized, market-oriented approach' to the sovereign debt restructuring process. This approach would require creditors to incorporate new clauses into their sovereign debt contracts, for example, 'a majority action clause, an engagement clause, and an initiation clause' to provide the basis for collective action, a 'roadmap for restructuring' debt, if necessary (ibid., p. 3). Moreover, such clauses would entail 'a minimum of direction or discretion by the official sector' and thereby help to reduce, but not eliminate, uncertainty (Taylor, 2004, p. 3).

During the Bush administration's second term, the US Treasury has successfully initiated a Strategic Review of the IMF. This is part of what has been depicted as 'periodic stock taking' to ensure that the IMF adapts to the needs and challenges of the international monetary system. The project should be one of restoration rather than renewal, returning the IMF 'to its core mission of promoting international financial stability and balance of payments adjustment' (Snow, 2005, p. 1). Timothy Adams, US Under Secretary for International Affairs, has publicly reaffirmed his faith in the IMF, asserting 'I am a believer in the IMF – that is, an IMF as a facilitator of international monetary cooperation'. Having pledged that 'There is a role for the Fund', Adams has once again repeated the familiar US Treasury mantra that the IMF can best strengthen its relevance by refocusing upon its core mission, as envisaged by the founders at Bretton Woods, namely international financial stability and balance of payments adjustment (Adams, 2005b, p. 1). In so stating, Adams has overlooked the fact that, for the founders of the IMF, the core mission of economic stability necessitated both capital controls and fixed exchange rates.

For the Bush administration, there are now five key priorities for the IMF. First, the reform of the IMF's quota allocation and representation. Korea is 66 per cent underweight, Mexico about 35 per cent underweight, and Turkey 32 per cent underweight, and the US having only 17 per cent when its GDP is 29 per cent of global economy. To resolve this issue, there must be a voluntary rebalancing of quotas, but within the existing total; the poorest countries, while actually being among 'the most overweight', nevertheless 'should be held harmless and so their quota does not fall'; and the IMF's Executive Board should better reflect the full membership by consolidation of the European chairs to give a greater voice to developing and emerging market economies (ibid., p. 2).

The second priority for the IMF is 'far more ambitious' IMF exchange rate surveillance to promote regimes in emerging markets that allow

for 'substantial exchange rate flexibility'. While the Treasury has acknowledged that this might be 'politically difficult for the IMF', and could
intrude upon self-determination and national autonomy, it has insisted:
'Nevertheless, the perception that the IMF is asleep at the wheel on its most
fundamental responsibility – exchange rate surveillance – is very unhealthy
for the institution and the international monetary system' (ibid., p. 3). The
US Treasury has identified exchange rate flexibility as a key element of this
process, with China, above all, and other Asian states such as Malaysia the
target for demands to adopt more flexible exchange rates and further trade
liberalisation, especially in financial markets (for example, Snow, 2005,
p. 1). The Treasury has acknowledged the Chinese growth rate of 9.7 per
cent averaged between 1990 and 2003; that it is the world's seventh largest
economy; and that the US and China have been 'the engines of the global
economy, accounting for half of global growth in the last few years'.
However, addressing the global imbalances in the global economy must be
'a shared responsibility among the major economies'. For East Asia and
China this means three things: first, greater exchange rate flexibility;
second, a shift from export-orientated growth to a domestic demand-based
economy, because, according to the IMF, exports now account for 45 per
cent of emerging Asia's GDP; and third, the development of China's
financial sector, including capital markets. In this last regard, there must be
financial liberalisation, a move to risk-based lending, and capital market
development (Adams, 2005b, p. 1).

The third priority for the IMF identified by the Bush administration,
and also related to crisis prevention, is the achievement of public debt sustainability in emerging markets. High public debt is held to have kept
domestic borrowing costs high, and therefore become 'a tax on their citizens'. Consequently, the IMF should take advantage of benign conditions,
by deepening its traditional focus upon fiscal policy to help countries 'to
improve their debt structures and by stressing structural fiscal reforms in
its surveillance and programs' (ibid., p. 3). In so arguing, the administration has deflected its attention from its own budget deficit. The administration's fourth priority is that of crisis resolution. Crises cannot always be
prevented, but the IMF's own crisis resolution framework is 'a mix of
policy adjustment, official finance and private finance'. For the US
Treasury, 'The real unresolved question is private sector involvement',
especially in sovereign debt restructuring. The Bush administration has
abandoned its earlier twin-track strategy. It is now categorical, following
First Deputy Managing Director at the IMF, Anne Krueger's, November
2001 proposal of an 'international workout mechanism', based upon the
'model of a domestic bankruptcy court', that 'there remains no need for a
Sovereign Debt Restructuring Mechanism' (ibid., p. 3). Instead, there is

the need for creative thinking on how to improve market-based sovereign debt restructuring.

The Bush administration's fifth and final priority for the IMF, partly as a consequence of 'the historic G8 debt deal to end the lend-and-forgive cycle at the World Bank, African Development Bank, and IMF', is to help low-income countries establish 'a sound macroeconomic framework through surveillance, technical assistance [and] a new-non-borrowing program' for countries not needing IMF finance. Adams has reaffirmed the Bush administration's belief that 'the IMF is not a development institution, and that it is clear that the IMF's financial involvement in low-income countries has gone terribly awry'. IMF funding should in future therefore be confined to short-term loans in response to balance of payments needs (ibid., p. 4).

A NEW COMPACT FOR DEVELOPMENT: THE MILLENNIUM CHALLENGE ACCOUNT

While the United States has sought to narrow the role and reduce the funding of the IFIs, the most prominent example of its attempts to repatriate development policy, and its attendant conditionality to domestic policy makers, has been the MCA initiative. In effect, the administration has sought to relocate responsibility for development funding within the city of Washington from the headquarters of the World Bank to the federal government. Much more lofty rhetoric was used when Bush presented his MCA initiative to Congress on 5 February 2003. He described it as a powerful way to 'draw whole nations into an expanding circle of opportunity and enterprise' (Bush, 2003). Secretary of State Colin Powell described lifting humanity out of poverty as 'one of the greatest moral challenges of the 21st century' and whether the US rose to that challenge carried 'profound implications for freedom, growth and security worldwide' (State Department, 2003, p. 1). Powell claimed that the MCA reflected 'a new international consensus on assistance' forged at Monterrey, and 'America at its best: generous and pragmatic, compassionate and focused on results' (ibid., p. 2).

Bush's plans envisaged increasing core official development assistance by 50 per cent over three years to a total of $15 billion by FY2006. The objective was to reduce poverty by significantly increasing economic growth through a process of targeted investment in selected countries. The MCA was intended to steer aid to poor countries with 'good economic policies' to increase growth and reduce poverty. The new conditionality accompanying MCA loans would entail the demonstration of three things: first, 'ruling justly', that is, 'upholding the rule of law, rooting out corruption, protecting human rights and political freedoms'; second, 'investing in people', through education and health care; and third, 'encouraging economic freedom', through 'open markets, sound fiscal and monetary policies, [and] appropriate regulatory environments' (Taylor, 2002a, p. 3).

The State Department claimed that the policy focus of the MCA would be upon a number of key priorities. First, growth, through 'prudent investments in agriculture, private sector development, good governance, education, healthcare, and the mentoring of local officials and business people in management skills'. Second, selectivity, by only providing aid to those countries that had proven their willingness to govern justly, invest in their people, and encourage economic freedom, and with a score above the median on an anti-corruption indicator (and only those on incomes below $1435 would be eligible in 2004, and all countries below $2975 in FY2006. Third, genuine partnership, where countries would work closely with the MCA, but be responsible for identifying critical barriers to their own development, ensuring civil society participation, and the development of a tailored MCA program for their own specific needs. Fourth, a business approach, meaning a high level of commitment and a public contract identifying 'a limited number of measurable goals and the inclusion of a timeframe, benchmarks, baseline information, a financial oversight plan, evaluation system, and a plan to sustain goals when a contract ends'. Fifth, accountability, where failure to meet financial standards or attain benchmarks could mean cutbacks or withdrawal of funding (State Department, 2003, pp. 1–2).

The MCA has been attacked for critical omissions from its criteria and methodology for determining the eligibility of candidate countries for MCA assistance in FY2004. In its 16 indicators of ruling justly, encouraging economic freedom, and investing in people, the key concepts claimed not to be captured in the current methodology are entrepreneurship, property rights and political capacity to sustain reforms. These criteria and attendant methodology have been criticised for focusing 'too much on macroeconomic indicators as proxies for economic freedom, at the expense of microeconomic incentives: entrepreneurship, private property rights, and the structure of political institutions', which means that there was a tendency to miss 'the underlying structural, institutional factors that drive economic growth and development' (Boettke et al., 2005, pp. 5–6).

The MCA has also been attacked for its failure, thus far, to deliver the promised resources. By fiscal year 2006 the MCA was supposed to be spending $5 billion, amounting to a 50 per cent increase in the budget for US development assistance (Taylor, 2002a, p. 3). In the event, during FY2004, only $994 billion was allocated to the MCA and only $1488 billion in 2005, while $3 billion has been requested for 2006 (Executive Office, 2005, p. 234). Because the Bush administration did not receive its full requests for MCA funding in 2004 and 2005 (receiving only $1.5 billion instead of the $2.5 billion requested), it did not meet the President's pledge for additional spending to increase by $5 billion (to be allocated to the MCA) by 2006.

Quantitatively, the whole MCA initiative is insignificant. As Birdsall has noted, US aid amounts to only $0.16 for every $100 of its GDP, 'an embarrassingly low base for the leader of the free world'. Indeed, she has pointed out that the proposed increases in US aid are 'trivial in terms of [the] rich world's wealth' and well below aid levels in previous countries' history, such as South Korea having received nearly $100 per person (in contemporary dollars) in annual aid between 1955 and 1972, and Botswana, the world's fastest growing country between 1965 and 1995 received average annual aid flows of $127 per person, while Sub-Saharan Africa averages only about $28 per person (Birdsall, 2005, p. 4). The MCA also pales into insignificance when compared to the funding dispersed by the private Gates Foundation to tackle global poverty and iniquities in health and education. From its endowment of $29.2 billion, the Foundation has disbursed $10.5 billion since its inception in 2000, including $1.36 billion during 2005. Furthermore, with the pledge of an additional $37 billion from Warren Buffet in June 2006, the Foundation's future disbursements are likely to at least match those of the MCA.

CONCLUSION

During two terms of office, the Bush administration has sought to redefine the roles of the World Bank and the IMF so as to narrow the range of global public goods that they deliver. The retreat from multilateralism has been part of a wider agenda of repatriating policy from international institutions to domestic politics. This has been a massive and costly strategic error, not only financially, and in terms of the loss of human life, but also in terms of securing homeland security and international order in the wake of the 9/11 attacks. In financial terms, the priorities of the Bush administration are very stark. In his Fiscal Year 2006 Budget, Bush sought a 5 per cent increase in discretionary defence spending to $419.3 billion, amounting to a 41 per cent increase since 2001. This is compared with an almost 1 per cent cut in non-security discretionary programmes during the same period. Moreover, the administration requested only $18.5 billion or a 14 per cent increase in discretionary budget authority for its International Assistance programmes. Of this, $1.34 billion was requested for US contributions to the MDBs in the 2006 Budget.

The Bush administration continues to invest only a tiny fraction of its vast budgetary resources to the non-military dimension of the 'war on terror'. Paradoxically, in the immediate aftermath of September 11, the administration had acknowledged the need to accelerate economic development in underdeveloped countries because of their being prone to becoming 'hotbeds for terrorism' (Taylor, 2001, p. 4). To make that development possible, what was needed was an urgent expansion in, rather than a retreat from, multilateral cooperation. When the US Treasury justified fewer resources for the IFIs, on the grounds that there had been 'a history of repeated lend and forgive cycles' between 1989 and 2002, that had led to total debt relief of $40 billion and new loans amounting to more than $93 billion (Adams, 2005a, p. 2), what it had identified was the inability of poor countries to escape their poverty without the necessary development assistance, and within a neo-liberal global political economy that had denied their key agricultural and textile exports tariff-free access to major markets.

As Nancy Birdsall has contended during congressional testimony, 'As the world's only superpower and a leading "shareholder" in the international financial institutions and the United Nations, the US has a particular responsibility, and its own key security and other interests, in ensuring progress on this global developmental agenda' (Birdsall, 2005, p. 2). The US should not only 'lead by example in a unilateral way, but take leadership in what is an increasingly *multilateral* system' (ibid., p. 2, original italics). The US should lead the G8 in maximising new donor contributions to multilateral channels, because these are 'less subject to political and other sources of volatility', because it is the most bilateral of all donors, and because only about 15 per cent of its aid goes through multilateral channels. Moreover, 'bilateral programs are not sufficient – in ideas, leadership, or financing' because in an interdependent world, acting unilaterally does not help to foster international cooperation (ibid., p. 13). In this regard, the MCA promised to be 'innovative, entrepreneurial and transformational' but the current approach risks reducing it to the status of 'just another development program' (Herrling and Radelet, 2005, p. 6). To be truly transformational abroad will mean bringing transformational change in attitudes among Americans at home, and making them realise, above all, that offering others hope for a better future, is actually 'a smart investment in America's own security' (ibid., p. 7).

REFERENCES

Adams, T. (2005a), 'Statement of the Under Secretary of the Treasury for International Affairs, House Committee on Financial Services, Subcommittee on

Domestic and International Monetary Policy, Trade and Technology, 27 September.

Adams, T. (2005b), 'The IMF: Back to the Basics', Remarks by Under Secretary for International Affairs Timothy D. Adams, 'Reform of the International Monetary Fund', Institute for International Economics Conference, Washington, DC, 23 September, Washington, DC: The Department of the Treasury.

Birdsall, N. (2005), 'Debt and Development: How to Provide Efficient, Effective Assistance to the World's Poorest Countries', Testimony for the House Committee on Financial Services, Subcommittee on Domestic and International Monetary Policy, Trade and Technology, 8 June, Washington, DC: Centre for Global Development.

Boettke, P., P. Aligica and B. Hooks (2005), 'The Millennium Challenge Account: Property Rights and Entrepreneurship as the Engine of Development's: Public Interest Comment on the Millennium Challenge Corporation's *Report on the Criteria and Methodology for Determining the Eligibility of Candidate Countries for Millennium Challenge Account Assistance in FY 2004*, Mercatus Center, George Mason University Global Prosperity Initiative.

Bush, G.W. (2001), Speech to the World Bank, Washington, DC, 17 July.

Bush, G.W. (2002a), 'President Promotes Compassionate Conservatism', San José, California, 30 April.

Bush, G.W. (2002b), 'President Outlines US Plan to Help World's Poor: Remarks by the President at United Nations Financing for Development Conference', Monterrey, Mexico, 22 March.

Bush, G.W. (2003), 'Message to the Congress of the United States', Washington, DC, 5 February.

Bush, G.W. (2005), 'Address to the United Nations Security Council', New York, 14 September.

Center for Economic Justice (2005), *US Cuts World Bank Funding: Corruption, Secrecy Prompt 20% Cut*, Albuquerque, NM: Center for Economic Justice.

Dam, K. (2002), 'The Role of the United States in the Global Economy', remarks delivered by the Deputy Secretary, US Department of the Treasury, to the Centre for Strategic and International Studies, Washington, DC, 11 September.

Edgerton, D. (1991), 'Liberal militarism and the British state', *New Left Review*, **185**, 138–70.

Edgerton, D. (2005), *Warfare State: Britain, 1920–1970*, Cambridge: Cambridge University Press.

Executive Office (2005), *Budget of the United States Government Fiscal Year 2006: Historical Tables*, Washington, DC: Executive Office of the President of the United States.

Herrling, S. and S. Radelet (2005), *The MCC Between a Rock and a Hard Place: More Countries, Less Money and the Transformational Challenge*, Washington, DC: Centre for Global Development.

IFIAC (2000), *Report of the International Financial Institutions Advisory Commission (IFIAC)*, Washington, DC: United States Congress.

O'Neill, P. (2001a), Testimony before the House Committee on Appropriations Subcommittee on Foreign Operations, Export Financing and Related Programs, 15 May.

O'Neill, P. (2001b), Statement at the Pre-G7 Press Conference, Washington, DC, 27 April.

O'Neill, P. (2001c), 'Excellence and the International Financial Institutions', Speech to the Economic Club of Detroit, Michigan, 27 June.

O'Neill, P. (2001d), Statement by US Treasury Secretary to the International Monetary and Financial Committee, Washington, DC, 29 April.

O'Neill, P. (2002a), 'Governor's Speech' to the Annual Meeting of the IMF and World Bank, Washington, DC, 29 September.

O'Neill, P. (2002b), 'Globalization: Spreading the Benefits', Keynote address at the Washington International Trade Center, 18 April.

PFANAC (1997), *Statement of Principles*, 3 June, Washington, DC: Project for the New American Century.

PFANAC (1998), 'Letter to the President, 26 January', Washington, DC: Project for the New American Century.

PFANAC (2000), *Rebuilding America's Defenses: Strategy, Forces and Resources for a New Century*, Washington, DC: Project for the New American Century.

Reagan, R. (1981), 'Inaugural Address, West Front of the US Capitol, Washington, DC, 20 January, reprinted in R. Reagan (1990), *Speaking My Mind: Selected Speeches*, London: Hutchinson, pp. 59–66.

Sanford, J. (2001), *Multilateral Development Banks: Procedures for US Participation*, Washington DC: Congressional Research Service, Library of Congress.

Snow, J. (2005), Statement by US Secretary Treasury John Snow to the International Monetary and Financial Committee Meeting, Washington, DC, 24 September.

State Department (2003), 'The Millennium Challenge Account: A New Vision for Development', 22 September.

Taylor, J. (2001), 'Strengthening the Global Economy after September 11: The Bush Administration's Agenda', Speech to the Kennedy School of Government, Harvard University, 29 November.

Taylor, J. (2002a), 'New Policies for Economic Development', Remarks by the Under Secretary for International Affairs, United States Treasury, at the Annual World Bank Conference on Development Economics, Washington, DC, 30 April.

Taylor, J. (2002b), 'An Economic Growth Agenda at the IDB', Speech to the Board of Governors of the Inter-American Development Bank and the Inter-American Investment Corporation, Fortaleza, Brazil, 11 March.

Taylor, J. (2004), Remarks to the IMF Conference in honour of Guillermo Calvo, Washington, DC, 16 April.

USGOV (2002), *National Security Strategy of the United States of America*, Washington, DC: Office of the President of the United States.

USGOV (2006), *National Security Strategy of the United States of America*, Washington, DC: Office of the President of the United States.

US Treasury (2001), Report on Implementation of Recommendations made by the International Financial Institutions Advisory Commission, Washington, DC: Office of Public Affairs.

World Bank (2005a), 'Statements on Confirmation of Paul Wolfowitz as Tenth World Bank President', Washington, DC, 31 March.

World Bank (2005b), 'Further Statement by Group of Executive Directors on the World Bank's Presidential Selection Process', Washington, DC, 31 March.

10. Globalisation, terror and the future of 'development': citizenship beyond bare life?

Su-ming Khoo

This is the story of a crime – of the murder of reality. And the extermination of an illusion – the vital illusion, the radical illusion of the world.

Jean Baudrillard, *The Perfect Crime* (1996)

INTRODUCTION: THE VITAL ILLUSION OF DEVELOPMENT

'Development' has provided a central theme and organising concept for modern social and political thought. Although it is conventionally seen as a post-1945 concept, ideas of development are grounded in much earlier Enlightenment understandings of historical change as universal and progressive, a rolling-out or unfolding of human emancipation and freedom. The project of development is thus intimately bound up with understandings of citizenship and democracy – the 'social contract', and with the claims of the politically, socially and economically excluded.

The idea of development is partly what Marshall Berman (1982) calls the 'vital mode of experience' of modernity itself and, like modernity, it has both utopian and dystopian faces. Positivist traditions have shaped 'development' as a schema for thinking about people, nature and economy since French and English Enlightenment thinkers sought to discover, explain and prescribe universal principles for economic and political government. Universalising concepts of human progress emerged at the historical juncture when the capitalist world economy was expanding. Nation states consolidated their sovereignty and sought to manage economic, social and industrial transformation through territorial expansion and the intensified exploitation of nature and humans. As national economies pulled together, they formed part of an emerging international system of modern states (Wallerstein, 2004). Vast areas and peoples were integrated into this world system through colonial mechanisms of conquest, production and exchange.

The critical, or 'counterpoint' strand of development thinking is more preoccupied with the ills of progress and the negative effects of economic expansion and incorporation. These two strands of positivist and critical development thinking present the two dialectical faces of development. On one hand, development thinking envisages a utopian programme for progressive modernisation, but on the other hand, there is also a dystopian critique of the human and natural cost of capitalist incorporation and the elaboration of radical, reformist or sometimes nostalgic or reactionary alternatives.

The epigraph at the beginning of this chapter is from Jean Baudrillard's essay *A Perfect Crime* (1996). His rhetorical assertion is deliberately exaggerated and opaque, precisely to provoke us to ask what is the 'real' vision of society that we do not wish to be murdered. A vision of development as 'good change' must answer to the fundamental challenges posed by the real reconfiguration of wealth, well-being, citizenship, ill-being and violence that have taken place during the past decades in the name of development and globalisation.

This chapter discusses three central problems that have persisted as the project of development has given way to globalisation. It argues that the future of development depends on how these problems are addressed, given the current context of globalisation, accompanied by the 'war on terror'. First, the contradiction between *universalist* principles and *exceptionalist* (or 'realist') practice, especially in relation to the political and economic agendas of development's hegemonic power, the United States. Second, the debate over economic *means* versus the human *ends* of development, representing contrasting demands for *efficiency* on one hand, and *justice* on the other. The current development mantra of 'good governance' collapses the means–ends distinction, replacing citizens' demands for social and political entitlements with external demands for market efficiency. Third, how development should deal with *poverty* – and whether we should think of poverty as *absolute* or *relative* deprivation. This last debate is crucial as it makes a profound connection between inequality, development and democracy, since demands for equality and structural justice involve the reduction of relative as well as absolute deprivations through the 'thickening' and radicalisation of citizenship and democracy.

Bauman explains that globalisation divides as it unites, creating new forms of social and spatial segregation, separation and exclusion (1999, pp. 2–3). Differing definitions of citizenship are at the centre of the contradiction between universalism and exceptionalism – as individual buyers and sellers in markets, as subjects of sovereign states, as rights bearers and as abject 'bare life' (Agamben, 1998). The contrasting principles of sovereignty and justice create pull and push between development and states, development and markets and development and citizens. A basic contradiction stands between the universalising and egalitarian claims of market freedom and the structural inequalities that determine the outcome of market incorporation as beneficial to some, but violent and adverse for others. This discussion suggests that the egalitarian social model of citizenship has been severely eroded by neo-liberal globalisation. I offer a defence of social citizenship based on a human rights position as a model for the future of development, given that market subjection, inequality and structural violence add up to a particularly undesirable model of globalisation.

The final part of this chapter provides a critical analysis of the 'post-Washington Consensus' and the millennial efforts to rehabilitate international development to 'include' the abject poor within a template of globalisation that is 'morally flat', but drastically unequal in empirical terms (Nederveen Pieterse, 2002, p. 1040). Globalisation's models of market sovereignty and consumer citizenship require the 'bracketing out' of those who do not, and cannot, qualify as consumer citizens due to their lack of purchasing power. For the very poor, market subjection involves exclusion and the *politics of abjection*. The processes of global capitalism simultaneously constitute categories of social and geographical membership and privilege, while constructing and maintaining 'a category of *absolute non-membership*: a holding tank for those turned away at the "development" door' (Ferguson, 1999, p. 242, italics added). Lipschutz uses the economic term 'externality' to encapsulate the social and environmental impacts of globalisation that are the material outcomes of globalisation's core beliefs and practices, yet they are ignored (2005, p. 26). Once they are placed outside the 'system', externalities are rendered immune to systematic analysis or critique.

The contemporary rendering of abject poverty as a human emergency raises its profile as an action issue, but treats it as just such an externality, separating it from 'normal' politics. Aid for such emergencies allows the fundamental inequality and structural injustice that flows from market sovereignty to be set aside. Our attention is focused on 'poverty that kills' (Sachs, 2005) as an exceptional state, a state of emergency. The 'powers of horror' that are associated with the abject (Kristeva, 1982) are harnessed in the creation of this state of exception, othering the poor as tragic victims. Thus are the abject poor thrown downwards, cast aside, expelled and discarded (Ferguson, 1999, p. 236). Even though the abject poor are placed outside the normal parameters of politics, they are still most subject to the structural violence that flows from extreme inequality. For the abject poor, 'development' is still a radical idea, and for them the demand for 'development' is most vital, yet it is also most illusory.

COLD WAR: THE INVENTION OF DEVELOPMENT
AND THE GEO-POLITICS OF RIGHTS

At the end of the Second World War, the UN Temporary Commission of
Social Affairs observed:

> At least half of the peoples of the world are living, by no fault of their own,
> under such poor and inadequate conditions that they cannot, out of their own
> scanty resources, achieve decent standards of living. The deep gulfs existing
> between the standards of living of different nations are, in the opinion of the
> Commission, a main source of international discontent, unrest, crisis and, in the
> last resort, are causes of wars, ultimately endangering and devastating countries
> of high as well as low standards of living. (ECOSOC, 1946, cited in de
> Senarclens, 1997, p. 190)

Some authors contend that development was 'invented' as a project to
eliminate world poverty for both universal, moral humanitarian reasons
and exceptionalist demands by the United States for national security, the
containment of Communism and market expansion (for example, Rist,
1997). Groenemeyer (1992, pp. 61–3) describes the post-Second World War
regime of international development assistance as 'elegant power', offering
help that serves the helper's particular interests and yet presents it as a
project of universal moral obligation. 'Development' thus referred ambiva-
lently to US-driven Cold War strategy and to an emerging set of universalistic aspirations for human rights and international peace and
cooperation which gained institutional form in the United Nations. The
latter led to the historical codification of a vision of global citizenship
based on universal human rights principles, starting with the 1948
Universal Declaration of Human Rights (UDHR).

The principle of containment drove development efforts during the Cold
War, and in the post-Cold War phase the containment principle informs the
securitisation of development and pre-emptive management for the 'failed
states' that cannot be integrated through market discipline (Soederberg,
2004). Hegemonic 'soft power' management of the development consensus
has become more visibly supplemented with 'hard power' coercion in the
post-Cold War period, especially with the rise of doctrines of asymmetric
power and 'full-spectrum dominance'.

The UDHR formally established human rights as 'universal, interdependent and indivisible', but formal consensus was marred from the very
beginning by bitter disagreements over models of citizenship, specifically
which particular ideas of citizen rights should be prioritised and whether
the state or the market could best deliver them. The Western liberal
tradition emphasised negative conceptions of rights, privileging private

individual citizens freedom from state interference, particularly in relation to their ownership of private property and limited taxation. On the other hand, 'developmental' views emphasised positive conceptions of rights as citizens' entitlements to employment and economic welfare, assuming a strong role for the state as guarantor of such rights (Steiner and Alston, 2000, p. 237).

As the Cold War intensified, the contrasts between different conceptions of citizenship were highlighted as the UDHR became the subject of intensifying ideological conflict between the Western and Eastern blocs. Two separate human rights treaties were eventually agreed, nearly twenty years later in 1966 – one emphasising the civil and political rights (the International Convention on Civil and Political Rights: ICCPR) and another emphasising economic and social rights (the International Convention on Economic, Social and Cultural Rights: ICESCR). In theory, these two 'pillars' were interdependent and interconnected, since the disagreement was 'not over the ultimate goals of universal human rights, only about how to achieve it' (United Nations, 1995, p. 42 at 122). Both covenants affirmed the inherent universality and egalitarianism of human rights, stressing the 'inherent dignity of the human person' and the 'inalienable rights to freedom and equality' (ibid., p. 42 at 222). However, a hierarchy of rights was historically established, privileging the liberal view of citizenship within the international system. Civil and political rights gained recognition in international law as 'justiciable' rights, while economic, social and cultural rights were considered softer and less justiciable, 'emergent' and 'gradual'.

THE END OF THE GOLDEN AGE: TOWARDS POST-DEVELOPMENT

Despite these ideological differences, states implemented 'development' in ways that enlarged social citizenship across the ideological spectrum. For nearly three decades, capitalist and socialist development models in both advanced and developing countries were based on a model of assimilation, inclusion and convergence, with economics being subordinated to politics and substantive development of social models of citizenship (see Marshall, 1992). Favourable economic conditions provided the possibility of growth and stability to most states within the international framework. The 1950s and 1960s represented a 'Golden Age' of capitalist development with relatively high overall rates of economic growth (Marglin and Schor, 1990, p. 1). A broadly Keynesian 'developmental' state provided the predominant policy model for economic growth. Development entailed state-protected industrialisation, the expansion and modernisation of the public sector and infrastructure as well as the state expansion of education and social welfare.

New critical perspectives arose in the 1960s as debates emerged about economic growth and import-substitution industrialisation as the chosen means of development and its ability to achieve the desired ends. The Latin American experience seemed to show that the state-led model of industrialisation was neither economically efficient nor sustainable as a growth strategy. Where economic growth had occurred, it was accompanied by increasing social inequality, while visible deprivation persisted. Critiques of poverty and inequality came to the fore and the 'trickle-down' theory of redistribution was criticised (Seers, 1969). The 'redistribution with growth' strategy offered a social democratic solution, suggesting that economic growth could be accompanied by specific measures to reduce poverty through more progressive income distribution and employment creation (Chenery et al., 1974).

The late 1960s marked the beginning of a wider 'cultural revolution' in development thinking as a diversity of humanist, environmental, feminist and anti-militarist critiques emerged, influencing the search for alternative models and strategies. An expansive debate opened up around the meaning and goals of development, providing new dimensions to oppositional and 'counterpoint' thinking (see Hettne, 1995). Important conceptual revolutions had begun to take place, but the search for 'another development' remained on the margins as state-led economic growth and modernisation continued to dominate development policy orthodoxy.

Mainstream development policy continued to be synonymous with state action until the 1980s. However, the state-driven model had begun to unravel in the 1970s under the pressures of oil price shocks and world economic downturn. The USA's growing fiscal deficits led to the destruction of the Bretton Woods system of fixed exchange rates in 1973, ushering in a new era of economic uncertainty. The value, cost and price of money became detached from production processes and the door was opened for the globalisation of finance capital. States became more vulnerable to external pressures, just as external conditions were deteriorating. World economic growth slowed to 3 per cent in the 1970s and to 2 per cent in the 1980s, with more frequent recessions (Marglin and Schor, 1990, p. 1). These global shocks and shifts shaped the new development orthodoxy of globalisation, based on export-orientad industrialisation and foreign direct investment. In the new international division of labour driven by transnational corporations, states became 'competition states', forced by global pressures to trade off domestic demands for the welfare state against the need for international economic competitiveness and the demands of mobile capital. A new social contract emerged – the exclusive society 'where the steady increment of justice began to falter' (Young, 1999, p. 1). By the mid-1970s, the primary engine for economic growth and development had shifted from state to market. Political accountability continued to reside in the nation state, but external conditions were more challenging and less accommodating.

Development encountered massive theoretical and practical challenges during the 1980s, as globalisation, socialism's collapse and the end of the Cold War undermined the very political and intellectual foundations of the idea, while the debt crisis led to the simultaneous collapse of financing for development. Jeffrey Alexander observed that a second Great Transformation had taken place: 'we are witnessing the death of a major alternative not only in social thought, but in society itself. In the fore-seeable future, it is unlikely that either citizens or elites will try to struc-ture their primary allocative systems in non-market ways' (Alexander, 1995, p. 65). The Keynesian idea of a coordinated international system of nationally regulated economies no longer seemed like a concrete possibil-ity (Leys, 1996). A further big question for development emerged as the environmental limitations of economic development became apparent in the early 1970s. Neo-Malthusian analyses of population growth, pollution and resource depletion informed the 'limits to growth' debate, leading to the sustainable development debate in the 1980s.

The 1980s became a decade of disenchantment for development thinkers and practitioners as the neo-liberal macroeconomic reforms pre-scribed by the 'Washington Consensus' downsized the state and many countries began to experience 'de-development'. The introduction of monetarist policies in the USA and the UK raised interest rates dramati-cally, causing the flows of capital from developed to developing countries to reverse (Figure 10.1). Indebted developing countries that had been net receivers of investment capital now became net disbursers of capital in the form of debt service.

The high interest rates under monetarism effectively forced the present generation to discount their future at a higher rate (UNDP, 1992, p. 50), and subjected debtor governments to creditor institutions and the new policy fundamentalism of neo-liberalism. Indebted states were forced to tear up their social contract and become the opposite of developmental states as 'economic shock therapy' became the new development ortho-doxy. The economic and welfare gains to development that had been incremental up to the 1970s began to reverse in some countries and regions (particularly in Sub-Saharan Africa), though they continued to advance in others (mainly East Asia). Many developing states had attempted a collective approach to redress the legacy of colonial inequal-ities even as globalisation and competition were beginning to undermine

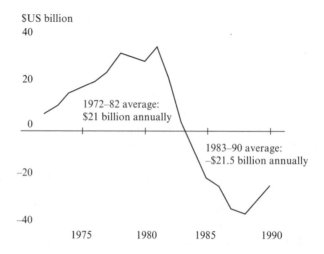

$US billion

Source: UNDP (1992, p. 50). Reproduced by permission of Oxford University Press, Inc.

Figure 10.1   Net financial transfers to developing countries, 1970–90

their newly-found political power. In 1974, developing country demands for a New International Economic Order rocked the United Nations system 'to its very core' (O'Rawe, 1999, p. 28) with their demands for structural inequality and historical injustice to be redressed and these demands continue to form the core of 'development issues' today. Yet by the 1980s, the widening differences between countries and regions lessened the coherence of the 'Developing World' or 'Third World' as a shared reality, making collective aspirations and hopes for convergence much more unlikely.

The 1990s saw the emergence of the deconstructive and critical 'post-development' school, contributing to a further conceptual implosion. 'Post-development' critics rejected development as an empty promise and an illusion:

> The idea of development stands like a ruin in the intellectual landscape. Delusion and disappointment, failures and crimes have been steady companions to development and they tell a common story: it did not work. Moreover, the historical conditions which catapulted the idea into prominence have vanished: development has become outdated. (Sachs, 1992, p. 1)

Post-development thinking reflected the very real difficulties of reconciling the progressive and critical strands of development thinking. The progressive view is largely positivist and optimistic in its view of social change, while the critical view is more pessimistic and polemic, presenting development as critique rather than as 'project'. The post-development school angrily rejected the entire concept of 'development' as a Eurocentric template for domination. Their alternative was a romantic, culturally essentialist and anti-Eurocentric vision based on the 'vernacular' cultures of the Third World (see, for example, Rahnema and Bawtree, 1997). They looked to indigenous 'pre-development' societies as sources of non-capitalist ways of life, post-materialist ethics, and indigenous wisdom.

Post-development's reified conception of cultural traditions as the 'answer' leads towards communitarian rather than social interpretations of citizenship. Its nostalgia and Occidentalism suggest a neo-traditionalist stance (Nederveen Pieterse, 2001, p. 110) that emphasises particularistic collective culture rather than universal individual rights, and tends to ignore problems of existing need and inequality.

A HISTORIC OPPORTUNITY TO RECONNECT RIGHTS AND DEVELOPMENT AND TO RETHINK 'SECURITY'

The disarray of development studies since the 1980s reflects the changing reference points for macrosocial analysis brought on by globalisation (Robinson, 2002, p. 1048). However, the social processes that 'development' tried to explain and mitigate had certainly not ground to a halt, but were quickening, making alternative approaches and exit from the 'paradigmatic quagmire' (ibid.) ever more necessary. As globalisation continues apace, development's promise remains vital, in both senses of being alive and necessary. While some saw the 'end of history' as synonymous with the triumph of the market, the end of the Cold War also presented a new historic opportunity to renew the human rights vision as there was no longer the need to preserve the historical antinomy between 'rights' and 'development', civil or political freedoms and socio-economic entitlements. The fundamental principles of indivisibility and the interdependence of rights could be recovered, presenting a holistic project for progressive change through the development of an international human rights framework.

Since the 1970s, several international conventions have already gone some way towards making indivisible and interdependent human rights a reality. These include the Convention on the Elimination of Discrimination against Women (CEDAW) which entered into force in 1981, the Declaration on the Right to Development (DRD) adopted in 1986, the Convention on the Rights of the Child (CRC) which entered into force in 1990 and the Convention on the Rights of All Migrant Workers which came into force in

2003 (United Nations, 1995, pp. 71–2 at 328, 331, 332). These conventions all broke ground by integrating the 'pillars' of human rights that had been driven apart by the Cold War. They marked a practical step towards the convergence of human rights and human development, starting with the most vulnerable and disadvantaged groups.

The 1986 DRD marked a potentially important turning-point because it redefined development in the age of globalisation, in terms that privileged human goals and subjectivity, placing the human being 'at the very centre of development'. Its emphasis on human beings as both the starting-point and ultimate ends of development marked a shift, away from the economism of growth and towards more ethical and humanistic goals and definitions (see Gasper, 2004).

The 1990s saw the emergence of the human development idea, arising from the 'basic needs' approach of the 1970s and Amartya Sen's theory of human capabilities and freedoms (Sen, 1999). This involved the redefinition and measurement of development using the Human Development Index (HDI). While economic growth continued to be recognised as an important component of development, it was put in a wider context of its contribution towards improvements in human development, defined more expansively as 'the process of enlarging the range of people's choices' (UNDP, 1992, p. 2).

The human development approach has continued to evolve and deepen since the 1990s. The clarification of ends and means, the fundamental concern with human freedoms and dignity, and concern for human agency characterise this emergent field of thinking (Fukuda-Parr, 2004). These core concerns underpin the demand for a participatory ethos to 'thicken' citizenship and democratise development. Participatory approaches emphasise egalitarian demands for fairer distribution of the benefits of development, and place a high value on development objectives being determined by people themselves.

By the early 1990s there were concerted efforts to close the Cold War gap between security and development thinking. The 'New Security Debate' proposed that a fundamental re-thinking of security was needed, re-orientating the concept of security away from hard power militarism and towards the achievement of human security, by redirecting resources towards development goals such as the eradication of poverty, hunger and disease instead of the traditional focus on state military capability (Johnson, 1999; Owen, 2004). However, post-Cold War global decreases in military spending and hopes for the diversion of states' resources towards development ('the peace dividend') were short-lived. Global military spending rose again from the late 1990s and by 2002 had again reached peak Cold War levels (Sköns, 2005, p. 3).

THE POST-WASHINGTON CONSENSUS

The neo-liberal Washington Consensus had incited internal and external critique since its rise in the early 1980s, but cracks became more visible in the consensus by the mid-1990s as its 'one-size-fits-all' macroeconomic approach came under greater theoretical and empirical strain from two angles – human poverty and governance.

The publication of the 'Adjustment with a Human Face' studies by Cornia et al. under the auspices of UNICEF (1987) signalled considerable dissent around the human cost of structural adjustment policies and their impact on human development, particularly for the poorest, women and children. The advent of James Wolfensohn's presidency of the World Bank also marked a sea-change in the mid-1990s as he incorporated a greater concern for the poor, initiating a 'Voices of the Poor' research project within the World Bank, involving 60 000 poor people in 'Participatory Poverty Assessments' across 60 countries (Narayan, 2000).

On the governance side of the argument, the East Asian countries had been pressed by the World Bank and the IMF to prove that their 'economic miracle' could be attributed to neo-liberal macroeconomic policies. However, the East Asian specialists within the Bank argued that this was not the case. East Asian success was really attributable to strong state intervention and active regulation, not weak states and deregulated markets as prescribed. East Asian countries had liberalised foreign trade and international finance according to neo-liberal prescriptions, however, the Asian financial crisis of 1997 provided dramatic evidence that this could lead to market failure, underlining the risks of deregulation in developing countries where state controls over the banking and finance sector were weak.

Arguments for stronger state institutions and the 'developmental state' started to re-enter the development orthodoxy. By the end of the1990s, a 'post-Washington Consensus' had appeared in relation to both governance and poverty issues, partially rehabilitating the role of states in the project of 'development', though in a limited and ambivalent manner. Mawdsley and Rigg's study of the World Bank's own literature found more evidence for a continuity with neo-liberal orthodoxy than radical change. The difference between 'soft talk' and 'hard policies' means that the post-Washington Consensus is more 'Washington Consensus' than 'post'. Development orthodoxy remains 'neoliberal, economistic and technocratic at heart' (2002, p. 108). 'Good governance' dominates development policy, and some state capacity is recognised as necessary, especially for the poorer and least-developed countries of Sub-Saharan Africa. A 'capable state' was now accepted as a requirement to facilitate the market and to help avoid market failures. However, actual development policies are not that much different from the neo-liberal policy conditionalities of the past. What is different is that these policies are now couched in the language of partnership and poverty reduction, giving each underdeveloped country the responsibility 'to manage managing its own underdevelopment wisely' (Abrahamsen, 2004, p. 1461).

The conclusion of the World Bank 'Voices of the Poor' study was that poor people's problems lay not just in their lack of income, but more importantly in the combination of their lack of assets and their powerlessness and lack of political voice (Narayan, 2000). Wade (2001) chronicled a growing chasm between neo-liberal and developmental perspectives in the struggle over the draft 2000–1 World Development Report, subtitled 'Attacking Poverty'. Ravi Kanbur had been appointed by the World Bank's Chief Economist, Joseph Stiglitz, to direct the team in charge of the report. Drawing on the 'Voices of the Poor' project and on the lessons from the 1997 Asian crisis, the draft report 'contained much that was anathema to [US] Treasury thinking' (Wade, 2001, p. 131). It allocated some of the blame for the Asian crisis to too-rapid opening of financial markets and advocated that other developing countries should follow the Chilean and Malaysian strategy of strict capital controls. The draft report was uncontroversial in supporting economic growth as 'the engine of poverty reduction', but it placed greater priority on empowerment and security for the poor, instead of putting growth first. It advocated that effective social 'safety-nets' had to be in place before free market reforms were pushed through, and it contained a section of policy proposals to empower the poor by scaling up organisations such as trade unions, cooperatives and networks, to enable them to articulate their political and economic interests and demand more responsiveness and accountability from state organisations.

The wider political context for these struggles at the dawn of the millennium was one of increasing civil society mobilisation and protest against neo-liberal policies and institutions, including the massive anti-globalisation protests against the World Trade Organisation in Seattle in 1999, and at the subsequent World Bank and IMF Spring Meetings. The US Treasury and the IMF criticised Kanbur's draft report, demanding that it be rewritten to remove the parts that they felt were '[pandering] to noisy and nosy NGOs [non-governmental organisations]' and to refocus the report more squarely on growth. Both Kanbur and Stiglitz departed from the World Bank and the final report was amended to emphasise the growth message and de-emphasise empowerment for the poor, as well as omitting the recommendation on capital controls. Kanbur later published an article in *World Development* contrasting the views from what he termed the 'Finance Ministry' versus 'Civil Society' (2001).

THE MILLENNIUM DEVELOPMENT AGENDA

The Millennium Summit in 2000 in New York saw the formal restatement of international aid commitments. The initial agreement at the United Nations First Decade of Development in 1961, was for the advanced countries to provide 1 per cent of their gross national income in assistance to developing countries. This obligation was reduced in 1970 to 0.7 per cent, but to date this existing promise has only been met by five countries: Denmark, Norway, Luxembourg, Sweden and the Netherlands (UNDP, 2005, p. 85).

The millennium development agenda as it stands today is a call to honour the levels of international assistance agreed in 1970 and for limited state cooperation to deliver basic social services to the abject poor. Mawdsley and Rigg (2003) discern a gradual weakening over time of the concept of development as shared responsibility. The 'post-Washington Consensus' marks a partial return to the idea of the state as a guarantor of social welfare not as an entitlement of citizenship, but as a minimal precondition for market functioning. It is supplemented by largely depoliticised and utilitarian conceptions of 'empowerment' (ibid.), and 'partnership' (Abrahamsen, 2004) more often employing arguments for poverty reduction based on efficiency rather than justice, that is, because it is a *cheap* measure, not because it is *right*.

'Development' as articulated by the UN's Millennium Development Goals means a project of poverty alleviation for the 1.2 billion people classified as the 'extreme poor', on incomes of less than one US dollar a day. Eight million people constitute what Sachs terms the 'voiceless dying' (Sachs, 2005). These are persons whose immediate vulnerability places them completely beyond the question of political consent or citizenship. They are consigned to space outside politics, the injustice of their voicelessness is overridden by the human emergency of their imminent death.

DEVELOPMENT, INEQUALITY AND STRUCTURAL VIOLENCE

As Nederveen Pieterse observes, the data on inequality under globalisation is 'dramatic and widely known . . . Overall discrepancies in income and wealth are now vast to the point of being grotesque' (2002, p. 1023). Global inequalities are 'so large that they are without historical precedent and without conceivable justification – economic, moral or otherwise . . . Global inequality has increased sharply since the 1980s, in a clear rupture with the pattern over previous decades'; '30 postwar years of growth with

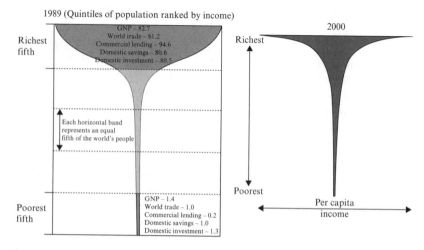

1989 (Quintiles of population ranked by income)

Richest fifth

GNP – 82.7
World trade – 81.2
Commercial lending – 94.6
Domestic savings – 80.6
Domestic investment – 80.5

Each horizontal band
represents an equal
fifth of the world's people

Poorest fifth

GNP – 1.4
World trade – 1.0
Commercial lending – 0.2
Domestic savings – 1.0
Domestic investment – 1.3

2000

Richest

Poorest

Per capita income

Sources: 1989: UNDP (1992, p. 35); 2000: UNDP (2005, p. 37); Dikhanov (2005, p. 43).
Reproduced by permission of Oxford University Press, Inc and Yuri Dikhanov

Figure 10.2   World distribution of income, 1989 and 2000 (percentage of world total)

improving equality have been succeeded by a pattern of growth with increasing inequality' (ibid., pp. 1028, 1034).

Putting the picture of inequality today side by side with that of a decade and a half ago, we can see that global inequality has worsened in shape, from what was described as a 'champagne glass' in 1989 to a shape approximating that of a 'g-string' brief in 2000. Comparing the shapes of inequality over the past decade or more, we see that the relative income share of the global majority, the bottom 80 per cent of the world, has not changed much – they still command a very small portion of world income. However, the top 20 per cent has changed shape quite dramatically, reflecting the fact that a tiny fraction of the top 20 per cent are capturing more and more income share, while the relative position of the upper-middle class is getting more precarious (Figure 10.2). What does this mean in terms of justice as well as efficiency and how does it relate to what might be termed 'structural violence'?

In 1992, the UNDP optimistically predicted that the 1990s would shape up 'as the decade for human development, for rarely has there been such a consensus on the real objectives of development strategies' (p. 74). In reality, unprecedented reversals and divergence have taken place in human development terms since 1990. Fifty-four countries were poorer in 2003 than they were in 1990 and life expectancy fell in 34 countries. The under-five mortality rate increased in 14 countries and primary school enrolments declined in 12 countries. In 21 countries the proportion of hungry people increased (UNDP, 2003).

There is little doubt that the 'war on terror' has resulted in the 'securitization of development' since 2001, replacing egalitarian humanitarian development aspirations with military and counter-terrorism goals (see Tujan et al., 2004). This has involved the militarisation of the bilateral aid policies of major donors, with a greater emphasis on foreign military financing instead of social development outcomes. The criteria of 'good governance' required by recipients of development aid have been redefined to include counter-terrorism measures. New aid initiatives have been focused on Pakistan, India, Indonesia and the Philippines as the most important fronts of the war on terror, or channelled to strategically important countries such as Djibouti, which received $31 million in US aid in return for permission for to set up a new US military base. There are fears that these changes may result in lowered arms control standards and lessened democratic accountability, with greater potential for human rights abuses (Human Rights Watch, 2002, p. 14).

While such measures focus on the containment of 'terrorist' violence, proponents of human security and human development continue to highlight the relationship between the trends of extreme inequality and structural violence and the causes of war (see, for example, Johnson, 1999). Structural violence can be defined as 'the political, economic, and social structures that maintain gross disparities of wealth and power within a country . . . [T]here are intimate links between structural violence and direct violence, because direct or physical violence is often used against those who resist or overcome structural violence' (Atack, 2005, p. 97). Farmer (2005) does not resort to precise definitions of structural violence, but explains it by 'bearing witness' to the suffering of the powerless. He illustrates the ways in which political, economic and social inequalities structure risks for infectious disease, but also 'most forms of extreme suffering, from hunger to torture to rape'. The conclusion is that the violence of poverty is not exceptional – the suffering of the abject is the expression of structural relations of inequality, manifested as violence on the bodies of the poor.

RETURN TO STARK UTOPIA: DEVELOPMENT REDUX OR DEVELOPMENT REDUCED?

An NGO campaign poster around Galway, Ireland proclaims that 'Poverty is the Real Emergency'. The visible 'realness' of the emergency, reflected in the eyes of the African child on the poster, paradoxically reinforces the invisible death of a more radical illusion – that of equality and justice, not charity. The new development consensus for poverty alleviation sits against a new conventional backdrop of predictable and well-known statistics about the extent of the 'new' emergency of poverty. Poverty alleviation exists 'in an awkward consensus' alongside neo-liberal policies (Nederveen Pieterse, 2002, p. 1026). Within the community of development experts, research and policy have been refocused on poverty and the 'Millennium Development Goals', including first and foremost the halving of absolute poverty and hunger by the year 2015. However, the discussion of inequality is purposefully sidelined. It is precisely the bracketing out of the very poorest and their treatment as an 'emergency case' that denies the vital and radical egalitarian promise of development as emancipation from structural violence, agreeing instead on a promise of palliative care for the abject.

Over the past decades, the concept of development itself has been seriously challenged, empirically and conceptually, externally and internally. Something like a Baudrillardian defence of the real is a necessary strategy if development is to have a future. The future of development hinges on how the key political questions of sovereignty and legitimacy are addressed – through democracy, citizenship and rights. The question of legitimate and illegitimate violence, raised by the war on terror cannot be insulated from wider questioning of the everyday terror of structural violence.

Brennan notes the striking similarity between George W. Bush's definition of terrorism and the terror of routine market incorporation, subjecting people to 'an unseen hand that strikes from nowhere without accountability, destroying innocent lives' (2002, p. 1). There is a stark contrast between the highly visible and politically dramatised human losses that unleashed the war on terror and the almost invisible, yet equally human, losses of structural violence. According to UNICEF estimates, a number of children equivalent to 12 Twin Tower tragedies die every day from hunger, malnutrition and preventable diseases. Increasing prosperity for the 'winners' of globalisation has been accompanied by the scaling down of consideration for the 'losers': 'Since 1990 increased prosperity in rich countries has done little to enhance generosity: per capita income has increased by $6,070, while per capita aid has fallen by $1' (UNDP, 2005, p. 8).

'Stark utopia' was a phrase coined by Karl Polanyi in *The Great Transformation*, to describe the fact that self-regulating free markets had not, and could not, be achieved:

> The goal of a self-adjusting market economy, 'disembedded' from society, culture and nature is a Utopian project. 'Such an institution could not exist for any length of time without annihilating the human and natural substance of

society; it would have physically destroyed man and transformed his surroundings into a wilderness. (2007, p. 3)

Polanyi's insight was that state coercion and repression are required to 'free' markets since the human and natural costs of market subjection are so high. Yet too much progress towards stark utopia could result in total social disintegration, as evidenced by the descent into two world wars. Fascism, for Polanyi was an example of a 'protective countermovement' brought on by the global freeing of market forces. Patel and McMichael (2004) point to the strong family resemblance between nationalism and fascism – both are capital's response to systemic threats.

DEVELOPMENT AS AN 'ANTI-POLITICS' MACHINE

Ferguson characterised development as an 'anti-politics machine', an apparatus that manages the 'suspension of politics from even the most sensitive of operations' (1994, p. 256). 'Development' involves 'étatization', the expansion of bureaucratic state power, with the conceptual and ideological effect of depoliticising both poverty and the state. The anti-politics machine reduces poverty to a technical problem for the bureaucratic state apparatus, a problem that requires technical solutions, not political ones. State power expands and becomes entrenched – even when it fails to deliver on its promises, more state action is required to eliminate poverty and deprivation.

In the era of globalisation and the post-Washington Consensus, the reference points for the anti-politics machine have been changed to a new accommodation between the market, states and civil society. Lipschutz argues that globalisation returns us to Polanyi's 'stark utopia' of politics via markets (2005, p. 62). Neo-liberalism has resulted in a generalised hegemony of utilitarian, technical and managerialist concerns on a world scale, accepting the fundamental constitutive questions of politics as a 'done deal'. As stark utopia advances, Lipschutz asks 'where have all our politics gone'? (ibid., p. 49). Faulks notes that citizenship is a concept that contains inherent demands for its benefits to become 'ever more universal and egalitarian', gaining in extent, content and depth over time (2000, p. 3). Yet the reconstitution of politics under globalisation has promoted the hollowing-out of the social contract and an acceptance of inegalitarian outcomes.

By raising economic growth to the status of simultaneously national, *and* global ideology, a technique was achieved for deterring *both* constitutive and distributive political questions. Attention is trained on economic growth and market efficiency, avoiding the distributive question of fairness and the constitutive questions about the nature of the social contract under market sovereignty, where 'benefits accrue to producers as well as consumers; but costs are imposed on those who are politically and economically powerless and too weak to resist those changes' (ibid., p. 27).

During the 'Golden Age' of welfare capitalism, 'development' was *the* project of states. It represented a social contract between states and former colonial subjects, who wished to become citizens. The achievement of self-rule provided a constitutive moment of political legitimacy for the post-colonial state. Post-colonial developing-country states could attribute poverty and inequality to the injustices of colonial exploitation. However, independence promised a post-colonial social contract – a state that could deliver people from their unchosen status as colonial subjects to a new status as modern citizens. Post-colonial states delivered independence and state sovereignty as a first step of 'citizenship-in-progress' through political rights and representation, while development promised a second step of citizenship through participation in employment, and through entitlements to health and education.

Yet, in many post-colonial situations, the national question remains unresolved. 'Development' meant 'catching up' for new states as well as social improvement for their citizens, involving the achievement of a parity of power and esteem with the more advanced nations and previous colonial masters (Gasper, 2004, p. 35). Mamdani argues that we must understand the historical specificity of the mode of rule in post-colonial situations, because while there may have been a break with the formal institutions of colonial power, there was no such break with the forms of that power (1996, p. 298). He characterises the post-colonial experience as 'history by analogy', 'a series of approximations, as replays not quite efficient, understudies that fell short of the real performance' (ibid., p. 9). Developing nations fall into the classification of the 'not yet' – 'not yet modern', 'not yet capitalist' and not yet democratic with regard to its 'not-yet citizens'.

Developmental states are typically not democratic, but simultaneously authoritarian and populist, with elites driving a programme of national 'development' in the name of the masses. The project of 'nation-building' cements the two objectives of self-rule and democracy, but it has contradictory tendencies since elites often sacrifice improvement for the poor in favour of improvement for 'the nation' defined through their own class-specific (often ethnically defined) interests. Mamdani shows that self-rule continues from 'native rule', itself a product of colonial subjection, and not fully reconcilable with citizenship. Post-colonial developmental elites often represent the choices of the coloniser, not the colonised, who remain subjects to customary and despotic forms of power that historically developed under colonialism. The post-colonial attempt to address the legacy of colonial rule must attend to both the native question and the subject question, questioning the hyphenation of the subject-citizen and the lack of fit between participation and representation.

To some extent, national elites can slip past these contradictions by invoking development according to the principles of economic nationalism and appealing to technocratic strategies of economic growth. The principle of solidarity for national competitiveness in a globalising world contains the distributive question, just as the quest for growth contains the demand for equality.

CONCLUSIONS: SOME QUESTIONS FOR CRITICAL AND HUMAN DEVELOPMENT

'Development' provides a critical means by which to pursue the real questions of equity, justice and human ends, if it is able to escape the immediate concerns of efficiency, growth and technical means. Critical development thinking must connect technocratic concerns to more fundamental questions about inequality and the social contract. It must pay proper attention to how citizens are made subject, and abject, by the sovereign power of states and markets. Development must provide a route out of abjection and a rights-based approach enables this by asserting the fundamentally egalitarian claim of persons to their dignity and rights.

Exceptionalism is a necessary mode of operation for all sovereign power. Even democracy requires exceptionalism and a degree of coercion, since 'the very idea of democracy is violent . . . the concepts of a people, a border, and of foundation are violent *in themselves*, in that they must be *imposed*, in spite of their impossibility, in order to get democracy going' (Ross, 2004, p. 151, original italics). Subjection and exceptionalism are essential constituents of the political doctrine of sovereignty. Coercion is most visible and subjection most problematic when sovereign power overturns citizen consent, for example by declaring a state of emergency. In cases of emergency, citizens lose their constitutive power and become subjects as the bottom-up flow of consent is overridden by top-down forms of coercion.

The status of persons in relation to the market, the state and violence – as political subjects, citizens or as abject 'bare life', pushed outside the normal parameters of political life – stands at the centre of development's futures. Neo-liberal globalisation has aggravated the existing legitimacy problems inherent in statist models of development by demanding the rollback of the state, and scaling down political expectations of what citizens may legitimately demand from their states. The needs not attended to are reconfigured as market externalities, not citizen entitlements, treated as residual and returned to 'civil society'. In practice this means leaving the problems up to 'charity' and at the door of NGOs. The fig leaf of legitimacy in developmental states has been further compromised by the decisive shift towards authoritarian forms of governmentality since the 'war on terror'. The accounting for the human cost of the war on terror has served, for some, to highlight the exceptionalist double standards that define the normatively human: what counts as a livable life and a grievable death? (Butler, 2004, p. xv). The combination of neo-liberal globalisation and the war on terror erodes development's 'vital illusion', its potential for human recognition, realisation and emancipation, putting in its place political subjection and human abjection, enforced by an increasing supplement of coercion and violence.

The post-Washington consensus and the millennium development agenda carry less visible, but no less significant risks. The everyday terror of violence, abjection and suffering endured by the very poor have not been recognised as structural and systemic effects of violently unequal globalisation, but as 'externalities', emergencies and exceptions to it. Efforts to alleviate poverty in the name of development are increasingly taking the shape of technical discourses, policed to exclude or at least marginalise the real questions of structural injustice, political and economic subjection and exclusion. There is the risk that the new development agenda of millennial poverty reduction will focus exclusively on the abject poor to the neglect of structural injustice. It is precisely because the needs of the abject poor are so unarguable that development must preoccupy itself with their present suffering, instead of turning to an analysis of root causes or imagining more egalitarian alternatives in the long run.

REFERENCES

Abrahamsen, Rita (2004), 'The power of partnerships in global governance', *Third World Quarterly*, **25** (8), 1453–67.
Agamben, Giorgio (1998), Homo Sacer: *Sovereign Power and Bare Life*, Stanford, CA: Stanford University Press.
Alexander, Jeffrey (1995), 'Modern, anti, post, neo', *New Left Review*, **1** (210) (March–April), 63–101.
Atack, Iain (2005), *The Ethics of Peace and War*, Edinburgh: Edinburgh University Press.
Baudrillard, Jean (1996), *The Perfect Crime*, London: Verso.
Bauman, Zygmunt (1999), *Globalisation: The Human Consequences*, London: Verso.
Berman, Marshall (1982), *All That Is Solid Melts into Air: The Experience of Modernity*, New York: Simon & Schuster.

Brennan, Teresa (2002), *Globalisation and Its Terrors: Daily Life in the West*, London and New York: Routledge.

Butler, Judith (2004), *Precarious Life: The Powers of Mourning and Violence*, London and New York: Verso.

Chenery, H., M.S. Ahluwalia, C.L.G. Bell, J.H. Duloy and R. Jolly (1974), Introduction to 'Redistribution with Growth', reprinted in S. Corbridge (ed.), *Development: Critical Concepts in the Social Sciences*, London: Routledge, pp. 214–22.

Cornia, Giovanni, Richard Jolly and Frances Stewart (eds) (1987), *Adjustment with a Human Face Vol. 1: Protecting the Vulnerable and Promoting Growth*, Oxford: Clarendon/UNICEF.

de Senarclens, Pierre (1997), 'How the United Nations promotes development through technical assistance', in Rahnema and Bawtree (eds), pp. 190–203.

Dikhanov, Yuri (2005), 'Trends in global income distribution, 1970–2015', http://hdr.undp.org/hdr 2006/statistics/documents/globalincometrends.pdf, accessed 14 June 2007, p. 43.

Farmer, Paul (2005), *Pathologies of Power: Health, Human Rights and the New War on the Poor*, Berkeley, CA: University of California Press.

Faulks, Keith (2000), *Citizenship*, London: Routledge.

Ferguson, James (1994), *The Anti-Politics Machine: 'Development', Depoliticization and Bureaucratic Power in Lesotho*, Minneapolis, MN: University of Minnesota Press.

Ferguson, James (1999), *Expectations of Modernity: Myths and Meanings of Urban Life on the Zambian Copperbelt*, Berkeley, CA: University of California Press.

Fukuda-Parr, Sakiko (2004), 'Rescuing the human development concept from the HDI: reflections on a new agenda', in Fukuda-Parr and A.K. Shiva Kumar (eds), *Readings in Human Development: Concepts, Measures and Policies for a Human Development Paradigm*, Oxford and New Delhi: Oxford University Press, pp. 117–24.

Gasper, Des (2004), *The Ethics of Development*, Edinburgh: Edinburgh University Press.

Groenemeyer, Marianne (1992), 'Helping', in Sachs (ed.), pp. 53–69.

Hettne, Björn (1995), *Development Theory and the Three Worlds*, Harlow, Essex: Longman.

Human Rights Watch (2002), 'Dangerous dealings: changes to U.S. military assistance after September 11', *Human Rights Watch*, **14** (1) (G), 1–15.

Johnson, Rebecca (1999), 'Post Cold War security', *Disarmament Forum*, Vol. 1, United Nations: UNIDIR.

Kanbur, Ravi (2001), 'Economic policy, distribution and poverty: the nature of disagreements', *World Development*, **29** (6), 1083–94.

Kristeva, Julia (1982), *Powers of Horror: An Esssay on Abjection*, New York: Columbia University Press.

Leys, Colin (1996), *The Rise and Fall of Development Theory*, Oxford: James Currey.

Lipschutz, Ronnie D. with James K. Rowe (2005), *Globalisation, Governmentality and Globalisation: Regulation for the Rest of Us?*, London and New York: Routledge.

Mamdani, Mahmood (1996), *Citizen and Subject: Contemporary Africa and the Legacy of Late Colonialism*, Princeton, NJ: Princeton University Press.

Marglin, Stephen and Juliet Schor (eds) (1990), *The Golden Age of Capitalism: Reinterpreting the Postwar Experience*, Oxford: Clarendon.

Marshall, T.H. (1992), 'Citizenship and social class', in Marshall and Tom Bottomore, *Citizenship and Social Class*, London: Pluto, pp. 3–51.

Mawdsley, Emma and J. Rigg (2002), 'A survey of the World Development Reports I: Discursive strategies', *Progress in Development Studies*, **2** (2), 93–111.

Mawdsley, Emma and J. Rigg (2003), 'A survey of the World Development Reports II: Continuity and change in development orthodoxies', *Progress in Development Studies*, **3** (4), 271–86.

Narayan, Deepa (2000), *Can Anyone Hear Us?*, Oxford and New York: Oxford University Press/World Bank.

Nederveen Pieterse, Jan (2001), *Development Theory: Deconstructions/Reconstructions*, London: Sage.

Nederveen Pieterse, Jan (2002), 'Global inequality: bringing politics back in', *Third World Quarterly*, **23** (6), 1023–46.

O'Rawe, Mary (1999), 'The United Nations: structure versus substance', in A. Hegarty and S. Leonard (eds), *Human Rights: An Agenda for the Twenty First Century*, London: Cavendish, pp. 15–23.

Owen, Taylor (2004), 'Challenges and opportunities for defining and measuring human security', *Disarmament Forum*, No. 3, 15–23.

Patel, Rajeev and Philip McMichael (2004), 'Third Worldism and the lineages of global fascism: the regrouping of the global South in the neoliberal era', *Third World Quarterly*, **25** (1), 231–54.

Polanyi, Karl (2nd edn, with a foreword by J. Stiglitz) (2001), *The Great Transformation: The Political and Economic Origins of Our Time*, Boston, MA: Beacon Press.

Rahnema, Majid and Victoria Bawtree (eds) (1997), *The Post-Development Reader*, London: Zed Books.

Rist, Gilbert (1997), *The History of Development: From Western Origins to Global Faith*, London and New York: Zed Books.

Robinson, William I. (2002), 'Remapping development in light of globalisation: from a territorial to a social cartography', *Third World Quarterly*, **23** (6), 1047–71.

Ross, Daniel (2004), *Violent Democracy*, Cambridge: Cambridge University Press.

Sachs, Jeffrey (2005), *The End of Poverty: How We Can Make It Happen in Our Lifetime*, London: Penguin.

Sachs, Wolfgang (1992), *The Development Dictionary: A Guide to Knowledge as Power*, London: Zed Books.

Seers, Dudley (1969), 'The meaning of development', reprinted in S. Corbridge (ed.), *Development: Critical Concepts in the Social Sciences*, London: Routledge, pp. 189–213.

Sen, Amartya (1999), *Development As Freedom*, Oxford: Oxford University Press.

Sköns, Elisabeth (2005), 'Military expenditure', *Disarmament Forum*, No. 3, 3–10.

Soederberg, Susanne (2004), 'American Empire and "excluded states": the Millennium Challenge Account and the shift to pre-emptive development', *Third World Quarterly*, **25** (2), 279–302.

Steiner, Henry J. and Philip Alston (2000), *International Human Rights in Context: Law, Politics, Morals*, Oxford: Oxford University Press.

Tujan, Antonio, A. Gaughran and H. Mollett (2004), 'Development and the global war on terror', *Race and Class*, **46** (1), 53–74.

UNDP (1992), *Human Development Report 1992*, New York: Oxford University Press.

UNDP (2003), *Human Development Report 2003 Millennium Development Goals: A Compact among Nations to End Human Poverty*, New York: Oxford University Press.
UNDP (2005), *Human Development Report 2005 International Cooperation at a Crossroads*, New York: Oxford University Press.
United Nations (1995), *The United Nations and Human Rights 1945–1995* (UN Blue Books Vol. VII), New York: UN Department of Public Information.
Wade, Robert (2001), 'Showdown at the World Bank', *New Left Review*, 7 (January–February), 124–37.
Wallerstein, Immanuel (2004), *World-Systems Analysis: An Introduction*, Durham, NC and London: Duke University Press.
Young, Jock (1999), *The Exclusive Society: Social Exclusion, Crime and Difference in Late Modernity*, London: Sage.

11. Globalisation, surveillance and the 'war' on terror

Michael McCahill

INTRODUCTION

This chapter aims to explore the relationship between 'globalisation', the 'war on terror', 'surveillance' and 'citizenship'. Firstly, the chapter argues that the rapid increase in the use of 'new surveillance' technologies has been driven by wider global trends which pre-date the 'war on terror'. Secondly, it shows that following the attacks on September 11 in the United States these developments have intensified as the 'rush to surveillance' has become a 'global' phenomenon (see Ball and Webster, 2003; Lyon, 2003a). Thirdly, the chapter draws upon theoretical debates on 'panopticism' and 'post-panopticism' to argue that the rush to a 'technological fix' may not have the desired effects in terms of preventing 'global terrorism'. Finally, the chapter goes on to show how the 'globalisation' of surveillance may have serious unintended consequences which threaten civil liberties and community cohesion.

SURVEILLANCE BEFORE SEPTEMBER 11

It has become a commonplace that following the attacks in the US on September 11 2001, 'everything changed'. Exceptional circumstances, it is argued, call for exceptional measures, hence the rapid introduction of new legislation (for example, The Patriot Act), new practices (for example, detention without trial), and the deployment of 'new surveillance' technologies (CCTV, biometrics, message interception, data mining, etc.). However, the rapid introduction of new legislation and surveillance practices in response to 'terror' is not an entirely new phenomenon. Consider the UK reaction to the Feinian bombings in 1883, for example, when Parliament introduced the Explosive Substances Act, or the introduction of new legislation and surveillance practices in response to the 'troubles' in Northern Ireland during the 1970s. The Prevention of Terrorism (Temporary Provisions) Act 1974 was subject to a mere 17 hours of debate in the House of Commons before its new powers were approved. In this instance, 'Parliamentary debate was driven by the public outrage caused by the Birmingham pub bombings which resulted in the deaths of 21 people and the injury to a further 180' (*Guardian*, 11 September, 2002). During this period, policing in Northern Ireland shifted from a 'reactive' to a 'pro-active' or 'pre-emptive' approach where large sections of the community were 'regularly and systematically monitored and surveilled' (Hillyard, 1987, p. 290).

Meanwhile, as Norris, McCahill and Wood (2004) have pointed out, the first large-scale public space CCTV surveillance system deployed in the UK was erected in Bournemouth in 1985 when the town was hosting the annual Conservative Party Conference. The previous year's conference in Brighton was marked by an attempt by the IRA to assassinate the Conservative Cabinet, by bombing the conference hotel: 'The explosion, while leaving Mrs Thatcher unscathed, killed five people and injured many more. As a result, additional security was provided to the conference venue by introducing CCTV along the sea front' (ibid., 2004). These developments accelerated during the 1990s when 'new' surveillance technologies were introduced in a number of major cities in response to 'terrorist' attacks. The original catalyst for CCTV expansion in central London, for example, came in 1993 in response to the IRA's terrorist attack on Bishopgate. In 1995, CCTV was deployed throughout urban public transport networks in Tokyo following attacks by followers of the *Aum Shinrikyo* cult using sarin nerve gas (Sorensen, 2003, p. 3). In the same year, laws governing the use of surveillance in public places were significantly relaxed in France amidst fears of urban unrest and terrorist attack (Anon, 1994).

The measures introduced in the USA PATRIOT Act 2001 (for example, wiretapping, widening government access to data held by Internet Service Providers (ISPs), etc.) are not entirely new either. As Haggerty and Gazso (2005) point out, the FBI and the National Telecommunications and Information Systems Security Committee had a lengthy shopping list of desired surveillance-related measures long before the events of September 11. These included legal enhancements to their wiretapping capabilities and provisions for governmental agents to compel ISPs to provide information on their customers. These measures were recycled from earlier legislative efforts which were said to be essential for the international 'war on drugs' or 'money laundering'. Thus, measures previously regarded as unpalatable on civil liberties grounds, have since been legitimated and rushed through parliament against a background of widespread fear among the public induced by terror attacks.

The 'new punitive' rhetoric exemplified by declarations of a 'war on drugs' is, for some writers, bound up with wider transformations in 'penality' which have been taking place for a number of years. David Garland (2001), for example, argues that over the last two or three decades there has been an increasing recognition on the part of central state actors in western societies that they are unable to exercise sovereignty over the problem of crime, particularly as it takes on characteristics associated with globalisation ('money laundering', 'international drugs trade', 'terrorism', etc.). The government response to this predicament has resulted in a series of policies that are highly contradictory. Garland notes that on the one hand the state appears to be attempting to reclaim the power of sovereign command by the use of phrases like 'zero tolerance', 'prison works', 'tough on crime', and 'three strikes'. However, at the same time there has been an attempt to face up to the predicament and develop new pragmatic 'adaptive' strategies including the 'rationalisation of justice', the 'commercialisation of justice' and a 'redistribution' of the responsibility for crime control (2001, p. 113). However one interprets these developments, it seems clear that one of the main reasons for rapid increase in the use of 'new surveillance' technologies in recent years, is because they manage to straddle these conflicting discourses on crime control: on the one hand, the 'sovereign state' approach with its 'expressive' gestures and 'punitive' sentiments, and on the other, the 'adaptive' strategies with their emphasis on 'prevention' and 'partnership' (Norris and McCahill, 2006).

This latter approach is clearly evident in the measures introduced under the PATRIOT Act 2001 which aims to 'pre-empt' crime through 'message interception'. The same could be said of the Computer Assisted Passenger Profiling System (CAPPS) which performs a 'risk assessment' and assigns a score to passengers entering the US. Other 'adaptive measures' include 'responsibilisation' strategies which increasingly are addressed not to central-state agencies such as the police, 'but *beyond* the state apparatus, to the organisations, institutions and individuals in civil society' (Garland, 1996, p. 451, original italics; O'Malley, 1992). In the United States, a whole range of 'Watch Programs', such as 'CAT Eyes' (Community Anti-Terrorism Training Institute), as well as more diffuse campaigns of 'citizen awareness' encourage members of the community 'to be alert for "anyone who does not appear to belong"' (ACLU, 2004, p. 7). These developments are mirrored in the UK with the launch by Scotland Yard of the Life Savers campaign which asks people 'to consider whether the behaviour of those they encounter, through work or socially, gives them any reason to think they might be planning terrorist attacks' (*The Guardian*, 22 March, 2004). As Peter Clarke, the Deputy Assistant Commissioner of the Metropolitan Police put it, 'all communities have a role to play in tackling the terrorist threat' (*The Guardian*, 22 March, 2004). Further evidence that crime prevention today involves a whole range of agencies 'beyond-the-state' was also evident in the aftermath of September 11 when central state authorities quickly compiled data from a whole range of databases (air traffic control, bank records, credit card records, e-mails, employment records, ferry records, flight school records, hotel booking records, intelligence databases, medical records, passport, student records, surveillance camera video tapes, telephone calls, visa records, wire taps, and so on) to track down those involved in the attacks (Haggerty and Gaszo, 2005).[1]

At the same time, however, government responses to the threat of 'terrorism' also reflects the 'sovereign state' approach with its 'expressive' gestures and 'punitive' sentiments. As David Lyon points out, these include the 'swashbuckling words' used by politicians which 'go hand-in-hand with a willingness to place suspects in a Cuban prison camp' (Lyon, 2003b, p. 103). Similarly, the network of surveillance cameras known as the 'ring of steel' introduced in response to the IRA's terrorist attack on Bishopgate to monitor the entrances to the City of London could be seen as a 'symbolic gesture' designed to reassure international finance about the security of the city (Norris and McCahill, 2006). Moreover, in the 'global media age', 'expressive gestures' and 'punitive sentiments' send messages to those beyond the confines of national borders. As Baker and Roberts (2005) have argued, the political slogans associated with the 'new punitiveness' (for example, 'three strikes and you're out', 'life means life' etc.) travel easily across national borders and have become familiar features of the penal landscape (2005, p. 123). It could be argued that a similar process has occurred with the global 'war on terror' which, like the 'new punitiveness', carries a clear symbolic aspect, arises in response to exceptional cases, becomes highly mediatised and assumes a high public profile across different jurisdictions which are rapidly adaptable from one country to another (Baker and Roberts, 2005, p. 133). The rapid dissemination of 'ideas', 'images' and 'news' via the mass media means therefore that 'distant events' can have significant 'local impacts'. In this respect, the images of September 11 that were constantly displayed on television screens throughout the world and the subsequent use of slogans with global currency like the 'war on terror', has taken the 'new punitiveness' on to a wider stage as the intensification of surveillance has become a 'global' phenomenon.

THE GLOBALISATION OF SURVEILLANCE

The principal legislative response to the attacks of September 11 was the legislation entitled Uniting and Strengthening of America to Provide Appropriate Tools Required to Intercept and Obstruct Terrorism Act of 2001 (USA PATRIOT Act). The legislation was introduced by House

Judiciary Committee Chairman, F. James Sensenbrenner, on 2 October 2001 and became law 24 days later (*The Guardian*, 11 September, 2002). This was a record-breaking activity made possible only by forcing the pace to the point where serious debate and discussion was made impossible by the restricted timescale and the public demand for political action. The new powers introduced through this act include expanded powers to require businesses to turn over records to the FBI; the requirement that ISPs preserve all data specific to a client or for a specified period of time; proposals to require college administrators to provide authorities with records of foreign students suspected of being involved in terrorism; proposals to make medical records of suspects available to investigators; and an expansion of government powers to spy by wiretaps.

Following the lead shown by the USA PATRIOT Act, anti-terror bills that restrict freedom of expression have been introduced in Indonesia, China, Russia, Pakistan, Jordan, Mauritius, Uganda and Zimbabwe (Hamilton, 2002). To further tighten Internet controls in Saudi Arabia, all service providers are now required to keep records of all Internet users in order to track access to forbidden web sites. Several European countries have also extended the length of time web users' data can be held by ISPs. In the UK, the Anti-Terrorism Act, 2001, required ISPs and phone companies to retain traffic data for up to a year. In November 2001, the French parliament voted for a law forcing ISPs and telecoms companies to retain traffic and locations data for a maximum period of one year (*The Guardian*, 12 September, 2002). The French parliament has since extended this to up to three years, and new procedures will give police access to them without the permission of an investigating magistrate (*The Guardian*, 28 July, 2005). Germany had one of the strictest data protection laws in the European Union before September 11, but in October 2001, the government voted to require telecoms providers to install tapping technology for the police and security services. In Spain, anti-globalisation protestors have complained of monitoring by security forces since September 11 who equate them with terrorists. Plans being drawn up by Europol, the police and intelligence arm of the European Union, propose that telephone and Internet firms retain millions of pieces of data – including details of visits to Internet chat rooms, and of calls made on mobile phones and text messages. The information retained about emails will include who sent the message, where the email went, its contents and the time and date it was sent (*The Observer*, 9 June, 2002). Meanwhile in response to the July 7 attacks in London in 2005, the Italian cabinet endorsed a package of measures including the easing of restrictions on surveillance of the Internet, giving investigators broader access to telephone records and clearing the way for DNA samples to be taken without consent (*The Guardian*, 28 July, 2005).

Since September 11 there has been a rapid increase in the use of 'biometric' surveillance systems. Biometric systems rely on having access to various physical characteristics (gait recognition, fingerprint and palm print recognition, facial recognition, and iris recognition) and then on algorithms that enable the verification process to be automated. An example is the 'iris recognition' system installed at Schipol Airport in Amsterdam a month after September 11 (Lyon, 2003b). As Zureik and Hindle (2004) have pointed out, within a few weeks of the terrorist attacks almost 9 bills were introduced in the United States Congress, including measures to allow tax benefits to companies that use biometrics. In the US, the use of biometric systems at borders actually began before September 11 in 1997 with the Computer-Assisted Passenger Profiling System (CAPPS), which looked at a traveller's overall flight history to flag potential security risks for more detailed baggage checking (Bennett, 2005). In 2001 the Aviation Security bill introduced a new version (CAPPS II) which was to include all passengers, not just those with checked baggage. On 5 June 2002, United States Attorney General John Ashcroft announced the National Security Entry–Exit Registration System (NSEERS). The initiative captures and archives biographic data and images of the faces and fingerprints of select foreign nationals visiting or residing in the United States on temporary visas. On 5 January 2004, this was replaced by the United States Visitor and Immigrant Status Indicator Technology program (US-VISIT) which collects biometric identifiers, fingerprint scans and digital photographs of foreigners entering and exiting the USA (Bennett, 2005). The latest system, Secure Flight, includes a 'passenger threat index' which evaluates the threat each passenger poses. Already, 'no fly lists' have led to the holding and questioning of US anti-war activists on domestic flights (*New Internationalist*, March 2005).

A number of other countries are issuing, or planning to issue, biometric passports to their citizens and biometric visas and residence permits to third-country residents. The European EURODAC system, for example, authorises the fingerprinting of all individuals aged over 14 who apply for asylum in an EU country, or who are found illegally present on the EU borders and in the EU territory. Meanwhile, Ass (2006) points out that 'the Norwegian government has made it standard procedure to X-ray photograph the hands and teeth of young asylum seekers in order to verify their age' (2006, p. 147). As Hayes (2006) points out, from 2007 all EU citizens will have to be fingerprinted to get a passport and 'with some member states pushing for the introduction of biometric ID cards as well we are now fast approaching a time in which everyone in the EU will be registered and fingerprinted by the state' (Hayes, 2006, p. 30).

Since September 11 there has also been an expansion in the number of countries planning to introduce CCTV surveillance systems. As Norris,

McCahill and Wood (2004) have reported, following the terrorist attacks in the USA there has been a rapid growth in the use of both CCTV surveillance and biometric technologies. In September 2004, Chicago city announced plans to install more than 2,000 surveillance cameras in public places. The authors go on to suggest that following the attacks of September 11 some industry officials predicted that the sale of CCTV surveillance cameras in the USA could soar to nearly $5.7 billion by the end of 2001. CCTV surveillance has also been instigated in at least five airports in India (*Times of India*, 2002). Meanwhile, despite being the most (visually) surveilled country in the world with around 4.2 million surveillance cameras in operation (Norris and McCahill, 2006), the response to the July 7 bombings in the UK from the Mayor of London, Ken Livingstone, 'was to double the number of CCTV cameras on London's tube network and ensure there were cameras on both decks of every London bus by the end of the year' (*The Guardian*, 14 September, 2005). Impressed by the speed and relative ease with which the London bombers and suspects were identified using video surveillance, the French government announced plans to install CCTV cameras in every Paris bus and metro corridor before the end of 2005 (*The Guardian*, 28 July, 2005). The July 7 bombings in London also prompted the German parliament to call for increased surveillance of airports, train stations and underground networks (*The Guardian*, 28 July, 2005).

THE 'GLOBAL INTEGRATION' OF DISCRETE SURVEILLANCE SYSTEMS

The integration of discrete surveillance systems across different national jurisdictions is not a new phenomenon. For example, Europol was established in 1993 as an agency for intelligence exchange and gathering between European states criminal intelligence services, such as the National Criminal Intelligence Service (NCIS) in the UK. This agency included analysis files covering drug trafficking, illegal immigration and 'Islamic extremist terrorism' well before September 11 (*The Guardian*, 10 September, 2002). Similarly, the Schengen Information System (SIS), set up in the early 1990s, created a widespread network of police cooperation, data registration and surveillance across Europe (Mathiesen, 2000). The Schengen agreement also introduced the Supplementary Information Request at the National Entries, otherwise known as SIRENE. Through SIRENE, police authorities in one country who have arrested a person who is registered in the SIS by another country, may require supplementary information, not stored in the SIS, from the latter country (Carerra, 2005).

Once again these developments have intensified since September 11 as the construction of new forms of information sharing and 'interoperability' increasingly connects discrete surveillance systems across different national jurisdictions. It is reported that data on two of the hijackers involved in the September 11 attacks already existed on different databases as suspected terrorists and yet no authoritative response was mobilised (Levack, 2003). Stung by this the US authorities set up The Total Information Awareness program (later changed to Terrorist Information Awareness) which aims to facilitate governmental collaboration. As Sam Cava, Director of the Department of Defence's Biometrics Fusion Centre in West Virginia, says, 'it doesn't do to have 50 systems that don't cooperate' (*The Guardian*, 18 June, 2004). Since September 11 there have been several other attempts to open up existing systems to new users. Canada and the USA, for example, have introduced Databank Integration which aims to integrate Police, Customs and Immigration databases both nationally and internationally; information sharing agreements between police, customs, immigration, grand juries and airlines; and the integration of immigration, customs and visa data between Canada and the USA at foreign locations (Haggerty and Gazso, 2005).

It could be argued that for a network of relationships to be considered 'global', it must include multi-continental distances, not simply regional networks between the USA and Canada or between European partners. It has been reported that British police will be given access in the near future to US intelligence databases containing DNA samples, fingerprints and digital images of thousands of foreign nationals seized around the world by the US as terror suspects (*The Guardian*, 18 June, 2004). The FBI, which has more than 75 million fingerprints on its criminal and civil computer records, is adding biometric details from suspects detained in Iraq, Afghanistan and elsewhere. Canada has already been given direct electronic access to such FBI databases and discussions with the UK are taking place through PITO (the Police Information Technology Organisation), about whether they should have (direct) access to US systems (ibid.). Meanwhile, soon after September 11, the European Union struck a deal allowing the USA to obtain personal data from the Europol law enforcement agency on suspects (*The Guardian*, 20 December, 2002).

The integration of discrete surveillance systems looks set to increase in the near future. One of the central aims of the EU Security Research Programme (ESRP), for example, is to achieve 'interoperability and integrated systems for information and communication', shorthand for linking national and international law enforcement databases and information systems (Hayes, 2006). The report also talks of the 'principle of availability', under which all data held by a law enforcement agency in one state should be automatically accessible/available to all the others (Hayes, 2006, p. 33–4). New measures proposed include widening access to the Eurodac database of asylum applicants' fingerprints from immigration authorities to security agencies. The Commission is also currently working on a proposal to interlink national DNA databases and in the longer term proposes a European criminal Automated Fingerprints Identification System (Hayes, 2006).

In his vision of what a 'total surveillance society' might look like, James Rule (1973) stressed the importance of the 'size of the files', the 'centralization of files', the 'speed of information flow' and 'number of points of contact' between the system and its subject population. To what extent is the 'globalization' of surveillance leading us towards this kind of 'surveillance society'? In terms of the 'size of the files', the UK Information Commissioner estimates in his 2005–6 report that information about each citizen is held on approximately 700 databases (BBC News, 13 July, 2006). Moreover, the digitalisation of this data means that it can easily be stored and processed, allowing a hitherto unimaginable level of detailed knowledge about individuals. For Rule (1973), the 'centralization of data' was also important because 'it prevents clients from escaping the effects of their past by moving from one place to another' (1973, p. 38). The construction of 'global' surveillance systems has resonance here with their ability to transcend national borders. As Whitaker (2006) points out, global databases 'create the capacity for decentralized "dataveillance", a surveillance society in which the "files" exist in no central location, and are under no central control, but which in their totality may exercise far more intrusive capacity to gaze into the private spaces of individuals than the Big Brother surveillance state of the past' (2006, p. 142). Also, as the ESRP makes clear with its emphasis on the principles of 'interoperability' and 'availability', the integration of discrete systems is now being systematically built into the policy agenda of transnational institutions such as the EU. 'Global' surveillance networks also produce information (profiles, DNA samples, images) that is '*controllable*, and not subject to the messiness or unruliness of time' (Simpson, 1995, p. 158, original italics). This increases the 'speed of flow' because information can be rapidly disseminated between one system and another. In the USA, police officers at airports now have handheld pocket PCs with software that allows real-time access to driver-license data, photographs, arrest warrants, weapon registrations and criminal databases (Solheim, 2005). Similarly, the 'number of points of contact' increases because deviant identities can be 'stored' in electronic spaces (for example, databases, computer files, videotapes), ready to be 'lifted out' so that an authoritative intervention can be mobilised at some future, as yet unspecified, time and place.

However, Rule (1973) was also well aware of how in practice 'real' surveillance systems always fall short of a 'total surveillance society'. This is no less true of the integration of 'global' surveillance systems. For instance, an internal note of a meeting between European and American officials in Dublin on 'the new transatlantic agenda' revealed 'that the FBI prefers to deal with individual EU states rather than Europol' (*The Guardian*, 25 March, 2004). It has also been reported that even the former head of the US Department of Homeland Security, Tom Ridge, may not have had 'proper access to intelligence even from within his own country' due to the tendency of the CIA and the FBI 'to hold on to their intelligence and secrets' (Stephan, 2004). As these examples show, there are limits to the construction of 'global' surveillance networks.

THE LIMITS OF GLOBAL PANOPTICISM

As David Lyon (1994) has pointed out, the sociological response to the general issue of surveillance has been dominated by images of the Panopticon, Jeremy Bentham's proposal, written in 1787, for an architectural system of social discipline, applicable to prisons, factories, workhouses and asylums. As Foucault (1977) argued, the architectural design of the Panopticon created a state of conscious and permanent visibility that assured the automatic functioning of self-control and self-discipline. The 'disciplinary' practices found in the institutional setting of the prison are situated at the 'sharp end' of the panopticon spectrum (Lyon, 2006) and clearly has resonance for the 70,000 detainees (Amnesty International, 2005, p. 4) held in Guantánamo Bay, Bagram and Kandahar, Camp Bucca and Abu Ghraib and other institutions that make up the 'global archipelago of exceptionalism' (Neal, 2006, p. 45). For Foucault though disciplinary power was not confined to the institutional setting of the prison. Instead, he argued that the principles of panopticism served as a model for understanding the operation of power in modern societies and that these principles would 'seep out from their institutional location to infiltrate non-institutional spaces and populations' (Smart, 1985, p. 88).

The advent of time–space transcending technologies, many writers believe, reflects this dynamic, extending the disciplinary potential of the Panopticon to non-institutionalised public space. Thus, while historically the 'direct supervision' of individuals was limited to the enclosed and controlled spaces of modern organisations (Giddens, 1985, p. 15), the development of CCTV systems in public spaces means that the 'direct supervision' of the subject population is no longer confined to specific institutional locales, nor does it require the physical co-presence of the observer. In this respect, the power of the Panopticon has been dramatically enhanced by technological developments which have allowed the disciplinary gaze to extend further and further across the entire social fabric. Meanwhile, the emergence of powerful computers and telecommunications networks has allowed for the systematic categorisation of whole populations. Oscar Gandy (1993) refers to this as a 'panoptic sort', whereby individuals in their daily lives as citizens, employees and consumers are continually identified, classified and assessed and the information then used to coordinate and control their access to goods and services. As David Lyon (2003b) points out, in the aftermath of September 11, the 'panoptic sort' was quickly co-opted by central state actors who used marketing devices such as Customer Relationship Management (CRM), data-mining and data-warehousing to tackle 'terrorism'. The central aims of the Pentagon's Total Information Awareness (TIA) Office set up in 2002, for example, was to create new algorithms for mining, combining and refining data that would allow them to successfully pre-empt and defeat terrorist acts (2003b, p. 91).

However, while the expansion of surveillance described in the previous section could be interpreted as a 'global dispersal of discipline', there are a number of problems with the ideas of 'panopticism' and 'dispersal of discipline' in relation to the 'war on terror'. Firstly, as Haggerty (2006) points out, in Foucault's work:

> The movement of panoptic principles into new settings is presented as entirely frictionless. Surveillance appears to proliferate because it represents a self-evident increase in the functionality of power. Entirely missing form this account is any sense of a surveillance politics. (p. 34)

We should remember, for example, that 'globalising' forces are always filtered through domestic politics. For instance, while research conducted on the rise of surveillance in Europe by the URBANEYE project found a general diffusion of CCTV throughout European society, the growth of open street CCTV systems has been restricted in a number of countries due to the legal/constitutional environment. In Germany, for instance, the Constitutional Court has declared that 'the knowledge of being under surveillance, why and by whom is crucial for a democratic society and the autonomy of its citizens' (Töpfer *et al.*, 2003, p. 6). Similarly, in Norway, where privacy rights are constitutionally enshrined, there is a strong data protection regime that has explicitly concerned itself with regulating CCTV through a licensing requirement (Wiecek and Rudinow-Saetnan, 2002, p. 11ff).

Also, while 'panopticism' and ideals of 'omniscience' may help us understand the appeal of surveillance systems for control agents, Foucaldian notions of 'anticipatory conformity' and 'normalisation' can also be questioned. As Haggerty and Gazso (2005) point out, terrorists themselves are aware of the different configurations of surveillance and security that surround particular targets. It has been reported that Dhiren Barot and his co-conspirators, for example, went to great lengths to avoid surveillance by not using phones and sending coded emails (*The Guardian*, 7 November, 2006, p. 3). Similarly, in a foiled al-Qaeda plot to hijack an airliner and fly it into the US Bank Tower in Los Angeles, Khalid Sheikh Mohammed recruited Jemaah Islamiyah for the mission 'because it was thought that south-east Asian hijackers would be less likely to arouse suspicions than Arab Muslims' (*The Guardian*, 10 February, 2006). As Vincent Cannistraro, former Director of the CIA's counter-terrorism centre explained, 'this was going to be the follow-up to September 11 [and] we weren't looking in south-east Asia. We were looking at the stereotype of Arab Muslims' (ibid., 2006).

For other theorists, Foucaldian notions on the connection between 'visibility' and 'power' can also be questioned especially when people 'want to be seen' (Koskela, 2006). As Anne Marie Oliver has pointed out, portraits of dead suicide bombers in the West Bank and Gaza are plastered all over the walls and videos of their last interviews are on sale on street stalls (*The Guardian*, 14 July, 2005). In relation to the 7 July bombings in London, she suggests that we should not underestimate the 'star factor' and the acquiring of glory that could have motivated the 'Yorkshire bombers'. As she says, 'it does not matter whether it is Britain or Syria or the West Bank, they are highly romantic figures . . . and the fact that they carried with them credit cards and other personal ID suggests *they wanted to be known*' (emphasis added, *The Guardian*, 14 July, 2005).

Other writers point out that in the 'information society' access to information technology and the mass media has become 'globalised' and that this transforms 'hierarchies of surveillance' by allowing the wider society to scrutinise the activities of the powerful (Haggerty and Ericson, 2000). Thus, while information technologies may extend the surveillance capacities of the central state and modern organisations, it has also increased the global reach of terrorist groups, such as al-Qaeda, who can use computer and telecommunication links, email, cellular and radio networks to conduct operations over long distances while minimising the need for fixed physical presence (Paul, 2005). Meanwhile, in a recent interview on the Al-Arabiya News Channel (24 October, 2006) a former radical who had a self-revision process claimed that more than half of young Saudis who had embraced radical ideology were recruited through the Internet. He revealed that there were more than 5,800 sites for radicals on the Internet.[2]

The rapid proliferation of surveillance systems may not, therefore, have a significant impact on the reduction of 'global terrorism'. However, in the following section I want to consider another issue: that once surveillance systems are introduced to monitor 'external' threats posed by 'terrorists' and other serious 'criminals', they can soon be used to monitor the behaviour of the wider civilian population.

BRINGING THE WAR BACK HOME

As Zureik and Salter (2005) have pointed out, long before the so-called 'war on terror' during an earlier phase of globalisation now known as 'colonialism', new surveillance systems were often tried and tested in a colonial setting before being imported to the mother country. The authors point to the work of Timothy Mitchell (1988) who noted that Jeremy Bentham's visit to Egypt in the nineteenth century was prompted by his desire to assist the Turkish ruler of Egypt at the time to instil obedience and discipline in the Egyptian population through surveillance techniques. Thus, Bentham's 'panoptic principle was devised on Europe's colonial frontiers with the British empire, and examples of the panopticon were built for the most part not in Northern Europe, but in places like colonial India' (quoted in Zureik, 2001, p. 8). Similarly, in Southwest Africa, the German government developed in the course of its domination of colonial populations a number of the techniques later applied against the Jews (Torpey, 2005, p. 157).

Global politics continued to shape surveillance practices during the twentieth century when external threats to the British state became inexorably entwined with internal threats to capitalism (Higgs, 2001). As Higgs (2001) explains, with the establishment of communist regimes in the USSR and China, many of the international threats to the British state could be seen as meshing with internal opposition to capitalism posed by trade unionists, peace activists and other 'left wing' groups. In the course of the twentieth century and particularly during the Cold War, the resources and surveillance technologies at the disposal of the security forces and Special Branch were increasingly used to target these groups as 'the distinction between geo-politics and internal class politics [became] blurred' (ibid., 2001, p. 191). Following the end of the Cold War, surveillance of the civilian population increased when global security companies sought to expand their operations into civil rather than military markets. For Racal-Chubb, GEC-Marconi, and other high-tech companies with their origins as defence contractors, this meant an expansion into the civilian markets of CCTV, electronic tagging for convicted offenders, intelligent scene monitoring and integrated database management (Norris and Armstrong, 1999, p. 33). These technologies soon became a common feature of the urban landscape as 'electronic monitoring' was used in the UK to track offenders (Nellis, 2003) and 'intelligent scene monitoring' was introduced on the London Underground (Heath *et al.*, 2002).

Since the 'global war on terror' was announced some commentators have begun to talk of the emergence of a 'security-industrial complex'. Hayes (2006), for example, argues that 'the traditional boundaries between external security (military) and internal security (security services) and law enforcement (policing) have eroded' (2006, p. 3). As part of the ESRP, EU officials, Hayes points out, have promised Europe's biggest arms and IT companies substantial funding to ensure that they can compete with US multinationals. Arms companies have also been joined in the emerging 'security-industrial complex' by the IT sector and its large multinationals, the IT revolution having thrown-up novel possibilities for the surveillance of public and private places. As Stephen Graham (2004) has shown, the blurring of 'external' security and 'law enforcement' is becoming visible at the urban level 'as globe-spanning, geostrategic concerns blur into very local, urban spaces, [and] all of a sudden it seems normal for Western cities to face a palpable militarization previously more common in cities of the global South' (2004, p. 12). Police chiefs in Liverpool, for example, are planning to use unmanned aerial vehicles (UAVs) similar to those used by the CIA to assassinate 'terror suspects' and innocent villagers in Afghanistan (Hayes, 2006), 'to hover over problem estates as part of plans for Britain's first "yob squad" to tackle anti-social behaviour' (Lusher, 2006). These developments had already taken off in the United States when, in April 2006, police used unmanned 'surveillance drones' to monitor a large gathering of bikers in Charles County, Maryland (Lusher, 2006). As Graham (2004) states:

> Here we confront the latest stage in a long history where disciplinary devices are developed to try and assert control and dominance for colonizing powers within colonized cities being later transmuted back into 'homeland' cities by military and political elites. (p. 264)

The use of surveillance systems to monitor the wider population has been greatly facilitated by the broad legal definition of 'terrorism' in the 'anti-terror' legislation. The European Union's 'Framework Decision' on combating terrorism, which came into force on 1 January 2003, has a definition that includes activities designed to seriously 'alter political, economic, or social structures' (Lyon, 2003, p. 50). In the UK, for example, anti-terror laws are being used to arrest people protesting peacefully against arms fairs and neo-liberal globalisation. Section 44 of the 2000 Terrorism Act, which allows police to stop and search anyone in a designated area, has been used to obstruct demonstrations against the Iraq war, global capitalism and arms fairs and even those who heckled speakers at last year's Labour party conference (*The Observer*, 22 January, 2006). Similar concerns have been voiced by American civil liberties groups who have denounced the FBI for using new counter-terrorist powers to spy on anti-war demonstrations (*The Guardian*, 24 November, 2003).

Meanwhile, there is also evidence that information on a number of individuals is being stored in global 'anti-terror' databases or what we might call 'just-in-case databases'. After September 11 the EU embarked on an extension of the Schengen Information System (SIS) and proposed four new categories of people to be included: 'violent troublemakers' such as protestors and suspected football hooligans; terrorist suspects; people to be prevented from leaving the EU; and people whose visas have expired, who would be subject to arrest and expulsion (*The Guardian*, 10 September, 2002). In Canada, it has been reported that a recently constructed 'anti-terrorist' database will be used to help monitor tax evaders and catch domestic criminals (Haggerty and Gazso, 2005). Also, the photographic database of the facial recognition system in Tampa, Florida, contains a list of people 'who might have "valuable intelligence" for the police' (Stanley and Steinhardt, 2002, p. 1). Introna and Wood (2004) meanwhile describe a case at the Fresno Yosemite International Airport when 'a man *who looked as if he might be from the Middle East*' (original italics) triggered the alarm of a facial recognition system and (although clearly a 'false positive') was detained and questioned by the FBI 'just in case' the system saw something they did not see. The authors wondered 'if these false positives may be stored in a database "just in case" and become targets for further scrutiny' (ibid., p. 234).

CONCLUSION

The rapid growth in the use of 'new surveillance' technologies over the last two decades has been driven by social, political and economic forces which pre-date the 'war on terror'. However, as we have seen in this paper since the attacks of September 11 these developments have both 'intensified' and 'globalised'. This concluding section considers the likely 'social impact' of these developments, focusing particularly on issues of 'social sorting', 'discrimination' and 'community cohesion'.

Since September 11, the 'war on terror' has highlighted issues of immigration, nationality and race, and widened the divide between 'insiders' and 'outsiders'. In the immediate aftermath of the attacks on September 11 in the USA, it is reported that up to 5,000 men, aged between 18 and 33 from Middle Eastern countries, were rounded up for questioning in what has been described as 'a dragnet based on ethnic profiling, not evidence' (*The Guardian*, 22 June, 2002). Other countries report that ID cards have become associated with police abuses and repression of minority groups. Mouloud

Aounit, the Secretary General of the French anti-racism group MRAP, says of the cards: 'they aren't in themselves a force for repression, but in the current climate of security hysteria they facilitate it'. He goes on to state that 'young people of Algerian or Moroccan descent are being checked six times a day' (*The Guardian*, 15 November, 2003). Similarly, in the UK, the uneven impact of surveillance 'is writ large through the seven-fold increase in the number of Asian people stopped and searched by the British Transport Police following the July 7 bombings' (Mythen and Walklate, 2006, p. 132).

The powers of 'stop and search' are applied during street encounters between the suspect population and the police and decisions are often heavily influenced by the subjective evaluations and discretionary powers of the latter. However, many of the surveillance practices discussed in this paper are not conducted by human agents but by the use of biometric devices, computer profiling and other 'automated' surveillance systems. As Lianos and Douglas (2000) have suggested, the proliferation of 'auto-mated socio-technical systems' means that subjective evaluations and discretionary powers are becoming much less significant as 'deviants' and 'law-abiding citizens' are replaced with efficient users of 'the system'. However, as the author has argued elsewhere (McCahill, 2002, p. 191), there is still room for discretion and subjective evaluations in the operation of 'automated' systems. For instance, when 'intelligent image processing systems' identify 'unusual events' and trigger an alarm, it still requires a knowledgeable social actor to decide whether or not any action should be taken to investigate the 'event'. Similarly, in relation to automated facial recognition systems computers need to be told (by software designers) how to recognise faces. But what criteria do software designers use when decid-ing how to differentiate between faces? Are computers programmed to recognise that certain facial expressions or gestures may be indicative of deviance? In other words, is it possible that subjective evaluations can be inscribed into an algorithmic formula? (McCahill, 2002, p. 192; Graham and Wood, 2003).

Empirical research suggests that discriminatory practices can in fact become an in-built feature of some automated surveillance systems. In their research on facial recognition systems, Givens *et al.* (2003) examined a data set of 2,144 images (two images for each of 1,072 people) and con-cluded that 'white subjects are harder to recognize than Asian, African-American or other subjects, even when the system is trained with racially balanced data sets' (2003, p. 2). As Introna and Wood (2004) have explained, this could have serious consequences in terms of the dispro-portionate targeting of certain ethnic groups. As they point out, facial recognition systems are prone to make a number of 'false positives' (that is, where the software mistakenly matches an innocent face in the crowd to one of the images on the database of suspects). One way of dealing with this problem is to increase the identification threshold thereby requesting the system to reduce the number of false positives. However, 'with an increased threshold, small differences in identifiability will mean that those that are easier to identify by the algorithms (African-Americans, Asians, dark skinned persons and older people) will have a greater probability of triggering the alarm' (2004, p. 234).

Similarly, in relation to the use of automated systems at border controls, David Lyon (2003b) points out that 'racial profiling' is being coded into the software and has given rise to a new category of suspicion – 'flying while Arab' (2003b, p. 99). For more affluent, low-risk populations, on the other hand, the same technologies used at airports and borders, actually speed up their travel through various fast-tracking programmes for frequent travellers. In Amsterdam, frequent travellers can purchase a fast pass called Privium, which utilises 'iris recognition' technology to allow them to enter the country through a kiosk turnstile without talking to an immigration officer. For the cost of membership and a short interview, Privium members may check in late at close parking facilities, enjoy increased velocities through security and immigration checks and enjoy VIP lounges with air-side access to their flights (Adey, 2004). Thus while 'low-risk' passengers enjoy all the privileges of 'speedy global-local citizenship' (Adey, 2004, p. 1371), others may have to endure the indignity of being taken out of the queue for a more detailed examination.

Clearly more empirical research on the 'social construction of suspicion' in the post-September 11 environment is required, but we can guess at both its likely contours and subsequent impact on community relations. If new surveillance technologies are used to disproportionately target many innocent individuals because they fit the profile of 'terrorist', further alienation is likely to occur as ideological 'fence sitters' begin to take sides and loose collectivities become more cohesive groupings whose unwarranted targeting reinforces the view that they do not belong.

NOTES

1. Once again, we could question the novelty of these developments because there is a long history of co-operation between central state actors and private-sector surveillance programmes. For instance, during the Cold War US telegraph companies (Western Union, RCA and ITT) provided the government with copies of cables sent to or from the United States everyday (ACLU, 2004).
2. The author would like to thank Ibrahim Al-haider (PhD student) for this reference.

REFERENCES

Adey, P. (2004), 'Surveillance at the airport: surveilling mobility/mobilising surveillance', *Environment and Planning A*, **36**, 1365–80.

American Civil Liberties Union (ACLU) (2004), 'The surveillance industrial complex: how the American government is conscripting businesses and individuals in the construction of a surveillance society', August.

Amnesty International (2005), 'Guantánamo and beyond: the continuing pursuit of unchecked executive power', AMR 51/063/2005, 13 May, http://web.amnesty.org/library/Index/ENGAMR510632005.

Anon (1994), 'Identity checks in France', *Immigration Laws*, November, **9**, www.migrationint.com.au/news/qatar/nov_1994-09mn.asp.

Ass, K.T. (2006), ' "The body does not lie": identity, risk and trust in technocultures', *Crime, Media, Culture*, **2**,(2), 143–58.

Baker, E. and J.V. Roberts (2005), 'Globalization and the new punitiveness', in Pratt, J., Brown, D., Brown, M., Hallsworth, S. and Morrison, W. (eds), *The New Punitiveness: Trends, Theories, Perspectives*, Cullompton: Willan.

Ball, K. and F. Webster (2003), 'The intensification of surveillance', in Ball, K. and Webster, F. (eds), *The Intensification of Surveillance: Crime, Terrorism and Warfare in the Information Age*, London: Pluto Press.

Bennett, C.J. (2005), 'What happens when you book an airline ticket? The collection and processing of passenger data post-9/11', in Zureik, E. and M.B. Salter (eds) (2005), *Global Surveillance and Policing: Borders, Security, Identity*, Cullompton: Willan.

Carrera, S. (2005), 'What does free movement mean in theory and practice in an enlarged EU?', *European Law Journal*, **11**(6), 699–721.

Foucault, M. (1977), *Discipline and Punish: The Birth of the Prison*, London: Allen Lane.

Gandy, Oscar, H. Jr (1993), *The Panopticon Sort: A Political Economy of Personal Information*, Oxford: Westview Press.

Garland, D. (1996), 'The limits of the Sovereign State: strategies of crime control in contemporary society', *The British Journal of Criminology*, **36**(4), Autumn, 445–71.

Garland, D. (2001), *The Culture of Control: Crime and Social Order in Contemporary Society*, Oxford: OUP.

Giddens, A. (1985), *The Nation State and Violence: Volume Two of a Contemporary Critique of Historical Materialism*, Cambridge: Polity Press.

Givens, G.J.R., J.R. Beveridge, B.A. Draper and D. Bolme (2003), 'A statistical assessment of subject factors in the PCA recognition of human faces', www.cs.colostate.edu/evalfacerec/papers/csusacv03.pdf.

Graham, S. and D. Wood (2003), 'Digitizing surveillance: categorization, space, inequality', *Critical Social Policy*, **23**(2), 235–56.

Graham, S. (2004), 'Introduction: cities, warfare, and states of emergency', in Graham, S. (ed.), *Cities, War and Terrorism: Towards an Urban Geopolitics*, Oxford: Blackwell.

Guardian, The (2002), 'The EU's surveillance network', 10 September.

Guardian, The (2002), 'Draconian laws passed in the UK and the US after September 11 threaten the very democracy they are meant to protect', 11 September.

Guardian, The (2002), 'How the world's electronic privacy changed', 12 September.

Guardian, The (2002), 'Civil wrongs', 22 June.

Guardian, The (2002), 'EU agrees to pass on intelligence to FBI', 20 December.

Guardian, The (2003), 'ID cards may cut queues but learn lessons of history, warn Europeans', 15 November.

Guardian, The (2003), 'FBI uses new powers to bug anti-war groups', 24 November.

Guardian, The (2004), 'Biometrics – great hope for world security or triumph for Big Brother?', 18 June.

Guardian, The (2004), 'Met urges public to use new terror hotline', 22 March.

Guardian, The (2004), 'EU set to agree sweeping counter terror policies', 25 March.

Guardian, The (2005), 'The suicide bomber is the smartest of smart bombs', 14 July.

Guardian, The (2005), 'Fearful Europe steps up security', 28 July.

Guardian, The (2005), 'Police victim's family refuse to meet Met chief', 14 September.

Guardian, The (2006), 'Bush tells of al-Qaida plot to fly jet into tallest building in Los Angeles', 10 February.

Guardian, The (2006), 'Buried inside a Bruce Willis video, the evidence of a plot to kill thousands', 7 November.

Haggerty, K.D. and R.V. Ericson (2000), 'The surveillant assemblage', *British Journal of Sociology*, **51**(4), 605–22.

Haggerty, K.D. and A. Gazso (2005), 'Seeing beyond the ruins: surveillance as a response to terrorist threats', *Canadian Journal of Sociology*, **30**(2), 169–87.

Haggerty, K.D. (2006), 'Tear down the walls: on demolishing the panopticon', in Lyon, D. (ed.), *Theorizing Surveillance: The Panopticon and Beyond*, Cullompton: Willan.

Hamilton, S. (2002), 'September 11th, the internet, and the affects on information provision in libraries', 68th IFLA Council and General Conference, 18–24 August, http://eric.ed.gov/ERICDocs/data/ericdocs 2/content_storage_01/0000000b/80/28/25/a6.pdf.

Hayes, B. (2006), 'Arming big brother: the EU's security research programme', Transnational Institute, TNI Briefing Series, No. 2006/1.

Heath, C., P. Luff and M.S. Svensson. (2002), 'Overseeing organizations: configuring action and its environment', *British Journal of Sociology*, **53**(2), 181–201.

Higgs, E. (2001), 'The rise of the information state: the development of central state surveillance of the citizen in England, 1500–2000', *Journal of Historical Sociology*, **14**(2), 175–97.

Hillyard, P. (1987), 'The normalization of special powers: from Northern Ireland to Britain', in Scraton, P. (ed.), *Law, Order and the Authoritarian State: Readings in Critical Criminology*, Milton Keynes: Open University Press.

Introna, L.D. and D. Wood (2004), 'Picturing algorithmic surveillance: the politics of facial recognition systems', *Surveillance and Society*, **2**(2–3), 177–98, www.surveillance-andsociety.org.

Koskela, H. (2006), ' "The other side of surveillance": webcams, power and agency', in Lyon, D. (ed.), *Theorizing Surveillance: The Panopticon and Beyond*, Cullompton: Willan.

Levack, K. (2003), 'TIA: terrorism information awareness or totally inappropriate'?, *Econtent*, October, www.econtentmag.com/Articles/ArticleReader.aspx?ArticleID=5550.

Lianos, M. and M. Douglas (2000), 'Dangerization and the end of deviance: the institutional environment', in Garland, D. and Sparks, R. (eds), *Criminology and Social Theory*, Oxford: OUP.

Lusher, A. (2006), 'Police want spy planes to patrol troubled estates', www. syndication@telegraph.co.uk.

Lyon, D. (1994), *The Electronic Eye: The Rise of the Surveillance Society*, Cambridge: Polity Press.

Lyon, D. (2003a), 'Surveillance after September 11, 2001', in Ball, K. and Webster, F. (eds), *The Intensification of Surveillance: Crime, Terrorism and Warfare in the Information Age*, London: Pluto Press.

Lyon, D. (2003b), *Surveillance after September 11*, Cambridge: Polity Press.

Lyon, D. (2006), 'The search for surveillance theories', in Lyon, D. (ed.), *Theorizing Surveillance: The Panopticon and Beyond*, Cullompton: Willan.

Mathiesen, T. (2000), 'On the globalisation of control: towards an integrated surveillance system in Europe', in Green, P. and Rutherford, A. (eds), *Criminal Policy in Transition*, Oñati International Series in Law and Society, London: Statewatch.

McCahill, M. (2002), *The Surveillance Web: The Rise of Visual Surveillance in an English City*, Cullompton: Willan.

Mitchell, T. (1988), *Colonising Egypt*, Cairo: American University of Cairo Press.

Mythen, G. and S. Walklate (2006), 'Communicating the terrorist risk: harnessing a culture of fear', *Crime, Media, Culture*, **2**(2), 123–42.

Neal, A.W. (2006), 'Foucault in Guantánamo: towards an archaeology of the exception', Special Section: Theorizing the Liberty-Security Relation: Sovereignty, Liberalism and Exceptionalism, *Security Dialogue*, **37**(1), March.

Nellis, M. (2003), ' "They don't even know we're there": the electronic monitoring of offenders in England and Wales', in Ball, K. and Webster, F. (eds), *The Intensification of Surveillance: Crime, Terrorism and Warfare in the Information Age*, London: Pluto Press.

New Internationalist (2005), 'They are watching you', March.

Norris, C. and G. Armstrong (1999), *The Maximum Surveillance Society*, Oxford: Berg.

Norris, C., M. McCahill and D. Wood (2004), 'The growth of CCTV: a global perspective on the international diffusion of video surveillance in publicly accessible space', *Surveillance and Society*, **2**(2/3), www.surveillance-andsociety.org.

Norris, C. and M. McCahill (2006), 'CCTV: beyond penal modernism?', *British Journal of Criminology*, **46**(1), 97–118.

Observer, The (2002), 'Police to spy on all emails: fury over Europe's secret plan to access computer and phone data', 9 June.

Observer, The (2006), 'We don't live in a police state yet, but were heading there', 22 January.

O'Malley, P. (1992), 'Risk, power and crime prevention', *Economy and Society*, **21** (3), August, 252–75.

Paul, T.V. (2005), 'The national security state and global terrorism: why the state is not prepared for the new kind of war', in Aydinli, E. and Rosenau, J.N. (eds), *Globalization, Security and the Nation State: Paradigms in Transition*, New York: State University of New York Press.

Rule, J. (1973), *Private Lives and Public Surveillance*, London: Allen Lane.

Simpson, L.C. (1995), *Technology, Time and the Conversations of Modernity*, London: Routledge.

Smart, B. (1985), *Michel Foucault*, London: Tavistock.

Solheim, S. (2005), 'Airport arms with ipaqs', www.eweek.com/article2/0,1759, 1780278,00.asp, accessed 23 August 2006.

Sorensen, A. (2003), 'Building world city Tokyo: globalization and conflict over urban space', *The Annals of Regional Science*, **37**, 519–31.

Stanley, J. and B. Steinhardt (2002), 'Drawing a blank: the failure of facial recognition technology in Tampa, Florida', ACLU Special Report, 3 January, www.epic.org/privacy/surveillance/spotlight/1105/aclu0302.pdf#search=%22Drawing%20a%20blank%3A%20the%20failure%20of%20facial%20recognition%20%22.

Stephan, A. (2004), 'America', *New Statesman*, 12 Jan, www.newstatesman.com/nssubsfilter.php 3?newTemplate=NSArticle_NS&newDisplayURN=200401120004.

Times of India (2002), 'Cameras to be installed at city airport', 20 July, http://timesofindia.indiatimes.com/articleshow/16593947.cms.

Töpfer, E., L. Hempel and H. Cameron (2003), *Watching the Bear: Networks and Islands of Visual Surveillance in Berlin*, Urbaneye Working Paper no. 8., Centre for Technology and Society, Technical University of Berlin, www.urbaneye.net/results/results.htm.

Torpey, J. (2005), 'Imperial embrace? Identification and constraints on mobility in a hegemonic empire', in Zureik, E. and Salter, M.B. (eds), *Global Surveillance and Policing: Borders, Security, Identity*, Cullompton: Willan.

Whitaker, R. (2006), 'A Faustian bargain? America and the dream of total information awareness', in Haggerty, K.D. and R.V. Ericson (eds), *The New Politics of Surveillance and Visibility*, Toronto: University of Toronto Press.

Wiecek, C. and A. Rudinow-Saetnan (2002), *Restrictive? Permissive? The Contradictory Framing of Video Surveillance in Norway and Denmark*, Urbaneye Working Paper no. 4., Centre for Technology and Society, Technical University of Berlin, www.urbaneye.net/results/results.htm.

Zureik, E. (2001), 'Constructing Palestine through surveillance practices', *British Journal of Middle Eastern Studies*, **28**(2), 205–27.

Zureik, E. and K. Hindle (2004), 'Governance, security and technology: the case of biometrics', *Studies in Political Economy*, www.queensu.ca/sociology/Surveillance/files/biometrics%20in%20SPE%20Final%20Published.pdf.

Zureik, E. and M.B. Salter (2005), 'Introduction', in Zureik, E. and Salter, M.B. (eds), *Global Surveillance and Policing: Borders, Security, Identity*, Cullompton: Willan.

PART 3

Reflections

12. Elias, organised violence and terrorism

Tony Ward and Peter Young

INTRODUCTION

What contribution can criminology make to the explanation of terrorism? The growth of terrorism and the global war on it are two of the most significant social changes of late modern society. Terrorism is a type of violent crime and the war on it marks a distinct type of global control response. The subject matter of criminology is the study of crime and its control, so a criminological explanation of both ought to be possible; it ought to come from its core.

This chapter offers a suggestion as to how criminology might address that explanatory task, by taking a step back from what many in the discipline would see as some of its central contemporary concerns. Criminology is a diverse discipline, and the study of state violence that interests some of us (Green and Ward, 2004) may seem far removed from the central preoccupations of mainstream criminology, which focus on why individuals engage in routine forms of 'ordinary' law breaking. Many criminologists are centrally concerned with constructing empirically rooted explanations of how crime fits into the daily routines of life. In some respects this focus upon the ordinary, routine nature of criminal activity is to be understood as a reaction to a tradition in criminology that started from the assumption that criminals are different in a number of ways from non-criminals. David Garland (2001) has described these different strains in criminology graphically as, on the one hand, 'a criminology of the self' and on the other, as 'a criminology of the other'. The 'criminology of the self', with its understanding of everyday crime and deviance as activities of ordinary people pursuing mundane goals in a particular social context, resonates to some extent with those studies of genocide and other major forms of organised violence which emphasise the 'banality of evil' (Arendt, 1965), the role of 'ordinary men' (Browning, 1993) and commonplace motives in crimes of extraordinary horror.

How would an explanation of terrorism fit here? Few see terrorism as an ordinary crime grounded in the routines of everyday life and thus explicable in terms of a vocabulary that treats it as prosaic and mundane. Rather, terrorism tends to be seen as exceptional behaviour. This may appear to justify pushing criminology back to its strategy of seeking for accounts that begin from an assumption of difference – that terrorists are different and that an explanation consists of a display of this. There is, however, no compelling reason or empirical evidence to approach the matter in either of these ways. On the one hand, terrorism does appear to be like any other crime. Terrorists belong to subcultures; they are certainly motivated to offend; terrorism needs planning – it is a highly organised form of activity; there is a routine aspect to it – skills have to be learnt and transmitted (see, for example, Elster, 2005). On the other hand, terrorism seems distinct by its very nature. A decision to cause such a degree of harm as is caused, for example, by many suicide bombings, to so disregard the common bonds of everyday sociability, seems to make terrorism and terrorists distinctive. Perhaps criminology does not possess the tools adequate to the task.

Explaining terrorism thus poses a problem for criminology (as it does for social science generally). So, how should we approach the matter? The strategy used here proceeds from two assumptions. First, we see terrorism as a type of intentional, patterned, normally violent, behaviour. Second, we see terrorism as behaviour that directly challenges prevailing conceptions of when it is legitimate to use violence and physical force. Terrorism is distinct from other forms of criminal activity, violence included, in that one of its purposes is to challenge the modern state's presumption that it possesses a monopoly of legitimate force. Ordinary crime, of course, often uses violence as a means to achieve an end but terrorism is distinct in that the primary end sought is political. Terrorism seeks a re-distribution of power by means outwith those regarded as legitimate. This suggests that a fruitful account of terrorism can be found in an explanation of the way in which violent behaviour and conceptions of legitimacy interact.

Such an account shifts the ground considerably as it makes the concept of political legitimacy central to explanation in a way that is not the case in ordinary crime and criminal violence. Terrorism is lodged in the space where contests over conceptions of legitimacy and violence overlap. Legitimacy must be regarded as a central concept in describing the how and why of terrorism and the response that national and international communities have to it. Legitimacy, however, is a notoriously slippery concept (Beetham, 1991; O'Kane, 1993). It is a phenomenological concept that is most closely associated with the Weberian tradition in sociological analysis and thus clearly points to the importance of context in the understanding of meaning and action. Actions make sense in contexts and derive meaning from them. This is crucial to understanding the dynamics of terrorism; terrorism as a type of violent action draws upon the social context in which it is performed. Terrorism begs questions about who has the power to define actions as legitimate.

This is where the work of Norbert Elias becomes relevant. Elias worked within a broad Weberian tradition in which the modern state is defined in terms of its monopoly over the use of force. He set out to provide an historical and developmental theory of the relationship between the emergence of the modern, Western state and the use and place of violence. His central contention is that this relationship is mediated by the growth of a characteristic sensibility that abhors the use of interpersonal violence and cedes to the state a monopoly of it. For us, it is this linking of the 'micro' and 'macro' that gives Elias's work a potential that most other analyses of violence lack.

For Elias, the relationship between state formation and sensibilities is dynamic and somewhat volatile. At its heart, however, is the creation and sustaining of what he calls 'pacified social spaces'. These are social spaces in which individuals feel secure and protected from the direct use of violence (see Garland, 1996). Terrorists use violence intentionally to disrupt these pacified social spaces; the point of terrorism is to create fear and to challenge who defines action as legitimate (Gambetta, 2005; Ruggiero, 2006). This raises important further questions that we discuss later; what sort of sensibility contextualises and justifies the use of violence by terrorists? How are we to understand this sensibility? We discuss this with particular reference to suicide bombing.

These questions raise difficulties for Elias's theory (of which he was aware) and we intend to explore these in the chapter. Nevertheless, we believe that his theory provides a useful framing device for understanding the dynamics of terrorism. One of its great advantages is that it encourages research into terrorism to be placed in a long-term perspective and in a framework that removes it somewhat from what Elias described as the politics of 'involvement and detachment' (Elias, 1987). Many accounts of terrorism and the response to it are driven, understandably, by the need to come to terms with the immediate problems that it poses for nation states, for terrorist populations and for the international community. In this sense, accounts of terrorism are often 'involved' in the action they explain. Using Elias's work, however, helps social scientists to 'step back' and become (relatively) more 'detached'. The understanding of contemporary terrorism is enhanced, we suggest, by perceiving it in the context of enduring social processes that create and sustain pacified social spaces and challenges to this. From this perspective, the globalisation of human rights culture, for example, may be seen as a mechanism by which to generalise a particular version of what a pacified social space ought to be like and terrorism as a rhythmic disruption to its boundaries.

The first part of the chapter uses Elias's work in this way. We also wish, as was said, to begin the discussion of what sort of sensibility goes along with the use of terrorist violence – what social conditions give rise to it and how it may be described. Elias's work is useful here also, although very often mostly in counterpoint. The chapter begins, however, with a brief exposition of Elias's theory. This is not a comprehensive account, not least because there are readily available texts that do this (Mennell, 1992; van Krieken, 1998; Smith, 2001). Rather, we wish to sketch the role that the concept of pacified social space plays in Elias's work and also to describe, again briefly, his later work in which he tries to account for the use of violence, including terrorism, in late modern societies.

ELIAS, THE CIVILISING PROCESS AND THE IMPORTANCE OF PACIFIED SOCIAL SPACES

Elias's work exists in a conceptual space bounded by Max Weber and Sigmund Freud. From Weber, Elias takes, above all, the concept of the modern state as being defined in terms of the probability of its monopoly of the use of physical force. He also takes from Weber a stress upon contingency in explaining long-term social change. As in Weber, there is always a sense in which, for Elias, things can be different – there is no inevitability or general direction to social change. Rather, change has to be accounted for specifically. There is an interesting difference between Weber and Elias in that for Weber, it is the monopoly of legitimate violence that is crucial, whereas for Elias it is a simple monopoly of physical force. From Freud, Elias takes a view of human nature in which humans are portrayed essentially as driven by instinctual urges that create a continuing potential for violence. Elias also takes from Freud a developmental view of physic growth in which humans gain control over these instinctual urges by coming to terms with the restrictions that flow from living in communities. Elias, however, contextualises this radically by describing in great detail the particular contingencies of social change that 'tame' or direct these urges in concrete ways.

Elias's theory of the civilising process consists of a detailed description of the precise historical changes that have given direction to this process of physic development and given rise to a generalised type of sensibility in Western societies. Elias, in *The Civilizing Process* (1978, 1982), first published in 1939, presents an account that revolves around two interconnected social processes. One of these is the gradual, but increasing, monopoly of violence by a centralised state and the other is the diffusion of a particular code of morality that first emerged among the courtly elites of European society. This code stressed the importance of the individual controlling and increasingly privatising all bodily functions, including using violence or physical force. Elias contends that in Western European states, this code was gradually spread down social hierarchies so that by the nineteenth century 'civilised' behaviour came to be defined in terms of carrying out bodily functions in private and avoiding the use of violence in interpersonal relationships in public. Rather, it came to be seen that it was the nation state that controlled the use of force through specific agencies (military, police and so on) charged with this role.

It is within this general picture that Elias's concept of 'pacified social spaces' is placed. Pacified social spaces are, as was said, social spaces in which the individual can feel secure. Security is defined essentially in terms of the relative absence of physical force as a governing feature of social behaviour. The boundaries of these spaces are maintained, not by individuals alone, but are also, perhaps primarily, the responsibility of the nation state. The nation state comes to be seen as the guardian of peace and individual well-being. The result of this, according to Elias, is not that violence disappears from society but that it goes outward and upward. It is nation states that are seen to be the legitimate users of violence, not individuals. If states cannot either maintain boundaries or guarantee internal peace and security, then, as the contemporary case of Iraq shows, there is a sense in which it no longer makes sense to describe the space as a society.

Pacified social spaces thus are a basic ingredient of the social for Elias but, ironically, their very existence is defined in terms of the control of violence. There is a sense, then, in which for Elias there is a continuing and dynamic relationship between violence and its control that is at the heart of all societies. The 'civilised' assumption in modern Western society that it is the state that has a monopoly of physical force, combined with forms of sensibility that distance the use of violence in personal relationships, provide the key mechanisms that police this relationship. The very fact that the control of violence is so central to modern society, however, provides in its turn, the space within which terrorism can have such a significant effect. Terrorism uses violence in an organised way to induce fear and insecurity and so undercuts or disrupts the very mechanisms that create pacified social space.

As with any major statement, there have been different critical responses to Elias's work. One response has been to read Elias in a rather too general and deterministic way by interpreting him as describing a general theory of social change in which there is a certain direction to history. Another has been to interpret Elias as saying that violence disappears from society and that individuals have no experience of it. Again, as with all major statements, evidence for these interpretations can be found in *The Civilizing Process*. Our interpretation of Elias, however, maintains a stress upon the contingent and even unstable nature of the social process that he describes. Elias's preferred theoretical metaphor was that of the dance. Change comes about by the interweaving of social bodies, constantly in motion. In this sense, pacified social spaces are not quiet havens where individuals have no experience of violence; rather they are spaces that provide a degree of insulation. As van Krieken argues, for Elias, the civilising process is 'permanently unfinished' and pacified social spaces thus need constant reinforcement and re-creation (van Krieken, 1998, pp. 84–135).

In this vein, Elias reacted directly to interpretations of his work that portray it as giving no place to violence within modern society. In *The Germans* (1997), he introduces a new concept of what he calls 'decivilising processes'. Decivilising processes are met with primarily as the result of particular power struggles that give rise, among other things, to increased levels of violence within rather that just between nation states. These specific power struggles disrupt pacified social spaces and so provide room for interpersonal violence to become more common. It is in this context that Elias provides an account of terrorism.

Elias takes two examples of terrorism in German society. The first is the right-wing *Freikorps* in the Weimar Republic and the second is the emergence in Germany in the 1960s of radical dissenting groups that embraced violence. Elias contends that there are common social processes involved in each. He points to two that underpin the emergence of terrorist groups. First, there is a perceived denial by the powerful of access to legitimate democratic processes or meaningful careers, combined with a rejection of the demands made by those who dissent. Essentially, the dissenters perceive their position to be the result of a lack of justice. For Elias, there is often a generational element to this. It is the young, or those who are marginalised, who are denied access by a powerful elder generation. The result of this, he claims, is a withdrawal of legitimacy by the powerless to the right of the powerful to monopolise power and make judgements that have to be accepted.

The second underpinning social condition is the existence of an ideology that presents a viable alternative view of social arrangements. Elias contends that terrorist activity emerges only if this alternative view of the world and of justice within it exists. If there is no developed ideological alternative then there may be protest but actions stop short of organised terrorism.

THE LIMITS OF ELIAS

Elias's most important contribution to understanding present-day terrorism lies not in his analysis of specific episodes of German history but rather in the way he ties sensibilities to social institutions. For Elias, it is the relationship between sensibilities and institutions that accounts both for the long-term decline in violence that constitutes the civilising process and the development of decivilising processes, of which terrorism is an example. This creates a context in which the use of violence and its control are to be explained as inter-related aspects of a dynamic process at the very heart of modern society. In this sense, there is more in common between Elias's explanation of violence and some other influential accounts of its place in modern history than some of his critics allow (see Smith, 2001). For example, for Bauman, Elias's theory fails to provide an adequate account of the holocaust precisely because, according to Bauman, it places violence at the margins of modern society rather than at its heart (Bauman, 1989). Our reading of Elias is clearly different from this and, from one point of view, makes the centrality of violence and its control, the central tension or problem to be resolved for modernity. Social institutions and sensibilities work together and this provides the nexus for explaining violence and terrorism; a nexus that we focus on in the later sections of this chapter.

Nevertheless, there are some clear problems in using Elias's theory. Some of these derive from his use of Freud. Elias ties the emergence of terrorism to specific social conditions that give a crucial role to the place of ideology, but where does this leave the Freudianism that is a deep structure in his wider theory? Elias's attempt to resolve the tension between the socio-historical and psychoanalytic aspects of his theory (1978, pp. 190–91) is not a model of clarity. Human beings unquestionably have a *capacity* for aggressive behaviour and a capacity for taking pleasure in cruelty, but whether these should be interpreted as drives or instincts eternally bubbling away below the surface of civilised life is much more debatable.

Second, for Elias, it is the nation state that provides the primary context in which to explain social and physic change. How does this emphasis sit with the central place given to globalisation in so many accounts of late modern or post-modern society?

Although the national state remains the context within which much political action is played out and while it still constitutes a key political and economic actor on the world stage, the ever-gathering forces of globalisation mark a new and unfolding social space. This new space is defined by growing dependencies and inter-relationships that cut across national boundaries. Law and cultures of law, such as human rights, have become crucial ingredients of this new social space and a degree of 'legalism' can be regarded as one of its characteristics. Human rights culture, arguably, is one of the institutional structures that aim to pacify this new social space. While human rights depend, in part, on state law, they also constitute one of the vectors that aim to 'civilise' the 'global'. The ostensibly global nature of the 'war on terror' may seem to raise a crucial problem for Elias's theory. If terrorist and counter-terrorist violence operate at this level, what conceptual room is left for the nation state?

One answer to this question is that we are moving in a direction that Elias foresaw in the conclusion to *The Civilizing Process*: the merging of nation states into 'larger hegemonial units' (Elias, 1982, p. 321). Globalisation can, however, be interpreted in quite the opposite way: as a 'decivilising' process in which anarchic market forces gain increasing sway as the power of nation states declines (Smith, 2001, pp. 124–7). We should not be carried away by either of these visions of globalisation. In reality, the exercise of organised violence is still overwhelmingly the prerogative of nation states, except in those 'failed states' where the monopoly of violence has broken down. Moreover, terrorist violence is predominantly directed against nation states. The dynamic by which state and anti-state violence respond to and feed one another remains crucial to understanding the nature of terrorism, and it is in this context that Elias's insight into the relation between the organisation of violence and the formation of sensibilities provides a helpful framework for analysis.

ELIAS AND STATE CRIME

Elias's main concern is with the psychological effects of state formation on those individuals who do not participate in the state monopoly of violence; but what of the effects on those who do? Modern states do not rely upon a specialised warrior caste, but recruit their police and soldiers from men, and increasingly women, who have presumably been socialised into a civilised sensibility of self-restraint and empathy. As Elias (1987, p. 81) notes, this socialisation gives rise to 'a contradiction between the code of non-violence within states and the code of permitted violence in inter-state affairs' and to 'a permanent tension within societies between the code of total non-violence valid for the majority of citizens and the code of licensed violence, more or less under public control, valid for the police and other armed forces'.

Elias says less than one might expect about how this 'permanent tension' is resolved, but there appear to be two possibilities. State agents may learn to exercise violence in a way that is compatible with civilised sensibilities because it is disciplined, rationally calculated, and even in certain respects humane. Or they may learn to consider themselves exempt from the restrictions on violence that apply to the rest of the population; they may even learn to enjoy the pleasures of violence which are denied to others (as in the case of the officer class and other elite males in Imperial Germany: Elias, 1997, p. 52).

These possibilities are not mutually incompatible. The disciplined violence of the police, for example, can coexist with a subculture of 'action-oriented hedonism' and the occasional excesses that it inspires (Holdaway, 1984). Abram de Swaan, building on Elias's work, has noted how these processes may come together in what he calls a 'bureaucratization of barbarism'.

> The most barbarous acts are perpetrated, sometimes in a calculated and detached manner, sometimes wildly, with passion, lust and abandon. What matters is that the barbarism occurs in demarcated spaces, in delineated episodes, well separated from the rest of society, from the everyday existence of the other citizens. (De Swaan, 2001, p. 268)

De Swaan notes how in Bosnia, for example, rapes and murders which individual soldiers performed with drunken abandon at the same time served as part of a deliberate strategy on the part of their officers. He coins the term 'dyscivilization' to refer to societies in which 'wild' violence is practised in segregated enclaves, against minorities marked out from the rest of the population who continue to enjoy a more or less pacific, civilised existence. De Swaan's extension of Elias's theory is of great interest for the study of state terror and genocide, and seems to us to capture the interplay of bureaucratic rationality and 'wild' violence much better than the influential work of Bauman (1989). What concerns us here, however, is its relation to anti-state terrorism: the actions of those who seek to challenge a state's monopoly of violence by attacking those not directly involved in exercising that monopoly.

DYSCIVILISATION AND TERRORISM

What de Swaan writes about 'an archipelago of enclaves where cruelty reigns while being reined in all the while' has an obvious resonance with developments in the 'war on terror' since then: Guantánamo Bay, Abu Ghraib, 'extraordinary rendition'. And yet his description does not quite fit these developments. They are not 'almost invisible and well-nigh unmentionable' (ibid., p. 269): they are constantly discussed and, especially in the case of Abu Ghraib, images of their barbarity are seen around the world. Nor is it entirely true that these enclaves are 'compartmentalized' through '*disidentification* from the designated victim population, the withdrawal of identificatory affect, the denial that the target population might be similar to oneself and the repression of emotions that result from identification, such as sympathy, pity, concern, jealousy' (ibid., p. 269, original italics). Clearly there are people in the UK, the US and elsewhere (particularly, but

not exclusively, within the Muslim population) who identify strongly with
the victims. Moreover, in addition to the tightly segregated 'enclaves of barbarism' there are what we might call 'unpacified spaces', such as much of
Iraq and Gaza, where no state enjoys either an uncontested monopoly of
violence, or the ability to conceal its own or its enemies' violence from the
outside world. (This is a matter of degree, but the stranglehold that the
Russian state has achieved over information from Chechnya probably
qualifies that country as an 'enclave of barbarism'. See Boykewich, 2005.)

One link between terror and globalisation is that what happens in these
enclaves and unpacified spaces affects not only adjacent, pacified spaces,
but also individuals at a great distance. American and British families are
bereaved in Iraq; Muslims and Jews on other continents can identify with
the sufferings of their co-religionists in the Middle East. Of course, this is
not a new phenomenon. The novelty of globalisation is often exaggerated.
But global media (including the Internet) significantly amplify the impact
of acts of violence by and against states, and the scope for developing
global networks united by solidarity with their victims or perpetrators
(Bauman, 2006, ch. 4). For example:

> Bin Laden's gripping and powerful pre-recorded video clip, delivered before the
> US air raids on Afghanistan and broadcast by al-Jazeera within hours of their
> inception, epitomized the inadequacy of the response the most powerful state in
> the world could muster in the face of basic modern telecommunications used
> well. . . . There is now a far greater sense of community among the world's
> Muslims . . . than at any time since the Western colonial powers broke up the
> remains of the Islamic empire eighty years ago. (Burke, 2004, p. 39)

And yet, despite the widespread awareness of violence, civilised life goes
on. Most of us, most of the time, are able to dissociate our peaceful everyday lives from the horrors of the television news.

This particular form of 'dyscivilisation', with its partial and leaky
compartmentalisation of violence, may be particularly conducive to anti-
state terrorism. One of the goals of terrorism is, we suggest, to shatter the
'compartmentalisation' of pacified social spaces from the enclaves of
barbarism – by creating new sites of barbarism at places and times not of
the state's choosing. If this seems to be attributing too much sophistication
to the terrorists, consider the terse and lucid statement of the London
suicide bomber, Mohamed Siddique Khan:

> Your democratically elected governments continuously perpetuate atrocities
> against my people all over the world. And your support of them makes you
> directly responsible, just as I am directly responsible for protecting and avenging
> my Muslim brothers and sisters. Until we feel security, you will be our targets.
> And until you stop the bombing, gassing, imprisonment and torture of my

people we will not stop this fight. We are at war and I am a soldier. Now you too will taste the reality of this situation. (BBC News, 2005)

Commentators have expressed bewilderment at the 'normality' of Khan, 'with all his trappings of Western culture' (Suleaman, 2005), and his fellow bombers. But perhaps it is precisely this that makes their actions intelligible. How does it feel to be outwardly at home in the pacified spaces of Western Europe, and at the same time to identify passionately with the victims of state violence in the Middle East? Not so very different, perhaps, from the feelings Elias ascribed to the young Germans attracted to the Red Army Faction in the 1960s and 1970s: an acute awareness that the world is full of atrocities, a disgust at the hypocrisy of the political class and the older generation in general, the 'loss of a positive national we-image' and an attraction to a subculture with its own strong sense of morality (Elias, 1997, pp. 262–7, 282).

Of course, it is irrational to hold passengers on the Underground responsible for what happens in Abu Ghraib or Gaza. Khan must have been aware that hundreds of thousands of Londoners had publicly demonstrated their rejection of 'their' government's policy. His perverse idealisation of democracy was no doubt influenced by other Islamist justifications of terror such as a statement issued in 2002 in the name of bin Laden and al-Qaeda:

> It is a fundamental principle of any democracy that the people choose their leaders, and as such, approve and are party to the actions of their elected leaders . . . By electing these leaders, the American people have given their consent to the incarceration of the Palestinian people, the demolition of Palestinian homes and the slaughter of the children of Iraq. This is why the American people are not innocent. The American people are active members in all these crimes. (Quoted by Blanchard, 2006, p. 7)[1]

Chechen propagandists give a similar justification for killing Russian civilians (Bloom, 2005, p. 99).

RETALIATION AND RITUAL

Another theme that Khan's statement shares with many other acts of suicide terror is that of mimesis (Girard, 1972 [2005]): the symbolic re-enactment, on a smaller scale, of the violence to which it is a response. As Bloom (2005, pp. 86–7) notes, many suicide bombers in Palestine, Chechnya and Sri Lanka have lost husbands or siblings at the hands of the state they attack. Khan of course had not, but he spoke of 'avenging my Muslim brothers and sisters', symbolically putting himself in the same position. His statement that 'you will taste the reality of this situation' echoes the rhetoric of Hamas in its most strident vein:

> Given the methods used by the Israelis, we consider the door to Hell is open. Their assassination policy and the bombardment – all this theatre of war inside Palestinian villages and homes – we respond to that by seeking to make Israelis feel the same, insecure inside their homes. (Sayeed Siyam, *New York Times Magazine*, 3 February 2002, quoted by Pape, 2005, p. 32)

Vengeance is an apparently universal way of gaining satisfaction from another's pain, and its appeal persists even in the most pacific of societies (Katz, 1988; Scheff, 2000). Mimetic forms of vengeance are characteristic of many acts of state terror meted out in response to terrorist or insurgent actions (Aretxaga, 2000; Keppley Mahmood, 2000), and also of much anti-state terrorism. As Holmes (2005, p. 165) points out:

> The backward looking principle of retaliatory justice – *do unto others as they have done unto you* – recurs obsessively in al-Qaeda statements. The 9/11 plotters adapted this norm to the age of mass communications: *Show the world that you can harm others as they have harmed you.* (Original italics)

According to Osama bin Laden, it was the sight of tower blocks destroyed in the 1982 Israeli invasion of Lebanon that inspired him 'to destroy towers in America so that it would have a taste of its own medicine and would be prevented from killing our women and children. . . . Self-defence and punishing the oppressor in kind: is this shameful terrorism?' (bin Laden, *The Towers of Lebanon* (2004) in Lawrence, 2005, pp. 239–40).

The relation between harm and retaliation is, then, one of ritual appropriateness as least as much as of instrumental calculation (Zulaika and Douglass, 1996). While there is a certain affinity between the ritual aspects of terrorism and of religious practice (Juergensmeyer, 2003, p. 127), the same ritual or symbolic character can be discerned in overtly secular acts of state, nationalist, or revolutionary terror. The ritual aspect of terrorism – the fact that it vividly *symbolises* the goal that it may or may not instrumentally contribute to attaining – seems to be essential to the particular sensibility that makes terrorism possible.

Elias argues that ritual or magical practices are a natural response to events that one does not understand but desperately needs to control: 'One must do *something*', and if one thinks of disease or disaster as produced by living agents, 'One can pit one's will against theirs' (1987, p. 105, original italics). Even if a scientific world-view (a product of the rationally calculative sensibility fostered by state formation) allows individuals to take a more 'detached' view of natural phenomena, this is much harder to do, argues Elias, when dealing with dangerous social phenomena since these really do involve 'wilful and deliberate acts' (ibid.). Although not discussed by Elias, the persistence of retributive punishment in 'civilised' societies is an obvious example,[2] as is the tendency of states fighting terrorism to engage in counterproductive acts of terror.

If the state itself is seen as the source of 'wilful and deliberate' violence against oneself or those with whom one strongly identifies, the impulse to 'do something', even if it has no rationally calculable positive conse-quences, is no more surprising than the impulse to punish criminals (which is not to say that the actions they inspire are morally equivalent). Since the 'will' of the state is embodied in its monopoly of legitimate violence, *any* challenge to that monopoly can be a way both of 'pitting one's will' against the state's and of cultivating a new sensibility which rejects state-imposed civilisation. Ruggiero (2006) brings this out well in his analyses of the German Red Army Faction[3] and the Italian Red Brigades:

> According to this ontology of the act [that is, that espoused by Ulrike Meinhof and other would-be revolutionaries], violence is a means not only to challenge state authority, but also to build new revolutionary subjects who defy their own internalized legalistic constraints. In other words, violence is an act of extreme transgression, a form of practical self-creation. . . . Violent protest is victorious by the mere act of existing. (Ruggiero, 2006, p. 126)

If terrorism involves the creation of a new sensibility at odds with that of 'civilised' subjects, that sensibility must also be a very different one from that of the pre-modern warrior, with his life of 'incurable unrest, the perpetual proximity of danger . . . in which there are at most small and transient islands of more protected existence' (Elias, 1982, p. 238). Elias suggests that modern soldiers may, albeit with difficulty, enter temporarily into a similar state of untrammelled pleasure in violence (1997, pp. 209–11). In general, however, neither professional soldiers nor terrorists can indulge in a sensi-bility of exuberant passions, violent mood swings and impulsive actions. Planning and self-control over long periods are called for. The terrorist, unlike Katz's (1988) perpetrators of 'righteous slaughter', or the soldier 'going berserk' in battle (Shay, 1995), cannot derive emotional satisfaction from an instantaneous conversion of pent-up humiliation into violent rage. Ritual violence (as in the duels of ruling-class men in imperial Germany: Elias, 1997, pp. 71–3) can be both intrinsically satisfying and tightly con-trolled. The emotional satisfactions of contemplating one's violent act – and anticipating one's own death – can be intense:

> On the night before the operation, we had that feeling when you first get married, on the night of the wedding, so excited. . . . We were so excited, and we were full

of happiness. In that moment, we lived a sort of higher faith. It's a feeling like
you are in the sky, like you are flying up to the sky, and the dunya [earthly world]
gets smaller and smaller and smaller. This feeling gives you all the happiness.
(Salah Mustafa 'Uthman, Palestinian bus hijacker, quoted in Oliver and
Steinberg, 2005, p. 136)

As Gambetta points out, to embark on a suicide mission requires an
extraordinary degree of 'nerve', beyond even that required for spontaneous
acts of heroism in the heat of battle. The perpetrators must sustain 'a "dissociative" state of mind which enables them at once to remain lucid and to
face the prospect of death' (Gambetta, 2005, p. 275). 'Uthman and his two
companions seem to have achieved such a state, remaining sufficiently self-
possessed, up to the moment when they boarded the bus – in an operation
which none of them expected to survive – to pass themselves off as an
Israeli student, businessman and off-duty soldier respectively. Exactly what
part the prospect of paradise plays in creating this dissociative state is
impossible to know, although we find plausible Gambetta's suggestion
(ibid., p. 277) that it acts as a 'visual mantra' helping to sustain the required
frame of mind. But the prospect of paradise is available only by virtue of
the symbolism that converts carnage and chaos into a ritual of 'righteous
slaughter', the just vindication of a humiliated people.

An instructive parable here is the one which provides Elias with the
central metaphor of *Involvement and Detachment* (1987, pp. 45–6): Edgar
Allan Poe's 'A Descent into the Maelström' (1841 [1978]). It is by detaching his mind from the fear aroused by his predicament that Poe's fisherman
is able to understand the pattern of natural forces at work in the maelstrom
and devise a means of escape. What Elias omits to mention is that the
fisherman achieves this state by viewing his situation in religious terms:

> I began to reflect how magnificent a thing it was to die in such a manner, and
> how foolish it was in me to think of so paltry a consideration as my own indi-
> vidual life, in view of so wonderful a manifestation of God's power. (Poe, 1978,
> p. 588)

The fisherman's state of 'light-headed' (ibid., p. 589) detachment is close to
that described by 'Uthman the bus hijacker: a state which does not involve
emotional disengagement, but rather derives emotional satisfaction from
understanding one's fate under the aspect of eternity.

It seems that many acts of terrorism embody some such sensibility, far
removed both from rational, bureaucratic violence and from the 'wild violence' discussed by de Swaan. The concept of ritual, as used by anthropol-
ogists like Zulaika and Douglass, explains how violence can result in
emotional gratification that is mediated by symbolism rather than resulting

(as Elias supposes of medieval warriors) from the simple satisfaction of aggressive 'drives'.

To stress the ritual elements of terrorist violence is not to deny that it can also form part of an instrumentally rational strategy. Zulaika and Douglass's argument is, rather, that:

> [The ritual aspects of terror are] crucial to the sustenance of the morale both of the organization and its individual members. . . . [S]ince each activist is aware that the outcome is quite in doubt, and that even if the quest is finally success-ful . . . its outcome will likely transpire at some distant time outside his/her own personal frame of reference, for the individual the game may become more important than the prize. (1996, p. 136)

A fortiori this must be true where any instrumental gain can only accrue after the militant's own death.

TERROR, DEMOCRACY AND SENSIBILITIES

While Bloom's (2005) study of suicide terrorism rightly stresses the element of retaliation against state violence, Pape (2005) makes the point that the states against which suicide attacks are directed are all democracies: Israel, the US, Russia, Sri Lanka – and now the UK. Bloom challenges Pape's rea-soning, pointing to 'the questionable label of Sri Lanka in the 1980s, Israel in the Occupied Territories, and the Russians in Chechnya as liberal demo-cratic societies' (Bloom, 2005, p. 84). In a way both Pape (who does not, in fact, label these societies 'liberal') and Bloom are correct. The point is not that such states act democratically in relation to those whose cause the ter-rorists espouse, but rather that they are to some extent democratic in rela-tion to the audiences the terrorists seek to influence. But this is hardly surprising. It would be pointless to attack the civilian population of an overt tyranny. Why kill people whose lives are as cheap to the enemy as they are to you?

From an Eliasian perspective, the crucial point may not be the tenuously 'democratic' character of the regime under attack, but the attackers' per-ception of its citizens' sensibilities. To achieve maximum effect, a terrorist attack needs to disrupt a 'pacified space' within a state that at least pretends to some humane concern for its population. In some cases, the terrorists – particularly when they are themselves the products of unpacified spaces or enclaves of violence – can celebrate and take advantage of the fact that they do not share such humane sensibilities. 'It is very difficult to expect human-ism from those who have been tortured' (Chechen statement quoted by Bloom, 2005, p. 92).

The Palestinian militant literature studied by Oliver and Steinberg (2005) makes a point of rejecting humane sensibilities. One Hamas communiqué tells its readers to bring up their children for 'jihad and the love of martyrdom', despite living in an 'era in which the [political] systems bring up their sons to celebrate the child of peace and to learn songs of peace by heart' (quoted in ibid., p. 83). The contrast between Israeli fear of death and Palestinian love of it is a constant theme of this literature (ibid., p. 32), as of al-Qaeda's ideology: 'It is the love of death in the path of Allah that is the weapon that will annihilate this evil empire of America' (Ayman al-Zawahiri, 2002, quoted by Burke, 2004, p. 35). Moreover, the militants' selective use of their Islamic heritage, reducing '[m]ore than a thousand years of history . . . to little more than a collection of paradigms and anecdotes' (ibid., p. 83) provides a direct link to a pre-modern warrior culture.

CONCLUSION

Where then, does this attempt to explain terrorism and its sensibilities leave us?

We have tried to present a view of terrorism that is 'detached' in the sense that, rather than viewing the phenomenon from the standpoint of those who are immediately threatened by it, we attempt to see the predicament of both perpetrators and victims as part of a larger pattern of forces (Elias, 1987). This brings with it a focus on the 'long-term context' in which patterns of violence and their relationship to the changing dynamics of legitimacy may be interpreted. In the long term, modern sensibilities have seen the nation state become the locus of legitimate violence and challenges to this come to be seen as aberrant. Viewed sociologically, the emergence of terrorism and the war on terror require us to rethink the relationship between states' power, the use of violence and legitimacy. Perhaps being 'detached' moves us in the direction of 'suspending belief' in what we think legitimacy means and instead seeing it as a consequence rather than an attribute of the way in which violence is organised.

We can now also see what is missing from the 'criminology of the self' as a way of approaching terrorism. If a habitual acceptance of the state monopoly of violence is, as Elias argues, a crucial element in the formation of the characteristic sensibility of Western modernity, then those who dedicate their life and death to defying that monopoly are in some sense truly 'other'. This is not to suggest that they suffer from any personal abnormality or defect as the 'criminology of the other' traditionally supposed (Ruggiero, 2006). It is, rather, to suggest that profound changes in an individual's way of thinking and feeling may be wrought by, and contribute to, changes in their relationship to the social order under which they live. If the account of these changes that we have tentatively sketched has any validity, its obvious implication – so obvious that, perhaps, we do not need Elias to teach it to us – is that it is by abusing its monopoly of violence that the state is most likely to bring into being the 'other' it so fears.

NOTES

1. Another text by bin Laden can be read as pointing up quite astutely the contradictions within Western democratic rhetoric: 'To the Americans' (2002) in Lawrence (2005, pp. 160–72).
2. Although not so obvious to Garland (1990, pp. 237–40), who ignores Elias's work on detachment and instead extrapolates from *The Civilizing Process* a Freudian account of retributive punishment.
3. An analysis which, as he acknowledges, shares considerable common ground with Elias's (Ruggiero, 1996, pp. 126–7).

REFERENCES

Arendt, H. (1965), *Eichmann in Jerusalem: A Report on the Banality of Evil*, Harmondsworth: Penguin.
Aretxaga, B. (2000), 'A fictional reality: paramilitary death squads and the construction of state terror in Spain', in J.A. Sluka (ed.), *Death Squad: The Anthropology of State Terror*, Philadelphia, PA: University of Pennsylvania Press, pp. 46–69.
Bauman, Z. (1989), *Modernity and the Holocaust*, Cambridge: Polity.
Bauman, Z. (2006), *Liquid Fear*, Cambridge: Polity.
BBC News (2005), 'London Bomber: Text in Full', http://news.bbc.co.uk/1/hi/uk/4206800.stm, accessed 24 April 2007.
Beetham, D. (1991), *The Legitimation of Power*, Basingstoke: Macmillan.
Blanchard, S. (2006), *Al Qaeda: Statements and Evolving Ideology*, Washington, DC: Congressional Research Service, www.fas.org/irp/crs/RS21973.pdf, accessed 24 April 2007.
Bloom, M. (2005), *Dying to Kill: The Allure of Suicide Terror*, New York: Columbia University Press.
Boykewich, S. (2005), 'Russia after Beslan', *Virginia Quarterly Review*, **81** (1): 156–88.
Browning, C.R. (1993), *Ordinary Men: Reserve Police Battalion 101 and the Final Solution in Poland*, New York: HarperPerennial.
Burke, J. (2004), *Al-Qaeda*, London: Penguin.
de Swaan, A. (2001), 'Dyscivilization, mass extermination and the state', *Theory, Culture & Society*, **18** (2–3): 265–76.
Elias, N. (1978), *The Civilizing Process. Vol. 1: The History of Manners*, Oxford: Basil Blackwell.
Elias, N. (1982), *The Civilizing Process. Vol. 2: State Formation and Civilization*, Oxford: Basil Blackwell.

Elias, N. (1987), *Involvement and Detachment*, Oxford: Blackwell.

Elias, N. (1997), *The Germans: Power Struggles and the Development of Habitus in the Nineteenth and Twentieth Centuries*, Cambridge: Polity.

Elster, J. (2005), 'Motivations and beliefs in suicide missions', in D. Gambetta (ed.), *Making Sense of Suicide Missions*, Oxford: Oxford University Press, pp. 233–58.

Gambetta, D. (2005), 'Can we make sense of suicide missions?', in Gambetta (ed.), *Making Sense of Suicide Missions*, Oxford: Oxford University Press, pp. 259–300.

Garland, D. (1990), *Punishment and Modern Society*, Oxford: Clarendon.

Garland, D. (1996), 'The limits of the sovereign state', *British Journal of Criminology*, **36**: 445–71.

Garland, D. (2001), *The Culture of Control*, Oxford: Oxford University Press.

Girard, R. (1972 [2005]), *Violence and the Sacred*, tr. P. Gregory, London: Continuum.

Green, P. and T. Ward (2004), *State Crime: Governments, Violence and Corruption*, London: Pluto.

Holdaway, S. (1984), *Inside the British Police*, Oxford: Blackwell.

Holmes, S. (2005), 'Al-Qaeda, September 11th, 2001', in D. Gambetta (ed.), *Making Sense of Suicide Missions*, Oxford: Oxford University Press, pp. 131–72.

Juergensmeyer, M. (2003), *Terror in the Mind of God*, (3rd edn), Berkeley, CA: University of California Press.

Katz, J. (1988), *Seductions of Crime*, New York: Basic Books.

Keppley Mahmood, C. (2000), 'Trials by fire: dynamics of terror in Punjab and Kashmir', in J.A. Sluka (ed.), *Death Squad: The Anthropology of State Terror*, Philadelphia, PA: University of Pennsylvania Press, pp. 70–90.

Lawrence, B. (ed.) (2005), *Messages to the World: The Statements of Osama bin Laden*, London: Verso.

Mennell, S. (1992), *Norbert Elias: An Introduction*, Oxford: Blackwell.

O'Kane, R.H.T. (1993), 'Against legitimacy', *Political Studies*, **41**: 471–91.

Oliver, A.M. and P. Steinberg (2005), *The Road to Martyr's Square*, Oxford: Oxford University Press.

Pape, R.A. (2005), *Dying to Win: The Strategic Logic of Suicide Terrorism*, New York: Random House.

Poe, E.A. (1841 [1978]), 'A Descent into the Maelström', in *Collected Works*, vol. II, Cambridge, MA: Belknap Press.

Ruggiero, V. (2006), *Understanding Political Violence: A Criminological Analysis*, Maidenhead: Open University Press.

Scheff, T. (2000), *Bloody Revenge: Emotions, Nationalism and War*, Lincoln, NE: iUniverse.com.

Shay, J. (1995), *Achilles in Vietnam: Combat Trauma and the Undoing of Character*, New York: Touchstone.

Smith, D. (2001), *Norbert Elias and Modern Social Theory*, London: Sage.

Suleaman, N. (2005), 'The Mystery of "Sid"', http://news.bbc.co.uk/1/hi/magazine/4354858.stm, accessed 24 April 2007.

van Krieken, R. (1998), *Norbert Elias*, London: Routledge.

Zulaika, J. and W.A. Douglass (1996), *Terror and Taboo*, New York and London: Routledge.

13. The oppressive discourse of global exclusion: the 'war on terror' as a war on difference and freedom

Andrew Robinson

INTRODUCTION

Globalisation has had ambiguous effects in relation to social exclusion. One of the effects of globalisation has been the reconstruction of nation states as transmission belts for neo-liberal policies and agendas, and the resultant reconstruction of national citizenship as conformity to a model of employability and productive usefulness (Sklair, 2000; Robinson, 2004; Moore, 2005). Another is the growth of hybridities on a global scale, such that discourses of homogeneity are rendered increasingly fictional and are defensible only as mythical impositions (Bhabha, 1993; Appadurai, 2001; Gilroy, 2004). The practice of state repression must be viewed as operating at the intersection of these logics, as an attempt to impose neo-liberal homogeneity in a context of centrifugal forces – an enforcement of economic globalisation in the face of social and cultural heterogeneity. It is in this context that the rise of new forms of repression must be viewed, as a project for reconstructing conformist and majoritarian identities so as to articulate these to the neo-liberal project and construct a social support base for the imposition of state control.

This duality in globalisation is constructing new kinds of social and class conflicts, with the concept of 'citizenship' one of several establishing a borderline between the in-group and its other. The conflict between included and excluded is superseding class conflicts among the included as the source of social antagonism today. Samir Amin refers to a massive extension of pauperisation, precarity[1] and social exclusion to the point where over half the global population is now precariously situated, and the precariously situated make up 40 per cent of the centre's popular classes and 80 per cent of the periphery's (Amin, 2004). Hence, a new division emerges which no longer follows lines of exploitation but rather of inclusion and exclusion. Alfredo Bonanno reconstructs the issue of class struggle in terms of 'the division of classes between dominators and dominated, between included and excluded' (Bonanno, 1993).

This chapter examines the spread of an increasingly pervasive form of state regulation of everyday life through the demonisation of minor deviance and nonconformity – a new problematic which reconstructs citizenship around an in-group–out-group binary, resulting in a situation of permanent social conflict. This problematic is conceived as a *project*, in the phenomenological sense – the actualisation in the social world of a particular way of constructing social reality. The purpose of the chapter is to offer an analysis and critique of this new problematic. In addition to mapping its structural origins, the effects of the project are assessed in terms of the emergence of resistance in everyday life.

The overall argument offered here is as follows. First, it is suggested that a new, especially insidious system of social control is being constructed in certain Western societies, instantiated by crackdowns on minor deviance and by the 'war on terror' and its domestic correlates. This system is shown to be not simply a response to particular problems but rather, an attack on difference in general, and on the 'right to have rights'. It is constructed around a demonisation of others, mainly by means of Barthesian myth, and in turn constructs social relations of voicelessness and domination. By constructing social problems in a way which precludes dialogue, this construction makes problems insoluble, and makes resistance both inevitable and necessary. It should be viewed as an outgrowth of a state logic of control inherent to state power as such and inimical to horizontal association. In this context, everyday deviance can often be interpreted as *resistenz*, and an insurrection in everyday life is constructed as the only possible response to pervasive voicelessness.

THE CREEPING GROWTH OF SOCIAL REPRESSION

A new repressive model, pushing back the boundaries of liberal and social-democratic regimes and redefining what it means to be a 'citizen' or socially included person, is taking root in certain core capitalist countries, among which Britain is one of the most obvious cases. The situation has been growing cumulatively worse since the early 1980s and has now reached the point where it is meaningless to speak of Britain as a society where rights are respected. The repressive model should be taken to include such measures and structures as the rise of gated communities, closed-circuit television (CCTV), radio frequency identification tags (RFID), identity (ID) cards, anti-social behaviour orders (ASBOs), dispersal zones, paramilitary policing methods, the 'social cleansing' of groups such as homeless people and street drinkers from public spaces, increasing restrictions on protests and attacks on 'extremist' groups, the use of extreme sentencing against minor deviance, and of course the swathe of 'anti-terrorism' laws which provide a pretext for expanded repression. Some of the new repressive laws and structures are connected specifically to the war on terror, whereas others are related to an increasingly intolerant attitude to everyday social deviance. While the legitimations are sometimes separate, the measures should be viewed as a continuum. For instance, the 'control orders' used against 'suspected terrorists' are basically an escalated extension of ASBOs, and measures such as CCTV and ID cards are often linked to both terrorism and everyday deviance. Such measures add up to a new paradigm of social control. The magazine *Datacide* analyses the wave of repression as 'the real subsumption of every singularity in the domain of the State. From now on if your attributes don't quite extend to crime, a judge's word suffices to ensure that crime will reach out and embrace your attributes' (Hyland, nd). To take an example, *Time* magazine writes of American Taliban fighter John Walker Lindh: 'nowhere in the statute books does there seem to be a law that precisely fits the crime he may have committed'.[2] This idea of a crime without a law is to say the least paradoxical, and fits perfectly the new discourse of repression.

The wave of repression is directed primarily against difference in all its manifestations, especially those associated with nonconformity and precarity. For instance, research reveals the extensive criminalisation of psychological difference among children, and intolerance-inducing and freedom-inhibiting effects of CCTV surveillance (Norris and Armstrong, 1997; Rosen, 2001; BIBIC, 2005). 'You do anything a little out of the ordinary here and they arrest you', remarked a protester at the Republican National Convention, reported by Reuters (Reuters, 2004). Computerised CCTV systems track abnormal action and label it as suspicious; even something like walking against the flow of pedestrians or standing around in one area is taken to be grounds for suspicion (Anon., nd).

The project is not simply an extension of liberal–democratic models of social control, but breaks with such models in directly criminalising nonconformity from a prescribed way of life and attempting to extensively regulate everyday life through repression. Beyond the shifting issues invoked by apologists for repression, there is an overarching principle driving the shift to authoritarianism, an almost totalitarian attitude to everyday life. To be sure, the external form of political polyarchy remains in place. But, in the aims of total intrusion into everyday life – the cumulative elimination of unconditional rights, unwatched spaces and spheres of autonomy – the drive to repression has more in common with totalitarian regimes than with any kind of open society. It is a regime of *gleichschaltung*, of top-down coordination of the whole of society by the state, the coordination of social space as if it were a single machine with the state at its head. Social space is homogenised and rigidified, activity ordered and regulated, difference labelled and criminalised or pathologised. Open spaces are attacked or regulated. The ways in which operations are coordinated worldwide, and people in Britain charged over actions in countries such as Israel, Canada and Pakistan, suggests an aspiration to construct a globally integrated control system irreducible to particular nation states. The breadth of 'anti-terror' laws denies any right to resist even the worst dictatorships, taking the claim to legitimacy of states to an extraordinary extreme and effectively making it a crime to support guerrilla movements anywhere in the world.

The novel, illiberal character of the new control regime is clear from the excess and exceptionalism of its concrete applications. Many of the 'terrorism' laws (regarding issues such as glorification, preparatory acts and failure to disclose) are extremely wide-ranging and vague, allowing innocuous actions to be read creatively as evidence of terrorism; this, combined with a climate of paranoia, is no doubt producing many wrongful convictions and malicious or dubious prosecutions. Two of these cases (Kamel Bourgass and Andrew Rowe) are discussed below; one should also consider dubious convictions of clerics such as Abu Hamza in which generic statements are taken as soliciting murder (BBC News, 2006a), and the continuing detention of Samar Alami and Jawad Botmeh in spite of an obviously flawed conviction (Guedella, nd). Given the breadth of the laws, it is virtually inconceivable that someone could not be convicted if there were substantial evidence of 'terrorism'. Yet in addition to these draconian laws, there are a whole raft of extrajudicial or summary measures which have been used against innocent people – from 'control orders' amounting to permanent house arrest and extradition proceedings ignoring human rights safeguards, to house raids amounting to ransacking and terrorising their targets, and prolonged detention 'on suspicion', during which psychological and physical abuse often takes place. The police often carry out dragnet-style mass raids and arrests on the basis of flimsy suspicion, with most of those arrested subsequently released without charge. Research covering the period from the September 11 attacks to April 2004 revealed that less than one in five of those arrested were actually charged with terrorism offences and little more than 1 per cent convicted (BBC News, 2004). These raids are also often accompanied by paramilitary incursions by groups of armed police into Muslim communities, terrorising neighbours and bystanders, threatening innocent people and disrupting local life (Akbar, 2006).

In fact there has been a pattern of collective punishment, with friends and relatives of 'terrorist suspects' themselves rendered 'suspect' and subjected to draconian measures such as prolonged imprisonment without

trial and house raids amounting to ransacking. One case involving a prominent Muslim cleric in Bradford, subjected to a house raid solely because
his son was declared suspect in Canada, despite being a well-known 'moderate', was particularly blatant (Dodd et al., 2006). The relatives of a British
suicide bomber who targeted Israel were also detained and charged on the
assumption that they should have known his plans, as were relatives of one
of the 7/7 suspects. And another person released without charge appears to
have been targeted because he was the relative of someone held in Pakistan
(Clarke, 2004; Cowan, 2005; BBC News, 2006b). Vaguely worded laws and
extra-legal sanctions such as detention on suspicion are thus used to punish
people for mere association with suspects, enabling the state to harm the
innocent either as a form of extortion against the guilty or as a kind of
guilt-by-association. This is once again typical of totalitarian regimes and
contrary to any consistent conception of rights.

Furthermore, the impunity surrounding police abuse has been covered
by a pattern of victimisation, as in the case of Babar Ahmad, who was
beaten and abused during a dragnet-style arrest. Medical evidence has been
produced to reveal that he was systematically abused while in detention. He
has subsequently been targeted for deportation to America, apparently
solely for online activities; it is suspicious that the first person to go public
and file charges over police abuse should be subjected to such apparently
baseless targeting. Since medical reports conclude that the mistreatment
was controlled and systematic, this suggests deliberation, which may in
turn mean that mistreatment is routine in 'terrorism' cases (Anon., 2004a,
2004b). In another case, prosecutors openly admitted to trying to convict
people before rather than after they do anything wrong; the case involved
the effective use of circumstantial and ambiguous evidence to convict
Andrew Rowe of terrorism offences (Freeman, 2005). Similarly, several
people acquitted by the ricin case jury have been subjected to extrajudicial
sanctions in contravention of the verdict, something jurors on the case have
condemned as government persecution, claiming the government is ignoring the verdict and being 'very vindictive and spiteful' (Campbell and
Norton-Taylor, 2005). Kamel Bourgass, convicted of murdering a police
officer during the raids surrounding the ricin affair, was convicted largely
because a prosecution account was upheld which directly contradicts the
outcomes of other trials – given that the state eventually admitted that there
was no terrorist or mass-murder plot, the motive given by prosecutors was
patently false, and Bourgass's defence – that he acted out of fear – was
effectively admitted to be true (BBC News, 2005; Carrell and Whitacker,
2005).

The idea of 'glorifying terrorism', and the broader idea of targeting so-
called 'spiritual leaders' who may have no organisational connection to

specific 'terrorist' actions, in fact involve the construction of categories of thought-crimes, criminalising people for adhering to a political ideology some of whose adherents practise 'terrorism', or for expressing views on certain issues which the government deems to be politically incorrect. After the passage of the law banning 'glorification', the political party al-Muhajiroun and two alleged offshoots have been banned for expressing views the government disapproves of (BBC News, 2006c). But in fact, the idea that advocacy of controversial or dissenting views constitutes a form of support for terrorism had already been implicitly asserted prior to this new prohibition. Mosques have been raided and closed, and individual clerics arrested for statements which amount to points of religious interpretation; even musicians such as Fun-da-Mental are at risk of persecution (BBC News, 2003, 2006d). People are facing 'solicitation to murder' charges simply for taking part in demonstrations (Press Association, 2006). In addition, political parties associated with armed opposition groups, such as Batasuna and Kongra-Gel, have been banned in Britain after similar prohibitions abroad (BBC News, 2006c). This kind of explicit prohibition of political beliefs and organisations is a recent tendency; previously, even parties such as Sinn Fein, the Irish Republican Socialist Party and the Ulster Democratic Party were able to operate legally despite allegations of links to armed groups. Had the current approach have been taken then, the eventual Northern Ireland 'peace process' would probably have been rendered impossible.

These new prohibitions amount to a kind of law previously found only in totalitarian regimes (the South 'African Suppression of Communism Act' being one precursor), in which certain political beliefs are forbidden by the state and people can be arrested simply for expressing such views. This kind of measure should also be taken as a threat by anyone who does not embrace the entire political project of the government. In Italy, similar laws have led to the persecution of critical intellectuals with no connection to actual incidents, simply for holding theoretical views similar to those of alleged perpetrators – for example, Antonio Negri and Alfredo Bonanno (Murphy, 2005).

The war against the 'anti-social' and against 'suspected terrorists' is becoming the 'touchy nodal point' of the current situation – the point at which a master-signifier is formed by means of the demonisation of a 'repressed Real'. Citizenship or social inclusion is constructed around a master- or despotic-signifier. A necessary structural effect of the master-signifier is the construction of at least one element as excluded other, standing for the elided contingency and instability threatening the social order – in Lacanian terms, a repressed 'Real' which is unsymbolisable in the framework of the existing system and through which the system's instability 'returns'. Slavoj Žižek has coined the term 'social symptom' to refer to those groups excluded by such social processes – refugees, the urban poor, and so on – 'the part which, although inherent to the existing universal order, has no 'proper place' within it' (Žižek, 1999, p. 224). Hence the irrationalism and dogmatism surrounding this issue, with representatives of the conformist position apparently unable to see any opposition to their views as anything but ignorance or evil.

CREATING THE ENEMY

If the new wave of repression is a state response to globalisation, the 'war on terror' can be seen as a re-globalisation of this phenomenon, both literally (in terms of the international extension of control regimes and the direct imposition of such regimes in occupied countries) and metaphorically (with 'rogue states', 'failed states', 'terrorists' and other bogeymen standing in relation to the 'international community' as a kind of global 'anti-social'). National and chauvinistic discourses rely on the same kind of mechanisms of othering and exclusion which construct the 'anti-social' as internal enemy or anti-nation (Benhabib, 1996; Jabri, 1996; Campbell, 1999). Again, the root problem is a problem of control faced by a striated world system when confronted by proliferating network forms of social organisation. This is clear, for instance, from the 'revolution in military affairs' literature, which emphasises the importance of combating oppositional networks in a situation of asymmetrical power (Arquilla and Ronfeldt, 2001). The construction of official discourse – for instance, the 'axis of evil', and the reactive misrepresentation of attacks on civil liberties as the 'protection' of liberty – is built around the same valuation of closure as internal repression. The only factor uniting the 'axis of evil' (two of which were at war twenty years ago) is the incompletion of their subsumption into the world system.

In the discourse of the 'war on terror', as in many forms of militarist discourse, particular enemies are usually reduced to a mythical figure of the Enemy, infused with all kinds of negative projections and imagined characteristics. The role of such a figure, as E.P. Thompson argues, is 'closing up people's minds and mouths' (Thompson, 1980, pp. 46–7). As Marcuse puts it, political linguistics is 'the armour of the establishment'; it 'not only defines and condemns the Enemy, it also *creates* him; and this creation is not the Enemy as he [sic] is but rather as he must be in order to perform his function for the Establishment' (Marcuse, 1969, p. 78, original italics). The enemy is ascribed a series of invariant mythical characteristics, and questioning the carving of the field into friend and enemy is taken as being on the side of the enemy. For example, *Panorama* contrasts the 'UK majority' to a 'Muslim minority' who oppose the war (rather than a UK minority), and discusses 'British Muslims' who will fight 'against Britain'.[3] Since a British Muslim is by definition part of 'Britain', it is illogical to suggest that she or he could fight against it; the formula operates by attributing an essence to Britain and therefore projecting the contradiction onto the Muslims themselves. In the false certainty of myth, hybridity is elided and national identity is associated exclusively with the in-group.

The discourse used here is an extension of internal repression. Thus, according to Ben O'Loughlin, the US National Security Strategy 'deploys a consistent Self/Other dichotomy . . . The Other . . . is depicted using bio-logical metaphors and allusions to criminality', thus drawing on the same policing and psychiatric/health discourses which underlie broader exclu-sionary repression (O'Loughlin, 2006, p. 107). At the same time, one finds in official discourse a process of metonymical slippage between different instances of elements escaping control, linking terrorism, immigration, crime, protest, cultural otherness and the myriad resistances to globalisa-tion (Burton, 1997). As Deleuze and Guattari (following Paul Virilio) remark, 'this war machine no longer needs a qualified enemy but . . . oper-ates against the "unspecified enemy", domestic or foreign', and thereby constructs a situation of 'organized insecurity' and 'programmed catastro-phe' (Deleuze and Guattari, 1988, p. 467).

The result is that the totalitarian and inhuman effects of the project of repression become clearest in their re-externalisation as 'war on terror'. Take, for instance, the situation in Fallujah. After recapturing (and virtu-ally destroying) the former insurgent stronghold, occupation forces initi-ated a scheme from the wildest fantasies of ID card advocates, imposing ID cards, fingerprinting and retina scans on 'military-age men' as part of a scheme to track and monitor the civilian population. Returning refugees are allowed to travel only in areas near their homes, and are subject to 'deadly force' (extrajudicial execution) if they act outside the ID scheme's rules. The old imperial practice of 'strategic hamlets' is thus extended into a project of biometric micro-regulation, regimenting the lives of the colonised population to an unprecedented degree, revealing starkly the kind of society which is being constructed by the ever-escalating project of repression.

DISCOURSES OF EXCLUSION

It is important, first of all, to recognise that ideas such as 'crime', 'anti-sociality' and so on are not immediate outgrowths of experience but rather, social constructs which structure the experience they claim to explain. Discourses of exclusion dehumanise those they label and construct oppressive social relations. Subjectivities and desires seek expression in an active, creative role in the world; empty prohibitions and fixed externalities are thus experienced as impediments to be resisted – unconsciously if not consciously. A grouping of experiences which I refer to as 'the experience of oppression' can be seen to exist across a wide range of different situations in the modern world. Empirical evidence for this ranges from Paolo Freire's educational philosophy and James Scott's work with peasants to David Matza's theory of 'moods of fatalism' (Matza, 1964; Freire, 1970; Scott, 1990). Human autonomy depends on the ability to name the world, individually and in dialogue with others. Oppressive discourse operates to block this capacity, thereby constructing an asymmetry between an in-group, who have the right to speak, and an out-group, who are silenced and left vulnerable to other forms of oppression and exploitation.

The imposition of voicelessness on the socially excluded occurs via a variety of means, central among which is the operation of Barthesian myth. The basic structure of myth is that a 'first-order' sign is used to carry or connote a second meaning which is independent of its signified; as a result, particular discourses can be made to signify without reference to the discourse of those who are signified. First, myth operates by means of connotation and is unconscious. It is transferred between speakers as an underlying unconscious message implicit in a first-order signification to which it is attached. For this reason, it is 'received' rather than 'read' (Barthes, 1985, p. 231). This is why it tends to be viewed as self-evident or commonsensical, to be hidden from critical interrogation, and to be immune from the lively immanent deconstruction which often operates in everyday life – what Barthes terms 'writerly reading'. Second, it constructs an 'ideological' matrix of roles or positions which can be transposed structurally onto specific incidents or phenomena, giving these phenomena an imposed meaning from outside their actual operation. In the case of the Dominici trial for instance, myths were used to construct an entire portrayal of someone's motives and psychology which were projected onto them without reference to their own meaning-system (Barthes, 1957 [2000], pp. 43–7), while in another instance 'the man in the street' is constructed against the very possibility of agency and mobilised as a figure against ordinary people in their concrete actions (Barthes, 1979 [1997]). Having been robbed of a voice, people are nevertheless assigned a signification through myth.

An especially violent and exclusive form of ontological privileging underlies this war on difference – the self-styled decent majority defines itself as the only group which matters, defines itself as the community and others as individuals whose concerns are secondary, and identifies itself and its experiences with 'reality' so exclusively as to shut it off completely from other voices. The self-styled 'majority' (who need not in fact be numerically any such thing) defines itself as the only group which matters, and from its self-imposed standpoint of superiority, it wages endless war against out-groups of every kind, against any who resist the stultifying rigidity of its own life-world, or who are excluded from this world by the people who run it, and forced to seek survival beyond its 'moral' parameters of social control.

The violent othering of perceived deviants leads to an especially strong 'us and them' where 'they' are defined as a race apart and where the basic laws of causality are suspended, with the other treated as an extra-causal daemoniac evil – hence the assumption that the other is somehow outside society, which is misconceived as a whole rather than a set of relations. This 'us and them' model tends to eliminate all ethical consistency; what is condemned from 'them' is most often permitted to 'us'. Thus, Blair appeared on al-Jazeera news station saying that 'blowing up innocent civilians' must be condemned regardless of its cause, on the same day that British and American bombs killed four United Nations mine-clearance workers in Afghanistan.[4]

One also finds in relation to so-called 'anti-social behaviour', an extra-relational kind of analysis which suggests that such acts are not simply harmful to individuals but are a threat to some abstraction called 'the community'. This abstraction is then supposed to be transcendent over 'individuals', and to have overarching claims on everybody. In fact, there is never any such thing as 'the community', so these claims are actually an ideological cover for a self-privileging by one concrete group of people in relation to another. The idea of 'the community' against 'the individual' is always in fact a distraction – a means whereby one community or individual justifies violence against another. 'The community' is most often a fantasmatic entity defined by its integration or conformity; as a result it is simply a cover for dominance. The violence conceived as an act by 'the community' against an 'individual' is in fact simply the act of one individual (or rather, of one socially located person) against another.

The discursive function of the idea of 'community' is to operate as an ideological cover for interpersonal domination. As Iris Marion Young puts it,

[T]he ideal of community denies the difference between subjects and the social differentiation of temporal and spatial distancing. The most serious political consequence of the desire for community . . . is that it often operates to exclude or oppress those experienced as different. Commitment to an ideal of community tends to value and enforce homogeneity.

The idea of community 'often occurs as an oppositional differentiation from other groups', and it 'validates and reinforces the fear and aversion some groups exhibit towards others' (Young, 1990, pp. 234–5). Most often, people believe themselves to be part of a homogeneous community of similar people when, in fact, the area where they live contains a lot of diversity. The inaccurate image is politically harmful because it leads to defensive exclusionary behaviour, often of a racist or sectional character.

The repressive project may pose as a protection of 'security' or an attempt to prevent harm, but in fact it involves the imposition of an entire doctrine through the means of repeated instances of coercive action by state and non-state agents. It operates via the device of 'morality-dependent distress', hence importing an imposed morality through the back door. Take, for instance, the case of the 'full' veil (*niqab*), an issue where racist-tinged paranoia about Islam overlaps with a project of regulation which attacks individual freedom. How individuals dress is no business of a secular government, only of one seeking to regulate everyday life so as to impose its own conception. Freedom of religious dress in particular is a long-established liberal principle, having arisen previously around such issues as the wearing of turbans by Sikh motorcyclists. Yet women exercising a personal choice based on a religious belief are now being treated as a threat, simply because they look different. The issue of harm is invoked in this context, but in a disproportionate way; the kinds of harm veil-wearers are accused of doing are either morality dependent (such as 'promoting separation') or else involve alleged communication and identification problems which are at most extremely minor, and most often simply a pretext. The issue is also linked to an attempt to impose vulnerability to the gaze of the state; one reason for hostility to the veil is the relative anonymity it affords to wearers, which in turn limits the intrusion possible through mechanisms such as CCTV, and the recent debate may be linked to plans to ban face-coverings on protests so as to increase the effectiveness of police intimidation.

There are, of course, debates about the significance of wearing the veil and objections (such as those of feminists, and some Islamic theologians) which have to do with the comparison of ways of life rather than with the control project itself. But the crucial point is not whether women should wear the veil; it is whether they have a right to – or more broadly, whether individuals have a right to dress in accord with their own standards of propriety, or indeed their own preferences. The portrayal of the issue as a problem with the alleged deviant – or rather, the portrayal of difference itself as the 'problem' – serves to turn an issue of intolerance into an issue of deviance, channelling racism in support of the regulation of everyday life. The implicit idea behind the objection to the veil as a 'mark of separation'

is particularly sinister, in that it implies people should conform to homogeneous models of dress in order to be socially included, and further, that
failure or refusal to conform to dress norms is a valid ground for exclusion
and repression.

One result of myth is to ignore the ways in which deviance results from
social structures and conflicts. The result is a denial of basic dignity and
rights to those who fall outside 'society', who, in line with their metaphys-
ical status, are to be cast out, locked away, or put beyond a society defined
as being for 'us and us only'. The result is that the state, which carries out
this casting-out, can pose as the centre of society: as representing 'society'
against the 'anti-social'.

Another is to turn horizontal resource-use and lifestyle conflicts into
intractable 'social problems'. The point, made clearly by Colin Ward, is that
horizontal conflicts – which are in fact conflicts between two perspectives,
two projects, or two ways of seeing – are misrepresented as a unilateral violence by one side and thus become insoluble. Estates get turned into bat-
tlegrounds for a specific reason, says Ward – children have no place or voice
in their society, which 'does not even recognize a need to find a place for
them in social life', as a result of which, the reterritorialisation of urban
spaces as spaces of play becomes conflictual, a kind of 'jungle warfare'
against the contexts of home and school (Ward, 1978 [1990], pp. 89–90). To
say that this activity is simply play from the perspectives of the children,
and not at all irrational, is to recognise that there are two perspectives
in conflict here – not simply an in-group and its other. But the conflict
becomes intractable because of its inscription in the dominant discourse as
inexplicable anti-sociality versus unquestionable decency. One side is thus
given ontological primacy and the other denied a voice. It is also important
to recognise that the nihilistic or non-dialogical aspect of this activity is a
consequence of its discursive exclusion.

Supporters of the dominant ideology believe in a right or privilege of the
socially included not to be disrupted, inconvenienced, offended, 'alarmed or
distressed' by others. This supposed 'right' is in fact a privilege, denied to the
excluded. This expanded 'right' contrasts sharply with the near-absolute
rightslessness imposed on the excluded. 'Anti-terror' crackdowns are often
targeted at a particular milieu or target group which has previously been
demonised (Muslims in Britain, anarchists in Italy); otherwise the full weight
of the police state has to be controlled in order to prevent mass discontent.
But the loss of rights is generalised; everyone is potentially at risk, if only in
that any particularity could in principle be demonised and repressed.

At the root of repressive ideology is the idea that the privileged social
in-group has an unconditional entitlement to preferential treatment in
lawmaking, that all laws should be rigged exclusively for the benefit of the

in-group – in other words, a denial of generic rights as such. The excluded are similarly denied the 'security' so demanded by the included.

A certain level of critical literacy now seems necessary for one to see through the repressive agenda. Not only is this ability insufficiently widespread among those who fall prey to anti-'crime' ideologies, but the insistence on the idea that direct reference to 'experience' can bypass discourse operates as a block on its development. The categories used to demonise become ever vaguer, as do the supposed offences one has to commit to become part of this enemy. In the discourse constructing this other, the definition of otherness is taken as obvious and thus in no need of definition; this lack of precision is directly connected to its perceived immediacy, its identification in a series of cases with a particular instance of deviance taken to 'obviously' manifest it.

REPRESSION AND FREEDOM

One of the crucial issues here in fact does not involve a dispute between particular lifeworlds at all, but revolves around openness or closure of space. For a perspective focused on freedom or on active desire, open space is a necessary enabling good; but for advocates of micro-fascisms, openness is both surplus to necessity – the self-present self-satisfaction of the in-group can be entirely inscribed in a closed system – and potentially dangerous, since open space is space which can be used by demonised others to construct other relations and possibilities – hence space where 'crimes' can be prepared or committed. Openness is a necessity for the different, so the war on open spaces is also a war against difference. The overarching project is a project of the destruction of uncontrolled or potentially uncontrolled spaces, of residues of wildness and ungovernability in everyday life, of horizontal social relations – and hence a project to expand ever deeper the existing systems of production, consumption, spectacle and power.

Against the pseudo-community of the included, one should remember Peter Kropotkin's distinction between social and state (or political) logics – a division later repeated by Pierre Clastres, Colin Ward, Martin Buber, Gustav Landauer and others. Kropotkin counterposes the social logic of networks and voluntary associations to the hierarchic political logic of statism, in which people are fragmented and controlled. While networks are bubbling with life, states bring with them death and decay, for the state has to destroy horizontal relations wherever it goes, to arrogate social power to itself and stand in for the community which no longer exists (one of the paradoxes being that the state needs to create the scarcity and competition which then act as the legitimation of its existence):

> The State demands from its subjects a direct, personal submission without inter-
> mediaries; it demands equality in slavery; it cannot admit of a 'State within a
> State'. Thus as soon as the State began to be constituted in the sixteenth century,
> it sought to destroy all the links which existed among the citizens both in the
> towns and in the villages. (Kropotkin, 1897)

The irony of a recent British law which defines gathering together in a public place as 'anti-social behaviour' would not have been lost on Kropotkin. It stands in a long tradition of state bans and attacks on horizontal associa-tion. For statists, people can only relate through the intermediary of the state; to remove this mediation is inherently threatening to it.

One crucial aspect of the dominant mythology which should be rejected is the image of the state as problem-solver or protector. Rather, the state is a machine of control which operates by an almost automatic logic, as a bulldozer which attempts to crush whatever stands in the way of its own advancement. This internal 'tendency' of the state can only be counteracted or limited by external forces. The rich texture of everyday life depicted by historians and peasant studies authors such as Scott, Hoggart, Hecht and Simone, Galvan, and Guha (Scott, 1999; Hoggart, 1971; Hecht and Simone, 1994; Galvan, 2004; Guha, 1998) is anathema to the state. The state is thus able to reinforce itself via a double-bind – it constantly claims to be the source of sociality while in fact destroying horizontal social logics.

For the state, anything goes in achieving its objectives; any level of suffering and devastation is taken to be a small price to pay for social control, and the evil of the other is portrayed as so overwhelming as to outweigh any such effects. Neither the state nor its passive supporters seems to care how many people it harms – even innocent people – so long as some minimal risk reduction can be deduced. For the chance of getting lucky and stopping an attack, it makes a sacrifice of many innocent people probabilistically calculated as maybe posing a risk. Of course, this vicious utilitarian logic is utterly flawed on all levels – it increases the anger which motivates attacks, it commits harm which is almost certainly greater than what it ostensibly prevents, and its lack of ethics leaves it at best morally equivalent to what it condemns. It is also devastating to basic freedoms. The only way one can prosecute alleged crimes before they happen is if life is so tightly regulated that the preparatory actions or ten-dencies of belief are themselves both visible and grounds for punishment. This requires the construction of an extremely intrusive system of micro-regulation ensuring that every action and every flow is visible, legible and comprehensible. The issue here is thus not simply a matter of the propor-tionality or otherwise of the response, the balance of harms, or the scale of the alleged risk. The point is about whether a world worth living in is to exist at all.

Many of the new forms of repression are largely aimed against the existence of horizontal sanctioning activity, which is taken to be intolerable in and of itself. In other words – it is not that the state objects to social sanctioning, but rather, that it objects to its operation in everyday life in the hands of agents other than the state. This is the underlying meaning of the way in which laws on harassment are used to target political dissent and everyday social conflicts. The repressive agenda is a concerted attempt to take direct power away from all social agents and to decimate the power of social networks based on horizontality – to assert the political principle to the absolute exclusion of the social principle.

The onslaught of state violence creates a situation of everyday insurrection. *Gleichschaltung* in its original meaning refers to pushing an electric flow through a material which resists it; this was developed as an analogy for the attempts by fascist regimes to push state control through everyday life. To deal with the problem of lack of compliance or regime penetration despite the relative scarcity of political resistance, historians of Nazi Germany such as Martin Broszat and Hans Mommsen formulated a concept of *resistenz*. Posited against *gleichschaltung*, this term refers to a pattern of actions in everyday life which, through noncompliance, impeded the pushing-through of top-down imperatives and constructed everyday life as a relatively impermeable space. Similar resistance is documented in Kotkin's recent work on Stalinist Russia, while Scott's research that peasant societies constructed similar patterns of everyday resistance (Scott, 1985, 1990; Kotkin, 1995). Peter Hüttenberger claims that liberal democracies do not face *resistenz* simply because these kinds of everyday activities are not in any case treated as deviant, because an autonomous civil society exists (Kershaw, 1993). This may well be true of certain kinds of liberal democracy, but it is not true of the kind of neo-totalitarian regimes of control I am discussing. Everyday deviance becomes resistance because of the project of control which attacks it; it also becomes necessarily more insurrectionary in direct response to the cumulative attempts to stamp it out through micro-regulation. What the state gains in coercive power, it loses in its ability to influence or engage with its other.

The effect of social closure is to drive dissent which would otherwise take open forms underground; denied the status of voice, it emerges in the guise of apparent inert effects. Thus, rather than an absence of resistance, there is in fact a constant subtext of resistance which is not perceived as such because it is mis-categorised as social problems, deviance, criminality, apathy, problems of 'culture' and so on. Arguing against this tendency in totalitarianism, Gramsci argues that by reducing political questions to 'technical ones of propaganda and public order', struggles are constantly fought against adversaries rendered invisible by their lack of official voice, and 'political questions are disguised as cultural ones, and as such become insoluble' (Gramsci, 1971, p. 149). This should be remembered whenever politicians come out with rhetoric about for instance 'yob', gun, knife or drug culture – the impermeable 'culture' is itself a product of political exclusions.

RESISTENZ, THE DEATH OF DIALOGUE AND THE INSURRECTION OF EVERYDAY LIFE

As established above, the cause of social problems is not as is usually assumed the agent of deviance (either individual or collective). The social problem is already constructed, prior to the act of individual deviance, in the discursive asymmetry which renders one agent as excluded and her/his actions of revolt or deviance as dissimilar from others' actions of oppression or conformity. In constructing one agent as unquestionable and another as voiceless, the dominant discourse precludes dialogical conflict resolution and necessitates that the will to power of the excluded find voice in resistance, sabotage, use of force, and other horizontal actions of a conflictual nature. And the point is that this is what renders social conflict and unrest inevitable. The absence of social dialogue and the pervasiveness of exclusionary discourse lead to the necessity of social conflict, even social war, between included and excluded.

A dialogical situation in the Bakhtinian sense requires that everyone be viewed as the bearer of a perspective, of their own discourses, project or perspective which has the same a priori validity as any other on entering into the process of dialogue. The problem of absence of dialogue is thus really a lack of critical literacy on the part of the socially included. The situation is thus one of unlimited hypocrisy – the state and the included commit constant acts of warfare against the excluded, attacking others' ways of life and committing innumerable acts of petty interference, dehumanisation and violence – and then complain about any reaction they receive, from those they systematically oppress. In addition, the backlash which arises in the form of violence against the included, as deviance is amplified by repression, is not a threat from the outside but a symptom of the ideology of the included, an inevitable boomerang which can be traced back to social intolerance. Thus, while there may well be innocent victims of a sort, it is far more generally accurate and more productive to think in terms of 'complicit victims', of a system of control through which the included produce their own suffering by means of their elisions and exclusions.

The logic of *resistenz* can be seen not only in the practice of radical social movements, but in the acts of everyday resistance through which the socially excluded resist or react against their exclusion and oppression. Thus *resistenz* continues to occur, and takes the form of a constant low-intensity insurrectional social war. Sabotage of apparatuses of control such as CCTV cameras, defiance of authority figures, low-intensity confrontations and so-called 'public order incidents', all point to this situation of conflict which is necessitated by exclusionary discourse. In the 'war on terror', a similar dynamic constructs an ongoing incapacity to stabilise occupied societies such as Iraq, Afghanistan and Haiti, with everyday *resistenz* passing over into full-scale armed resistance.

There is also a constant possibility of mass unrest due to the polarisation produced by repression. The uprisings in France in November 2005 were largely precipitated by the introduction (albeit at the early stages by British standards) of 'anti-social behaviour' measures in the *banlieues*, in a context of pervasive social exclusion and the very public demonisation of minorities in general and Muslims in particular; the same can be said for previous urban uprisings in the northern England towns of Bradford, Oldham and Burnley. Trevor Phillips of the Commission for Racial Equality recently warned that the hysteria about the veil could lead to social polarisation culminating in mass revolts (ITV News, 2006). There was also an impromptu demonstration and warning of possible unrest after the aforementioned police raid on a moderate cleric in Bradford: 'Everyone in the community is horrified and shocked and feeling very angry with the police. I was down there just after the raid, there were 300 people outside the house. Somebody shouted "things are going to hot up" at the police' (Dodd et al., 2006). Insurrection is the last means to speak available to the excluded; its necessity is encoded in the discursive asymmetry which constructs social oppression.

The quagmire character of such exclusion-based conflicts is a result of their basis in elision and asymmetry. It is the statist gesture of exclusion which constructs asymmetry and thus social conflict. Furthermore, it is the increasingly totalitarian suppression of effective protest and social action by other means which constructs the insurrectionary mode of everyday resistance as the main site of social antagonism – just as occurred in fascism and Stalinism.

Empty condemnation, and use of terms like 'anti-social' and 'terrorist' which reproduce the system's logic, is not only pointless but counterproductive. Deviants are often kicking back against society – and rightly so. Unfortunately, this fightback is undirected – often people make sense of their situation in nihilistic terms, blaming 'society' as it is defined by the dominant discourse. They lash out in general, against any target which comes to hand. Indeed, there is a danger, exemplified in discourses such as those of the international jihadi movement and of identity-based 'gangs', that oppressive discourse will simply be inverted by those who resist, with excluded groups mapped onto unmarked terms in another discourse. Nevertheless, the point is not to condemn, but to construct more emancipatory discourses of rebellion to channel resistance more effectively.

Furthermore, there is a need to side with the marked against the unmarked term in social struggles in order to break down repressive binaries. The paradox here is that, while the goal is dialogical – the transmutation of a situation of mutual impenetrability into a situation where horizontal engagement becomes possible – the means may not be. Precisely because of the asymmetrical discourse, it is necessary as a precondition for dialogue that the marked term seize voice, and that the dominant majority be forced to give up its claim to unquestioned primacy, its tyranny of common sense, and admit the discourse of the other. Sometimes the means to this are through dialogue, education and social psychology; but often it requires conflict – defeat even – for the dominant group to disavow its epistemological privilege. The goal is discursive opening – the breaking apart of a false consensus which constructs exclusion through its elisions. The means must therefore often be dissensual – the explosive emergence almost as an 'Act-Event' of what is assigned the status of unspeakable Real in a particular discourse. It is only when the fact of difference, of heterogeneity, of multiplicity of voice becomes unavoidable that the surface of pseudo-consensus is broken; thus, the sharpening of antagonism can often be a means to construct the future possibility of dialogue and horizontality. This emerges clearly both in Gramsci and in Franz Fanon – dialogical resolution cannot occur without antithesis being openly posited; otherwise the apparent resolution is simply recuperation or transformism and does not undermine the discursive privileging which renders dialogue impossible.

As I suggested earlier, the state and conformists are engaged in a constant warfare against the excluded – a warfare of which they themselves are often unaware. For there to be dialogue there must be ceasefire; and for there to be ceasefire there must be a general awareness of the existence of social war. This requires an awareness of the discourse of the other, of the ways in which the unquestioned privileging of certain discourses is a violence against the discourse of the other.

Today, the other does not even have the dignity of an enemy in a fair fight, but is treated as unspeakable. Without overcoming this primary exclusion, social problems will remain intractable, and resistance in everyday life will remain both necessary and justified. The struggle of those labelled as anti-social is already a political struggle in its structural manifestation as *resistenz*. But its rearticulation as a struggle against systematic voicelessness would render it a constant, radical challenge to existing logics of political domination.

Of course, this politicisation of 'anti-sociality' is incompatible with any attempts to win over the 'decent majority' by appealing to their existing beliefs, attachments and discourse. The 'decent majority' can be faced only with the stark demand that it unlearn its dominance, its impositional discourse, and that it become other. But this demand is also emancipatory, for the 'decent majority' is itself trapped in its role, its conformity. The 'becoming anti-social' of the decent majority is also its breaking of its ties to the status quo, its refusal of the 'cops in our heads'. In this way, the liberation of the anti-social is simultaneously a 'universal' liberation.

The revolution-to-come is not a new order but a breaking down of all social orders based on asymmetry, in favour of a horizontality without borders. It is being built, often unconsciously, in the constant everyday resistance to social control. And it is this conflict – between included and excluded, between an implicit politics of affirmation of voice and an exclusionary discourse of ontological privilege – which defines the social conflicts of our era and of our future.

NOTES

1. Precarity refers to precarious labour; term first used in autonomist Marxism.
2. *Time* magazine, 17 December 2001, p. 84.
3. BBC *Panorama*, 14 October 2001.
4. Labour Left Briefing, November 2001, p. 30.

REFERENCES

Akbar, A. (2006), 'Asian families consider quitting Britain after terror raids by police', www.informationliberation.com/index.php?id=11850, accessed 15 January 2007.

Amin, S. (2004), *The Liberal Virus*, London: Pluto.

Anon. (2004a), 'Tourist Brochure Could Lead to Guantánamo', www.socialistworker.co.uk/article.php 4?article_id=2972, accessed 15 January 2007.

Anon. (2004b), 'Babar: beaten, abused and still denied justice', www.socialistworker.co.uk/article.php 4?article_id=2713, accessed 15 January 2007.

Anon. (nd), 'Inside the surveillance capital of Europe', www.325collective.com/social-control_surveillance_capital.html, accessed 15 January 2007.

Appadurai, A. (2001), *Globalization*, Durham, NC: Duke University Press.

Arquilla, J. and D. Ronfeldt (eds) (2001), *Networks and Netwars: The Future of Terror, Crime and Militancy*, Santa Monica, CA: Rand.

Barthes, R. (1957 [2000]), *Mythologies*, London: Vintage.

Barthes, R. (1979 [1997]), *The Eiffel Tower and Other Mythologies*, Berkeley, CA: University of California Press.

Barthes, R. (1985), *The Fashion System*, London: Jonathan Cape.

BBC News (2003), 'Q&A: Finsbury Park raid', http://news.bbc.co.uk/1/hi/england/ 2675983.stm, accessed 15 January 2007.

BBC News (2004), 'Too many arrests, too few charges?', http://news.bbc.co.uk/1/hi/ magazine/3590753.stm, accessed 15 January 2007.

BBC News (2005), 'Mystery still surrounds killer', http://news.bbc.co.uk/1/hi/uk/ 4440953.stm, accessed 15 January 2007.

BBC News (2006a), 'Abu Hamza "was wrongly convicted"', www.cageprisoners. com/articles.php?id=17291, accessed 15 January 2007.

BBC News (2006b), 'Man released after terror arrest', www.cageprisoners.com/ articles.php?id=16042, accessed 15 January 2007.

BBC News (2006c), 'Groups banned by new terror law', http://news.bbc.co.uk/1/hi/ uk_politics/5188136.stm, accessed 15 January 2007.

BBC News (2006d), 'Musician "willing to face prison"', http://news.bbc.co.uk/1/hi/ entertainment/5126152.stm, accessed 15 January 2007.

Benhabib, S. (ed.) (1996), *Democracy and Difference: Contesting the Boundaries of the Political*, Princeton, NJ: Princeton University Press.

Bhabha, H. (1993), *The Location of Culture*, London: Routledge.

BIBIC (British Institute for Brain Injured Children) (2005), 'Aint Misbehavin': young people with learning and communication difficulties and anti-social behaviour', www.bibic.org.uk/newsite/general/pdfs/campaign%20update.pdf, accessed 15 January 2007.

Bonanno, A. (1993), 'For an Anti-Authoritarian Insurrectionalist International', London: Elephant Editions, www.geocities.com/kk_abacus/ioaa/insurint.html, accessed 15 January 2007.

Burton, J. (1997), *Violence Explained: The Sources of Conflict, Violence and Crime and their Prevention*, Manchester: Manchester University Press.

Campbell, D. (1999), 'Justice and identity in the Bosnian conflict', in Jenny Edkins, Nalini Persram and Véronique Pin-Fat (eds), *Sovereignty and Subjectivity*, Boulder, CO: Lynne Rienner, pp. 21–37.

Campbell, D. and R. Norton-Taylor (2005), 'Jury anger over threat of torture', *The Guardian*, www.guardian.co.uk/crime/article/0,,1489156,00.html, accessed 15 January 2007.

Carrell, S. and R. Whitacker (2005), 'Ricin: the plot that never was', *The Independent*, originally http://news.independent.co.uk/uk/crime/story.jsp?story= 630187, archived at www.williambowles.info/spysrus/ricin_plot.html, accessed 15 January 2007.

Clarke, P. (2004), 'Pair face retrial in suicide bomber case', *The Scotsman*, archived at www.cageprisoners.com/articles.php?id=2394, accessed 15 January 2007.

Cowan, R. (2005), 'Relatives deny shielding Cowan from police', *The Guardian*, archived at www.cageprisoners.com/articles.php?id=8888, accessed 15 January 2007.

Deleuze, G. and F. Guattari (1988), *A Thousand Plateaus*, trans. Brian Massumi, London: Continuum.

Dodd, V., M. Wainwright and R. Norton-Taylor (2006), 'Youth arrested over links to Canadian terror plot is grandson of leading Islamic scholar', *The Guardian*, archived at www.cageprisoners.com/articles.php?id=14318, accessed 15 January 2007.

Freeman, S. (2005), 'Suspect jailed for 15 years over terror "plot"', *The Times*, archived at www.cageprisoners.com/articles.php?id=9695, accessed 15 January 2007.

Freire, P. (1970), *Pedagogy of the Oppressed*, London: Continuum.
Galvan, D.C. (2004), *The State Must Be Our Master of Fire: How Peasants Craft Culturally Sustainable Development in Senegal*, Berkeley, CA: University of California Press.
Gilroy, P. (2004), *After Empire*, London: Routledge.
Gramsci, A. (1971), *Selections from the Prison Notebooks*, ed. Quintin Hoare and Geoffrey Nowell-Smith, London: Lawrence & Wishart.
Guedella, D. (nd), 'Justice denied: the wrongful convictions of Samar Alami and Jawad Botmeh', www.freesaj.org.uk/deniedfront.html, accessed 15 January 2007.
Guha, R. (1998), *Elementary Aspects of Peasant Insurgency in Colonial India*, Oxford/Delhi: Oxford University Press.
Hecht, S. and M. Simone (1994), *Invisible Governance: The Art of African Micropolitics*, New York: Autonomedia.
Hoggart, R. (1971), *The Uses of Literacy*, Harmondsworth: Penguin.
Hyland, M. (nd), 'New Age policing: biology is ideology', http://datacide.c8.com/text/7-newage.html, accessed 15 January 2007.
ITV News (2006), 'Race chief in veil riot warning', www.itv.com/news/index_6467c5039a5a8512a45667594a4e00a0.html, accessed 15 January 2007.
Jabri, V. (1996), *Discourses on Violence: Conflict Analysis Reconsidered*, Manchester: Manchester University Press.
Kershaw, I. (1993), *The Nazi Dictatorship*, New York: Routledge.
Kotkin, S. (1995), *Magnetic Mountain: Stalinism as a Civilisation*, Berkeley, CA: University of California Press.
Kropotkin, P. (1897), *The State: Its Historic Role*, www.panarchy.org/kropotkin/1897.state.html, accessed 15 January 2007.
Marcuse, H. (1969), *Essay on Liberation*, Harmondsworth: Penguin.
Matza, D. (1964), *Delinquency and Drift*, New York: John Wiley & Sons.
Moore, P. (2005), 'Revolutions from above: worker training as transformismo in Korea', *Capital and Class*, **86**, 39–72.
Murphy, T.S. (2005), 'Editor's introduction', in Antonio Negri (ed.), *Books for Burning*, London: Verso.
Norris, C. and G. Armstrong (1997), 'The unforgiving eye: CCTV surveillance in public space', Hull: Centre for Criminology and Criminal Justice at Hull University.
O'Loughlin, B. (2006), 'The intellectual antecedents of the Bush regime', in Alejandro Colás and Richard Saull (eds), *The War on Terrorism and the American 'Empire' After the Cold War*, London: Routledge, pp. 91–113.
Press Association (2006), 'Man remanded over cartoon protests', *The Guardian*, archived at www.cageprisoners.com/articles.php?id=13792, accessed 15 January 2007.
Reuters (2004), Republican National Convention protest report, archived at www.vault.com/messages/The_Sandbox/The_Sandbox1201786.html, accessed 15 January 2007.
Robinson, W.I. (2004), *A Theory of Global Capitalism: Production, Class, and State in a Transnational World*, Baltimore, MD: Johns Hopkins University Press.
Rosen, J. (2001), 'Being watched: a cautionary tale', *New York Times Magazine* 7 October, www.globalpolicy.org/wtc/liberties/surveillance.htm, accessed 15 January 2007.
Scott, J.C. (1985), *Weapons of the Weak*, New Haven, CT: Yale University Press.

Scott, J.C. (1990), *Domination and the Arts of Resistance*, New Haven, CT: Yale University Press.

Scott, J.C. (1999), *Seeing Like a State*, New Haven CT: Yale University Press.

Sklair, L. (2000), *The Transnational Capitalist Class*, Oxford: Blackwell.

Thompson, E.P. (ed.) (1980), *Protest and Survive*, Harmondsworth: Penguin.

Ward, C. (1978 [1990]), *The Child in the City*, London: Bedford Square Press.

Young, I.M. (1990), *Justice and the Politics of Difference*, Princeton, NJ: Princeton University Press.

Žižek, S. (1999), *The Ticklish Subject*, London: Verso.

14. Power, resistance and 'anti-globalisation' movements in the context of the 'war on terror'

Michael S. Drake

INTRODUCTION

In the analysis of power and resistance there is an inevitable interaction between theory and its object, as political initiatives and empirical transformations are theorised and theoretical analysis further informs political action. Through an analysis of the positions, tactics and responses adopted by actors in the events around the Gleneagles G8 Summit of 2005, this chapter investigates the contemporary relations between theories and practices of power and resistance.

It is generally accepted among commentators that the 'war on terror' has been used to legitimate restrictive legislation and police practices of social control encroaching on civil liberties and citizenship rights which function as new conditions for power and resistance in the political sphere (for example, Lyon, 2003; Agamben, 2005, pp. 2–3; Beck, 2005). Rather than focusing on terrorism, the ostensible target of such tendencies, this chapter focuses on how the new conditions of power and resistance have affected the 'anti-globalisation' movement. Through this study, the chapter thus questions whether these new conditions are a consequence of the war on terror, or whether they represent deeper and longer-term developmental tendencies inherent in the state and sovereignty in the condition of globalisation. It argues that for these twenty-first century conditions, we need to radically rethink the terms of contemporary relations between individuals and civil society, and the state and its forces of order.

Critical reviews of the sociology of power and of social movement theory in conjunction with analysis of the frames of interpretation of key actors in the events around G8 reveal how contemporary sociological analysis falls short of a capacity to engage with developments under the conditions of globalisation and the war on terror due to an adherence to instrumental and representational models. Contemporary political sociology has reached an impasse because of its grounding in modern, twentieth-century sociological concepts. The chapter engages critically with attempts to revise the socio-logical analysis of social movements, arguing that we need to attend to developments across disciplines (for example, in political theory) and to the theoretical reflections generated by activists themselves.

POSITIONS AND REPRESENTATIONS

Prior to June 2005, the polarisation of representations of G8 appeared to be taking on a bipolar form of 'globalisation' and 'anti-globalisation', opposed ideological camps each containing a plurality of positions, ranging on one side from Earth First! ecologism through to traditional Marxian analysis, and on the other from Bushite unilateralism through to the conscience-led mission of Make Poverty History. This ideological bipo-larity could be conceptualised along a conventional left–right continuum and as such has been subject to critical analysis by Worth and Abbott (2006), in an essay that reveals the limitations of such static, positional con-ceptualisation for contemporary analysis. In their overview of ideological positions, Worth and Abbott attempt a critique of the anti-globalisation movement in the UK from the Gramscian Marxist perspective that was established by the 'New Times' group in the 1980s as an alternative to far left opposition to Thatcherism. They argue that British anti-globalisation movements, 'lack an overall ideological strategy to counter neo-liberalism', rendering them complicit in the wider accusation that the left, 'have failed to construct a counter-hegemonic project, largely due to a failure of ideo-logical contestation'. Activism such as summit protests are therefore dis-missed as 'adding to the spectacle' (ibid., p. 55).

However, these assessments are entirely conditioned by Worth and Abbott's dogmatic diagnosis, showing their analysis of globalisation to be itself almost entirely ideological; as Chandler responded: 'reproducing "critical" analysis as a hollow framework without analytical content . . . conflating empirical analysis with . . . normative assertion' (Chandler, 2006, pp. 65–6). The 'strategy' they prescribe is therefore idealist, and their objective becomes a reiteration of the goal of survival in retreat, the context from which Gramscian analysis originated in the 1920s and which was revived in the 1980s in the face of Thatcherism. It takes a considerable feat of dissembly to argue that those conditions were replicated in July 2005, and Worth and Abbott work hard to conjure a spectacle of looming neo-fascism which the anti-globalisation movements 'fail' to counter ideologic-ally, in the form not of corporate globalisation at all, but of the tiny neo-fascist British National Party. Worth and Abbott's accusation that the contemporary left's neglect of ideology has enabled fascism to appropriate left-wing themes is simply redundant when we consider that such appropriation is definitive of fascism *per se*, not a result of any particular conditions. Furthermore, Worth and Abbott's argument is supported by only one example – the maverick New Right and neo-fascist affiliations of Edward Goldsmith do not constitute evidence of latent fascist tendencies within anti-globalisation and ecology in general.

To urge the adoption of a positional hegemonic struggle because of a latent threat from neo-fascism seems misdirected, given the tendencies of corporate global corporate and political power to use its given authority to invoke authoritarian regulation which criminalises social and political opposition. It seems still more contrary to critique 'the left' for failing to adopt a positional struggle when the ideological frame has manifestly splintered, producing multifarious struggles beyond ideology, with forms of organisation, protest and direct action which manifest their alternative order directly in material (albeit nomadic and transitory) forms, rather than through representations. Worth and Abbott's call for us to understand anti-globalisation struggles in terms of hegemonic contestation thus remains mired in positional metaphors, while the struggle itself has become fluid, contesting not positions and representations, but life itself.

Even the crude ideological distinction between the two stances towards G8 as pro- and anti-globalisation was disrupted by the late intervention of the media-intoxicated brigade of celebrity personalities led by Bob Geldoff. These branded names appeared to offer a position that enabled individuals to participate in opposition to G8 as a form of consumption, that is, without disrupting the key contemporary social integer of post-modernity and with the prospect of instant gratification as reports of reforms agreed in the talks could be integrated into self-congratulatory celebratory global broadcasts from the concert stages.

Live8 was announced just as an earlier grouping, principally comprising non-governmental organisations (NGOs) and religious leaders, which sought to positively influence the Summit, had begun to disintegrate. Internal pressure within the Make Poverty History coalition had been produced as a consequence of a strategy of compromise and accommodation to the G8 'world leadership' in order to ensure the 'insider' status which the mainstream NGOs saw as a prerequisite for influence over the agenda and outcome of the Summit. Seeking to build a mass, moderate mobilisation, Make Poverty History planned actions which were designed to maximise media coverage as indirect legitimate pressure, taking care not to impinge directly on the Summit or its security. Ideologically, the coalition declared a neutrality which was effectively a disavowal of 'anti-globalisation'.

Make Poverty History had followed up an earlier mobilisation around G8 1998 in Birmingham and had begun to organise as early as 2003. On the other polarity, the Dissent network had also taken a long-term approach to preparation for G8 2006, with its organisational principles of horizontality and democracy and its functional structures emerging *ad hoc*, 'organically', from practice rather than strategy, in a process that was acknowledged by participants as fraught, problematic, and at times even contradictory (Trocchi et al., 2006). The network eschewed a priori objectives and the G8 Summit provided simply a focus for the organisation of events which were intended to effect their own appropriations and transformations. The network similarly sought to develop organisation as the manifestation of its principles, rather than as instrumental means. The network avoids the label 'anarchist', and though some see this as a concession to latent sectarianism and media prejudice (ibid., pp. 63–4), other statements articulate a more consistent argument: 'The ideology is secondary to the present itself, that is, to the existing practices of horizontality and openness and their condition now . . . it is the concrete practices that create the conditions of possibility in which the ideology is produced' (Nunes, 2006, p. 302). This network organisation produced a myriad of alternative events around G8, including the pre-summit Cre8-Summat intervention in the local M74 bypass protest, intended to realise positive interaction between Dissent and the local community, an eco-village (the Hori-Zone) providing base camp (kitchens, water, toilets) for G8 Summit protesters, and the Carnival for Full Enjoyment in Edinburgh (intended to realise a wider protest against the new capitalist organisation of life around precarious work), with a Counter-Spin Collective and an Info-Line to inform (not coordinate) tactics of the 'affinity groups' autonomously organising to protest or disrupt the Summit.

The other major grouping on the anti-globalisation end of the spectrum was G8 Alternatives, a coalition in which significant members at all levels alternated this participation with Socialist Workers Party membership, via the longer-term Globalise Resistance. Not a 'front' organisation in the classic conspiratorial sense, this is a form of organisation that allows an explicitly Leninist party to interact and organise with a wider margin including members of other parties and factions as well as unaffiliated individuals, without compromising its internal ideological integrity, as it operates also within the anti-racist Respect and the anti-war Stop the War coalitions. Apparently more naive than Dissent activists to the way that the politics around the G8 Summit were determined by the security imperative, G8 Alternatives was frustrated in a series of initiatives requiring the cooperation of local authorities, but subsequently built for a single mass march direct to Gleneagles, achieving the only breach of the Summit perimeter fence.

The ideological array thus already appeared to be less positional than Worth and Abbott's analysis would suppose, with broad, overlapping alliances, networks and coalitions constituting the field, rather than fronts with clearly demarcated parameters, rendering it problematic from the outset for any of these umbrellas, including even Live8, to represent themselves in a singular ideological form as the counter-hegemonic strategy of Worth and Abbott would require.

While we cannot therefore reduce the representational array of G8s ideologically, it is similarly difficult to analyse the 'globalist' end of the polarity. Positions here are rather assumed as given, as implicit in the representative function of the Summit itself, in the case of G8, and in the implicit claims to speak on behalf of those in whose interests they exist, in the case of the NGOs, effecting a double substitution for democracy, as G8 heads of particular states become 'world leaders', while NGOs substitute for disenfranchised civil societies and 'failed states'. The substitution of services hitherto considered the function of civil society or the state undermines the development of democratic institutions, just as the G8 Summit undermines prospects of the emergence of global democracy by reducing global politics to policy making by an elite which bypasses all legislative and deliberative assemblies, so that G8 summits become the equivalent of early modern absolutism in the territorial state, which similarly displaced pre-existing institutions such as parliaments and communes.

We can analyse those rival representations of the G8 Summit archaeologically, through their respective websites which can be read as a depository of understandings through which the experience of the G8s was mediated.

The conceptualisation of the event as a summit of world leaders is clearly represented in the Perthshire local authority website, 'Perthshire G8 2005' (Perthshire and Kinross Council). The site 'welcomes the world' to Perthshire as the ultimate exclusive golf club meeting, thus reducing 'the world' to the handful of leaders and their entourages, and enabling the site to publicise 'Gleneagles' as a global site for premier leisure consumption in the sense that its representation as host of the G8 Summit effectively dislocates the site from any other context, marketing Perthshire as a virtual location that can accommodate the significant personages who constitute 'the world'. The website thus represents the global lifeworld in which the political elite operate, in which any public representation is also an opportunity for self-promotion that is thus indistinct from the political. In using the G8 to promote itself as a disembedded elite tourist venue, the Perthshire Council G8 website thus illustrates how public authority at the local level becomes subsumed in the contemporary elite political condition in which private and public interests are assumed to be convergent, even synergetic, and thus mutually beneficial.

These conditions of the politics of G8 as a summit of world leaders are borne out by an attempt to apply the vision pedagogically, as governmental in the sense of the capacity to shape not only global policy development, but also the subjects of that development. The corporately-sponsored J8 Global Citizenship site (Morgan Stanley International Foundation) offered schoolchildren the opportunity to engage in competition, with the winners' communiqué on G8 topics to be presented to the assembled world leaders. It is clear also that while the summit is global, citizenship is national, a subcategory which has access to the global only by privileged routes, that may, moreover, be privatised: winners of the competition to draft a communiqué of G8 topics, 'will represent their country at the J8 Summit in St Petersburg in July 2006'. The construction of a learning opportunity around G8 thus carries the message that citizenship, like leadership, is neither expressive nor instrumental, but conditioned by personalisation and celebrity within a competitive context.

In J8, G8 2005 is presented as a package of pre-digested information, a representation that extends not only to the performative 'junior citizen', but also to the educators of tomorrow's virtual citizenry – teachers are provided with a resource pack containing nine detailed lesson plans, and an opportunity for them to also participate as consumers of governance, by entering another competition, to actually meet the world leaders at Gleneagles. This structure of participation and awards presents a hierarchical order of world leaders, educators and junior citizenry, sharing the subjective condition of functional role performance within the governmental framework. In this representation, G8 leaders 'run the world' both rationally and de facto, both as celebrity personalities and as occupants of public office, and those who engage most successfully with this understanding of global politics have a chance of elevation to the level of personification. This version of G8 corresponds to the elision of an exclusive, virtual politics with performative participation: 'J8 is . . . tailor-made especially for you, teachers of students in G8 countries'. It is tailored, furthermore, by corporate interests. This website represents the way that public citizenship becomes corporately appropriated through the private, contractual provision of services which define citizenship in the public domain.

The same performative, personifying and virtualising characteristics are also manifest in the celebrity-star campaign Live8, narrowly focused on Africa in continuity with the earlier Live Aid famine response campaign, once again reducing the issues to an emotional imperative in which the underdeveloped world appears as destitute and helpless. Instantly attracting media attention disproportionate to anything but its celebrity quotient, this entire publicity campaign was premised on the assumption that a meeting of eight men could remove social, economic and political inequality and injustice, if prevailed upon to do so by the virtual public. The campaign sought to conjure up a manifestation of global spirit via the magic of totemic representation in which ageing rock stars stood in for the *anima* of Durkheim's classical analysis of socio-cosmic reality-construction (Durkheim, 1976, p. 233).

The Live8 intervention readily corresponds to the political spectacle of G8, a virtual pressure group that merely functions to endorse the world-leadership claims of the Summit and the personification of power in its 'world leaders'. Thus, endorsement of G8 by the promoters of Live8 is not merely ideological. Here, too the shift of politics from its old instrumental functions and ideological, representational or positional forms renders positional analysis such as that of Worth and Abbott inadequate or even irrelevant. The self-elective status of the celebrity promoters functions as spectacle rather than as ideology. Reflecting and endorsing the self-electivity of the G8, its forms of celebrity are symmetrical with those of the Summit's virtual, self-promoted 'world leaders', its reduction of global conscience to moralised personalities mimics the reduction of global politics to a cigar-smoke debate among eight great men. While the G8 Summit represented a self-proclaimed world political leadership, the promoters of Live8 posited themselves as representing a global 'conscience collective'.

Immediate responsibility for the security of the G8 Summit fell on another local authority: 'Tayside Police is taking the lead on the G8 policing operation as the summit venue, Gleneagles Hotel, falls within the Force area' (Tayside Police G8 2005 website). On the pages of their website, personification and virtualisation again fill the foreground. The Group of 8 are here, as elsewhere, de facto and tautologically 'world leaders' by virtue of their appearance at the G8 Summit of world leaders. The importance of these virtual power-personalities thus demands their insulation. The ring of steel erected around the Gleneagles conference serves not merely to keep the protesters out, but (perhaps more primarily) to retain the purity of the image of the elect within.

Personification and virtualisation around the summit reproduces, in effect, the fiction of sovereignty. In his critical development of the work of Carl Schmitt, Giorgio Agamben has argued that sovereignty consists ultimately in the capacity to decide in the state of emergency, and thus:

> The point is that the police – contrary to public opinion – are not merely an administrative function of law enforcement, rather, the police are perhaps the place where the proximity and the almost constitutive exchange between violence and right that characterises the figure of the sovereign is shown more nakedly and clearly than anywhere else. . . . If the sovereign is in fact the one who marks the point of indistinction between violence and right by proclaiming the

state of exception and suspending the validity of the law, the police are always operating within a similar state of exception. The rationales of 'public order' and 'security' on which the police have to decide on a case-by-case basis define an area of indistinction between violence and right that is exactly symmetrical to that of sovereignty. (Agamben, 2000, p. 104)

The responsibility for security claimed by Tayside police, shows that sovereignty, now (re)invested in the elite global summit, has no need of forces of 'its own', since virtual sovereignty has transcended the reliance of territorial sovereignties upon a particular state apparatus. The context of virtual globalisation dissolves the local/global dichotomy, and for the duration of the Summit in the virtual global location of Perthshire, Tayside police become global police. One of the functions of their website, their presence in a virtual public domain, is to manage this 'glocalisation', but that function reveals the imperative precedence accorded to G8 security, as the website provides local citizens with bulletins from the police operation at the Summit, supplemented by a video circulated to 'let the local community know what to expect'.

The police function at Gleneagles is also spectacular, consisting of a double perimeter fence, a continuous cordon of officers, and high-profile surveillance, a spectacular form that is not distinct from the security function itself, since the significance of G8 is dependent on its security appearing as an overriding imperative which negates conventional liberties. G8, it becomes clear, is possible only on condition of such security. Its further corollary is the criminalisation of anti-G8 protests, so that the policing of the assembled protesters becomes informed by operational precepts relevant to the exigencies of the state of emergency, or even war, rather than the function of maintenance of a given public order.

Agamben's observation that this appearance of the core of sovereignty in its police function reveals the zone of indistinction in which protesters appear criminalised (ibid., p. 105), has been adopted to inform reflections on anti-G8 activism: 'Without wanting to confuse the experience of Camp X-Ray prisoners with that of protesters' treatment by the police, we should suspect that the same blurring of distinctions between criminal and suspect, terrorist and potential terrorist, is creeping into the domain of public protest' (Skrimshire, 2006, p. 287).

Conventionally, sovereignty in modern society is considered to be vested in the state, and police forces are conventionally understood as an instrument of potentially encroaching power of the state against which citizenship constitutes protection. It is also conventionally acknowledged that the condition of war temporarily suspends such internal checks and balances of democratic society, albeit exceptionally for purposes of the defence of society and its democratic norms. However, in the post-9/11 context of the 'war on terror', protection and defence become redefined as security, and unlimited police power comes to appear as a precondition of the possibility of a democratic society which always has to be compromised, because the *disregard* of institutions such as citizenship appears as the precondition for their security. Democracy then becomes predicate on policing, and what was instrumental for power becomes power in itself. We are left, then, with an increasing dichotomy between power and resistance which can be explored in its fullest sense not in the conflict of the 'war on terror', in which both 'sides' invoke the state of exception as virtual sovereign powers within their scope of action, but in the struggle against this mode of power by alternatives nominally called into action under the label of anti-globalisation, such as around the G8 Summit.

Much more was thus at stake there than the arguments over the agenda, ideology, or even the frame of the issues would suggest. Using the G8 Summit to reflect on the contemporary conditions of power and resistance in the context of globalisation and the war on terror thus illuminates a struggle over power itself, a struggle that is different from the previous struggles of sex, class and race because it is not a struggle for, but over power. Power in itself was essentially contested in the events around G8, which in turn provides merely a snapshot, a frame in which we can begin to glimpse the spectre of the twenty-first century: 'The emphasis is on creating our own worlds, not in seeking state power' (Summer and Halpin, 2006, p. 355).

POWER AND RESISTANCE

Mainstream sociological approaches to the analysis of power proceed through a distinction between power relations and relations of social control, after Dennis Wrong (Hindess, 1986, p. 143) and then break the residual phenomena down into analytical categories such as economic, political and ideological power. This approach displaces study of the exercise of power with analysis of the sources of power, producing a sociology at the cost of displacing the focus on power itself, with explanations which tend to ascribe power-holding to processes that take place elsewhere, for instance explaining political power in terms of ideology and the power to generate ideology in terms of economic power (for example, Mann, 1986).

The issue of whether we should not blur the distinction between power and social control is challenged by empirical as well as theoretical developments such as post-structuralism; 'identity' social movements in particular (for example, feminism) have developed understandings of power which locate it within culture and the social relations of control, and operate on that understanding, so that analysis which insists on a distinction between those relations and the exercise of power will only be able to analyse such movements reductively, disregarding the perspectives of agents themselves. In the face of theoretical and empirical contradictions, adherence to Wrong's analytical imperative becomes itself ideological, a liberal refusal to acknowledge power as embedded in culture, knowledge and social relations of control.

Consequently, the sociology of power has become incompatible with work on social movements that conceptualises power in theories of resistance and change. The European tradition of social movement analysis has developed in interaction with theories generated by the movements themselves, focusing on the function of movements in formation of identities and social processes of transformation, in contrast to the American tradition, which has developed more objectively to focus on movements in terms of resource mobilisation.

If we accept that new social movement theory contains a theory of resistance, and therefore implies a conceptualisation of power, then we see that the mainstream sociological model of power is implicit in the North American tradition of sociological analysis of new social movements, which focuses on movements as the mobilisation of resources to influence policy through political processes (McDonald, 2006; Ryan, 2006). It is thus a theory of the contention of established, constituted power, by social movements seeking to exert an equivalent power-from-below by mobilising resources that are more widely distributed in society but which share the same essential form, and may even coincide with, the resources of the power they contest. The American approach retains its tight focus through a relatively narrow concept of the political, leading some commentators to see it as a reflection of the character of the US political field (ibid.). In this approach, new social movements remain ultimately orientated towards the state, towards influencing policy (Meyer, 2001), and the model of power implied thus tends to conform to Wrong's analytical distinction between relations of power and wider relations of social control.

In contrast, the 'European' approach to social movement analysis adopts a much wider conception of the political to focus on the construction of identities and cultural change. Developing out of a focus on class and culture that was absent from US analysis, in the wake of the events of 1968, the European tradition developed the concept of 'new social movements', distinct from the old by virtue of a number of factors, such as their horizontal rather than hierarchical structure. In particular, it is characteristic of European analyses to engage with the subjective intentions of the movements themselves, producing a much greater focus on their aspirations to effect wider social and cultural change, beyond influencing specific policies

(Hamel and Maheu, 2001). Through attention to the way that movements change the lives of participants and through them may effect cultural change, such analysis has moved away from a strictly rationalised conception of action and tends towards acknowledgement of the personal and even the affective experience of activism, a dimension that has recently been advanced as a new modality of action peculiar to 'global movements' (McDonald, 2006). In the European analysis, the creative effects of new modes of political action (such as the production of new social identities or communities, new repertoires of action, new forms of organisation and the politicisation of issues or activities), tend to be considered as effective accomplishments in themselves, rather than as effective only in terms of their instrumental relation to political processes, implying a very different concept of power from that of the US approach.

The interrelation between theory and practice is stronger in Europe than in the USA. Foucault addressed his explicit rejection of the 'sovereign' model of power used in mainstream sociology and political science to the emergent social movements of the 1970s as an argument for new ways of thinking that might enable resistance which did not mimic existing structures of power in its discourse, practice, organisation, orientation and focus (Foucault, 1980, pp. 78–108). Foucauldian analyses of power look at how power functions, how it has its effects, and repudiate the analytical distinction between power and wider relations of social control on the grounds that such relations constitute power as it effects and structures the social itself, including identities, understandings, opportunities, and indeed resources. Criticism of Foucault for neglecting resistance thus misunderstands how his work, like the practice of the movements that it aimed to inform, has circumvented the old conceptualisation of power on the model of the sovereign. Foucault shows us how power needs to be thought of not in terms of forceful domination, but rather as a quality inherent in techniques of organisation of spaces and bodies and in the discourse and knowledge those arrangements produce. An oppositional category of 'resistance' would be simply misplaced in this theorisation. Rather, he argues, any countervailing power must be informed by alternative discursive constructs, other knowledges, which should be 'local', non-totalising, in order to avoid the determinantly subjectifying effect of power/knowledge as it operates within systems (Foucault, 1978, pp. 135–45). Foucault for this reason was not interested in resistance, but in alternatives.

Foucault subsequently appears to have understood his own work on disciplinary power as about domination rather than power (see Foucault, 1982), and developed a supplementary analysis of government that could be applied to neo-liberal strategies of the late twentieth century. It is where these political technologies come together with disciplinary techniques and the biopolitical power exercised over life that, Foucault says, modernity becomes truly 'daemonic' (Foucault, 1988; Agamben, 1998, p. 5). As a strategy of citizenship, neo-liberal governmentality functions to regulate conduct by constructing a choosing and performative subject and then providing a structure for choices and actions, thus producing 'freedom' in the classical liberal sense.

Such analyses of neo-liberal modalities of rule clearly find their limitation with the war on terror, in which (to use the phrase of one of the most skilful exponents of governmental political practice), the rules of the game are all changed. New modes of state repression in the 'war on terror' appear as a reversion to power as domination, and as Hindess (2001) has argued, the Foucauldian analysis of governmentality does not adequately enable us to theorise liberal authoritarianism. We may, however, find precursors in the liberal governance of subjects who are deemed unfit for 'free decision', as in colonial rule, where, as Arendt (1951) pointed out, government takes the form of rule by decree, a state of exception to the norm that is similarly applied to the government of individual subjects deemed unfit for full citizenship, such as criminals or the insane, and which enables it to suspend the rights of citizenship under conditions such as war and insurrection.

It is in precisely this state of exception that Agamben locates the 'hidden point of intersection between the juridico-institutional and the biopolitical models of power', a juncture which he identifies as nothing less than the condition of sovereignty (a concept quite distinct from Foucault's notion of sovereign power). Agamben's critical political theory develops Foucault's concept of biopolitics around the figure of *homo sacer*, the condition of 'bare life' stripped of all rights, and the state of exception, which introduces a 'zone of indistinction' between the norm and the exception such that 'all citizens can be said . . . to appear virtually *homines sacri*' (Agamben, 1998, p. 111), potentially reducible to the condition of bare life as subject to the sovereign imperative of security. In the state of exception, the line dividing the norm and the exception, the citizen and *homo sacer*, is not fixed. Rather, the distinction becomes *ad hoc*, arbitrary, and is made not by the sovereign in a contractual Hobbesian sense, but by whatever agency is 'sovereign' by virtue of its capacity to draw the line within the state of indistinction that accompanies every crisis of order, whether individual deviance or collective disorder:

> If there is a line in every modern state marking the point at which the decision on life becomes a decision on death, and biopolitics can turn into thanato politics, this line no longer appears today as a stable border dividing two clearly distinct zones. This line is now in motion and gradually moving into areas other than that of political life, areas in which the sovereign is entering an ever more intimate symbiosis not only with the jurist but also with the doctor, the scientist, the expert, and the priest. (ibid., p. 122)

Even if Agamben does dehistoricise and essentialise Foucault's concept of the biopolitical (Foucault, 1978), his analysis of the contemporary securitisation of the war on terror as a manifest example of the correspondence of biopolitics and sovereignty seems able to operate independently of that framework. Furthermore, we can understand Agamben's identification of sovereignty with the biopolitical as a development of Foucault's critique of the sovereign conception of power, since Agamben does not reify sovereignty but rather identifies it as an effect of the state of exception, predicate on the potentiality to invoke *homo sacer*: 'It can even be said that the production of a biopolitical body is the original activity of sovereign power' (Agamaben, 1998, p. 6). There is a link between the negativity of sovereign power of deduction, the power of death, and the biopolitics of the power over life.

BEYOND RESISTANCE

The networked anti-globalisation and anti-capitalist movement (the 'movement of movements') could be seen as part of the wider phenomenon theorised by McDonald (2006) as 'global movements' or even 'experience movements' (to include new humanitarian NGOs and religious fundamentalisms). Just as with the Dissent network, the 'resistance' of global movements as analysed by McDonald does not oppose itself to power as its primary orientation, it is not a mirror-image of power as it is given, yet it indicates a capacity to create, to produce, to constitute (rather than merely imagining and representing) new identities, new social relations, new ways of life; 'the whole idea wasn't really about protesting against G8 . . . It was about being and becoming human . . . This was living, this was being human' (The Free Association, 2006, p. 25).

Some recent sociological work has attempted to address this other moment of power, as in the distinction between 'power over' and 'power to' that Angus Stewart (2001) draws from the work of Hannah Arendt (1951). Stewart points out that we can distinguish between analyses of power which understand power as domination (power over) and those which understand it as the 'expression of collective autonomy' (power to). Stewart uses this distinction strictly to refer to two ways of analysing power, but the political theory tradition upon which he draws recognises that the way that actors understand themselves to be powerful has very real implications, so that this analytical distinction can have real consequences, and we can thus use it to refer to two distinct relations of power. This usage is reinforced by recognition of the limits of English, which has one word for power where most European languages have two: *pouvoir, Vermogen, potere* and the Latin *potestas*, referring broadly to 'the might of authority of an already structured and centralised capacity, often an institutional apparatus such as the state', and on the other hand, *puissance*, *Macht*, *potenza* and the Latin *potentia*, referring to 'implications of potentiality as well as . . . decentralized or mass conceptions of force and strength' (Binetti and Casarino, Translators' Notes in Agamben, 2000, 143n1). The correspondence between the different languages is not exact, but the overall distinction between two referents is evident. The distinction seems implicit in the understanding of power used by recent global social movements, particularly in the theory and practice of Dissent network: 'Summit protests are the product of a kind of activism that prefigures and embodies a wholly different kind of politics, a politics of everyday life that seeks to transform the way we envisage power and relate to it' (Tormey, 2006, p. 345).

Agamben has recently developed this distinction from the work of Walter Benjamin, who he says 'presented the relation between constituting and constituted power as the relation between the violence that posits the law and the violence that preserves it' (Agamben, 1998, p. 40). In the analysis and practices of social movements, however, we have seen a shift in the conception of power beyond the formal, constitutional framework in which even Agamben thinks of constituting power as 'the power from which the constitution is born' (ibid.), so that constituting power now becomes the power to realise entirely new social relations, new ways of living, new identities, independently of constituted power altogether, even seeking to escape from the tendency to crystallise power in a constituted form. Agamben also enables us to see how the problematics of constituting power for the 'movement of movements' are not new, but have attended all attempts in modernity to not only, 'conceive a constituting power that does not exhaust itself in a constituted power' (ibid., p. 41), but also to preserve it without setting up a 'police' of the movement and its ideas.

Agamben's critique of the tendency for constituting power to become constituted power encapsulates the problematic facing the anti-globalisation movement where it attempts to act other than simply as resistance to the globalisation managed by G8 and in its attempts to avoid the tendencies latent in political organisation to consolidate itself securely and to become positional by forming fixed identities and social relations, for example, activist/non-activist, globals/locals, hardcore/fluffy, by inadvertently creating a hierarchy of functions and thence of offices, and by codifying ideological parameters. But it also identifies the strategic void that movement thinkers recognise within their own political practice (Hewson, 2006).

With effective tactics for the struggle for space apparently emerging from spontaneously innovative practice, the temporal dimension becomes critical for the Dissent network's model of the conditions of political action – how to sustain, or preserve, that which was gained by refusing to come to be, seems to require the movement to either continue to exist only as a response to summits and to global sovereignty, so that the logical order is reversed and their constitutive power becomes predicate on the constituted power they protest, or itself becomes 'sovereign' in the way that Globalise Resistance seeks to establish a constituted order of resistance, a structure with its own precedence, priorities and internal sovereignty. Dissent G8's attempts to think otherwise are attempts to inaugurate a post-Aristotelian politics, which refuses the implications of its own refusal, to retain its own potential not to be. 'What is potential can pass over into actuality only at the point at which it sets aside its own potential not to be . . . an act is sovereign when it realizes itself by simply taking away its own potentiality not to be, letting itself be, giving itself to itself' (Agamben, 1998, p. 46).

The dimension in which this can be achieved is that of time rather than space; requiring a strategy of (dis)organisation rather of distribution, and of immediacy rather than strategy: 'the future is already here . . . the future of myriad molecular projects, plans and experiments that we see developing in force and influence across the world . . . we can use protests to remind ourselves that we have outworn a strategy, in favour of a practice of resistance here and now' (Tormey, 2006, p. 349). The movement around Dissent G8 and elsewhere seems to have begun to develop tactics which enable the reclamation of space, as Skrimshire argues (2006, pp. 289–90) in a temporary contingent sense which nevertheless functions to expand the potentialities for future protest and which has a wider effect on culture and social perceptions, but the transient actuality of this potential means that the movement is confronted with time. Werner Bonefeld's play on the term 'movement' brings this into sharp relief with the phrase, 'without movement there is certainty', and in pointing out that movement compels both dependence (since there is no 'place' for the movement, no certainty that will bring social reproduction, 'no free, autonomous spaces that provide bases for anti-capitalist struggles'), and the struggle for social autonomy (Bonefeld, 2006, pp. 266–7).

Bonefeld reiterates Agamben's warnings against 'the party' in favour of 'the carnival', but resort to the concept of 'the multitude' as an alternative simply reintroduces the subject, with all its conditions and implications. Bonefeld argues that the movements are already inside bourgeois social relations (and thus inside power) and cannot think themselves beyond, but have to practise a self-organised negation which requires an embrace of the uncertainty that is the political beyond the state, beyond constituted power, a potentiality for freedom which requires permanent uncertainty. However, organisation tends to produce organs, and carnival cannot last forever without ceasing to be carnival and becoming the norm:

> 'Moments of excess' are points at which possibilities open and anything could happen. Yet it is in the nature of this state that they are brief. These situations cannot last long. Sooner or later they will settle into something, and the very fact of becoming anything rather than a moment of openness, a jumping off point for an unknown future, must in a way feel like a disappointment. (Anonymous, 2006, p. 181)

Without constituting itself as a subject, then, the anti-globalisation network cannot act or think strategically, but remains in a liminal condition in which contingency substitutes for calculation, a situation corresponding to Habermas's concept of a lifeworld in which communication is free of distortion because of its immediacy. If only tactics need to be considered, and those only in contingency, then the movement can dispense with subjectification; but in order to bring about those moments, it has to think and act strategically, and thus not only subjectifies itself but becomes (criminal) subject for the other:

> In the final analysis the state can recognize any claim for identity . . . what the state cannot tolerate in any way is that singularities form a community without claiming an identity, that human beings co-belong without a representable condition of belonging. (Agamben, 2000, p. 87)

BEYOND SOLIDARITY

As a situation where the 'sovereign police' meet popular resistance in its 'ordinary' form of a social movement, but under the normalised extraordinary conditions of the war on terror, the G8 Summit thus provides an opportunity to analyse in concrete terms Agamben's claims:

> Faced with the unstoppable progression of what has been called a 'global civil war', the state of exception tends increasingly to appear as the dominant paradigm of government in contemporary politics. The transformation of a provisional and exceptional measure into a technique of government threatens radically to alter . . . the structure and meaning of the conventional distinction between constitutional forms. Indeed, from this perspective, the state of exception appears as a threshold of indeterminacy between democracy and absolutism. (Agamaben, 2005, pp. 2–3)

Resistance thus faces the dilemma of how to operate without symmetrically reproducing the form to which it is opposed. Such avoidance means the avoidance of totalisation, as Foucault pointed out in his lectures on power/knowledge from the 1970s (1980) directed at the post-1968 political activists, which in their call for local knowledges both foreshadowed and inadvertently delimited the subsequent development of a 'movement of movements'. Foucault's methodological refusal of symmetrism in refusing *analysis* of a totality is echoed in Dissent's dilemma:

> Every determination is a closure – even saying, 'this is the problem', 'this is where we stand', 'this is what we have to do now', narrows down the terms of debate and . . . excludes people who think differently . . . any determination of a goal, position, analysis, etc. beyond the constitutive terms of the open space is perceived a negative, because it reduces diversity. Discussions of this kind are only possible within smaller affinity groups, which means that more defined positions and strategies . . . do not belong in the debate of larger networks or spaces. In this way, horizontality always posits its own limit . . . (Nunes, 2006, p. 305)

The Dissent network was aware that asymmetry meant a shift in conditions of protest as well as of policing:

> The state has . . . unwittingly accelerated this drive toward more and more horizontal forms of organizing . . . ultimately we can never beat the state at its own game: we will always be militarily defeated. The alternative strategy is to remove any remaining layers of direction and control, and effectively create a peer-to-peer network. (The Free Association, 2006, p. 20)

It is worth remembering that some of the legislative measures opening a zone of indistinction in which the police function as sovereign (being excused from constraints of civil or human rights in order to allow them 'to get on with their job') preceded 9/11 and President George W. Bush's declaration of the war on terror, and have been deployed routinely against civil protests rather than against terrorist threats. In Agamben's terms, this outcome is teleological, the realisation of the truth of the liberal as much as of the absolutist state, an observation of Guy Debord that Agamben revived once again in the context of the Gulf war of 1990:

> The state of the integrated spectacle (or, spectacular-democratic state) is the final stage in the evolution of the state form – the ruinous stage toward which monarchies and republics, tyrannies and democracies, racist regimes and progressive regimes are all rushing . . . this global movement actually embodies a tendency toward the constitution of a kind of supranational police state . . . (Agamben, 2000, p. 86)

If the state of exception is a state where right and violence are indeterminate, contested, then it is also a condition where politics becomes open. However, those using Agamben as a guide, and indeed Agamben himself, often seem to imply that the state of exception is a condition that is actively sought by the state, its ideal condition because it is an inherent condition. Skrimshire, for instance, follows Hornqvist to argue that the state of emergency seeks to protect the public from politics, 'And if the public wishes to be politics . . . then they need to be protected from themselves' (Skrimshire, 2006, p. 287). So do the forces of public order seek containment, closure, rather than serial extension of the state of emergency? The problem here arises from the normative definition of politics or the political, since it is this very concept that is open to contention in the state of exception. The forces of public order seek to close that openness, to fix politics as institutional, as an exercise of constituted power. The state of exception, then is the condition of contemporary power, its own return to its constitutive source as security. Only by recognising that the state of exception is necessary to both constituted and constituting power, will it be possible to develop a strategy for a movement which seeks to realise its own condition of potentiality.

The problematic of constitutive power is thus how it can be grounded without falling into the trap of subjectification and rendering itself as another form of constituted power. Another way of putting this would be to ask how a global movement can maintain a state of becoming and never become. How can the transitory, the temporary, persist? It is on this question that Agamben's work becomes a critique not only of power as constituted, but also of tendencies within global movements that are focused upon more positively by McDonald.

While his work sometimes seems to attribute to 'global movements' characteristics that have earlier been identified as differentiating new social movements from old, McDonald nevertheless points out how in a further shift since the late 1980s, movements have increasingly come to adopt 'direct action' that is neither instrumental nor expressive, but which temporarily enables an alternative social order of experience in protest events:

> The forms of action . . . all involve a break from this paradigm where groups are constituted through the act of representation. Rather than the 'power to represent', we encounter other grammars of action . . . grammars of embodiment, as experience, as mode of presence and engagement with the world. (McDonald, 2006, p. 37)

The focus is on the immediate, rather than on the future, and thus the global movements and modernities studied by McDonald are beyond ideology, orientated by, 'an ethic of the present . . . committed to living differently now, as opposed to programmatic or linear attempts to shape the future' (ibid., p. 64). McDonald points out that the 'new humanitarianism' of NGOs such as Médecins Sans Frontières shares in this ethos of imme-diacy, of urgency, and shares also affective qualities that increasingly have characterised direct action protests since the 1980s.

I have already explained how the Dissent network, like other movements analysed by McDonald, developed novel modes of organisation through networks, affinity groups and personalised relationships of affiliation, which McDonald argues indicate 'a clear break with the paradigm of "identity correspondence" and "civic grammar" characteristic of even new social movements when they are understood by sociologists as constituting a group "through the act of representation"' (ibid., p. 86; pp. 84–92). While US analyses have tended to focus on this discursive dimension of emergent global movements, European approaches have often applied the terms 'tribe' or 'neotribe' in contrast to the older concept of subculture to conceptualise the fluidity of new movements, since, 'groupings which have traditionally been theorized as coherent subcultures are better understood as a series of temporary gatherings characterized by fluid boundaries and floating memberships' (Bennett, 1999, p. 599). Bennett argues that the concept of tribe incorporates the affective, emotional dimension of the contemporary phenomenon of 'resistance' or constituting power within global movements.

The distinction that McDonald draws between social and global move-ments in terms of affectivity requires more careful qualification, however, since social movements have always functioned on an emotional register (indeed, it was precisely the emotive elements that differentiated social movements from contemporary politics, as noted in Weber's (1948) rationalist critique of revolutionary ideologies of left and right, with their 'ethics of conviction'). It is not simply the existence of an affective and experiential quality that differentiates global from previous social move-ments, as McDonald suggests, but rather the way that affect is experi-enced. In the mass movements of the nineteenth and early twentieth centuries, affect was experienced as a collective, in which the personal was subsumed within the mass, not merely organisationally, but subjectively; the mass provided the frame for experience, and individual affect was gen-erated as part of the collective. This is of course akin to Durkheim's analysis of the sociological generation of a 'conscience collective', a concept developed in the analysis of primitive religion, but which was intended to be applied to phenomena as modern as party rallies, football spectatorship, and even the vicarious experience accessible through the consumption of mass media.

In McDonald's scenario, the crucial distinction is that affect and experi-ence are now not framed and constitutive of a collective identity, but rather consist in the social context of personalised relationships of affinity:

Through the affinity group, each person enters into a relationship with a concrete other (people you know and trust) as opposed to relating to a totality . . . The paradigm is closer to friendship in that each person recognizes the other as a person, as opposed to someone carrying out a function on behalf of a collectivity or organization . . . a friendship is not based on sharing a category: a friendship is an experience of the recognition of singularity. (McDonald, 2006, p. 87)

BODIES AND SPACES

This shift is related by McDonald to the new conditions of post-industrial capitalism, synthesised by Boltanski and Chiapello (2006) from a growing body of work, on the threshold of a major shift in sociology. We can trace how since the late 1980s, movements have increasingly adopted 'direct action' which inaugurates a social order in protest events. 'A key aspect of the anticapitalist direct action movement is our desire for a "prefigurative" politics that sees no separation between means and ends . . . we want to be the change that we want to see in the world' (Klepto and Up Evil, 2006, p. 247). In the UK, this can be traced in a genealogy which passes through the Greenham Common women's camp of the early 1980s, where anti-nuclear armaments protest fused with currents from 1960s social radicalism and esoteric mysticism, and with radical feminism and the punk DIY ethos from the late 1970s, manifesting an alternative social order of fluid boundaries and a floating membership who came to experience themselves and the world in radically new ways as they passed through the camp. Subsequently, UK anti-road protests, especially Twyford Down in Hampshire and London's A40, constituted similar spaces of emancipation from determinant social and cultural structures, fusing further cultural politics from the 'New Age travellers' and the UK rave and festival culture.

While these convergences can be traced intellectually to sources such as classical anarchism and the Situationist International, explicitly ideological links are weak. Rather, it is personal experience that articulates the linkages. For McDonald, this seems to imply that individuals carry the 'memory' of activism from one event to the next, leading researchers to use interviews and to trace networks in much the same way as police intelligence or pop journalism. Through this methodology, the 'beyond social movement theory' developed by McDonald tends to unintentionally produce a misleading elitist picture of movements. There is an assumption that in place of ideology, significant individuals rather than cultural practices constitute innovations and maintain movements over time, neglecting the theoretical reflections, practical communications, and other forms of discourse which constitute the 'movement'. The G8 Dissent network, however, seem acutely aware of the 'floating' nature of personal participation (Anonymous, 2006), of the diversity of sources, contexts and definitions of activism, and of the absence of a direct lineage of development of organisation and action. Their reflections on organisation recognise that McDonald's conceptualisation of movements in terms of flows rather than structures is more difficult to maintain in practice than in theory (see, for example, Nunes, 2006).

However, McDonald's theorisation of the new modality of protest participation in terms of embodiment is the most problematic aspect of his analysis. For McDonald, affective experience is grounded in a personalised conception of the body, attested by frequent sensory references in the personalised memoirs of 'experience movements' and from his critique of social movement theory:

> The instrumental (strategy and opportunity) accounts and the identity (expressive, community, *communitas*) theories mirror each other. The instrumental theories exclude the body in order to focus on the rational actor. The expressive theories introduce the body, but within theory where the person is dissolved in categories of holism. (McDonald, 2006, p. 216)

However, McDonald's focus on embodiment depoliticises the body by reducing it to experience and sensation, neglecting its social reality, the sense in which our bodies are conduits for social forces which frame our experience of sensation and even shape the physical body itself.

If the body is the medium of experience, then McDonald assumes that the body exists outside of social mediation, that the body as a purely 'personal' experience is acontextual. Such assumptions characterise the discourse of embodiment as a whole and have turned the project for a sociology of the body away from social bodies, towards attempts to articulate pure unmediated experience. In McDonald's application this turn to embodiment highlights those moments in the accounts of participants where experience becomes mediated by a sense of recovery of naturalistic experience. Hence, 'experience movements', such as the natural childbirth movement which claims to put women 'back in their bodies' (ibid., p. 216), or reports of how physical participation in symbolic activism has the effect of 'reconnecting' body and self (ibid., p. 217), and such movements' affinity with forms of music which 'remind us of something forgotten' (ibid., p. 224). The movements' politics through 'doing' he claims:

> are above all at work at the level of personal experience, from grammars of the Internet and practices of healing to the action of memory. But rather than the isolation of the individual monad and his capacity for sociality, the forms of

experience we have encountered can only be constructed through traditions, cultures, memory and religious subjectivities. (ibid., p. 226)

McDonald's theorisation of 'grammars of experience' of new 'experience movements' as grounded in a body-in-itself articulated through such media is not simply a theoretical construction. Such reflections appear in the accounts of G8 Dissent network activists, with references to a sense of connection with historical figures, with the sounds of musical instruments, with environment and with landscape, constructing a mythology of resistance that by reconceptualising protest as a temporary link with timeless experience of embodiment undoes much of the attempts to articulate a space for invention and a politics of becoming.

Attempts to ground 'experience movements' in the body thus appeal to a naturalistic body and its corollary, an ideology of romanticised 'resistance'. However, G8 Dissenters are aware, unlike McDonald, of the ambivalence of creating a culture of resistance, where celebration of the sensual element of 'moments of excess' is qualified by reflection:

> When forms of rebellion become ritualised it can mean they are repetitive, stale, repugnant. But it can also mean they are ingrained, have become customary, expected – which can be a big pain for those in power, but also simultaneously limiting for radicals. Things can become entrenched – with both the positive and negative sides of that – a position that is firmly held and very difficult for the enemy to shift, but also difficult to move forward from. (Anonymous, 2006, p. 183)

In contrast to cultural ritualisation and the naturalistic experience of the body, the Dissent network shows a keen sense of the political as openness to action, rather than experience, in which the body is creative, rather than merely sensitive, 'Global protest movements are waking up to the disembodied reality of global politics, through an exploration of mobility and fluidity of bodies' (Skrimshire, 2006, pp. 289–90).

For Agamben, the body thus conceived, in the situation of exception stripped of the social and political mediation of rights, is not a return to a given, but a construction. Moreover experience through the body does not open onto the realm of freedom, rather,

> [T]he concept of the 'body' . . . is always already caught in a deployment of power. The 'body' is always already a biopolitical body and bare life, and nothing in it or the economy of its pleasure seems to allow us to find solid ground on which to oppose the demands of sovereign power. (Agamaben, 1998, p. 187)

A similar ambivalence also applies to the spaces that the anti-globalisation activists create for the politics of becoming. The careful construction by G8

Dissent of exactly such spaces, such as the pre-summit Cre8-Summat and the eco-village or the appropriation of public space in Edinburgh for the Carnival for Full Enjoyment (Molyneaux, 2006), is intended not as a step on the way to overthrow capitalism or seize power in the state, but in itself, 'to open up spaces in which anything – briefly – appears possible, provide us with a glimpse of another possible world'. By calling into question, and thus politicising, the means by which experience of everyday life is constructed (Trott, 2006, pp. 216–17).

As G8 Dissenters make clear, such zones can be constructed anywhere, but these activities are conducted under police presence and intensive surveillance. Even in the debates in the G8 network before the Summit, there was an awareness that organising around summits ties such openings to heavily policed spectacular security events, as well as restricting action to activism and activism to the form of a confrontational response to power. Similarly, as Agamben points out, in conditions of ubiquitous and permanent security which displace politics into technical procedures, the state of exception can be instituted anywhere, 'an apparently innocuous space . . . actually delimits a space in which the normal order is *de facto* suspended and in which whether or not atrocities are committed depends not on law but on the civility and ethical sense of the police who temporarily act as sovereign' (Agamaben, 1998, p. 174).

CONCLUSION

Around G8 2005 the state of exception was ubiquitous, becoming spectacular with the arrival of the unmarked military Chinook helicopters which disgorged British police reinforcements to charge the demonstrators when the perimeter fence was breached on 6 July. It appeared also in the spectacle of the London bombings of 7 July, leaving Gleneagles a sideshow; again around the body of Jean Charles de Menezes at Stockwell Underground station in London on 22 July; and has become normalised in the free-fire zones of the 'war on terror' in Iraq, Afghanistan and the Gaza Strip.

Thus, the movements' 'Temporary Autonomous Zones', to use the term of neo-anarchist theorist Hakim Bey (2004), are best understood critically, as the flipside of zones of indistinction, the spaces where the definitive struggle between constituted and constitutive power appears. Just as the power of the state and sovereignty extends its state of exception to everyday life under the rubric of the 'war on terror', so the struggle to live and experience differently seeks to extend itself beyond 'summitism' into everyday life. Zones of indistinction are at once potentially moments of an opening onto alternative experience and of absolute unfreedom, of the camp as, 'a space in which power confronts pure biological life without mediation . . . the paradigm of political space at the point in which politics becomes biopolitics and the *homo sacer* becomes indistinguishable from the citizen' (Agamben, 2000, p. 40). The primary struggle of our times is thus not the terrorising struggle for security against terror, but between a power over space, time and bodies which seeks to secure the conditions for bare life, and a power which may open life and experience to becoming.

REFERENCES

Agamben, G. (1998), Homo Sacer: *Sovereign Power and Bare Life*, Stanford, CA: Stanford University Press.

Agamben, G. (2000), *Means Without End: Notes on Politics*, Minneapolis, MN: University of Minnesota Press.

Agamben, G. (2005), *State of Exception*, Chicago: University of Chicago Press.

Anonymous (2006), 'Inside and outside the G8 protests', in Harvie et al. (eds), pp. 175–83.

Arendt, H. (1951), *The Origins of Totalitarianism*, Orlando, FL: Harcourt Brace.

Beck, U. (2005), *Power in the Global Age: A New Global Political Economy*, Cambridge: Polity.

Bennett, A. (1999), 'Subcultures or neotribes: rethinking the relationship between youth, style and musical taste', *Sociology*, **33** (3), 599–617.

Bey, H. (2004), *The Temporary Autonomous Zone, Ontological Anarchy, Poetic Terrorism*, New York: Autonomedia, www.hermetic.com/bey/taz_cont.html.

Boltanski, L. and E. Chiapello (2006), *The New Spirit of Capitalism*, London: Verso.

Bonefeld, W. (2006), 'Notes on movement and uncertainty', in Harvie et al. (eds), pp. 265–72.

Chandler, D. (2006), 'Holding a looking-glass to the "Movement": a response to Worth and Abbott', *Globalizations*, **3** (1), March, 65–7.

Durkheim, E. (1976), *The Elementary Forms of the Religious Life*, Woking: Allen & Unwin.

Foucault, M. (1978), *The History of Sexuality: An Introduction*, Harmondsworth: Penguin.

Foucault, M. (1980), 'Two lectures', in C. Gordon (ed.), *Power/Knowledge: Selected Interviews and Other Writings by Michel Foucault, 1972–77*, Hemel Hempstead: Harvester, pp. 78–108.

Foucault, M. (1982), 'The subject and power', in H. Dreyfus and P. Rabinow (eds), *Michel Foucault: Beyond Structuralism and Hermeneutics*, London: Harvester Wheatsheaf, pp. 206–26.

Foucault, M. (1988), 'Politics and reason', in L.D. Kritzman (ed.), *Michel Foucault: Politics, Philosophy and Culture: Interviews and Other Writings, 1977–1984*, London: Routledge, pp. 57–85.

Hamel, P. and L. Maheu (2001), 'Beyond new social movements: social conflicts and institutions', in Nash and Scott (eds), pp. 261–70.

Harvie, D., K. Milburn, B. Trott and D. Watts (eds) (2006), *Shut Them Down! The G8, Gleneagles 2005 and the Movement of Movements*, Leeds and New York: Dissent and Autonomedia.

Hewson, P. (2006), 'It's the politics, stupid! How neoliberal politicians, NGOs and rock stars hijacked the global justice movement at Gleneagles . . . and how we let them', in Harvie et al. (eds), pp. 135–49.

Hindess, B. (1986), *Discourses of Power: From Hobbes to Foucault*, Oxford: Blackwell.

Hindess, B. (2001), 'Power, government, politics', in Nash and Scott (eds), pp. 40–48.

Klepto, K. and M. Up Evil (2006), 'The clandestine insurgent rebel clown army goes to Scotland via a few other places', in Harvie et al. (eds), pp. 243–54.

Lyon, D. (2003), *Surveillance after September 11*, Cambridge: Polity.

Mann, M. (1986), *The Sources of Social Power, Vol. 1: A History of Power from the Beginning to AD 1760*, Cambridge: Cambridge University Press.

McDonald, K. (2006), *Global Movements: Action and Culture*, Oxford: Blackwell.

Meyer, D.S. (2001), 'Protest and political protest', in Nash and Scott (eds), pp. 164–72.

Molyneaux, L. (2006), 'The carnival continues . . .', in Harvie et al. (eds), pp. 109–18.

Morgan Stanley International Foundation, The J8 Global Citizenship Programme, www.j8summit.com, accessed 2 April 2006.

Nash, K. and A. Scott (eds) (2001), *The Blackwell Companion to Political Sociology*, Oxford: Blackwell.

Nunes, R. (2006), 'Nothing is what democracy looks like: openness, horizontality and the movement of movements', in Harvie et al. (eds), pp. 299–319.

Perthshire and Kinross Council, 'Perthshire G8 2005', www.perthshireg8.com/, accessed 2 April 2006.

Ryan, L. (2006), 'Rethinking social movement theories in the twenty-first century', *Sociology*, **40** (1), February, 169–76.

Skrimshire, S. (2006), 'Anti-G8 resistance and the state of exception', in Harvie et al. (eds), pp. 285–90.

Stewart, A. (2001), *Theories of Power and Domination: the Politics of Empowerment in Late Modernity*, London: Sage.

Summer, K. and H. Halpin (2006), 'The end of the world as we know it', in Harvie et al. (eds), pp. 351–9.

Tayside Police, 'G8 2005', www.tayside.police.uk/g8/index.php?ref=1155226499, accessed 3 April 2006.

The Free Association (2006), 'On the road', in Harvie et al. (eds), pp. 17–26.

Tormey, S. (2006), 'After Gleneagles: where next?', in Harvie et al. (eds), pp. 337–49.

Trocchi, A., G. Redwolf and P. Alamire (2006), 'Reinventing dissent! An unabridged story of resistance', in Harvie et al. (eds), pp. 61–102.

Trott, B. (2006), 'Gleneagles, activism and ordinary rebelliousness', in Harvie et al. (eds), pp. 213–33.

Weber, M. (1948), 'Politics as a vocation', in H.H. Girth and C. Wright Mills (eds), *From Max Weber: Essays in Sociology*, London: Routledge & Kegan Paul, pp. 77–128.

Worth, O. and J.P. Abbott (2006), 'Land of false hope? The contradictions of British opposition to globalization', *Globalizations*, **3** (1), March, 49–63.

15. Between the bliss of the new consumer society and the new dark times

Maurice Mullard

The mid-term elections of November 2006 in the USA reinforced the hope of politics. The coalition of Christian leader, business and corporate interests that defined the conservative movement and shaped the thinking of the Republican Party and had come to dominate American politics was brought to a halt in November 2006. Despite declarations by President George W. Bush that a vote for the democrats was a vote for the insurgency in Iraq and referendums on gay marriage and stem cell research to mobilise the Christian votes, the Democratic Party still won 53 per cent of the vote – a landslide victory:

> We may be seeing the downfall of movement conservatism – the potent alliance of wealthy individuals, corporate interests and the religious right that took shape in the 1960s and 1970s. This alliance has become mainly a corrupt political machine, the movement is fundamentally undemocratic; its leaders don't accept the legitimacy of opposition.. And the determination of the movement to hold on to power at any cost has poisoned our political culture. Just think about the campaign that just ended, with its coded racism, deceptive robo-calls, personal smears . . . not to mention the constant implication that anyone who questions the Bush administration or its policies is very nearly a traitor. (Paul Krugman, *New York Times*, 10 November 2006, p. 27)

Although democracy is being corrupted and distorted by money in politics it would seem that as the discrepancy between the manipulated message and reality widens, citizens do use the democratic process to register the need for change. The adage that you can fool people some of the time but not all of the time was a statement used by the economist Milton Friedman to explain that the economics of fiscal illusion applies equally to politics. The primary concern of government is to construct a continuing image of competence, to attempt to manage the idea of public opinion and ensure that there is a correspondence between policy priorities and public concern.

The war on terror and economic globalisation define contexts and land-scapes while the commitments and claims on citizenship reflect the day-to-day personal human experience. The connections between the war on terror, globalisation and citizenship reflect the relationships between the contexts that seek to give shape to what is possible and the spaces for accountability of government. Second, there is the political dimension to both globalisation and the war on terror since both processes are inextri-cably linked with government, political parties and therefore political ide-ologies. In the context of globalisation the politics can be described as the disavowal of responsibility where the aim is to reinforce the idea about the limits of government and generating the debate for the 'personal responsi-bility crusade' society of individual health insurance accounts and private pension arrangements (Hacker, 2006). There is a politics of globalisation in the sense that the process of globalisation is not the exogenous event that is beyond the control of nation-state institutions but rather reflects a series of deliberate policy choices. Despite the claims that markets are the science equivalent in status to laws of gravity, the study of politics is an argument that points out that markets continue to be social constructs that are defined by policy making.

A common theme that emerges from the text is the issue of pacification in the sense that both the war on terror and globalisation seek to create a logic of inevitability and a climate that there are no alternatives. In policy making the emphasis of trust replaces transparency and dialogue. Electors are expected to have trust in their representatives. Trust creates passivity. Those in the workplace have to understand the laws of supply and demand. Employment and income inequalities are the natural outcomes of markets reinforcing the rewards for skills and resources. Rewarding higher incomes to CEOs, celebrities and sports personalities reflects their personal endowments and entitlements. Implicitly some forms of resist-ance including trade union militancy are dismissed as being illogical, non-rational or lacking in legitimacy. The war on terror reinforces pacification as it generates emotions of fear and insecurity. The fears of personal risk that are created by impersonal markets and economic globalisation are reinforced by the new risks of terrorism. These are two forms of fear that increasingly become conflated: the first is generated by the high risks of a highly privatised consumer citizen who is asked to cope with flexible employment, uncertainties of future earnings, higher costs for health insurance and retirement; and the second is the war on terror, rising crime and appearances of chaos. The appeals to the emotions of fear and hyste-ria leave little room for complex argument or reasoned debate. The war on terror and globalisation reflects the shift from the social state to the per-sonal safety state (Bauman, 2006).

The concern of this book has been the attempt to explain the possible connections of globalisation, the war and terror and citizenship. Ideas of citizenship do not obey the rules of definition. Definitions are static, unable to explain changes in expectations. Putting an emphasis on the constituent parts of citizenship as a form of clothing downgrades the importance of context. In the context of the war on terror, taken-for-granted civil and political rights are being re-written while the ascendance of a market liberal paradigm has eclipsed and downgraded the collectivist and Keynesian thinking that defined social rights. The making of social citizenship developed by Marshall (1992) depended on the optimism of government intervention in making commitments to full employment and the possibilities of social policy. By contrast, market liberals have since the mid-1970s sought to dismantle the pillars of the post-war consensus where the dependency of the social citizen is replaced by individualism and the responsible consumer citizen. Policy makers and policy advocates at the World Bank, the IMF and the WTO have pointed to the successes of nation states that have embraced free markets, free trade, liberalisation and privatisation. Putting the focus on the arithmetic of pluses and minuses they aimed to show that there are more winners than losers, leading to the implicit and logical conclusion that globalisation has to be celebrated.

The political dimensions of globalisation and the war on terror make the crucial connection that both these processes reflect a series of deliberate policy choices. Rather than defining globalisation as the exogenous factor that countries have to embrace the politics of globalisation points to political autonomy, policy choices and political priorities. The commitment to free markets is combined with an argument for less government and retreat from public spaces. Furthermore, market liberalism combined with aggressive militarism as articulated by neo-conservative thinkers in the USA have become the ideological underpinnings to both the politics of globalisation and the war on terror. The wars in Afghanistan and in Iraq were not 'inevitable' responses to the attacks on the World Trade Center, declaring a war on terror was not an inevitable policy response to the atrocities in New York and the Pentagon. The war on terror therefore represented a qualitative policy shift. The declaration of war needed clusters of allies and enemies, us and them; us the Christian democracies, and them the Islamic fascists who had previously committed criminal acts and now were defined as the enemy that has to defeated. That Bush was President and that his policy makers had shaped a global foreign and economic policy founded on neo-conservative thinking did make a difference. President Bush had already made up his mind to go to war in Iraq in 2002. It is now clearly evident that the intelligence on weapons of mass destruction had been reshaped in both the UK and USA to justify the war in Iraq

(Woodward, 2006; Gore 2007) and the ex-Prime Minister Tony Blair had pledged his support for the President at least 10 months before the UN Resolution of March 2003.

The underlying hope of this study is that it will make a contribution to the understanding of the human condition at the beginning of the twenty-first century. The war on terror and globalisation are generating different forms of fear and insecurity. In appealing to the emotions of fear, policy makers are downgrading the possibility for reasoned debate. The Patriot Act of 2001 reviewed in 2006 and the more recent Military Commissions Act have put into question the robustness of the US Constitution. Since 9/11, President Bush and Republican lawmakers have argued that since the United States was at war these were exceptional times that needed exceptional responses, surrendering more power to the President as Commander in Chief and where the checks on the executive written in the US Constitution have to be balanced with the new needs for the safety and security of US citizens. Removing the rights to habeaus corpus for detainees at Guantánamo Bay means that defendents can no longer apply to the US federal courts for judicial review. Justice will be delivered through military tribunals. Prosecutors will be able to bring forward evidence extracted under torture or hearsay. The President is able to use secret wire taps without seeking oversight from FISA (Foreign Intelligence Surveillance Act, 1978). The President can define any American citizen as an enemy combatant. According to Al Gore, Vice President to former President Bill Clinton and presidential candidate in the 2000 election, the war on terror has undermined democracy and the Constitution:

> Civil rights have been weakened since the Bush–Cheney administration chose to use the war against terror as a basis for both political argument in a partisan context and for an assault on the individual rights including the right to be free of government eavesdropping. The conversation of democracy has been degraded, emotions and appeals to fear have been given a priority over reasoned debate. (Henry Porter, Interview with Al Gore, *The Observer*, 5 November 2006, p. 45)

In their sociological imaginations on the human condition, Giddens (2007) and Bauman (2006) have come to some very contrasting conclusions. Giddens and what can be generally called the 'Third Way optimists' describe a world of individual consumer citizens who are more assertive, who use the Internet to collate information and who are now better informed than the bureaucracy of public sector professionals and bureaucracy. The new knowledge consumers have embraced the language of personal freedom of choice and now seek to have more choice in health care and their children's education:

> Choice is empowering for users and provides great incentives for providers, as
> long as money follows it. Choice is only effective if it has consequences – if
> rewords follow being chosen and unfavourable consequences follow those who
> are not chosen. But there must be real choice between providers. New kinds of
> providers must be introduced to develop such choice. (Giddens, 2007, p. 110)

By contrast, Bauman has sought to reinforce the argument of Hannah
Arendt and Richard Sennett that we are entering dark times when public
spaces have stopped being the places that bring light through dialogue and
instead create a culture of anti-politics and a retreat into quietism:

> Can the public space be made once more a place of lasting engagement rather
> than casual and fleeting encounters? A space for dialogue discussion confronta-
> tion and agreement. . . . That variety of public stage has been stripped of most
> of the implements and assets that enabled it to sustain the dramas staged in the
> past. Those public stages originally constructed for the political purposes of
> nation and state remain stubbornly local when contemporary drama is human
> wide and so obstreperously and emphatically global. (Bauman, 2006, p. 152)

The concern of the optimists is the new sovereign consumer – the individual situated in the new knowledge economy and where the working class
of Karl Marx has become a minority. From the middle of the nineteenth
to the late twentieth centuries, history was being shaped by the industrial
revolution, the shift from agriculture to industrial communities, the begin-
nings of state intervention in regulating public health and the continuing
compromises between capital and labour. Claims for democracy, trade
unions and the emergence of political parties that sought to represent the
interests of labour were integral to explaining the nature of social change.
For Giddens those contours of class and capitalism are no longer relevant
analytical concepts. The twenty-first century is being shaped by the individual, the flat organisation, the world that is dominated by the selling of
ideas and where knowledge rather than the ownership of capital defines life
chances. Equally, Keynesian economics, commitments to full employment
and the post-war welfare state are clustered as belonging to the now
eclipsed Soviet era.

By contrast, the dark times advocates point to new concentrations of
power and wealth on a global scale and the concerns raised by Marx of the
wasting of human lives and social injustice as still being highly relevant.
Bauman (2006) points to fear and insecurity and asserts that the emphasis
on consumer society represents the study of surfaces and appearances.
Individuals influence markets as consumers where the only power they
exercise is as consumers. Consumers in a market register approval or disapproval for goods and services. Jobs for life are a thing of the past.
Employment is becoming more of an individual journey and an experience

of continuing changes and disruption. In the meantime money, financial donations to political parties, and the influence of professional lobbyists create wider disconnections between citizens and public institutions. Public spaces are now increasingly occupied by an emerging political and business elite. Democracy is undermined because it stops being the site of conversation of governments listening to many voices. Elected politicians are becoming increasingly isolated from their electors, sheltered by high salaries and fringe benefits which keep them separate from the lived experiences of those who elect them. In a recent survey, UK members of parliament improved their parliamentary salaries of £50 000 by an additional income of £140 000 in allowances for housing, energy, transport and secretarial support costs. In 2001 and 2005, electoral turnouts in the UK were at their lowest levels since 1884. Voter turnout in Europe has declined by around 12 per cent during the past decade. In a recent report by McDonald and Saples (2006) for the Brookings Institution and the Cato Institute (2006) the authors have pointed out that since 1994, 98 per cent of incumbents for Congress are re-elected, while competitive races are in decline, making the accountability of political leaders to citizens less possible:

> Competition in the United States bears a strong resemblance to that in nations where candidates run unopposed or with token opposition – nations that American leaders criticise for lacking truly democratic or legitimate elections. (ibid., p. 6)

The process of electoral re-districting means that registered republicans and democrats are clustered by boundaries which continually change in accordance with which party controls the state legislature. In 2003, after the election of a Republican Congress in Texas, Tom Delay, who is at present being investigated for financial irregularities and who in 2006 resigned as Republican Congressman for Texas, had redrawn the map of Texas, ensuring that the state would elect four republicans and one democrat in 2004 in contrast to pre-re-districting when the state was electing three republicans and two democrats. Politicians in the US seem to be involved in choosing their electors rather than electors voting for their elected leaders. During the mid-term elections of November 2006, in seats that were defined as being competitive there were turnouts of between 50 and 70 per cent, while in some seats there were no challengers and turnouts were as low as 7 per cent:

> The system is broken. Big money and gerrymandering have placed government out of the reach of most Americans. Millions of thoughtful Americans have become so estranged from the political process that they've tuned out entirely. (Bob Herbert, 'The system is broken', *New York Times*, 30 October 2006, p. 42)

There is a need to re-examine the concept of public spaces and how issues enter and exit the public arena and become areas for public debate. Politics is increasingly becoming a form of spectacle, with political elites managing the world stages and citizens as the quiet audience. In democracies there is the held assumption that political leaders are connected to their electors since they listen to their concerns and make those concerns public. However, this assumes that political leaders and political parties are passive empty vessels to be shaped by their electors. Governments are not passive and political leaders are concerned about the message and ensuring that they are part of the definers of how the public space is defined.

In the war in Iraq, the US administration has misued images of heroes. In May 2003, Jessica Lynch emerged as that hero. Her rescue by Marine and Airborne Forces was relayed at prime time on global TV networks. Her heroism, her femininity and Iraqi torture chambers had to be fitted into one story. Lynch as the soldier hero had emptied the whole of her rifle on her enemies before she surrendered, while Lynch the female victim had been raped and tortured by her captors. The truth of Jessica Lynch was to be leaked six months after the event when it was acknowledged that she had been cared for by Iraqi medical staff and given blood transfusions despite shortages of blood. She had not fired her rifle because it had jammed. Private Lynch in an interview with ABC news eventually admitted that she had been used by both the military and political leaders:

> They used me to symbolise all this stuff. It is wrong. I don't know why they filmed my rescue or why they say these things. I did not shoot my rifle, not a round, nothing. I went down on my knees. (Jessica Lynch interview with ABC News, 20 July 2003)

Pat Tillman was also a necessary hero. Tillman, who had signed as line-backer for the Arizona cardinals, had rejected a $3.5 million contract to do his duty for his country. Tillman was killed in Afghanistan. Posthumously he was promoted to corporal and awarded the purple heart for bravery. Military leaders who knew the real story that Tillman had not died in a fire fight but had been shot in the head accidentally by another American soldier had held back the real story for another month after the memorial service.

The most recent attempt by the UK government to re-define the public space was a report in the *Lancet* in October 2006, which had estimated that some 650 000 Iraqis had died since the end of hostilities in 2003. Rather than dealing with that question, senior Labour ministers including the ex-Prime Minister Tony Blair turned their attention to the Muslim woman at a Kirklees school who had been dismissed for wearing the *Niqab* in the classroom. While the case was still pending a tribunal decision, the Minister for Race Relations, the Minister for Local Government and finally the ex-Prime Minister Tony Blair made statements that the council had been right in dismissing the assistant teacher but also used the occasion to make the case that Muslims were failing to integrate into the British community. The question of Iraqi dead had been successfully diverted to a relatively unimportant issue, especially when considered in the wider context that only about 2000 women actually wear the *Niqab* in Britain.

On the world stage of humanity of over 6 billion actors, there are around 600 million who can be defined as consumer citizens, members of the consumer society and who tend to live in the OECD area. There are an estimated 870 million who face life-threatening poverty and malnutrition. Yet those 870 million has become a political statistic – a benchmark for assessing the successes or failures of the Millennium Development Goals; but behind that statistic are real lives.

However, it would be misleading to polarise rich and poor in geographical spaces of North and South or in the categories of the 'developed' and the 'developing' world, of Africa and Europe. In the new emerging plutocracy of the 360 billionaires, there is an African, Arab and Chinese elite of business people, politicians and senior civil servants who reside in the affluent gated communities of Abuja, Riyadh, Beijing and Nairobi with high walls and razor wires, who benefit from policies of deregulation and privatisation as much as their counterparts in London, Paris and New York.

Present forms of globalisation are contributing to increases in global income inequalities, with the main beneficiaries being the top 0.01 per cent of the population. In the advanced economies the top 1 per cent of income earners have since the 1970s seen their income share as a percentage of GDP increase from 32 to 40 per cent. The incomes for the top 0.01 per cent have increased by 187 times while for the other 99 per cent of households, incomes have either remained stagnant or actually declined. In the UK a recent survey by Income Data has shown that executive pay over the past decade had increased from 39 to 100 times of average earnings. In the USA, incomes for CEOs have increased from 39 times of average earnings in 1976 to 369 times in 2006. By contrast, most recent surveys of disposable incomes show that real incomes have been rising at approximately 0.5 per cent per annum over the last decade, while personal savings as a ratio of GDP have remained at around 0.6 per cent. The consumer citizens of the advanced economies are faced with high mortgage costs, and higher costs of transport and energy. Consumer demand has been kept buoyant through higher levels of personal debt, encouraged mainly by the continuing rise in property prices. So while GDP has continued to grow over the past two decades, the proceeds of that growth have tended to be re-distributed to a narrow elite of high earners (Hacker, 2006; Piketty and Saez, 2003).

The process of globalisation is increasingly being judged as being a major factor representing a qualitative break with the past. The speed and intensity of present globalisation is different from other periods of global economic integration. Technology, capital flows and instant forms of communication are generating contradictory possibilities of hope and insecurity, and great interdependence but also the retreat into individualism. The citizenship that is being shaped can be the cosmopolitan and global citizen embracing difference diversity and arguments of common humanity. However, there is also evidence of the consumer citizenship model being shaped by the logic of market liberalism that puts emphasis on the individual, that reflects fear and insecurity, that seeks security, and that wants tighter borders, higher fences and the exclusion of the other, however that other is defined.

The tensions between the cosmopolitan and consumer citizen are most vivid in the study of housing markets. Property development is becoming highly segmented, with new versions of gated communities that seek to exclude others who do not share similar a income and lifestyle. The state of Florida is an example of that potential future. Housing development is directed mainly at residents from New York seeking second homes. Florida offers a diversity of gated communities that have their own security guards, shopping malls and leisure parks. Residents do not have to venture out into the unknown, geographical landscapes of run-down estates in Miami. In the meantime, migrants mainly of Hispanic origin are moving into the neglected housing estates. There are approximately 12 million people in the US who do not possess legal rights of entry, yet these migrants are an essential part of the construction industry and the agricultural economies of Florida. The politics of race was a major issue during the mid-term elections of November 2006, with the incumbent senator making speeches about stopping the invasion of migrants and giving support for great border control with Mexico.

Issues of race, immigration, surveillance and policing have become inextricably linked with the politics of globalisation and the war on terror. Bauman (2006) has argued that the personal safety state has displaced the social state. The emphasis on fear, insecurity, the presence of strangers and the need for securing borders seem to be vote-winning strategies, while accusations of being soft on terrorism, race and immigration are seen as vote losers. The political message is to be robust. Being tough on race and immigration, declaring the wearing of the *Niqab* or *Hijab* as a failure of the Muslim community to integrate, is certainly not a vote loser. Political leaders do not seek to minimise the fear of terrorism irrespective of the argument that being killed in a terror outrage is less likely than being killed in a traffic accident. In the meantime, daily stories of rape, burglary and murder together with the ghosts of juvenile crime, appearances of disorder and chaos have become blurred with the fear of the war on terror. Governments warn against the possibility of terrorists being able to get hold of weapons of mass destruction, of manufacturing risin and using liquid bombs on aircraft. The war on terror becomes more terrifying. Waterboarding and other forms of torture become acceptable in the war on terror. The personal safety state has the ability to find resources for policing and new surveillance techniques.

All those who look Muslim are under suspicion, accused of a failure to integrate. The question is, integrate into what? The assumption is that there is a tangible homogeneous Britsh culture, yet no one seems to ask what parts of British culture should Muslims aspire to join? The assumption that strangers and outsiders have to be integrated into some homogeneous culture or community that does not exist and yet is assumed to exist always puts the other on the defensive. There is no 'let-out clause' in the accusation of failure to integrate because the process of integration is itself an endless process. There is no benchmark for the success or failure to integrate. It is a commonsense argument, not an argument that seeks to be analysed, criticised or evaluated. The stranger has two possible strategies available: to be the parvenu and seek assimilation, vomit or deny his/her identity, or become the pariah making claims of the right to be different and yet being accused of failure to integrate.

The mid-term elections of November 2006 have been described as a watershed in American politics. The Democratic Party have regained the House of Representatives after 12 years of Republican control and also have taken control of the Senate. The Republican revolution announced by Congressman Newt Gringrich when the Republican Party took control of Congress in 1994 seems to have been brought to a halt. Corruption, the economy, the war in Iraq and terrorism were cited by the electors as the major issues of concern during the election campaign (*New York Times*, 9 October 2006, p. 42). Democrats have pledged to focus on economic issues including improving the minimum wage, not making permanent the tax reforms that they feel had benefited only the top income earners, providing more financial assistance to students and investigating the costs of medicine and drugs. Nancy Pelosi, the new Speaker, pledged that the 110th Congress would be the most honest and transparent in American political history.

The study of the election is important because it reinforces the essence of politics and democracy. While the Bush administration has aimed to use the terror attacks on New York and the Pentagon in a politically partisan attempt to benefit the Republican Party, it would seem that political manipulation has its limits. Equally, in spite of attempts to portray the opposition to the war on terror as being a form of betrayal and treachery, it would seem that the politics of fear and passivity does eventually give way to optimism and hope.

REFERENCES

Bauman, Z. (2006), *Liquid Life*, Cambridge: Polity.
Giddens, A. (2007), *Europe in a Global Age*, Cambridge: Polity.
Gore, A. (2007), *The Assault on Reason*, London: Bloomsbury.
Hacker, J. (2006), *The Great Risk Shift*, Oxford: Oxford University Press.
Marshall, T.M. (1992), *Citizenship and Social Class*, London: Pluto.
McDonald, M. and J. Saples (2006), *The Market Place of Democracy: Electoral Competition and American Politics*, New York: Brookings Institution and Cato Institute Publications.
Piketty, T. and E. Saez (2003), 'Income equality in the United States 1913–1998', *Quarterly Journal of Economics*, **118** (1), 1–39.
Woodward, B. (2006), *State of Denial: Bush at War Part III*, London: Simon and Schuster.

Index

Progressive Politics 130
progressive pre-emption 129–30
progressivism 130–31, 139
Project for the New American Century
  (PNAC) 8, 33, 35, 36, 152, 156,
  168
property ownership 108, 193
property rights 184
  see also intellectual property
    rights
Pryce, Sue 47
'public', concept of 104–12
public citizen model 82–3, 93–5
public debt sustainabilty 182
public opinion 26
  on Bush and Blair 162–3
  media used to influence 101–21
public-private partnerships 130–31
public space
  commitment to 93
  direct supervision of 221
  reclamation of 11, 117–18
  redefined by governments 306–7
  retreat from 82, 85, 93, 95, 302, 304,
    305
public sphere, citizenship after the
  death of 101–21
public values 107, 126, 139
punitive sentiments 215

quasi-state of emergency 138
quasi-states 37–8
Quayle, Dan 35
quotation marks, use of 16

Radelet, S. 186
radio frequency identification tags
  (RFID) 254
Rahnema, Majid 197
Rawls, John 42, 138
Reagan, Ronald 147, 148, 152, 170
Reaganomics 169, 173
realistic Wilsonianism 159
reciprocity principle 138–9
Red Army Faction 245, 247
Red Brigades 247
regimes
  distinction between states and
    126–7
  international 43

Reich, R. 149
Reid, John 138, 139, 145
Renegger, Nicholas 50
repetition 112
repressed Real 258–9, 270
Republican Party 3, 119, 300, 303, 305,
  309
reputation 62
resistance, theory and practice of 11,
  284, 285, 287, 288, 289, 290–91,
  293, 296
resistenz 11, 254, 267, 268–71
Respect 278
retaliation 245–7, 249
Reus-Smit, Christian 40, 43
Reuters 255
Rhodes, Martin 65
Rice, Condoleeza 157, 164
Richardson, Louise 46
Richelieu, Cardinal 108
ricin case 257
Ridge, Tom 221
Rigg, J. 199, 201
risk, attitudes to 68, 69
Rist, Gilbert 192
Ritchie, David G. 38
Ritter, Scott 34, 121
ritual 246–9, 296
Roberts, J.V. 215
Robinson, W.I. 197, 253
Rodrik, Dani 60
Roman Catholicism 140
Ronfeldt, D. 259
Roosevelt Corollary (1904) 36
Rosamond, Ben 68
Rose, David 34
Rosen, J. 255
Ross, Daniel 207
Rousseau, Jean Jacques 109
Rove, Karl 3
Rowe, Andrew 256, 257
Rudinow-Saetnan, A. 222
Ruggie, John Gerard 64
Ruggiero, V. 237, 247, 250
Rule, J. 220
Rumsfeld, Donald 35, 119, 157
Russia 60, 151, 179, 216, 244, 245, 249,
  267
Ryan, L. 284
Rycroft, Matthew 153